Surprise!

You may be reading the wrong way!

It's true: In keeping with the original Japanese comic format, this book reads from right to left—so action, sound effects and word balloons are completely reversed. This preserves the orientation of the original artwork— plus, it's fun! Check out the diagram shown here to get the hang of things, and then turn to the other side of the book to get started!

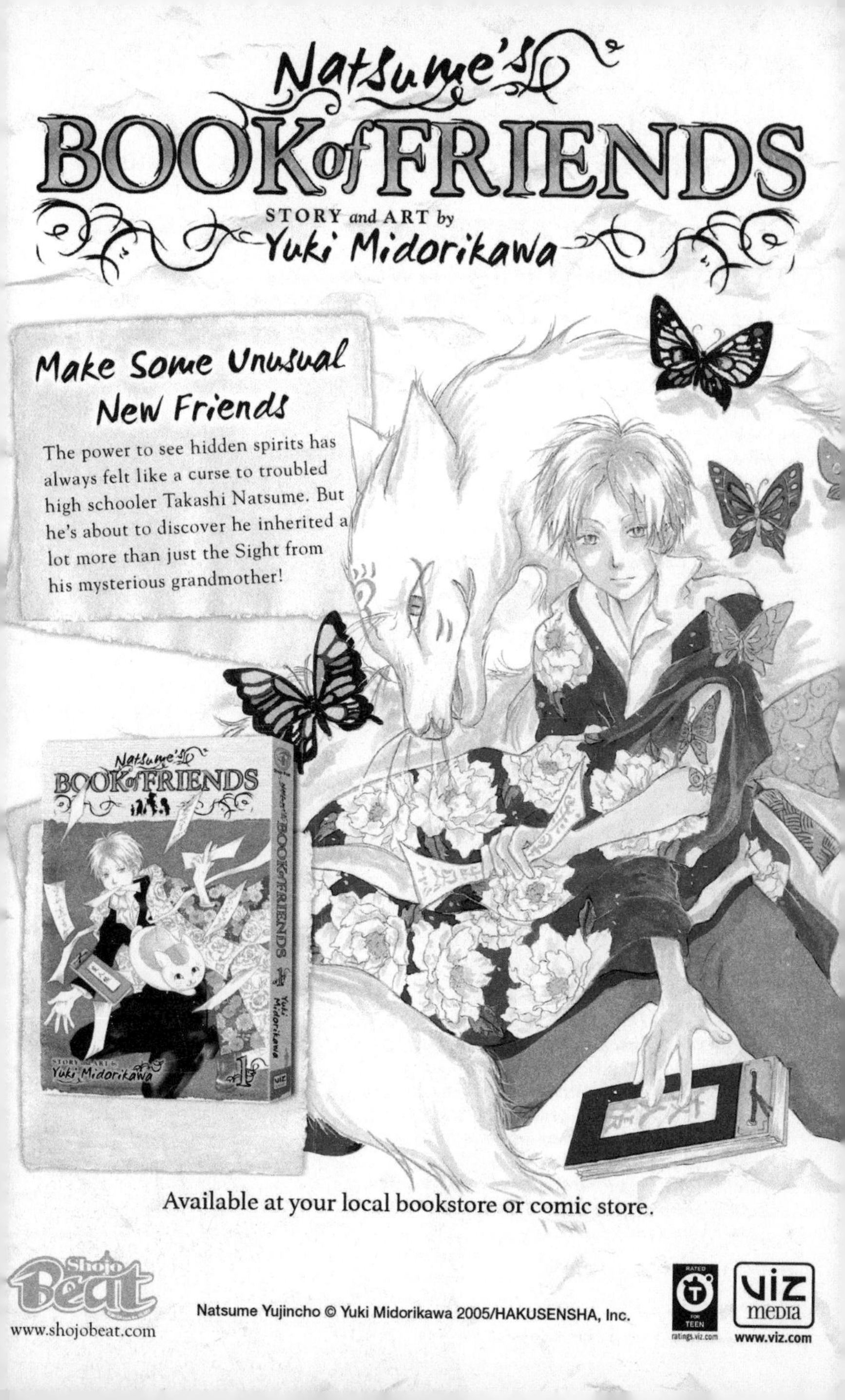
Natsume's
BOOK of FRIENDS
STORY and ART by
Yuki Midorikawa
Make Some Unusual New Friends
The power to see hidden spirits has always felt like a curse to troubled high schooler Takashi Natsume. But he's about to discover he inherited a lot more than just the Sight from his mysterious grandmother!
Natsume's BOOK of FRIENDS
Yuki Midorikawa
Available at your local bookstore or comic store.
Shojo Beat
www.shojobeat.com
Natsume Yujincho © Yuki Midorikawa 2005/HAKUSENSHA, Inc.
RATED T TEEN
ratings.viz.com
VIZ media
www.viz.com

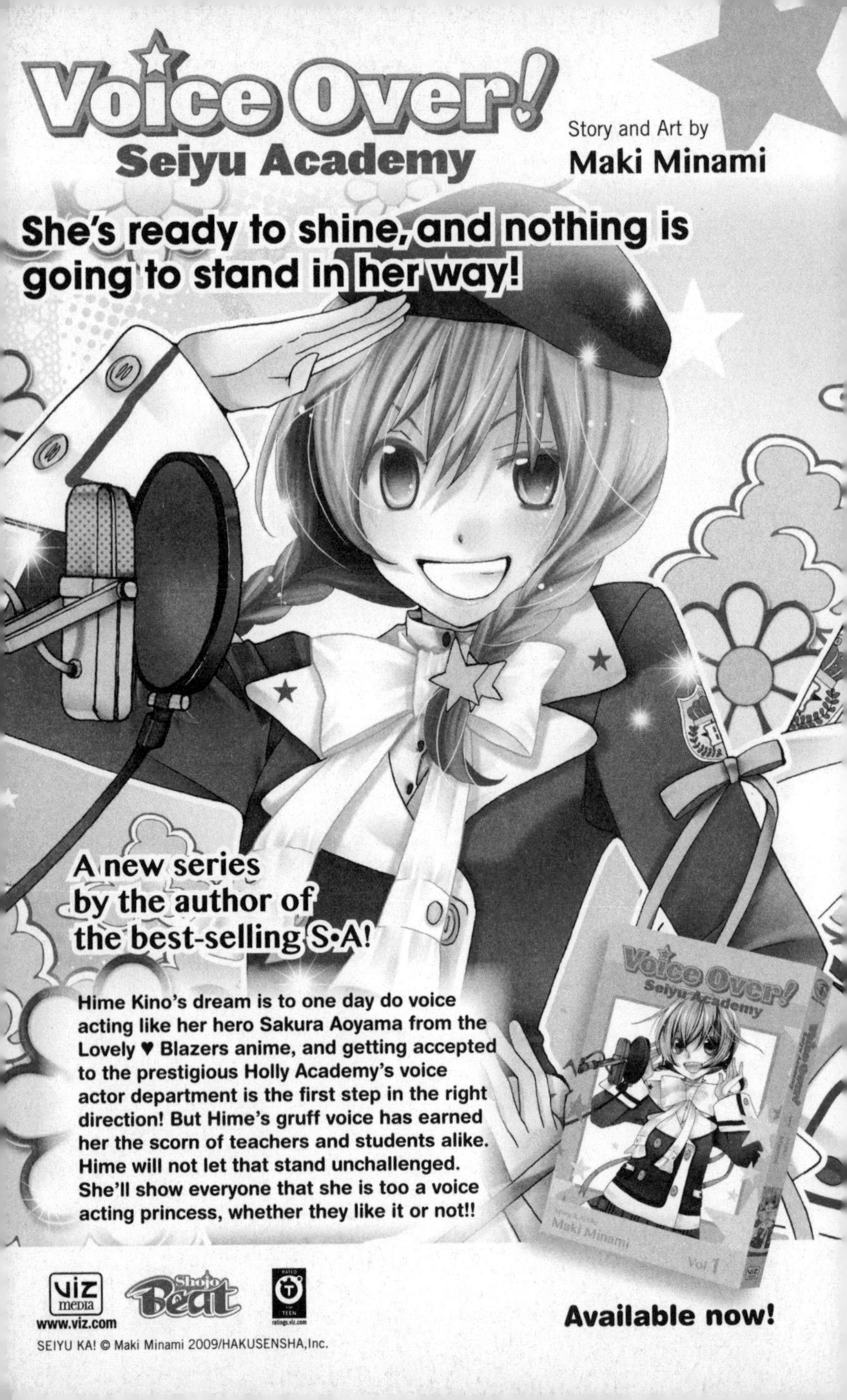
Voice Over!
Seiyu Academy
Story and Art by
Maki Minami
She's ready to shine, and nothing is going to stand in her way!
A new series by the author of the best-selling S•A!
Hime Kino's dream is to one day do voice acting like her hero Sakura Aoyama from the Lovely ♥ Blazers anime, and getting accepted to the prestigious Holly Academy's voice actor department is the first step in the right direction! But Hime's gruff voice has earned her the scorn of teachers and students alike. Hime will not let that stand unchallenged. She'll show everyone that she is too a voice acting princess, whether they like it or not!!
Voice Over! Seiyu Academy
Maki Minami
Vol. 1
viz media
www.viz.com
Shojo Beat
RATED T TEEN ratings.viz.com
Available now!
SEIYU KA! © Maki Minami 2009/HAKUSENSHA, Inc.

THE HEIRESS AND THE CHAUFFEUR
Vol. 2
Shojo Beat Edition

**STORY AND ART BY
KEIKO ISHIHARA**

English Translation & Adaptation/pinkie-chan
Touch-Up Art & Lettering/Rina Mapa
Design/Yukiko Whitley, Sarah Richardson
Editor/Amy Yu

Ojosama no Untenshu by Keiko Ishihara
© Keiko Ishihara 2012
All rights reserved.
First published in Japan in 2012 by HAKUSENSHA, Inc., Tokyo.
English language translation rights arranged
with HAKUSENSHA, Inc., Tokyo.

Printed in the U.S.A.

Published by VIZ Media, LLC
P.O. Box 77010
San Francisco, CA 94107

10 9 8 7 6 5 4 3 2 1
First printing, August 2016

www.viz.com   www.shojobeat.com

Shojo Beat

The Heiress and the Chauffeur

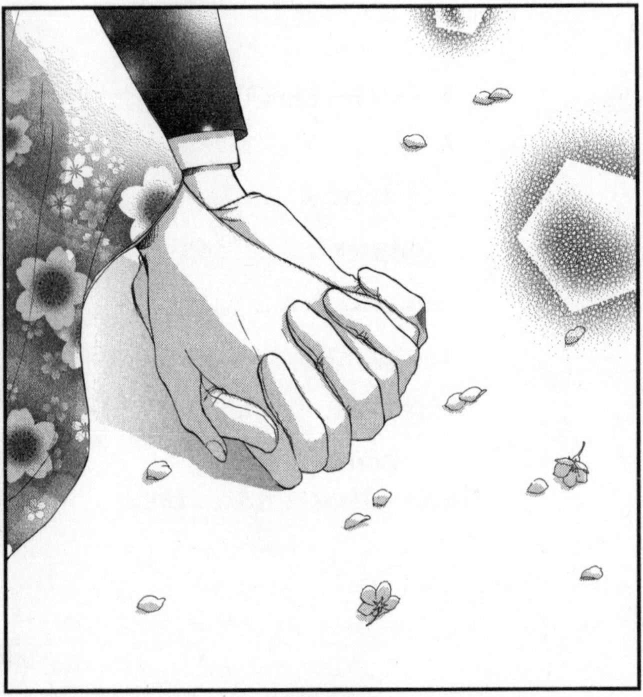

2

Story & Art by

Keiko Ishihara

The Heiress and the Chauffeur

2

CONTENTS

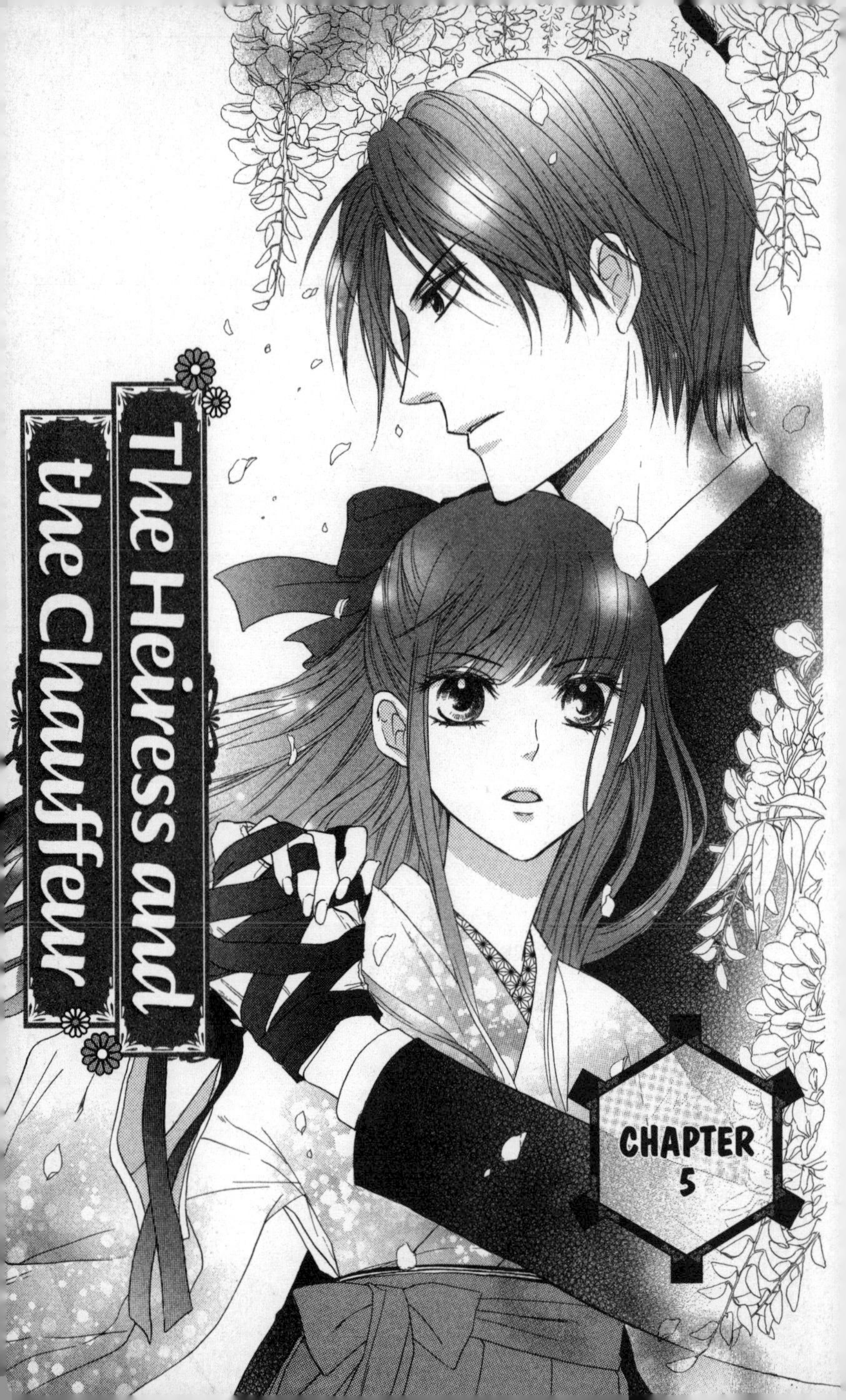
The Heiress and the Chauffeur
CHAPTER 5

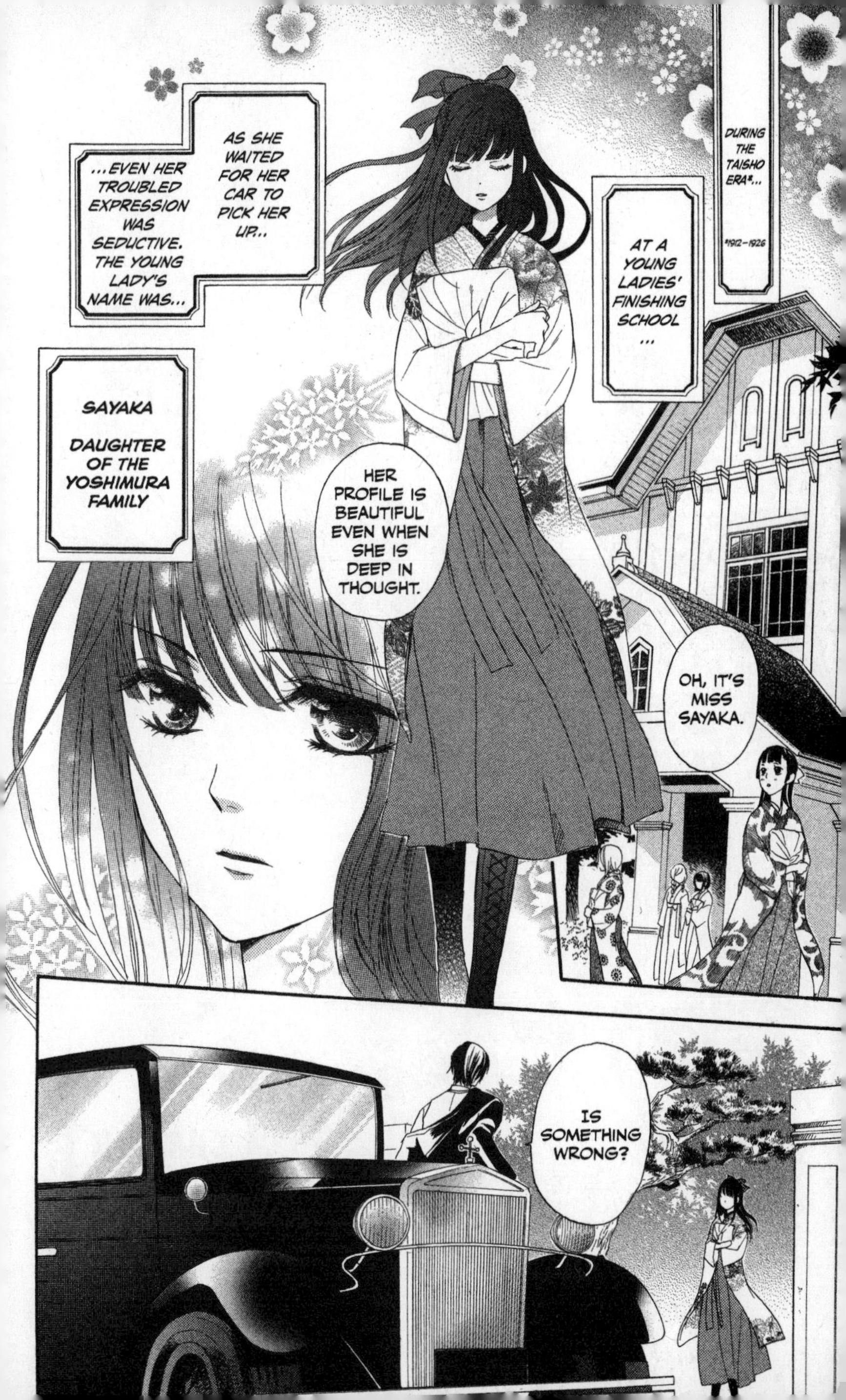
DURING THE TAISHO ERA*...
*1912–1926
AT A YOUNG LADIES' FINISHING SCHOOL...
AS SHE WAITED FOR HER CAR TO PICK HER UP...
...EVEN HER TROUBLED EXPRESSION WAS SEDUCTIVE. THE YOUNG LADY'S NAME WAS...
SAYAKA
DAUGHTER OF THE YOSHIMURA FAMILY
OH, IT'S MISS SAYAKA.
HER PROFILE IS BEAUTIFUL EVEN WHEN SHE IS DEEP IN THOUGHT.
IS SOMETHING WRONG?

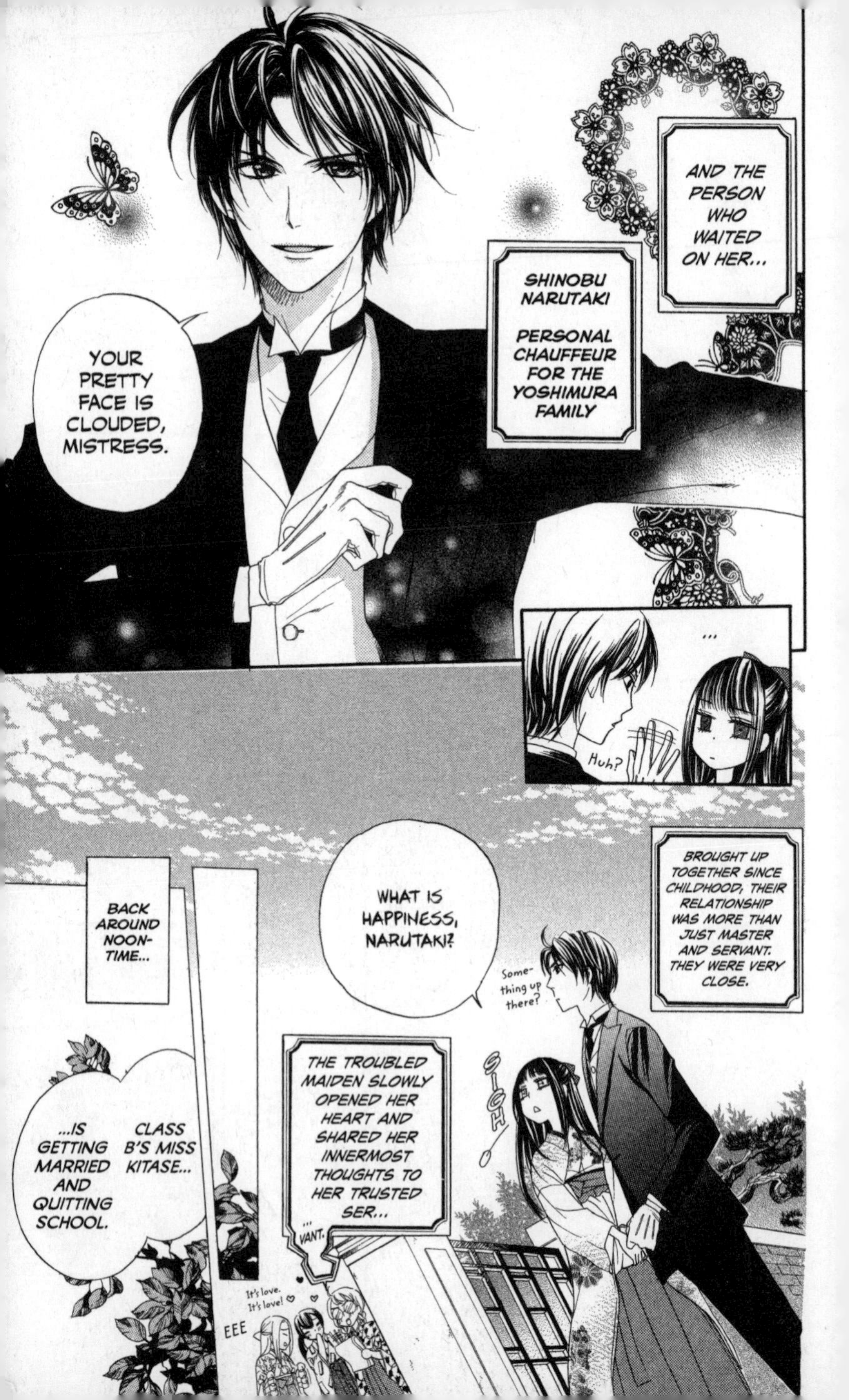
AND THE PERSON WHO WAITED ON HER...
SHINOBU NARUTAKI
PERSONAL CHAUFFEUR FOR THE YOSHIMURA FAMILY
YOUR PRETTY FACE IS CLOUDED, MISTRESS.
...
Huh?
BROUGHT UP TOGETHER SINCE CHILDHOOD, THEIR RELATIONSHIP WAS MORE THAN JUST MASTER AND SERVANT. THEY WERE VERY CLOSE.
Some-thing up there?
WHAT IS HAPPINESS, NARUTAKI?
SIGH
THE TROUBLED MAIDEN SLOWLY OPENED HER HEART AND SHARED HER INNERMOST THOUGHTS TO HER TRUSTED SER...
...VANT.
It's love. It's love!
EEE
BACK AROUND NOON-TIME...
CLASS B'S MISS KITASE...
...IS GETTING MARRIED AND QUITTING SCHOOL.

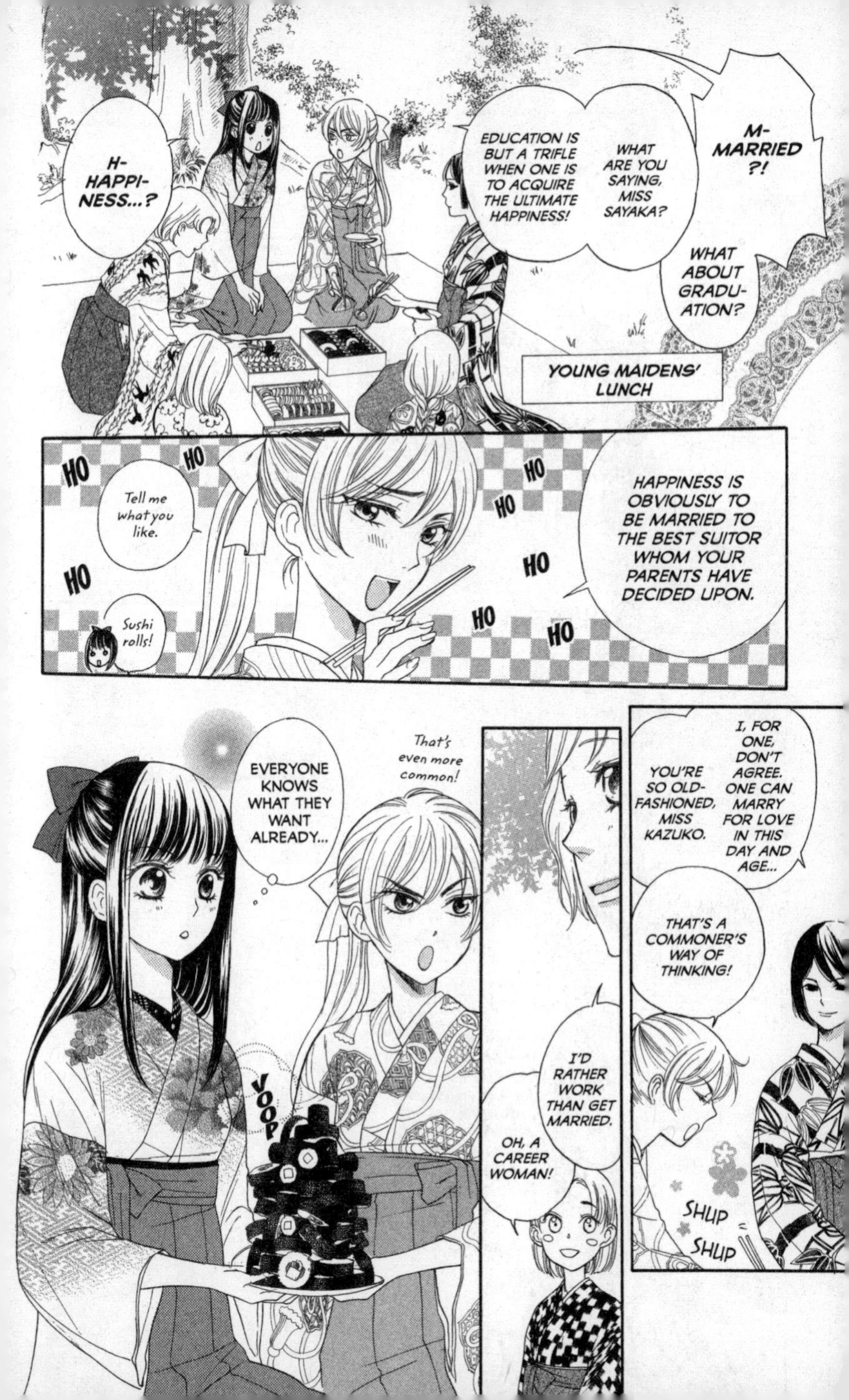
M-MARRIED?!
WHAT ABOUT GRADUATION?
WHAT ARE YOU SAYING, MISS SAYAKA?
EDUCATION IS BUT A TRIFLE WHEN ONE IS TO ACQUIRE THE ULTIMATE HAPPINESS!
YOUNG MAIDENS' LUNCH
H-HAPPINESS...?
HAPPINESS IS OBVIOUSLY TO BE MARRIED TO THE BEST SUITOR WHOM YOUR PARENTS HAVE DECIDED UPON.
HO HO HO HO HO HO HO HO
Tell me what you like.
Sushi rolls!
I, FOR ONE, DON'T AGREE. ONE CAN MARRY FOR LOVE IN THIS DAY AND AGE...
YOU'RE SO OLD-FASHIONED, MISS KAZUKO.
THAT'S A COMMONER'S WAY OF THINKING!
SHUP SHUP
I'D RATHER WORK THAN GET MARRIED.
OH, A CAREER WOMAN!
That's even more common!
EVERYONE KNOWS WHAT THEY WANT ALREADY...
VOOP

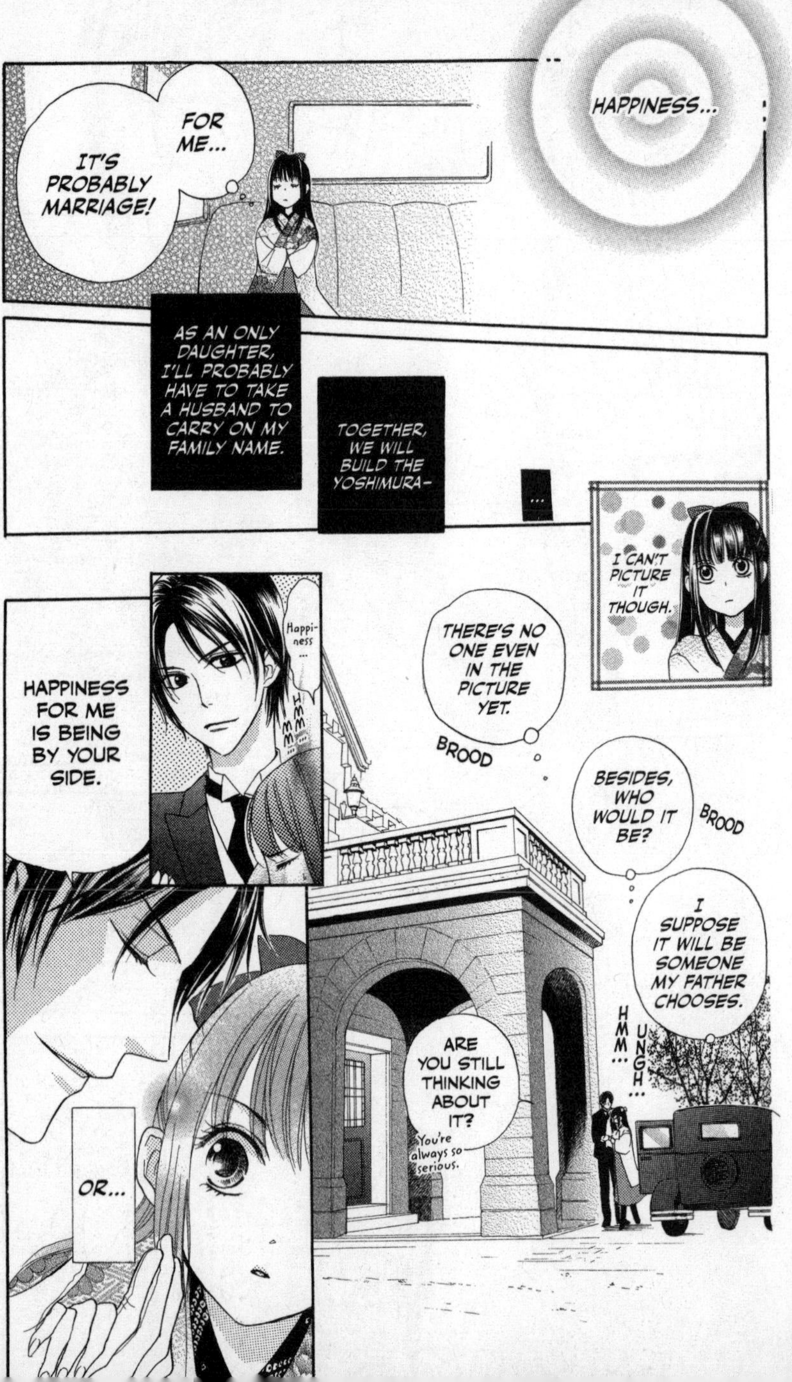

...HAPPINESS...?
FOR ME...
IT'S PROBABLY MARRIAGE!
AS AN ONLY DAUGHTER, I'LL PROBABLY HAVE TO TAKE A HUSBAND TO CARRY ON MY FAMILY NAME.
TOGETHER, WE WILL BUILD THE YOSHIMURA-
...
I CAN'T PICTURE IT THOUGH.
THERE'S NO ONE EVEN IN THE PICTURE YET.
BROOD
BESIDES, WHO WOULD IT BE?
BROOD
I SUPPOSE IT WILL BE SOMEONE MY FATHER CHOOSES.
HMM...
UNGH...
ARE YOU STILL THINKING ABOUT IT?
You're always so serious.
Happiness...
HMMM...
HAPPINESS FOR ME IS BEING BY YOUR SIDE.
OR...

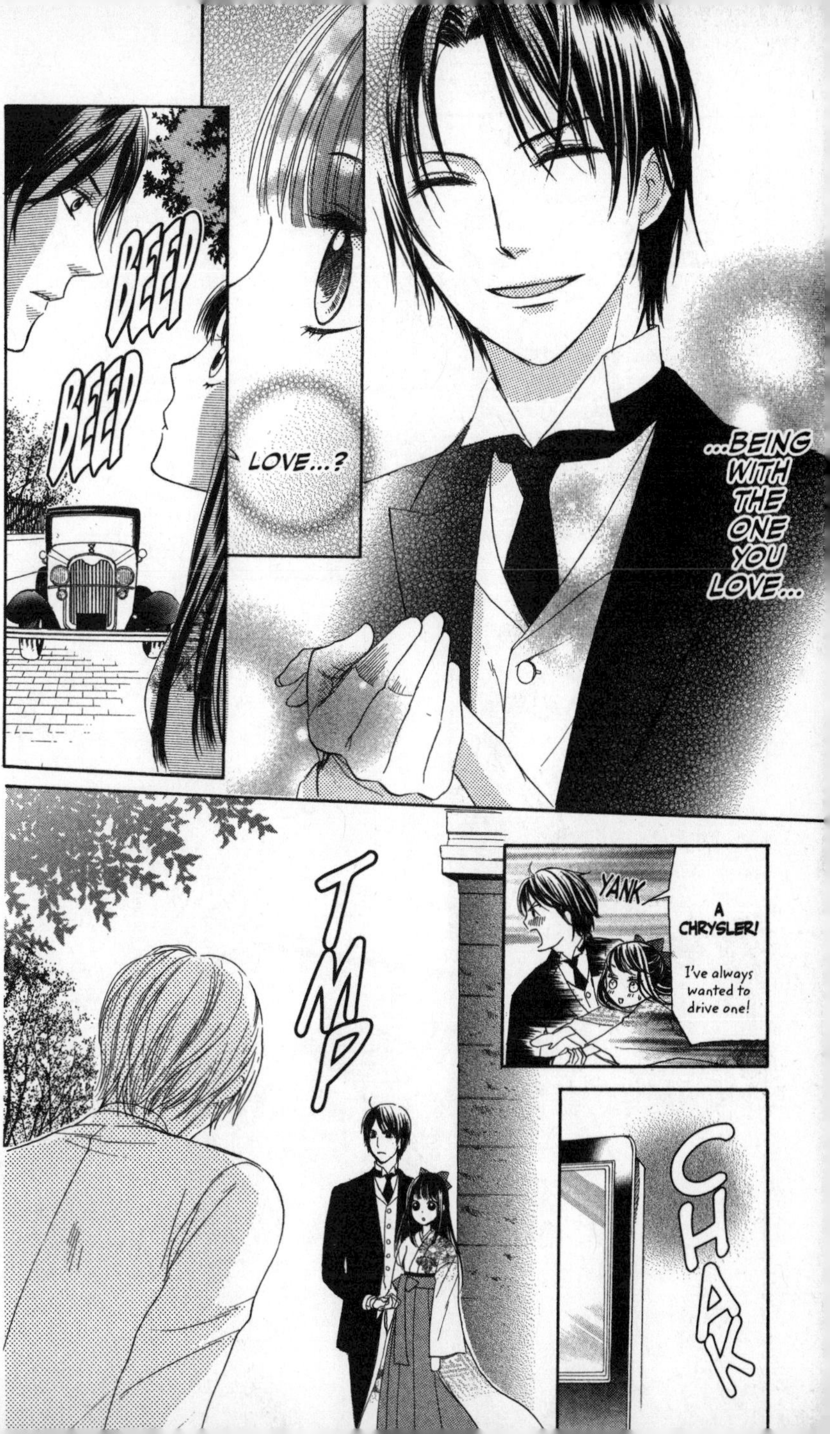
...BEING WITH THE ONE YOU LOVE...
LOVE...?
BEEP
BEEP
YANK
A CHRYSLER!
I've always wanted to drive one!
CHAK
TMP

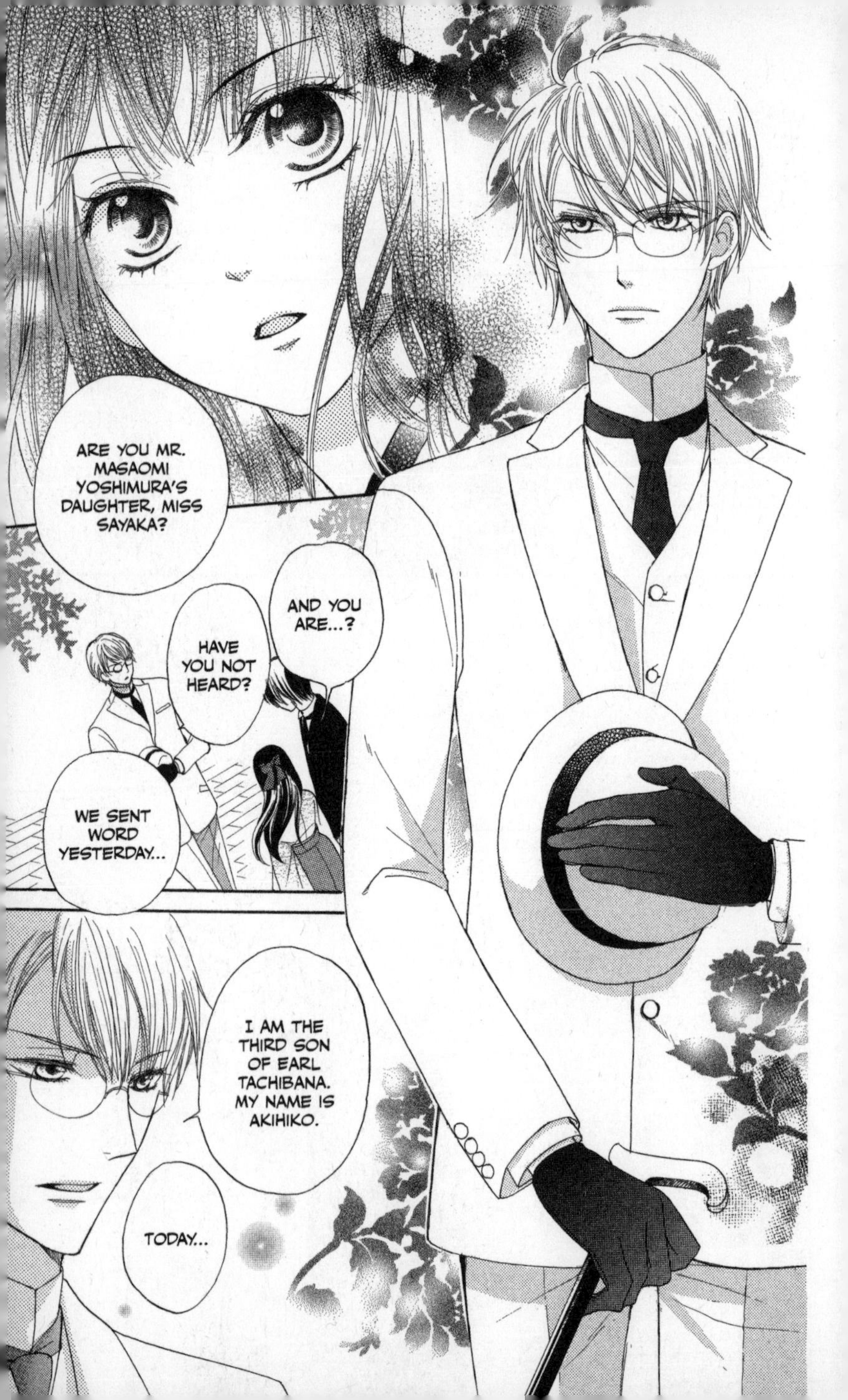
ARE YOU MR. MASAOMI YOSHIMURA'S DAUGHTER, MISS SAYAKA?
AND YOU ARE...?
HAVE YOU NOT HEARD?
WE SENT WORD YESTERDAY...
I AM THE THIRD SON OF EARL TACHIBANA. MY NAME IS AKIHIKO.
TODAY...

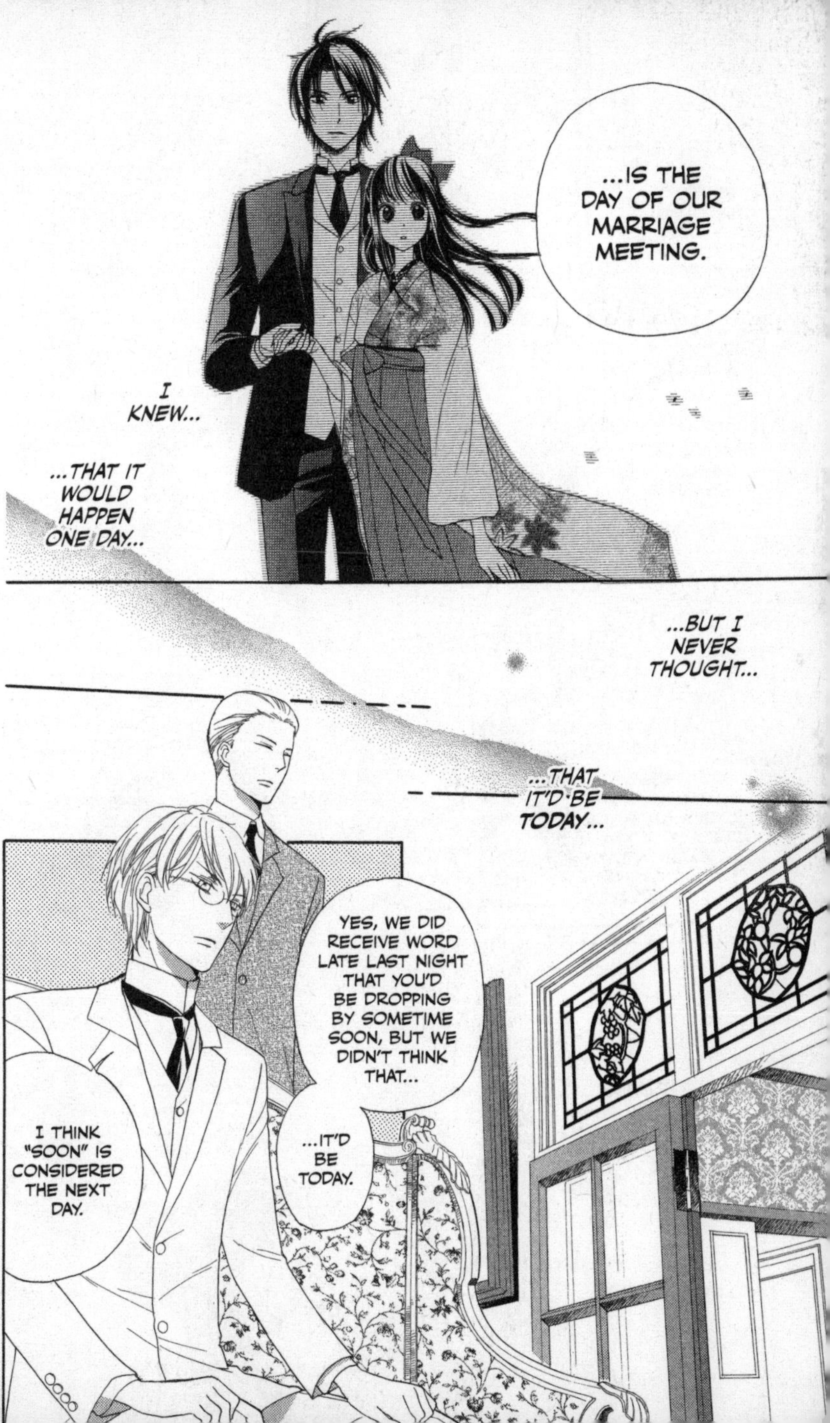
...IS THE DAY OF OUR MARRIAGE MEETING.
I KNEW...
...THAT IT WOULD HAPPEN ONE DAY...
...BUT I NEVER THOUGHT...
...THAT IT'D BE TODAY...
YES, WE DID RECEIVE WORD LATE LAST NIGHT THAT YOU'D BE DROPPING BY SOMETIME SOON, BUT WE DIDN'T THINK THAT...
...IT'D BE TODAY.
I THINK "SOON" IS CONSIDERED THE NEXT DAY.

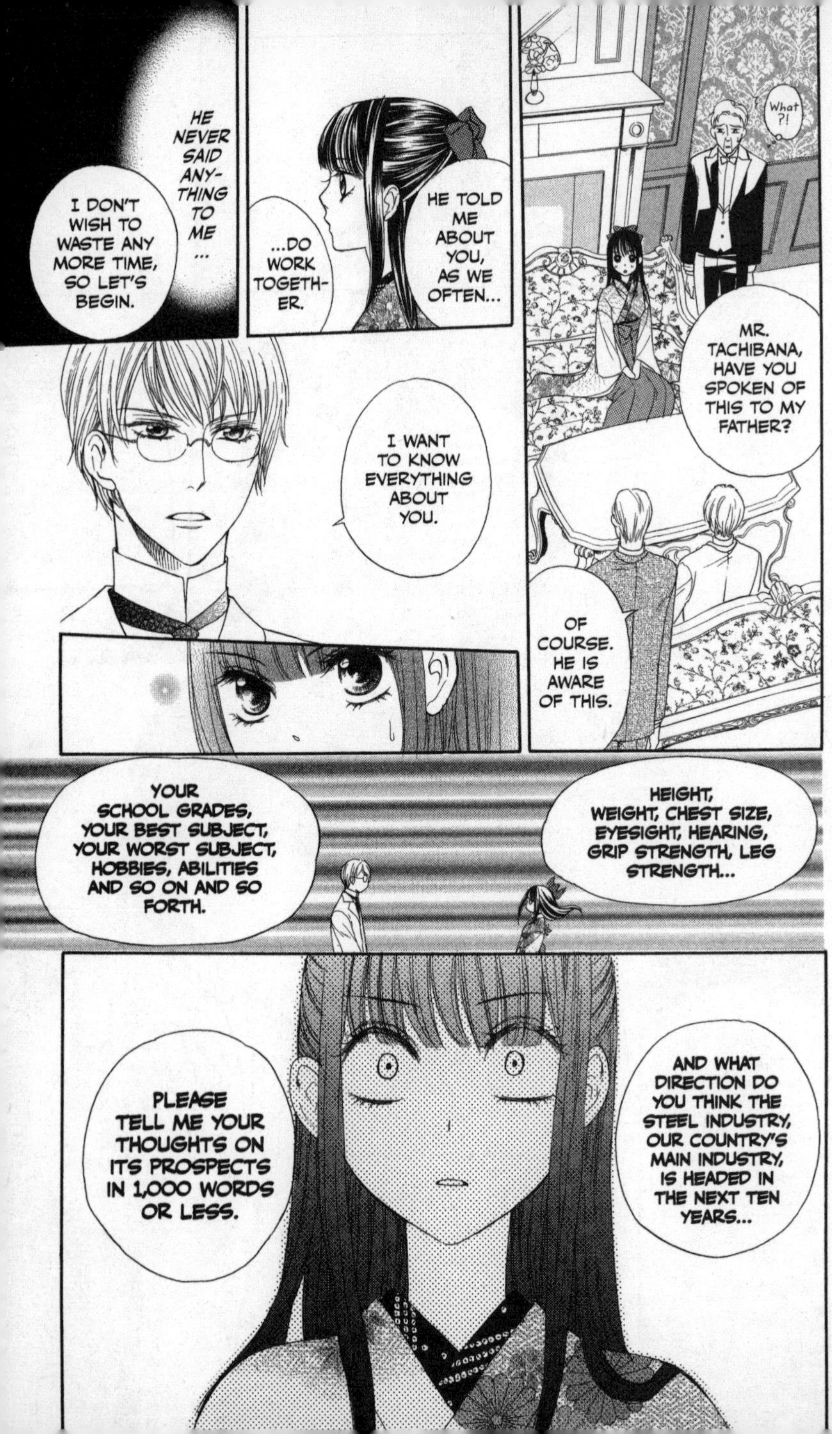
What ?!
MR. TACHIBANA, HAVE YOU SPOKEN OF THIS TO MY FATHER?
OF COURSE. HE IS AWARE OF THIS.
HE TOLD ME ABOUT YOU, AS WE OFTEN...
...DO WORK TOGETHER.
HE NEVER SAID ANYTHING TO ME ...
I DON'T WISH TO WASTE ANY MORE TIME, SO LET'S BEGIN.
I WANT TO KNOW EVERYTHING ABOUT YOU.
HEIGHT, WEIGHT, CHEST SIZE, EYESIGHT, HEARING, GRIP STRENGTH, LEG STRENGTH...
YOUR SCHOOL GRADES, YOUR BEST SUBJECT, YOUR WORST SUBJECT, HOBBIES, ABILITIES AND SO ON AND SO FORTH.
AND WHAT DIRECTION DO YOU THINK THE STEEL INDUSTRY, OUR COUNTRY'S MAIN INDUSTRY, IS HEADED IN THE NEXT TEN YEARS...
PLEASE TELL ME YOUR THOUGHTS ON ITS PROSPECTS IN 1,000 WORDS OR LESS.

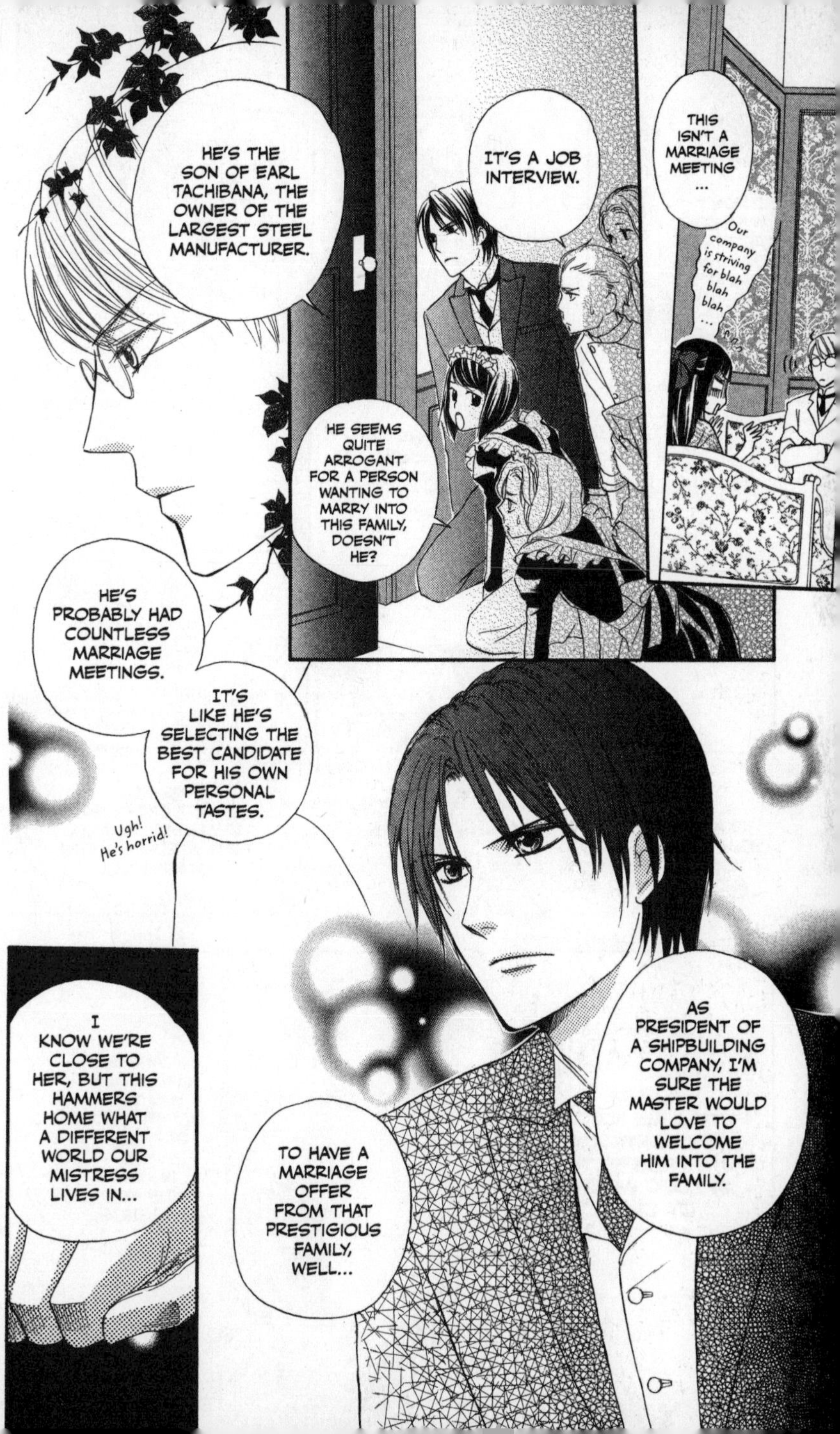
THIS ISN'T A MARRIAGE MEETING...
Our company is striving for blah blah...
IT'S A JOB INTERVIEW.
HE SEEMS QUITE ARROGANT FOR A PERSON WANTING TO MARRY INTO THIS FAMILY, DOESN'T HE?
HE'S THE SON OF EARL TACHIBANA, THE OWNER OF THE LARGEST STEEL MANUFACTURER.
HE'S PROBABLY HAD COUNTLESS MARRIAGE MEETINGS.
IT'S LIKE HE'S SELECTING THE BEST CANDIDATE FOR HIS OWN PERSONAL TASTES.
Ugh! He's horrid!
AS PRESIDENT OF A SHIPBUILDING COMPANY, I'M SURE THE MASTER WOULD LOVE TO WELCOME HIM INTO THE FAMILY.
TO HAVE A MARRIAGE OFFER FROM THAT PRESTIGIOUS FAMILY, WELL...
I KNOW WE'RE CLOSE TO HER, BUT THIS HAMMERS HOME WHAT A DIFFERENT WORLD OUR MISTRESS LIVES IN...

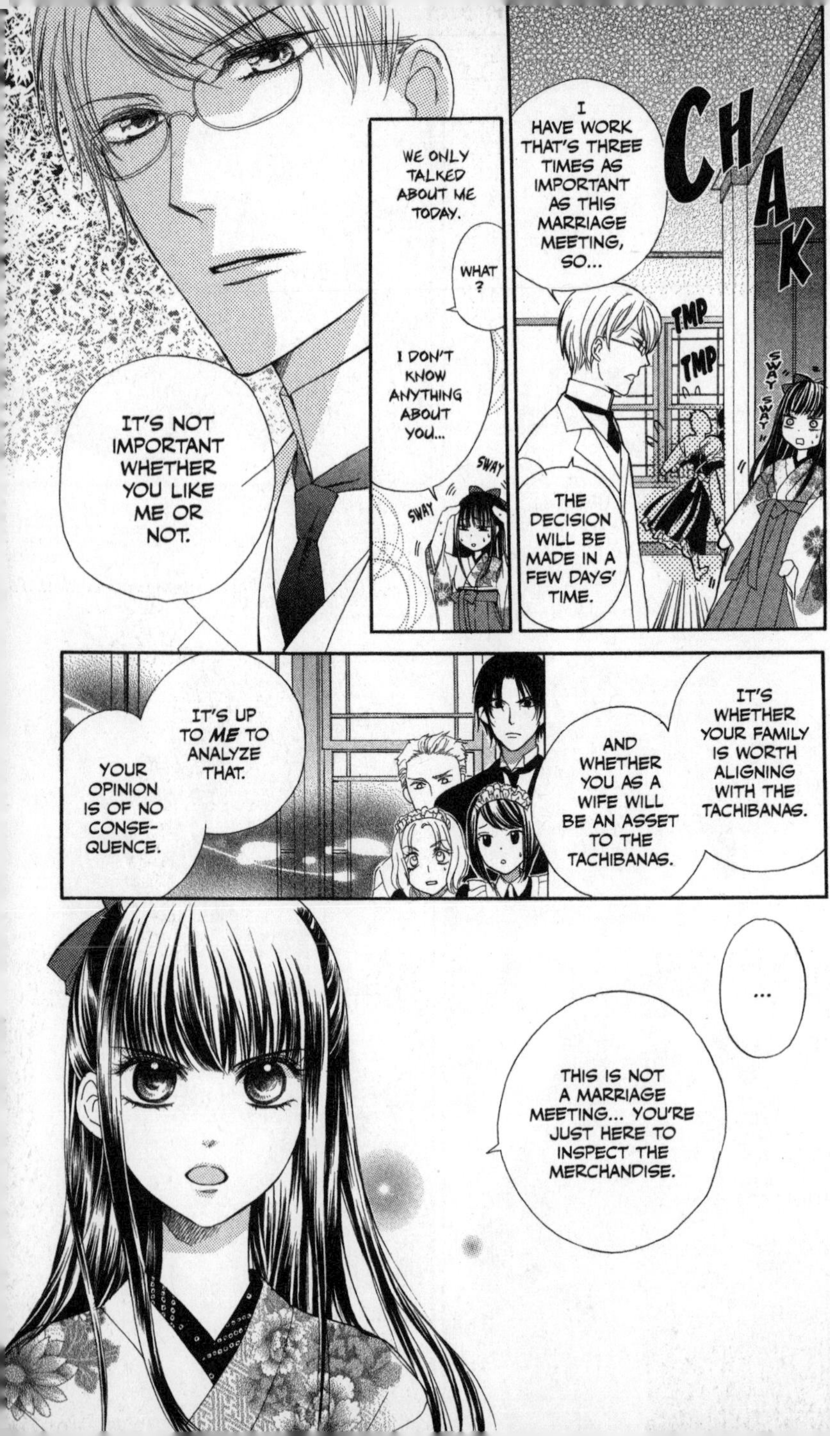
I HAVE WORK THAT'S THREE TIMES AS IMPORTANT AS THIS MARRIAGE MEETING, SO...
CHAK
TMP
TMP
SWAY SWAY
THE DECISION WILL BE MADE IN A FEW DAYS' TIME.
WE ONLY TALKED ABOUT ME TODAY.
WHAT?
I DON'T KNOW ANYTHING ABOUT YOU...
SWAY
SWAY
IT'S NOT IMPORTANT WHETHER YOU LIKE ME OR NOT.
IT'S WHETHER YOUR FAMILY IS WORTH ALIGNING WITH THE TACHIBANAS.
AND WHETHER YOU AS A WIFE WILL BE AN ASSET TO THE TACHIBANAS.
IT'S UP TO *ME* TO ANALYZE THAT.
YOUR OPINION IS OF NO CONSEQUENCE.
...
THIS IS NOT A MARRIAGE MEETING... YOU'RE JUST HERE TO INSPECT THE MERCHANDISE.

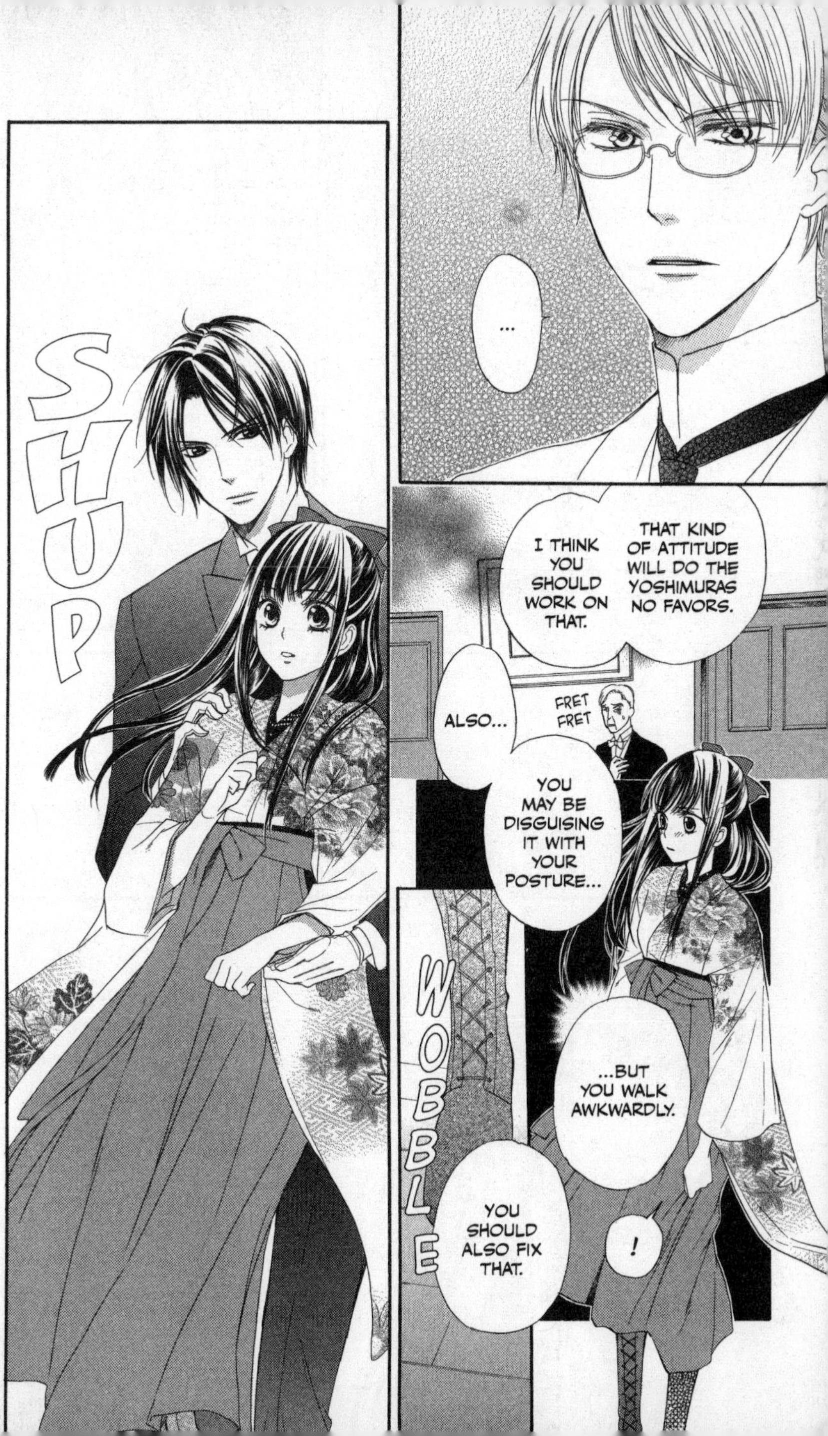
...
THAT KIND OF ATTITUDE WILL DO THE YOSHIMURAS NO FAVORS.
I THINK YOU SHOULD WORK ON THAT.
ALSO...
FRET FRET
YOU MAY BE DISGUISING IT WITH YOUR POSTURE...
...BUT YOU WALK AWKWARDLY.
!
WOBBLE
YOU SHOULD ALSO FIX THAT.
SHUP

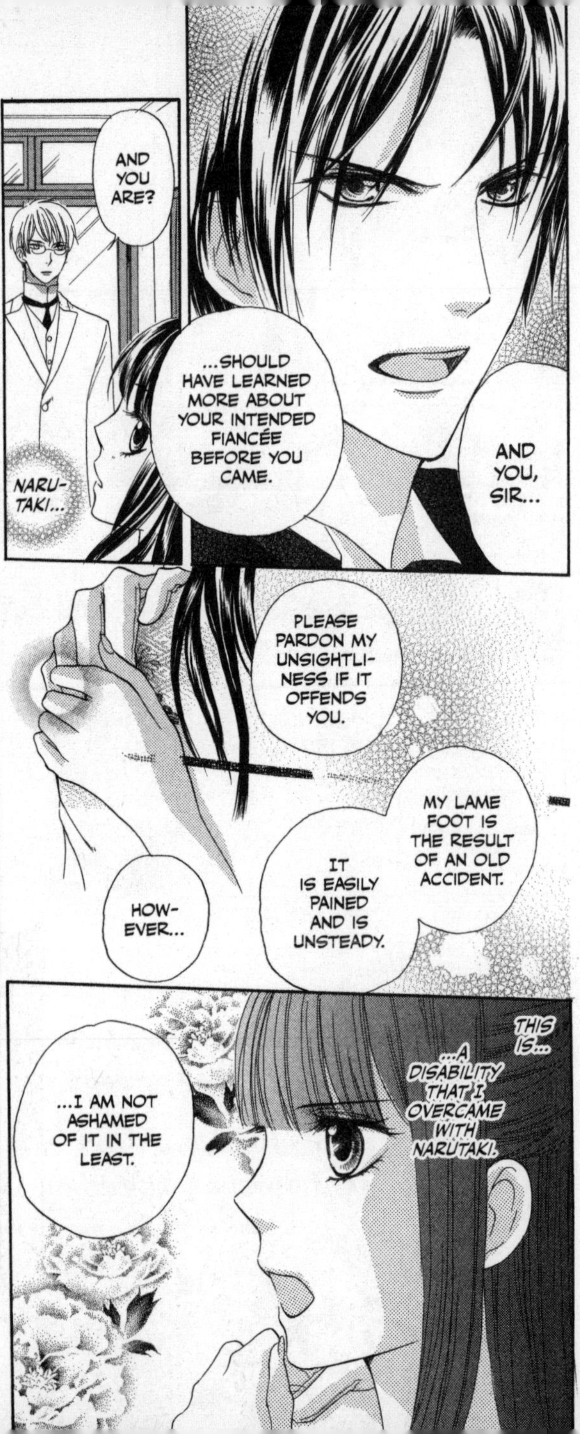
AND YOU, SIR...
...SHOULD HAVE LEARNED MORE ABOUT YOUR INTENDED FIANCÉE BEFORE YOU CAME.
AND YOU ARE?
NARUTAKI...
PLEASE PARDON MY UNSIGHTLINESS IF IT OFFENDS YOU.
MY LAME FOOT IS THE RESULT OF AN OLD ACCIDENT.
IT IS EASILY PAINED AND IS UNSTEADY.
HOW-EVER...
THIS IS...
...A DISABILITY THAT I OVERCAME WITH NARUTAKI.
...I AM NOT ASHAMED OF IT IN THE LEAST.

Hello. I'm Keiko Ishihara. Thank you very much for reading ***The Heiress and the Chauffeur.***

This is the final volume. I hope that you'll keep reading until the end.

CHAPTER 5

A rival has finally appeared in the fifth chapter. I initially created Tachibana as a shy and weak-willed character. But my editor said "That's repulsive! So gross!" about twenty times, so I changed his personality to this...

Also, I finally took some reference photos for the exterior of the Yoshimura house. So from this chapter on, I was able to trace them, and it made it a little easier to draw the backgrounds. Sayaka's house is mainly based on Hatoyama Hall in Tokyo.

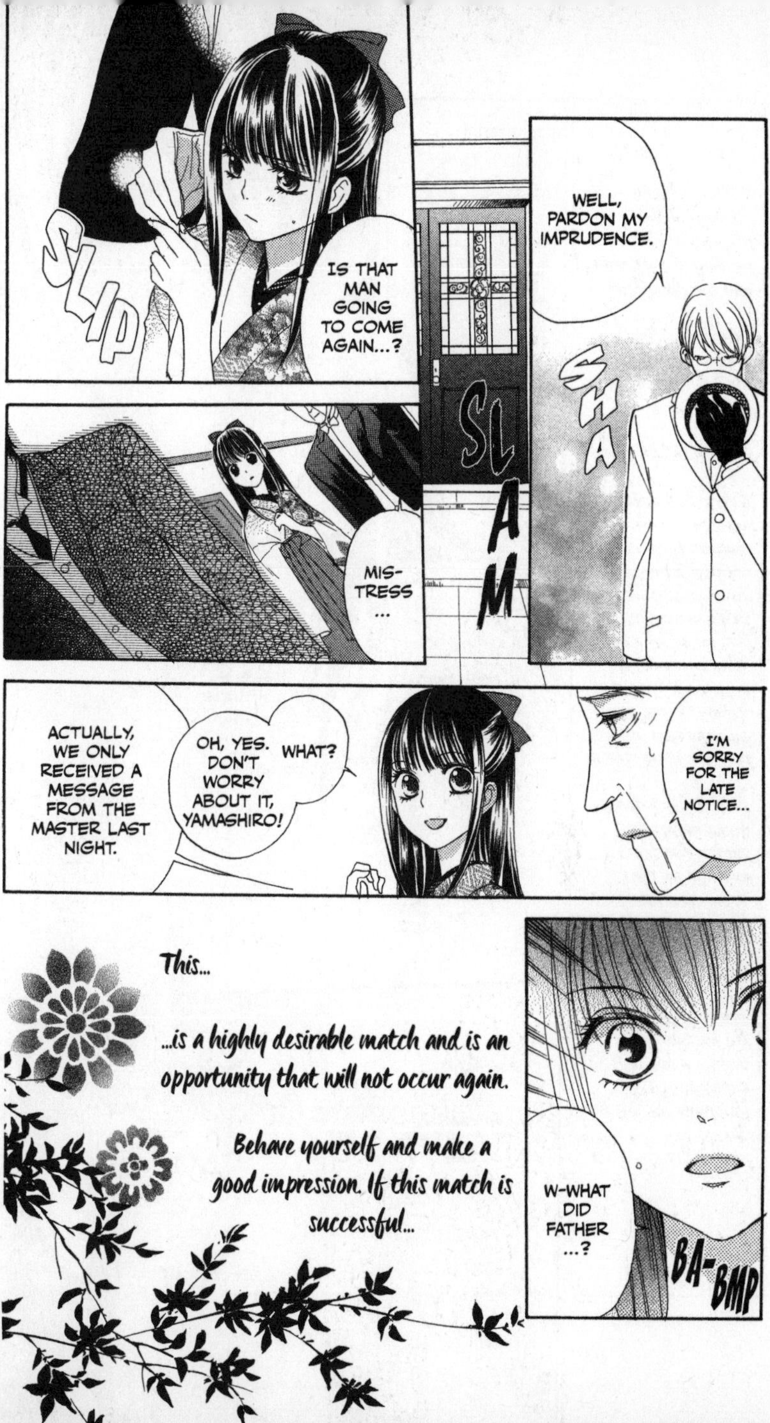
WELL, PARDON MY IMPRUDENCE.
SHA
SLAM
SLIP
IS THAT MAN GOING TO COME AGAIN...?
MIS-TRESS ...
I'M SORRY FOR THE LATE NOTICE...
WHAT?
OH, YES. DON'T WORRY ABOUT IT, YAMASHIRO!
ACTUALLY, WE ONLY RECEIVED A MESSAGE FROM THE MASTER LAST NIGHT.
W-WHAT DID FATHER ...?
BA-BMP
This...
...is a highly desirable match and is an opportunity that will not occur again.
Behave yourself and make a good impression. If this match is successful...

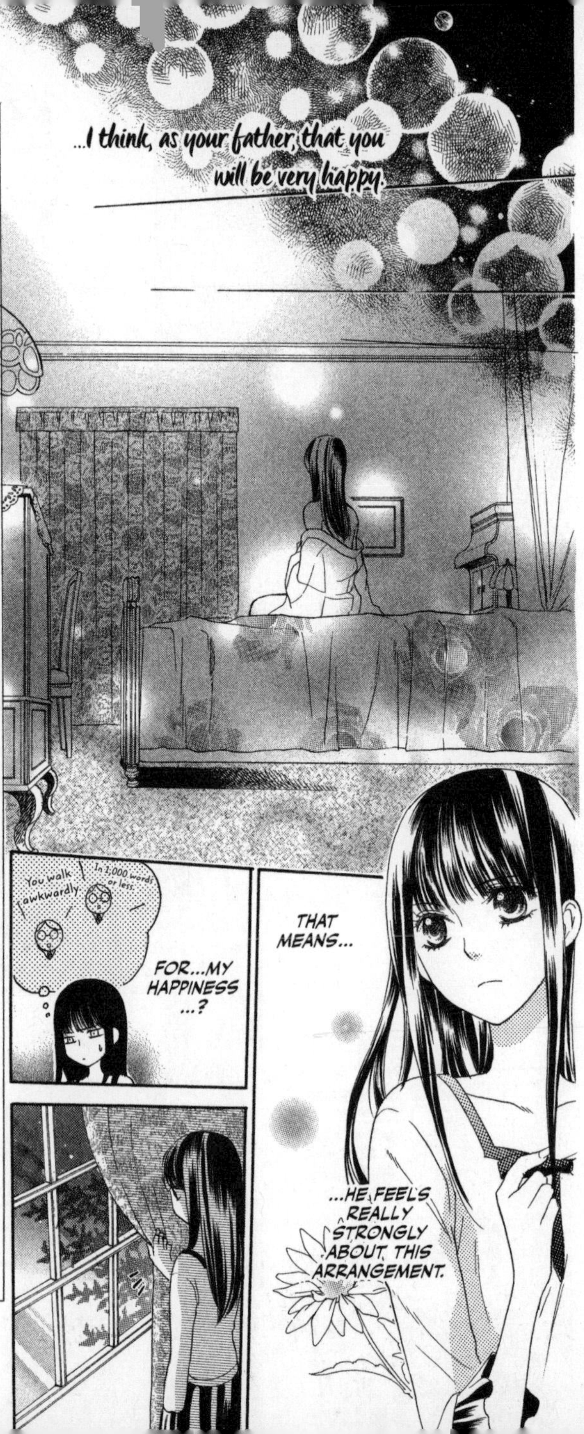
...I think, as your father, that you will be very happy.
THAT MEANS...
In 1,000 words or less.
You walk awkwardly.
FOR...MY HAPPINESS ...?
...HE FEELS REALLY STRONGLY ABOUT THIS ARRANGEMENT.

ABOUT SAYAKA

The young lady of the Yoshimura house. She's a 17-year-old student. The daughter of a wealthy man, she is both beautiful and intelligent. She is beloved by her older childhood friend / servant... However, I created a character who wants to go her own path in life and will fight against what is expected of her. She's so different from myself that I had a hard time creating her. I have no idea what she's thinking, so I struggled every time to come up with an ending that she would be content with.

But I was really happy that I got to show a pretty girl who could handle an older man. I wanted to do that most of all.

She's a tomboy, but I wanted to show that she was brought up properly. It was fun to think about her mannerisms and her facial expressions.

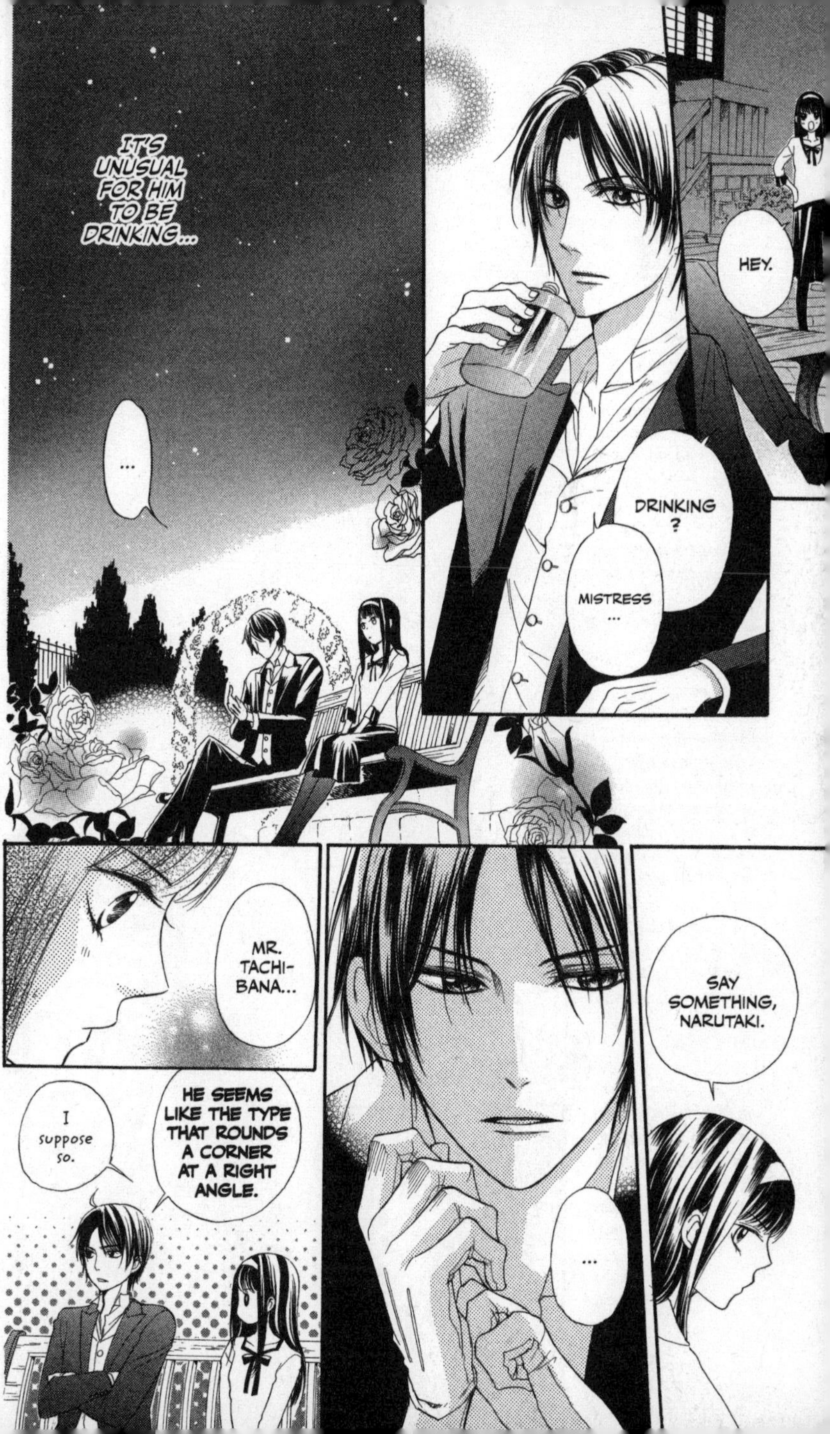
HEY.
DRINKING?
MISTRESS...
IT'S UNUSUAL FOR HIM TO BE DRINKING...
...
SAY SOMETHING, NARUTAKI.
...
MR. TACHIBANA...
HE SEEMS LIKE THE TYPE THAT ROUNDS A CORNER AT A RIGHT ANGLE.
I suppose so.

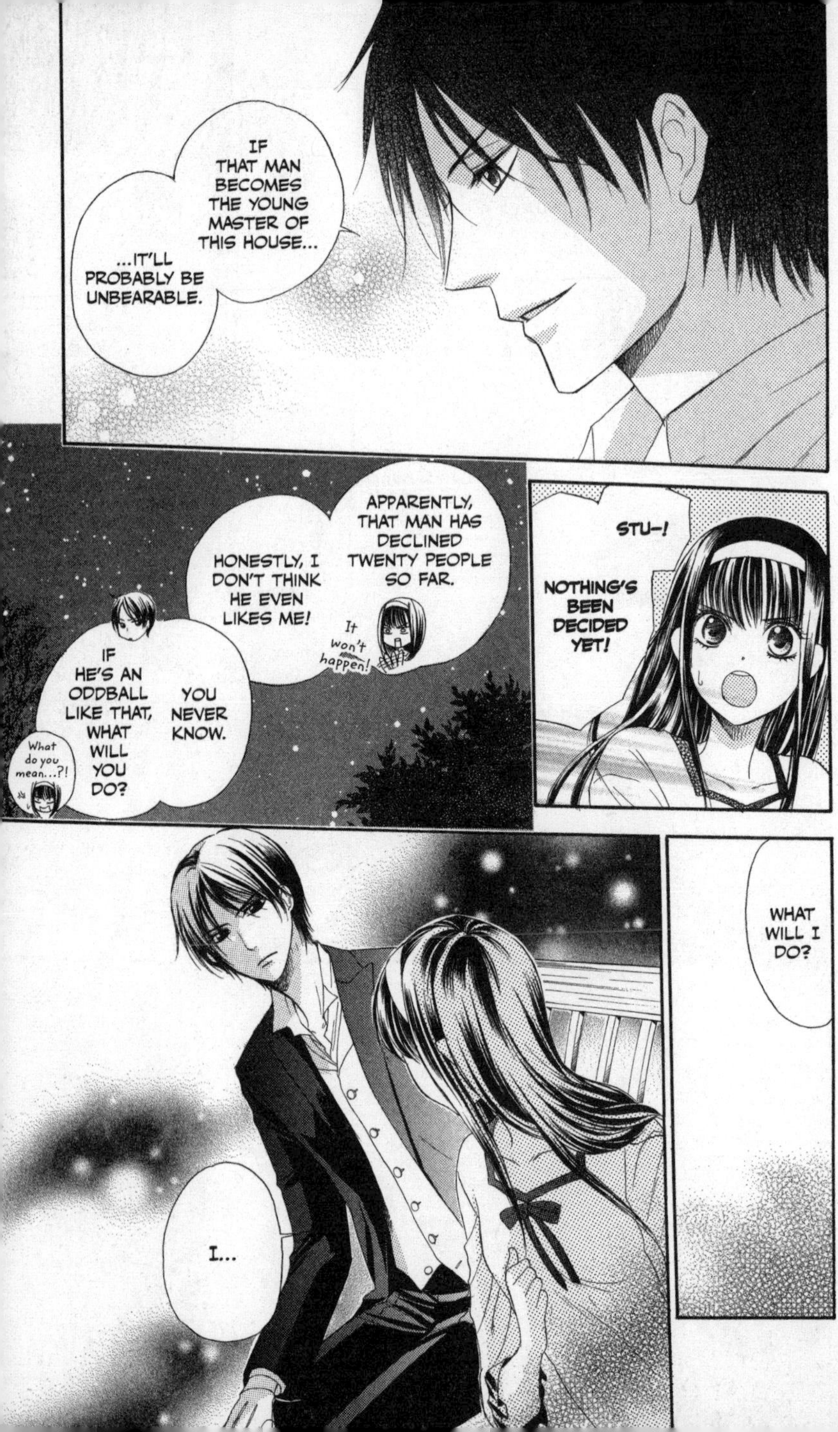
IF THAT MAN BECOMES THE YOUNG MASTER OF THIS HOUSE...
...IT'LL PROBABLY BE UNBEARABLE.
STU-!
NOTHING'S BEEN DECIDED YET!
APPARENTLY, THAT MAN HAS DECLINED TWENTY PEOPLE SO FAR.
HONESTLY, I DON'T THINK HE EVEN LIKES ME!
It won't happen!
YOU NEVER KNOW.
IF HE'S AN ODDBALL LIKE THAT, WHAT WILL YOU DO?
What do you mean...?!
WHAT WILL I DO?
I...

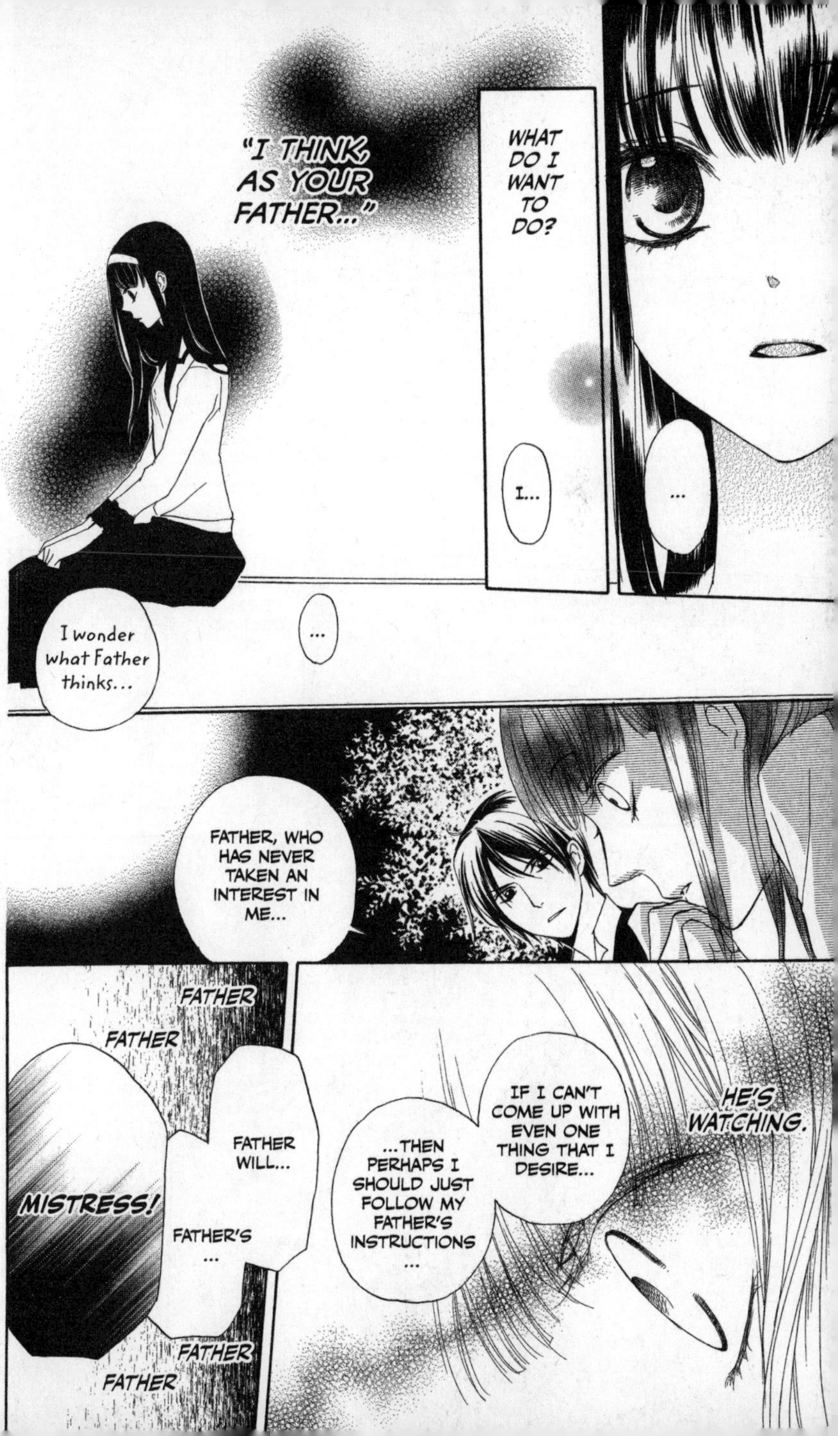
WHAT DO I WANT TO DO?
...
I...
"I THINK, AS YOUR FATHER..."
...
I wonder what Father thinks...
FATHER, WHO HAS NEVER TAKEN AN INTEREST IN ME...
HE'S WATCHING.
IF I CAN'T COME UP WITH EVEN ONE THING THAT I DESIRE...
...THEN PERHAPS I SHOULD JUST FOLLOW MY FATHER'S INSTRUCTIONS ...
FATHER
FATHER
FATHER WILL...
MISTRESS!
FATHER'S ...
FATHER
FATHER

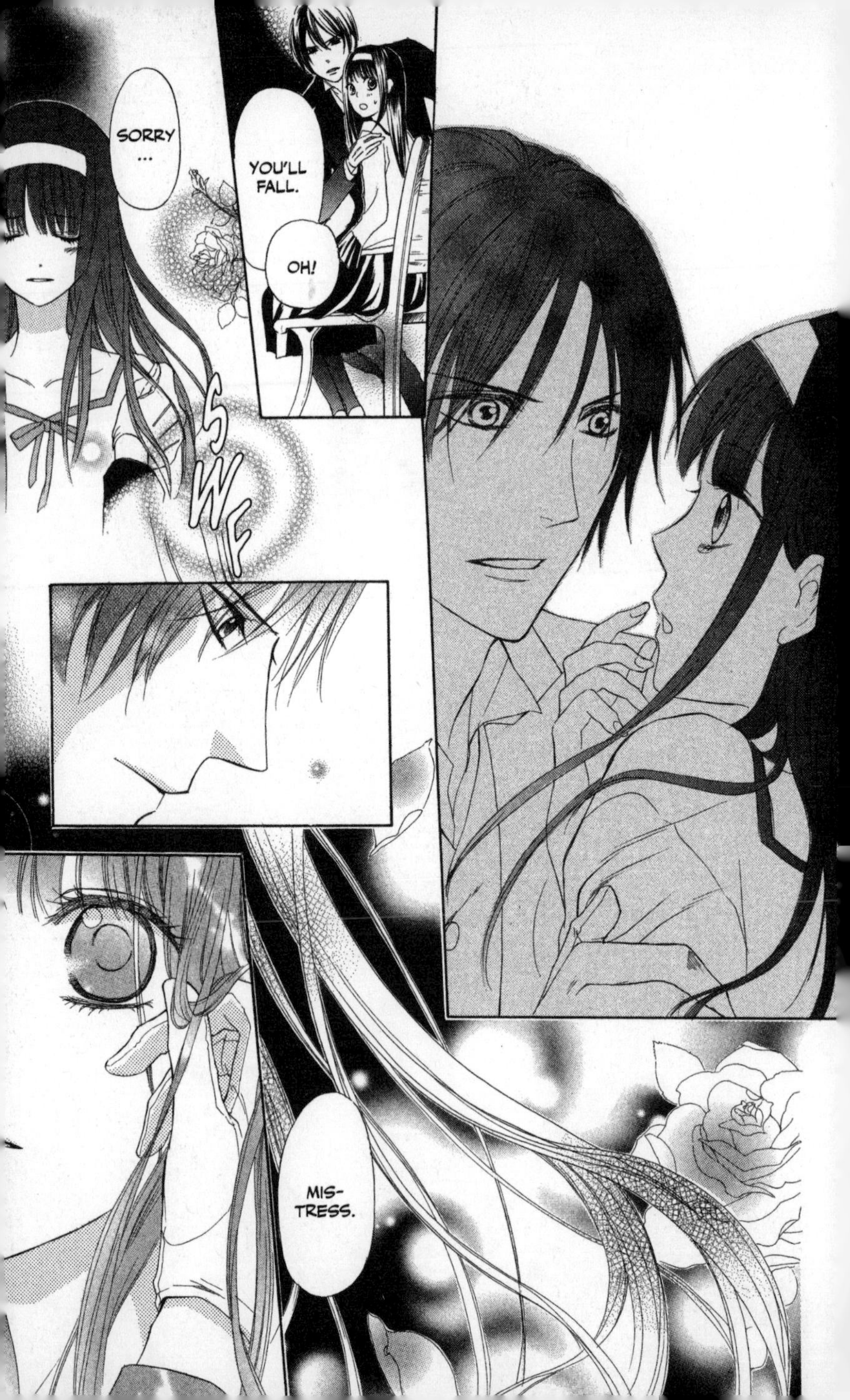
YOU'LL FALL.
OH!
SORRY ...
SWF
MIS-TRESS.

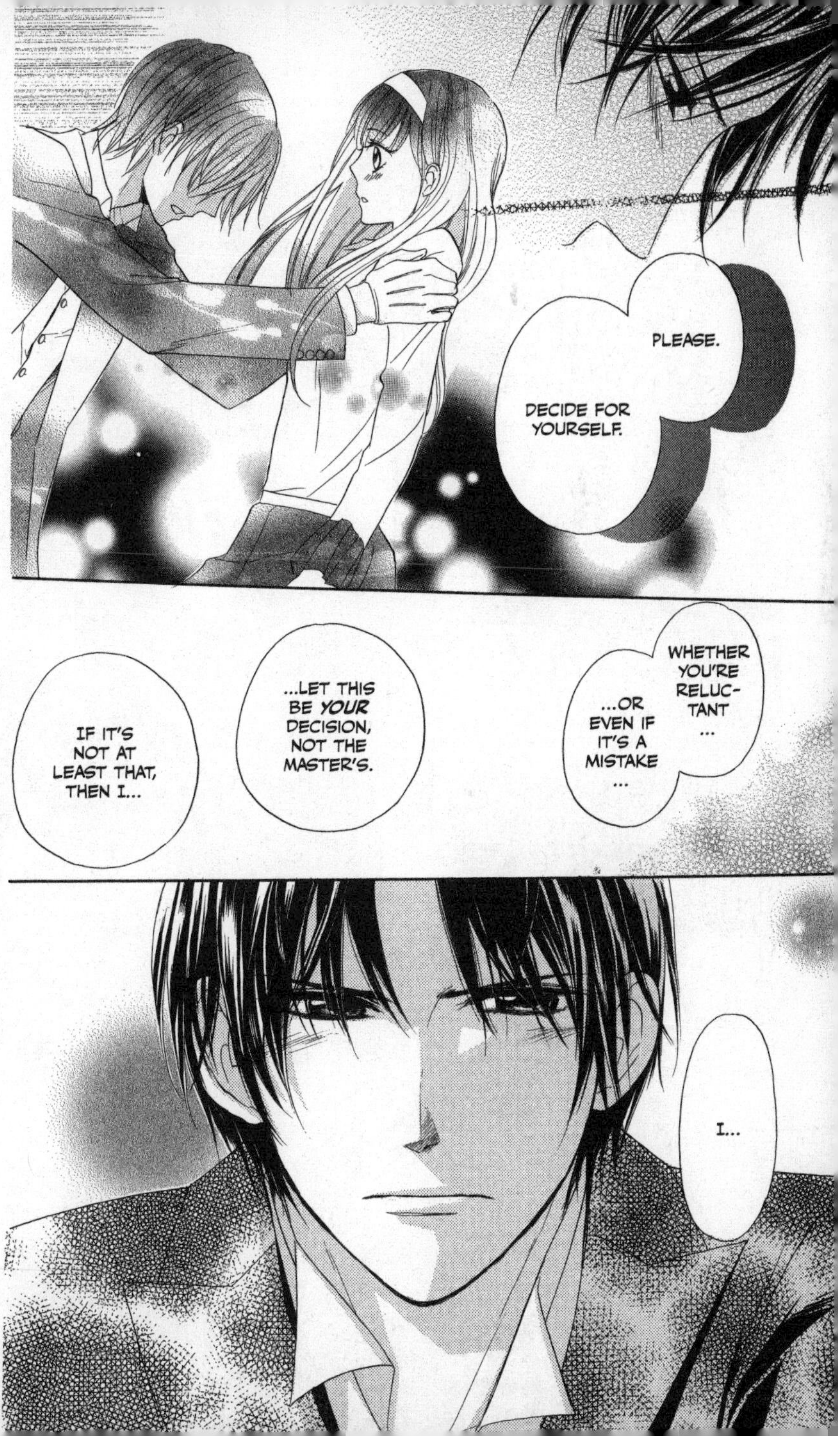
PLEASE.
DECIDE FOR YOURSELF.
WHETHER YOU'RE RELUC-TANT ...
...OR EVEN IF IT'S A MISTAKE ...
...LET THIS BE *YOUR* DECISION, NOT THE MASTER'S.
IF IT'S NOT AT LEAST THAT, THEN I...
I...

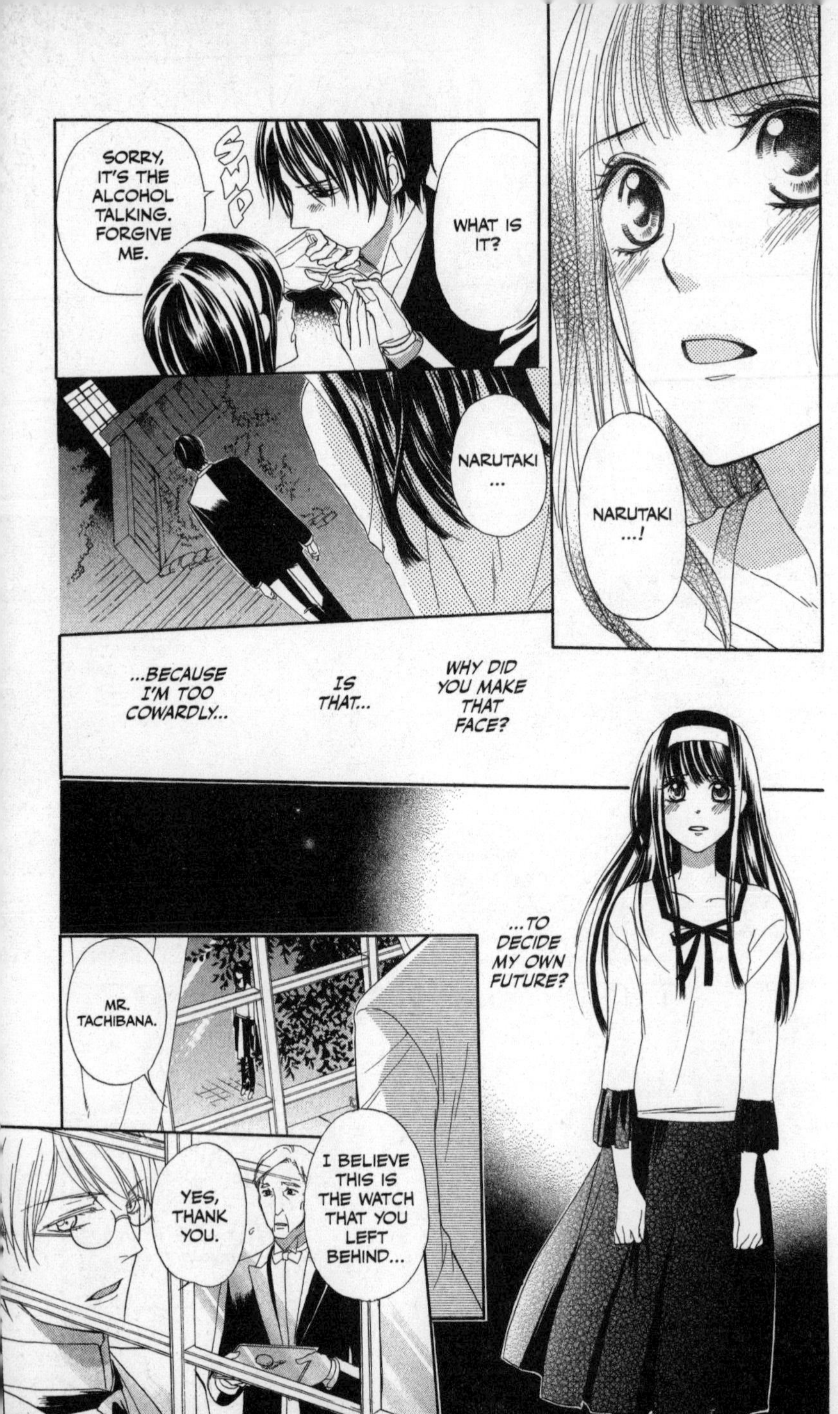
NARUTAKI ...!
WHAT IS IT?
SWD
SORRY, IT'S THE ALCOHOL TALKING. FORGIVE ME.
NARUTAKI ...
WHY DID YOU MAKE THAT FACE?
IS THAT...
...BECAUSE I'M TOO COWARDLY...
...TO DECIDE MY OWN FUTURE?
MR. TACHIBANA.
I BELIEVE THIS IS THE WATCH THAT YOU LEFT BEHIND...
YES, THANK YOU.

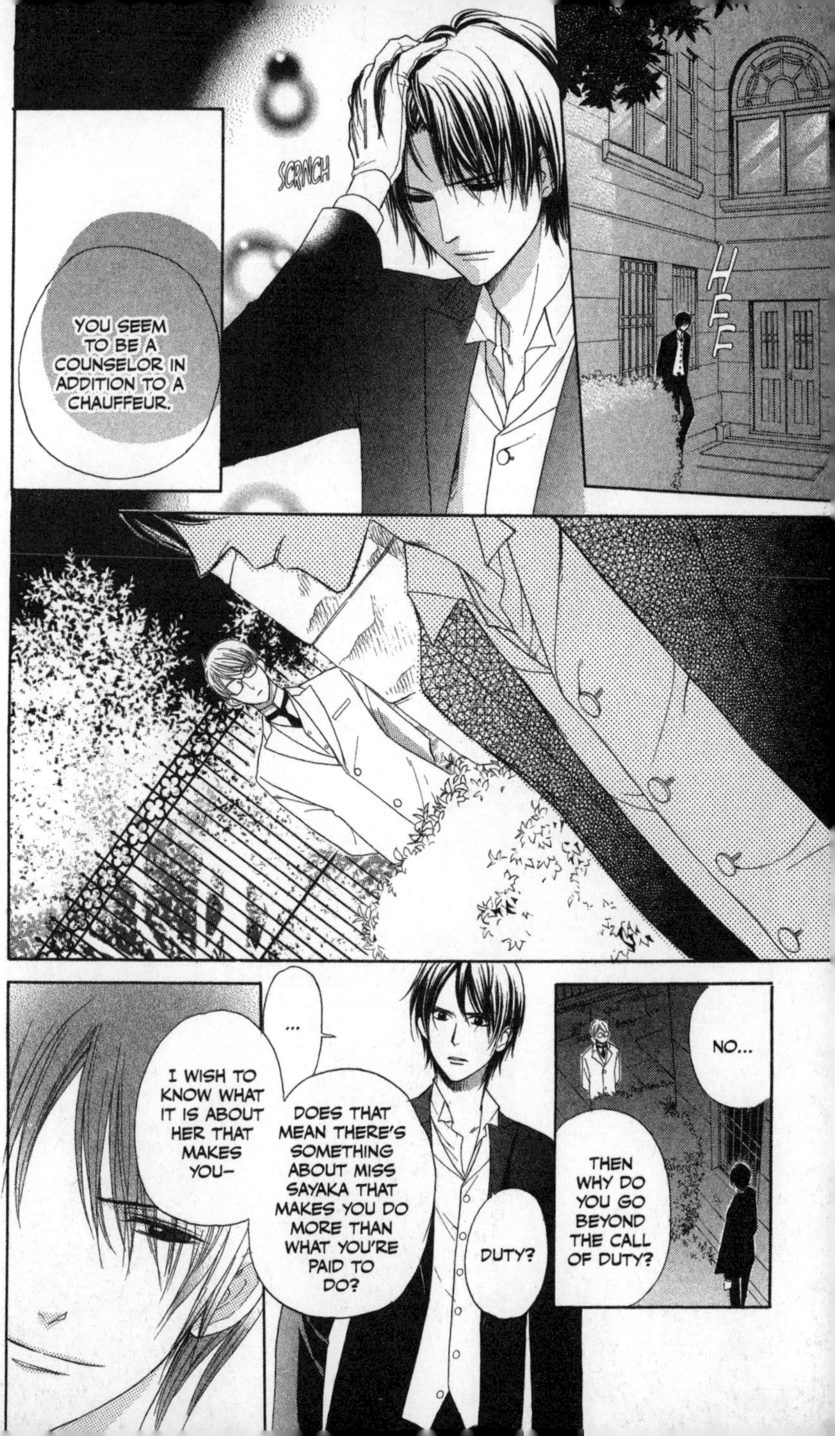
HFF
SCRNCH
YOU SEEM TO BE A COUNSELOR IN ADDITION TO A CHAUFFEUR.
NO...
THEN WHY DO YOU GO BEYOND THE CALL OF DUTY?
DUTY?
...
DOES THAT MEAN THERE'S SOMETHING ABOUT MISS SAYAKA THAT MAKES YOU DO MORE THAN WHAT YOU'RE PAID TO DO?
I WISH TO KNOW WHAT IT IS ABOUT HER THAT MAKES YOU–

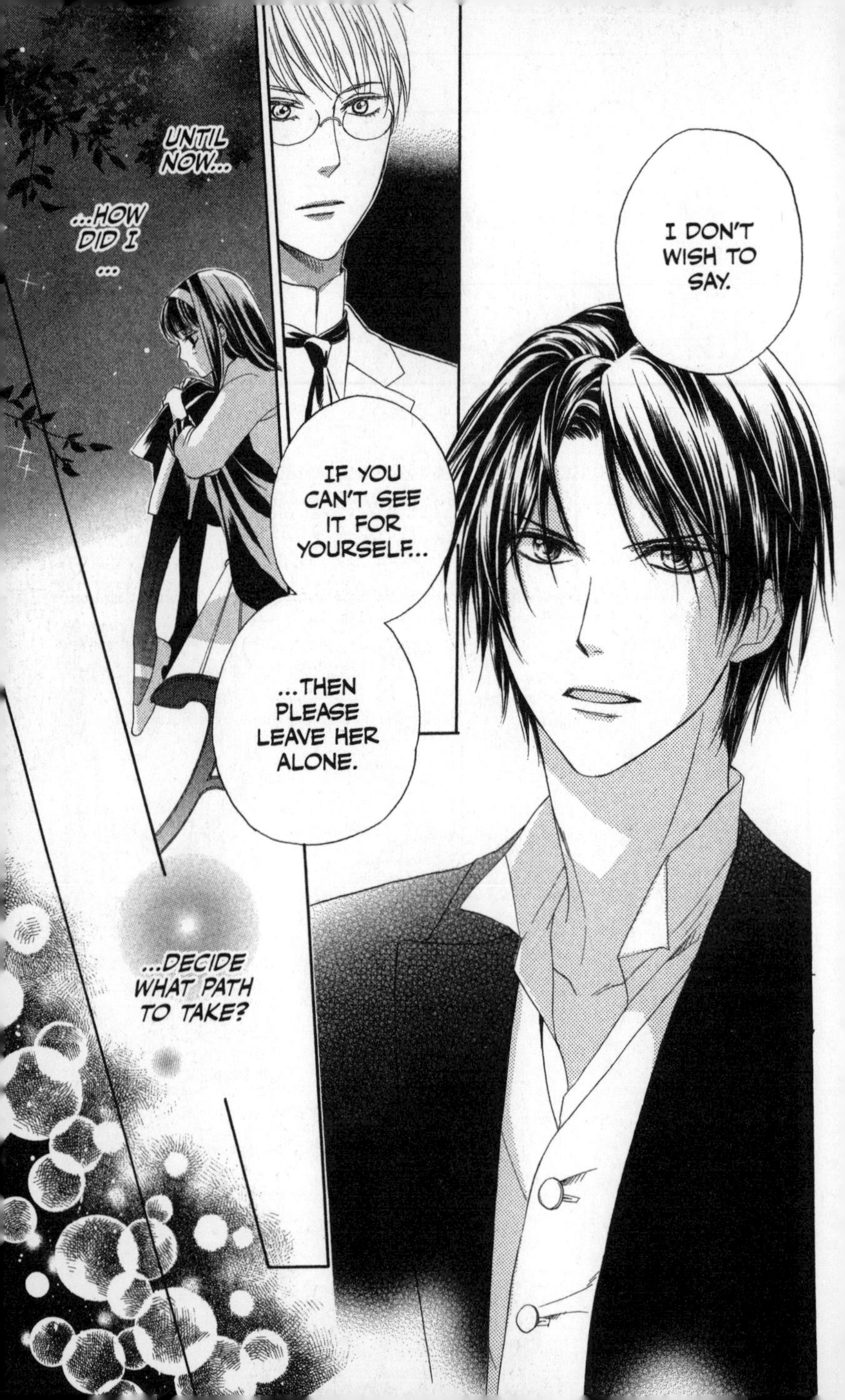
I DON'T WISH TO SAY.
IF YOU CAN'T SEE IT FOR YOURSELF...
...THEN PLEASE LEAVE HER ALONE.
UNTIL NOW...
...HOW DID I ...
...DECIDE WHAT PATH TO TAKE?

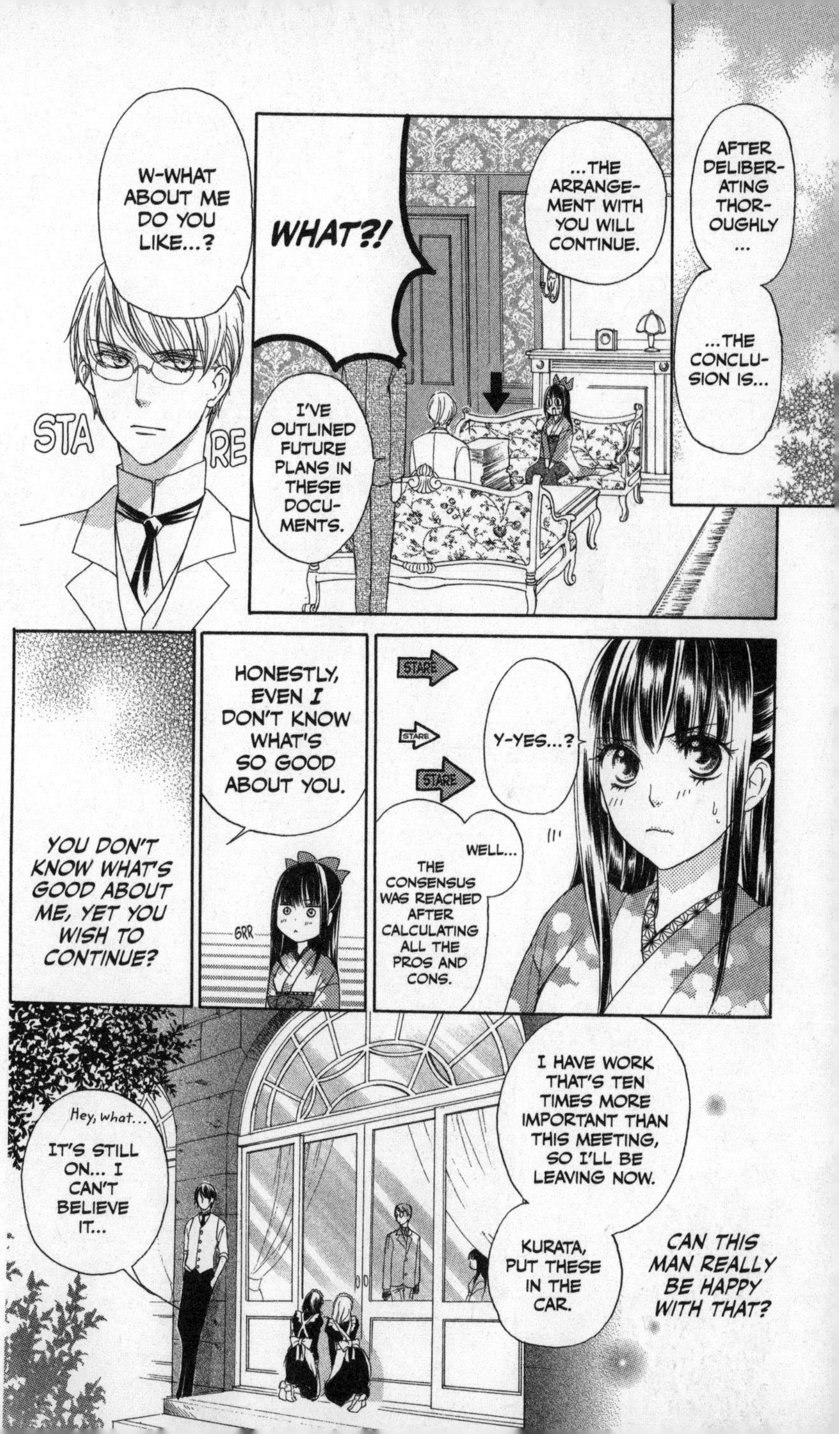
AFTER DELIBERATING THOROUGHLY...
...THE CONCLUSION IS...
...THE ARRANGEMENT WITH YOU WILL CONTINUE.
WHAT?!
I'VE OUTLINED FUTURE PLANS IN THESE DOCUMENTS.
W-WHAT ABOUT ME DO YOU LIKE...?
STARE
STARE
STARE
STARE
Y-YES...?
WELL...
THE CONSENSUS WAS REACHED AFTER CALCULATING ALL THE PROS AND CONS.
HONESTLY, EVEN *I* DON'T KNOW WHAT'S SO GOOD ABOUT YOU.
GRR
YOU DON'T KNOW WHAT'S GOOD ABOUT ME, YET YOU WISH TO CONTINUE?
I HAVE WORK THAT'S TEN TIMES MORE IMPORTANT THAN THIS MEETING, SO I'LL BE LEAVING NOW.
KURATA, PUT THESE IN THE CAR.
CAN THIS MAN REALLY BE HAPPY WITH THAT?
Hey, what...
IT'S STILL ON... I CAN'T BELIEVE IT...

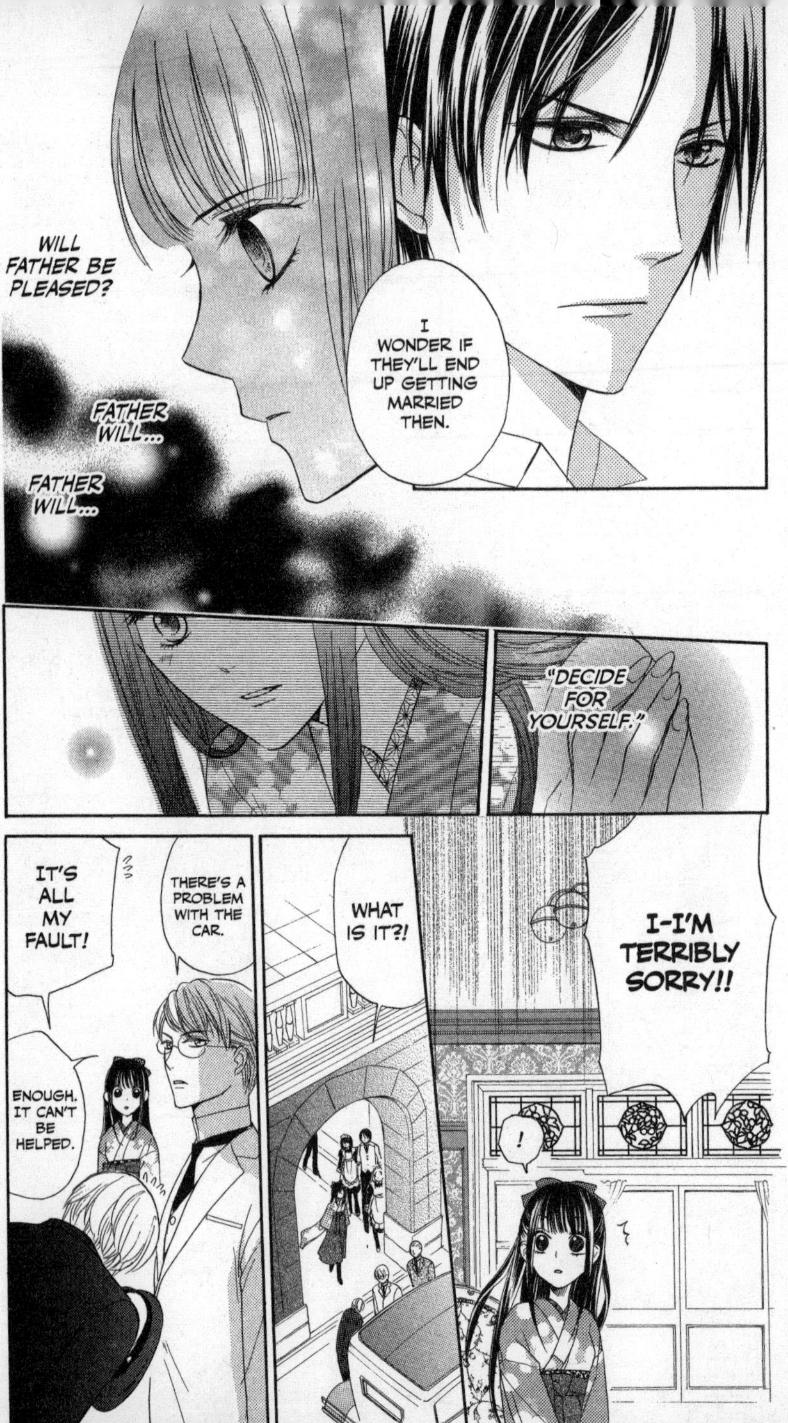
I WONDER IF THEY'LL END UP GETTING MARRIED THEN.
WILL FATHER BE PLEASED?
FATHER WILL...
FATHER WILL...
"DECIDE FOR YOURSELF."
I-I'M TERRIBLY SORRY!!
!
WHAT IS IT?!
THERE'S A PROBLEM WITH THE CAR.
IT'S ALL MY FAULT!
ENOUGH. IT CAN'T BE HELPED.

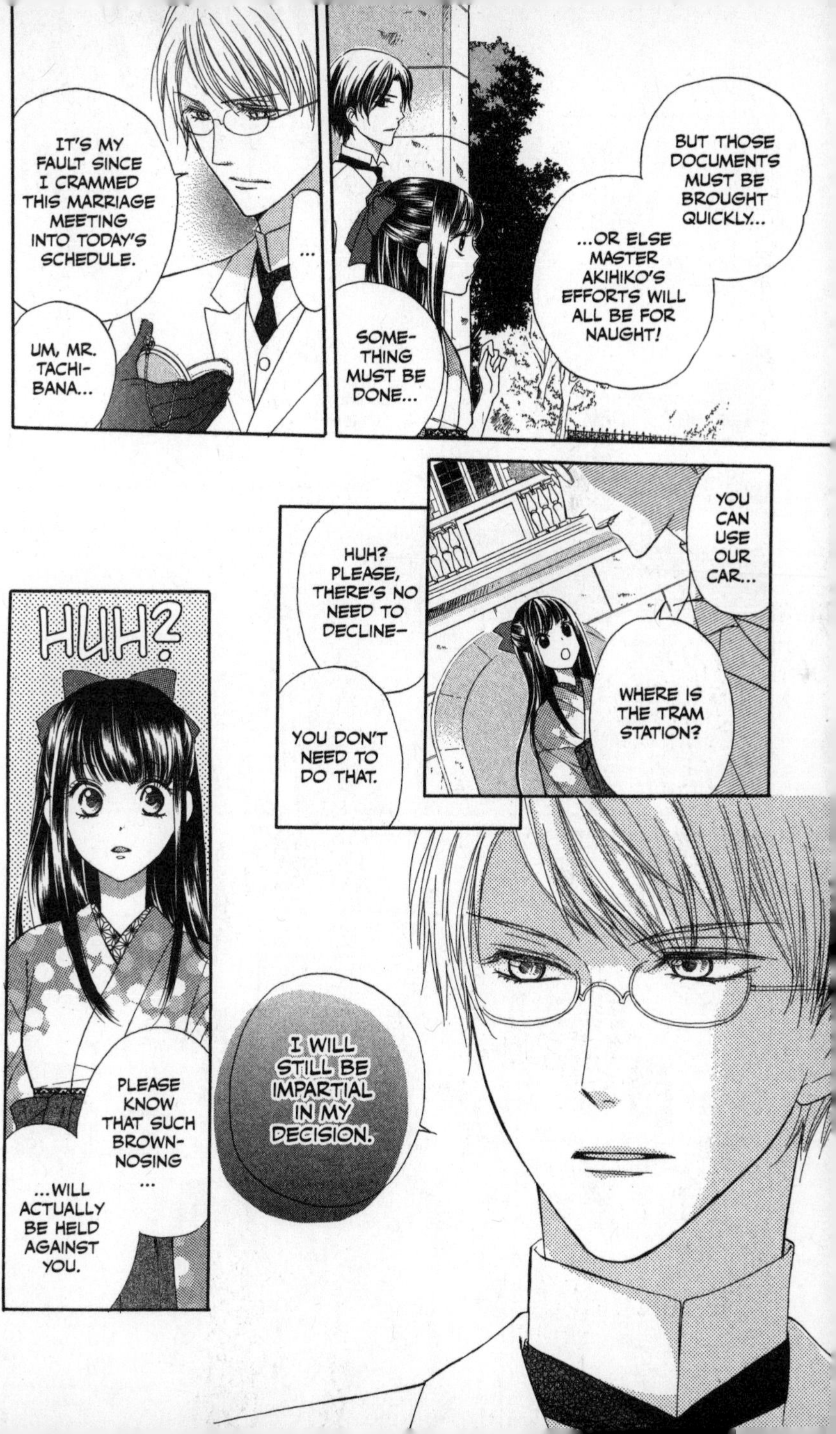
BUT THOSE DOCUMENTS MUST BE BROUGHT QUICKLY...
...OR ELSE MASTER AKIHIKO'S EFFORTS WILL ALL BE FOR NAUGHT!
SOME-THING MUST BE DONE...
IT'S MY FAULT SINCE I CRAMMED THIS MARRIAGE MEETING INTO TODAY'S SCHEDULE.
...
UM, MR. TACHI-BANA...
YOU CAN USE OUR CAR...
WHERE IS THE TRAM STATION?
HUH? PLEASE, THERE'S NO NEED TO DECLINE—
YOU DON'T NEED TO DO THAT.
PLEASE KNOW THAT SUCH BROWN-NOSING...
...WILL ACTUALLY BE HELD AGAINST YOU.
I WILL STILL BE IMPARTIAL IN MY DECISION.
HUH?

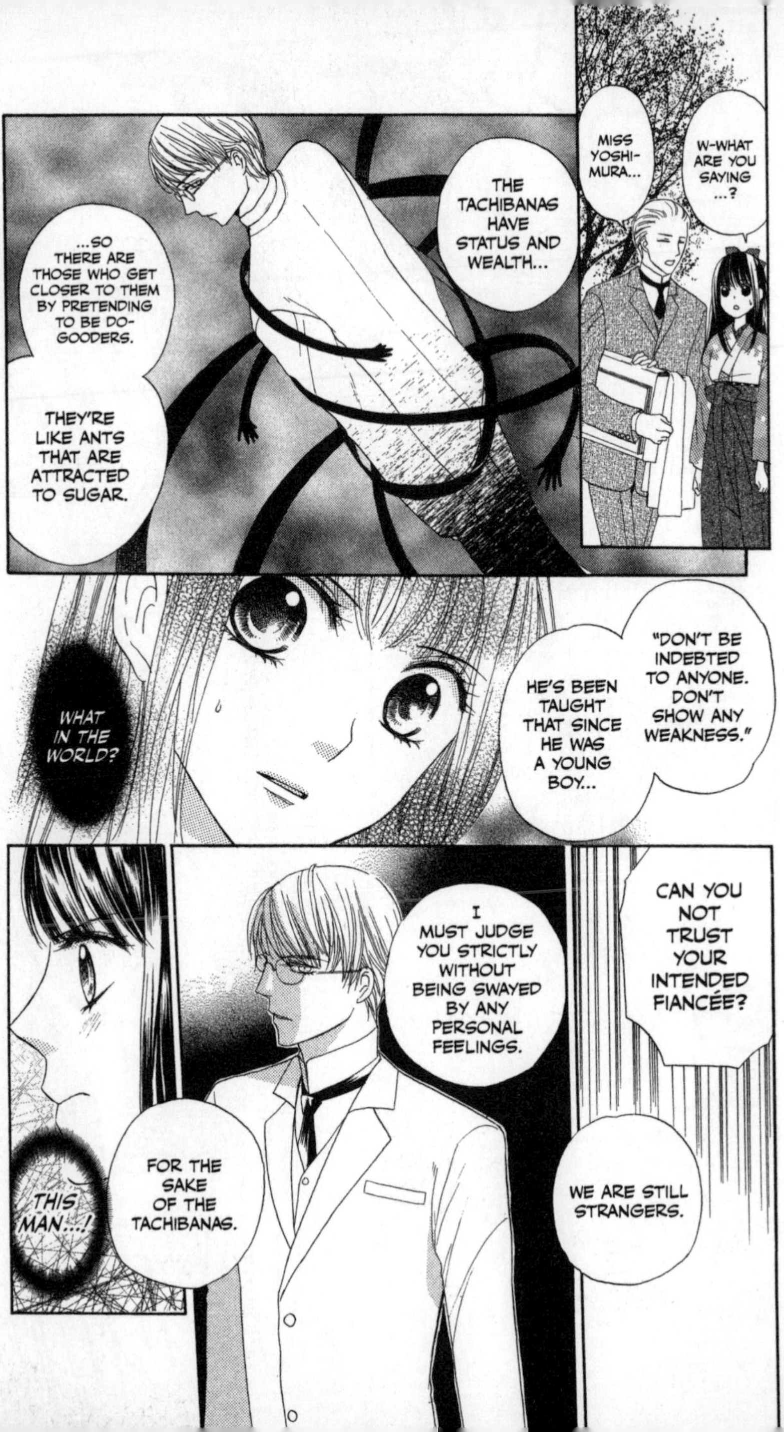
W-WHAT ARE YOU SAYING ...?
MISS YOSHIMURA...
THE TACHIBANAS HAVE STATUS AND WEALTH...
...SO THERE ARE THOSE WHO GET CLOSER TO THEM BY PRETENDING TO BE DO-GOODERS.
THEY'RE LIKE ANTS THAT ARE ATTRACTED TO SUGAR.
"DON'T BE INDEBTED TO ANYONE. DON'T SHOW ANY WEAKNESS."
HE'S BEEN TAUGHT THAT SINCE HE WAS A YOUNG BOY...
WHAT IN THE WORLD?
CAN YOU NOT TRUST YOUR INTENDED FIANCÉE?
WE ARE STILL STRANGERS.
I MUST JUDGE YOU STRICTLY WITHOUT BEING SWAYED BY ANY PERSONAL FEELINGS.
FOR THE SAKE OF THE TACHIBANAS.
THIS MAN...!

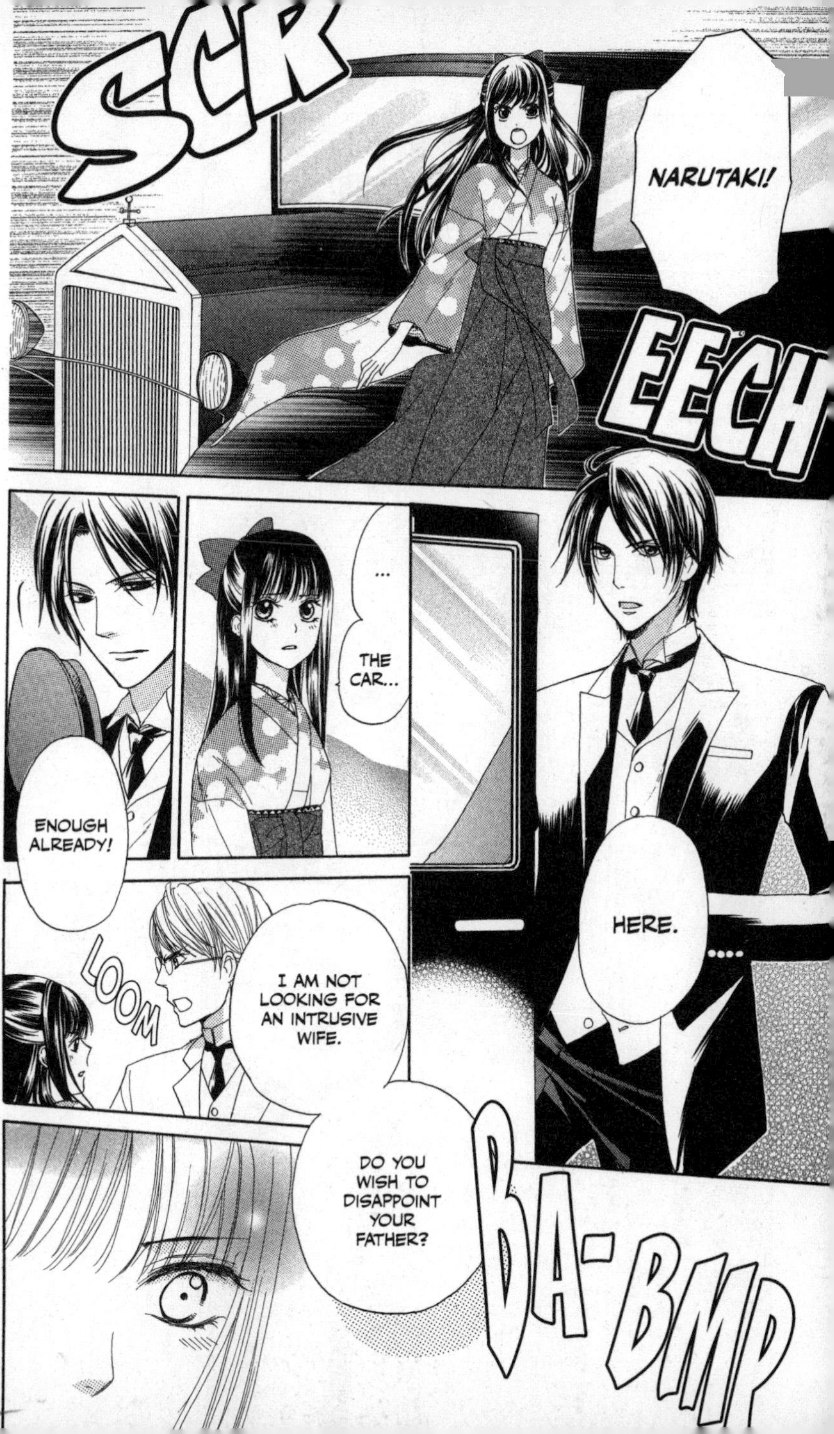
NARUTAKI!
SCR
EECH
HERE.
...
THE CAR...
ENOUGH ALREADY!
I AM NOT LOOKING FOR AN INTRUSIVE WIFE.
LOOM
DO YOU WISH TO DISAPPOINT YOUR FATHER?
BA-BMP

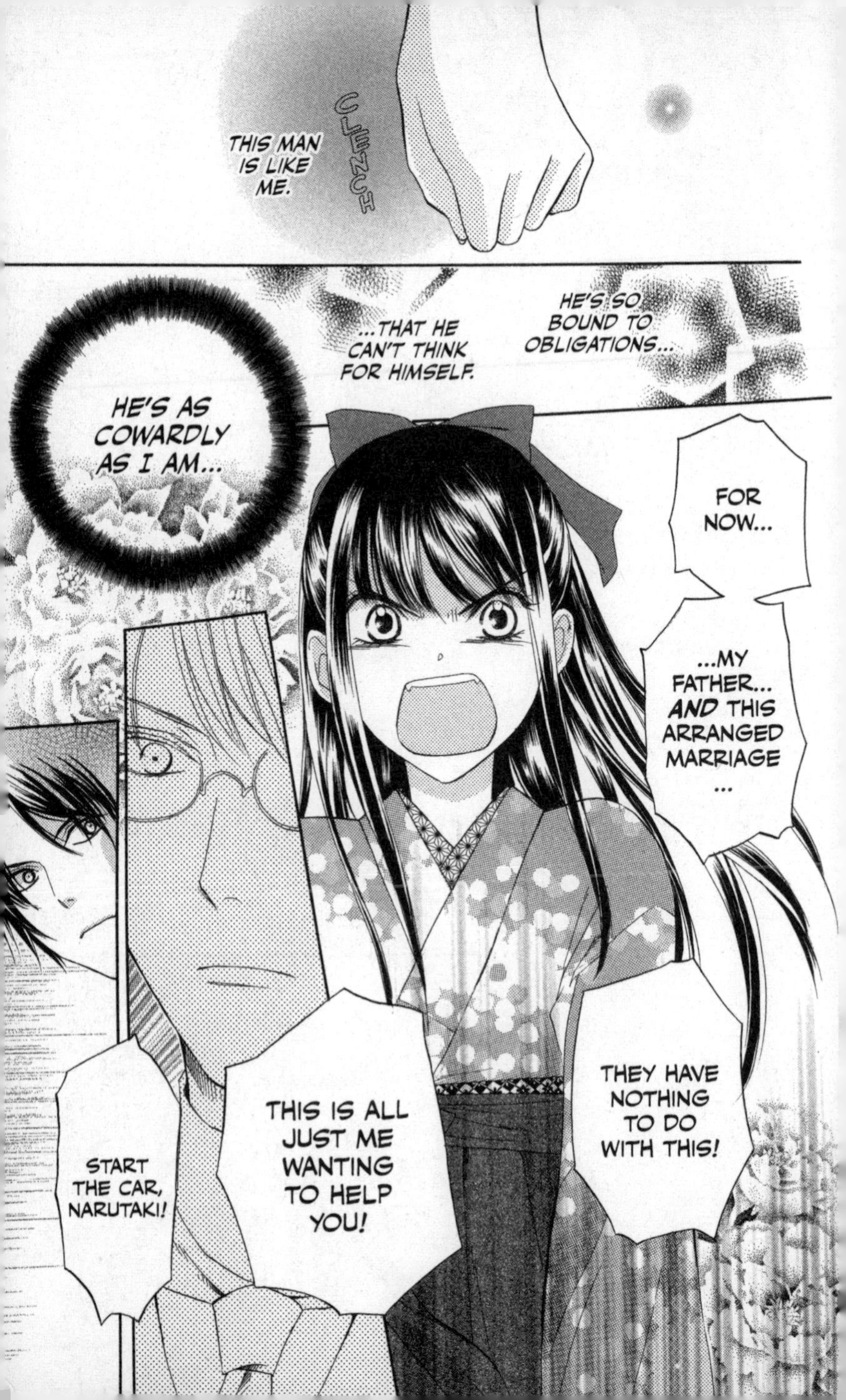
CLENCH
THIS MAN IS LIKE ME.
HE'S SO BOUND TO OBLIGATIONS...
...THAT HE CAN'T THINK FOR HIMSELF.
HE'S AS COWARDLY AS I AM...
FOR NOW...
...MY FATHER... AND THIS ARRANGED MARRIAGE ...
THEY HAVE NOTHING TO DO WITH THIS!
THIS IS ALL JUST ME WANTING TO HELP YOU!
START THE CAR, NARUTAKI!

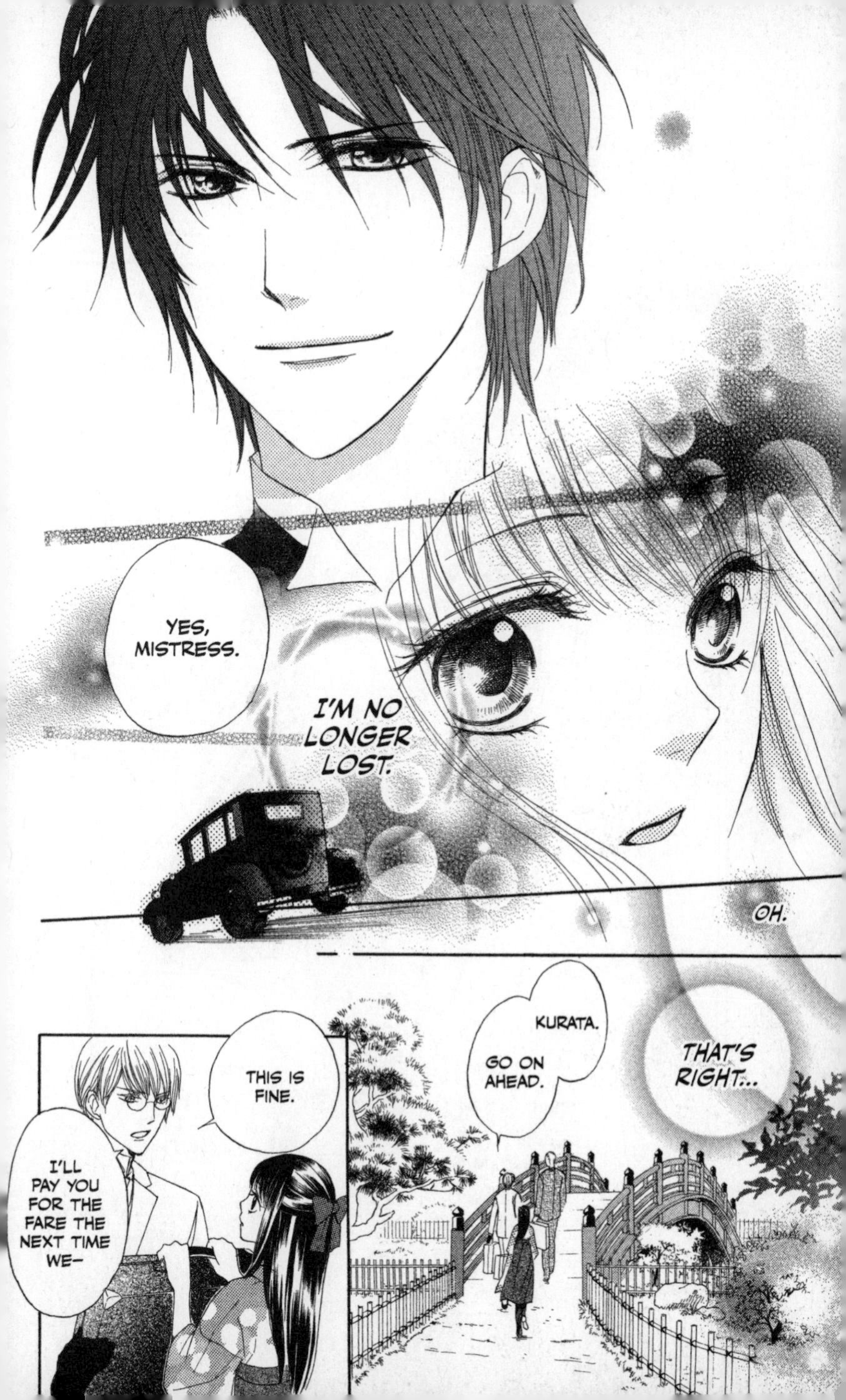
YES, MISTRESS.
I'M NO LONGER LOST.
OH.
THAT'S RIGHT...
KURATA.
GO ON AHEAD.
THIS IS FINE.
I'LL PAY YOU FOR THE FARE THE NEXT TIME WE–

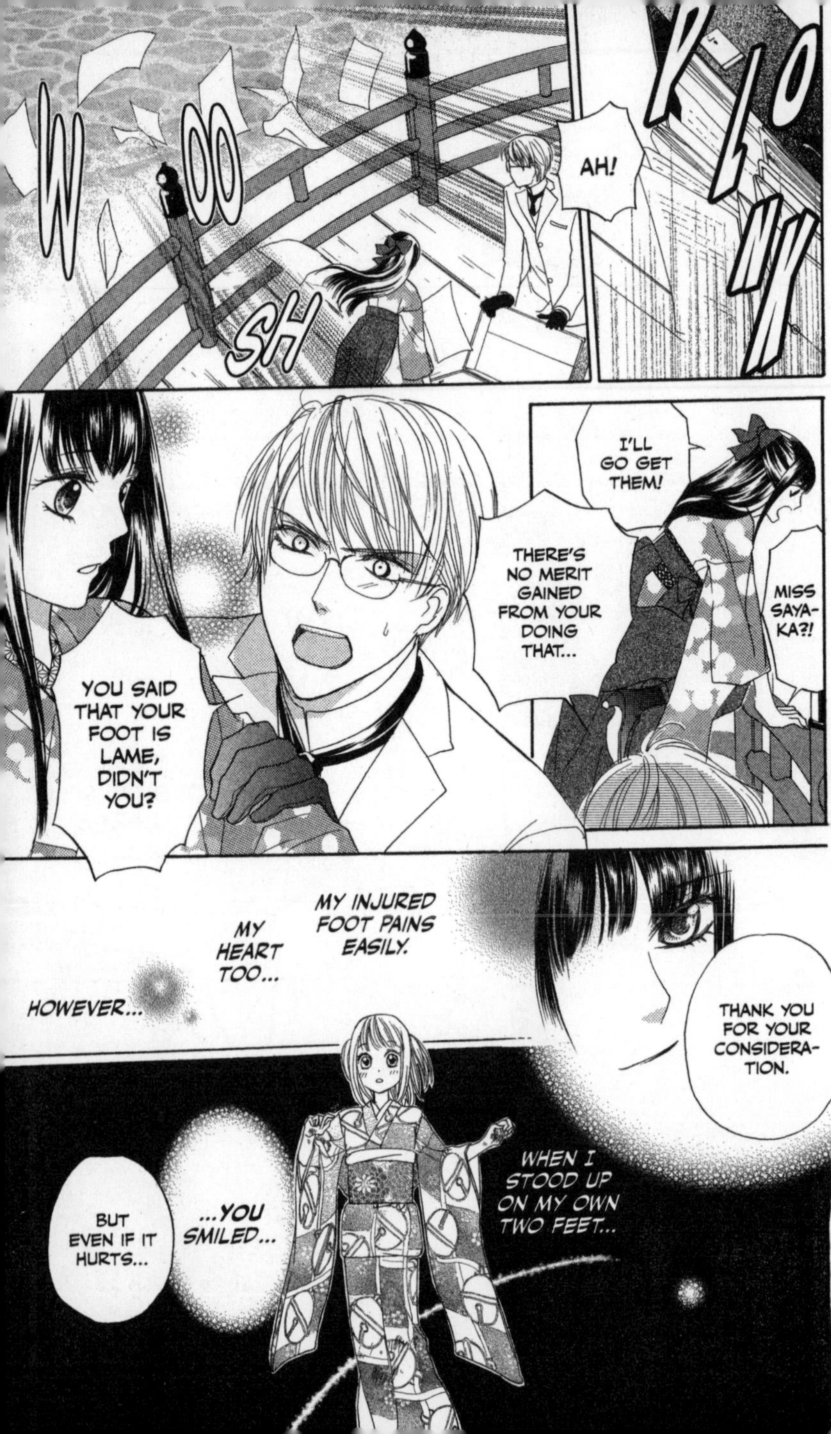
AH!
WOOSH
I'LL GO GET THEM!
MISS SAYA-KA?!
THERE'S NO MERIT GAINED FROM YOUR DOING THAT...
YOU SAID THAT YOUR FOOT IS LAME, DIDN'T YOU?
THANK YOU FOR YOUR CONSIDERA-TION.
MY INJURED FOOT PAINS EASILY.
MY HEART TOO...
HOWEVER...
WHEN I STOOD UP ON MY OWN TWO FEET...
...YOU SMILED...
BUT EVEN IF IT HURTS...

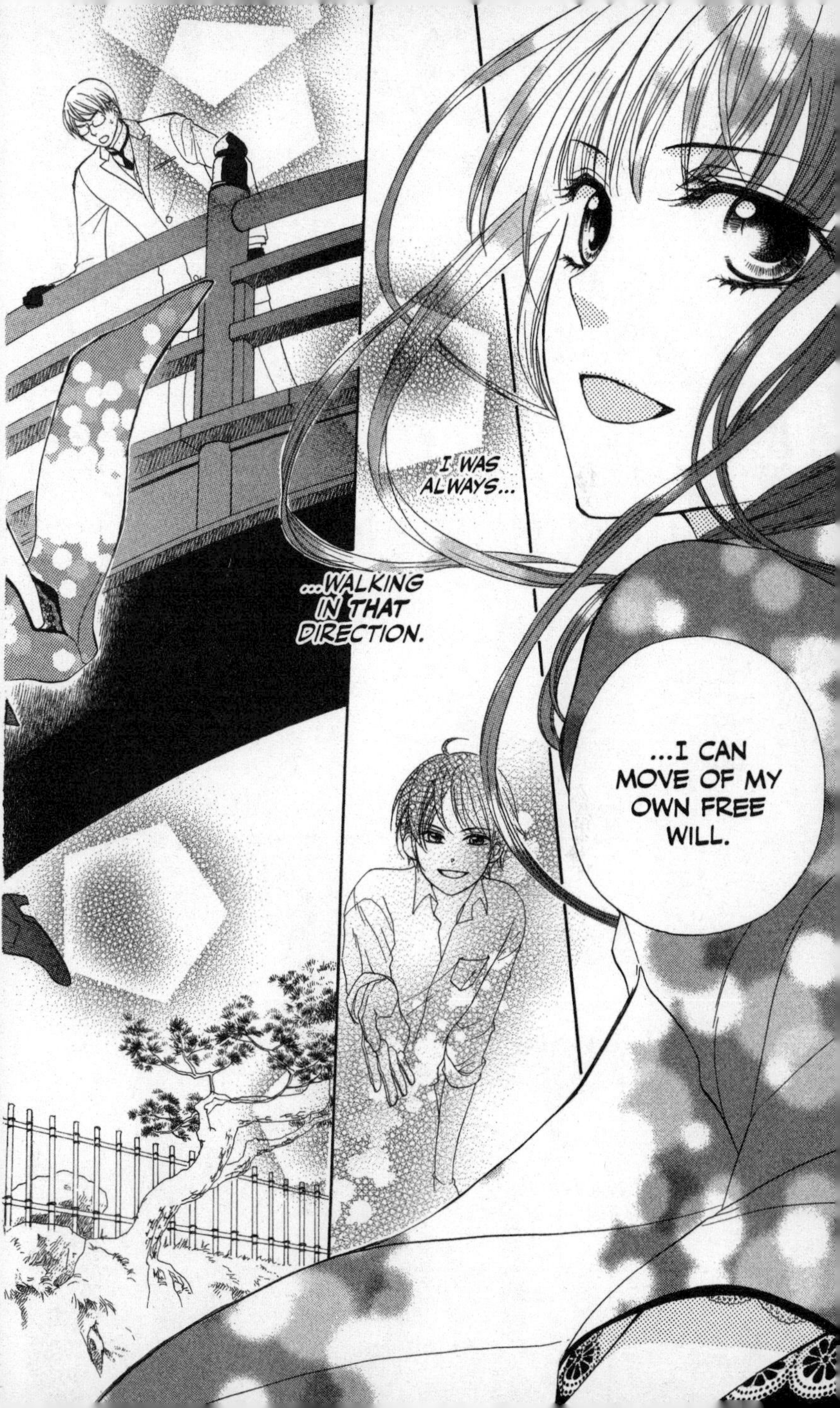
I WAS ALWAYS...
...WALKING IN THAT DIRECTION.
...I CAN MOVE OF MY OWN FREE WILL.

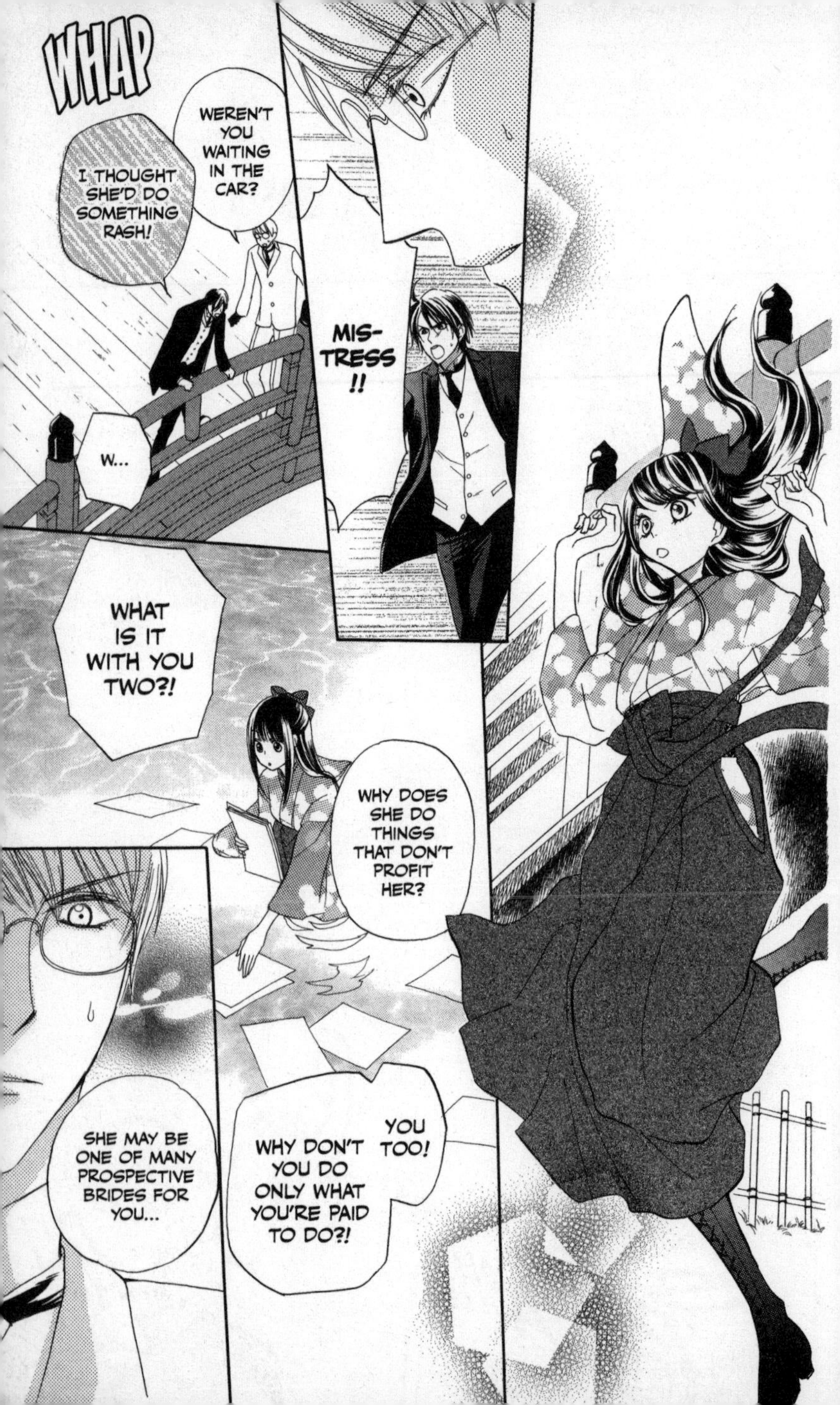
MIS-TRESS!!
WHAP
WEREN'T YOU WAITING IN THE CAR?
I THOUGHT SHE'D DO SOMETHING RASH!
W...
WHAT IS IT WITH YOU TWO?!
WHY DOES SHE DO THINGS THAT DON'T PROFIT HER?
YOU TOO!
WHY DON'T YOU DO ONLY WHAT YOU'RE PAID TO DO?!
SHE MAY BE ONE OF MANY PROSPECTIVE BRIDES FOR YOU...

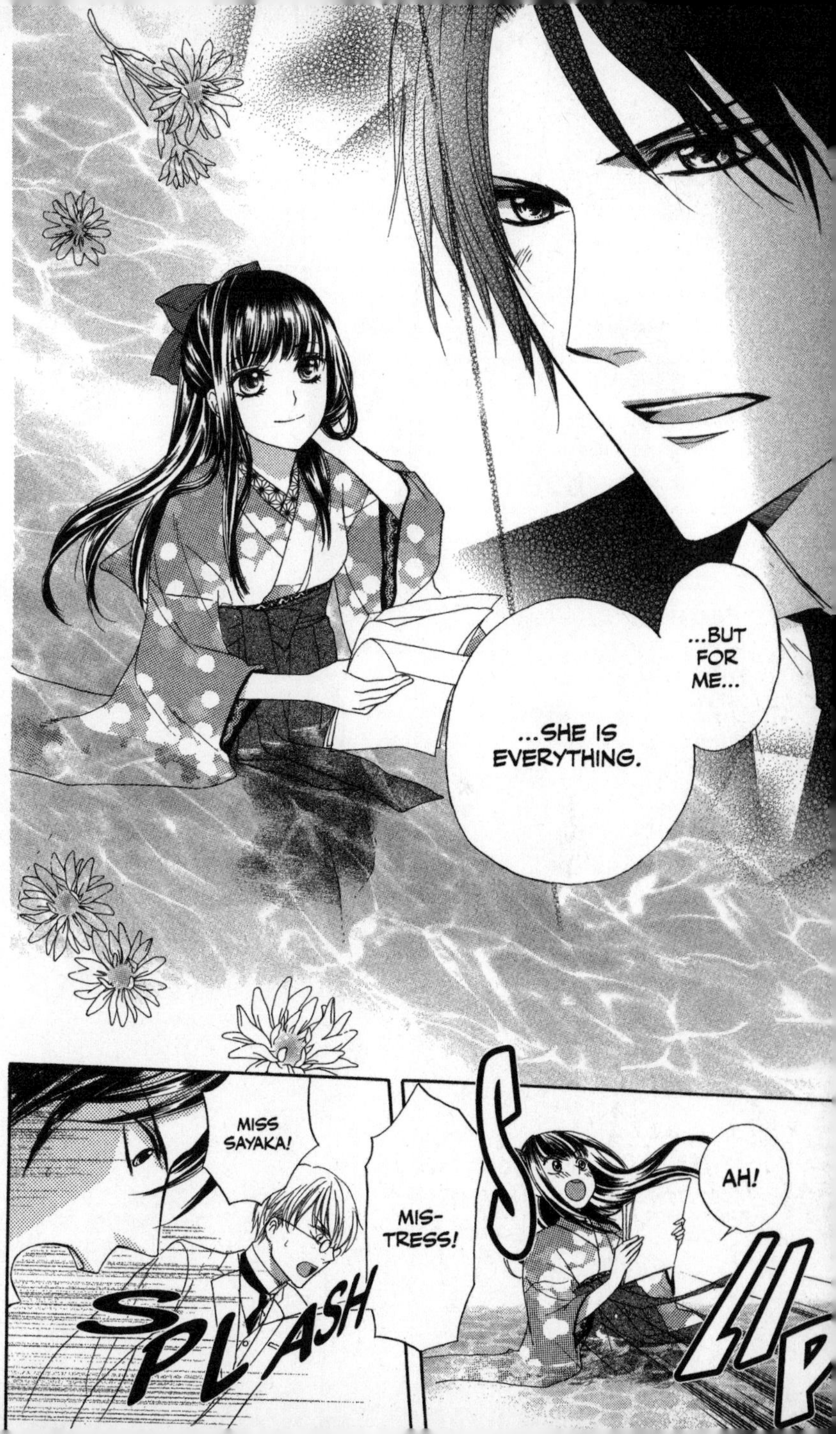
...BUT FOR ME...
...SHE IS EVERYTHING.
SLIP
AH!
MIS-TRESS!
MISS SAYAKA!
SPLASH

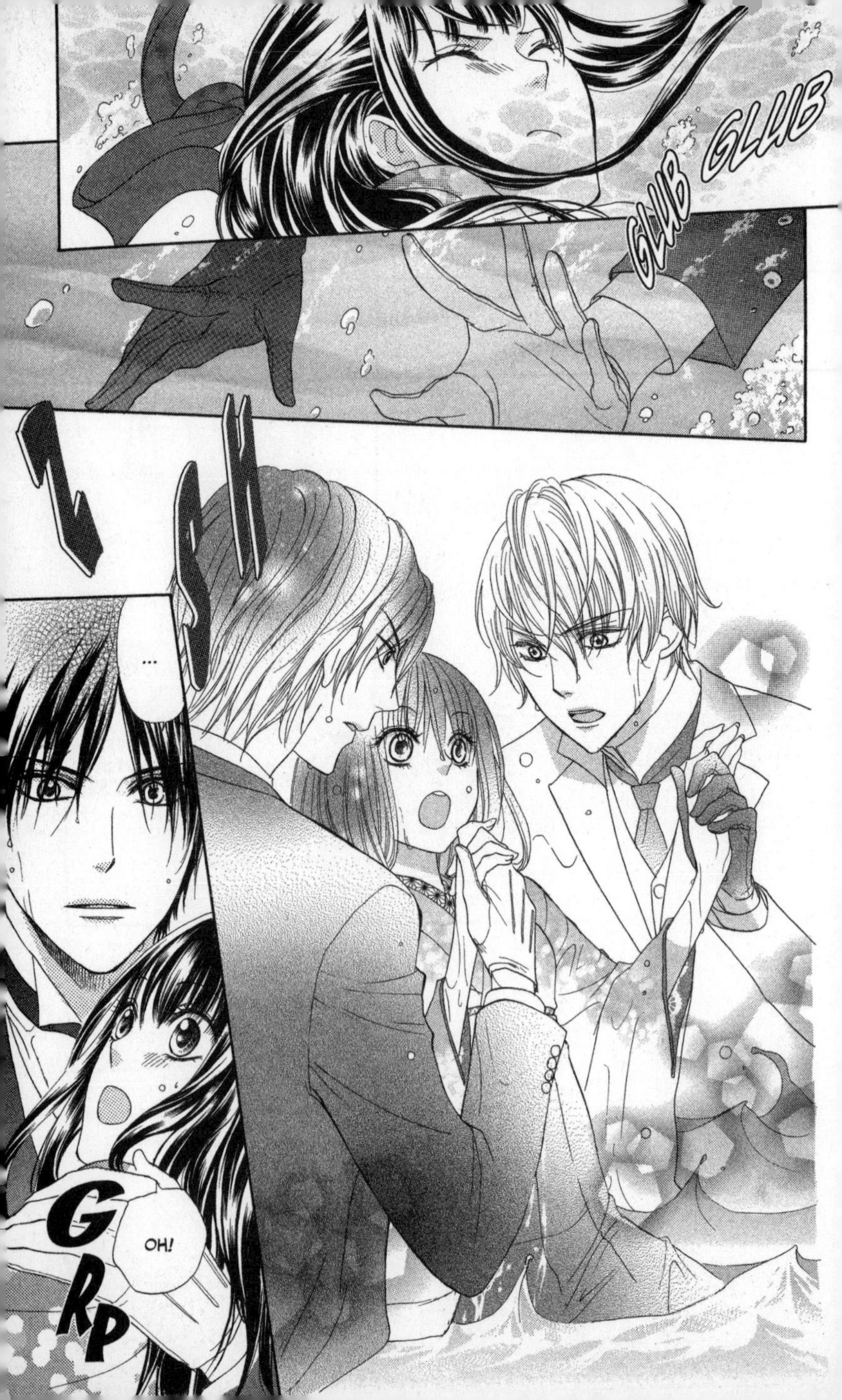
GLUB GLUB
...
GRP
OH!

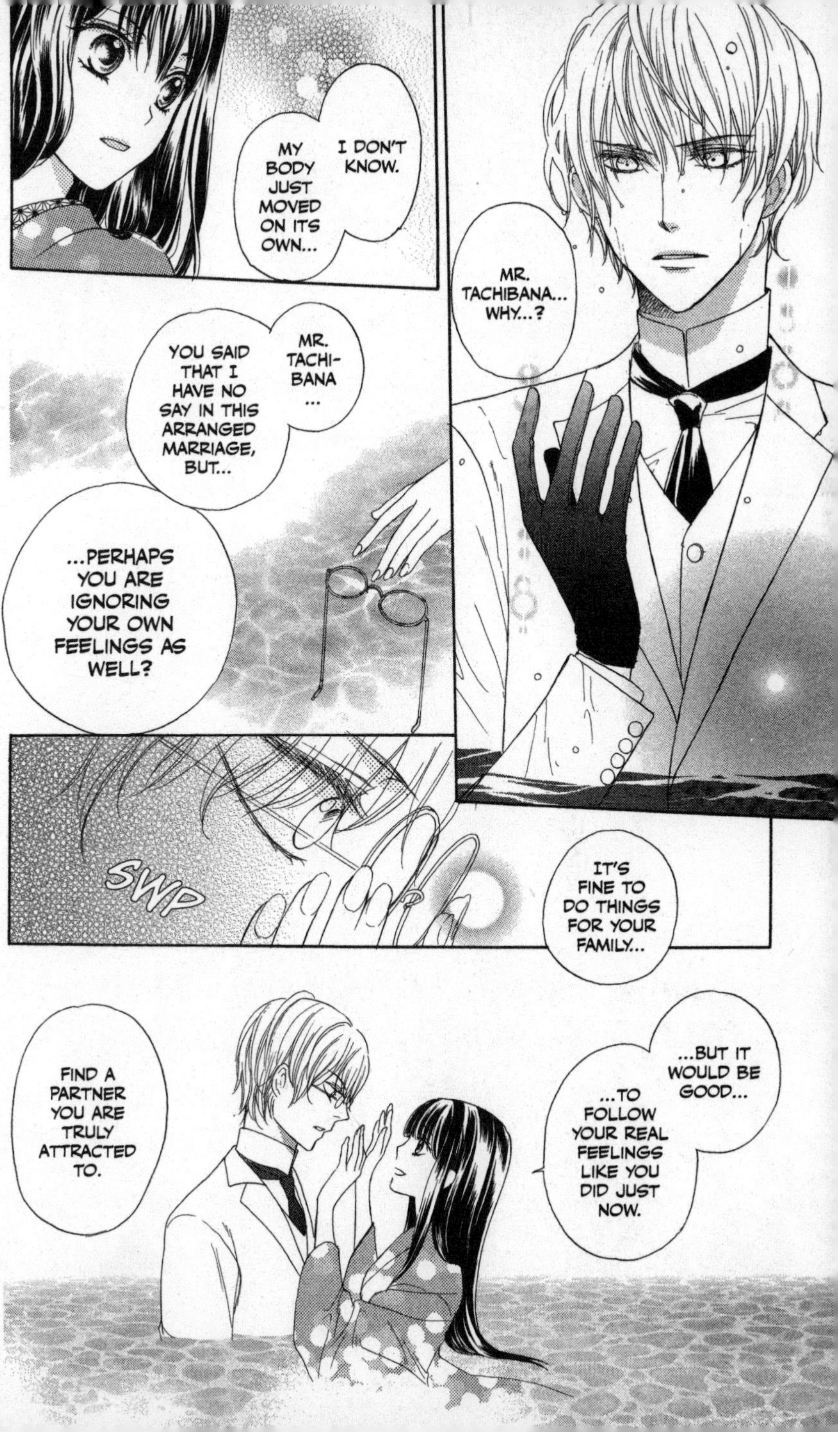
MR. TACHIBANA... WHY...?
I DON'T KNOW.
MY BODY JUST MOVED ON ITS OWN...
MR. TACHIBANA...
YOU SAID THAT I HAVE NO SAY IN THIS ARRANGED MARRIAGE, BUT...
...PERHAPS YOU ARE IGNORING YOUR OWN FEELINGS AS WELL?
IT'S FINE TO DO THINGS FOR YOUR FAMILY...
SWP
...BUT IT WOULD BE GOOD...
...TO FOLLOW YOUR REAL FEELINGS LIKE YOU DID JUST NOW.
FIND A PARTNER YOU ARE TRULY ATTRACTED TO.

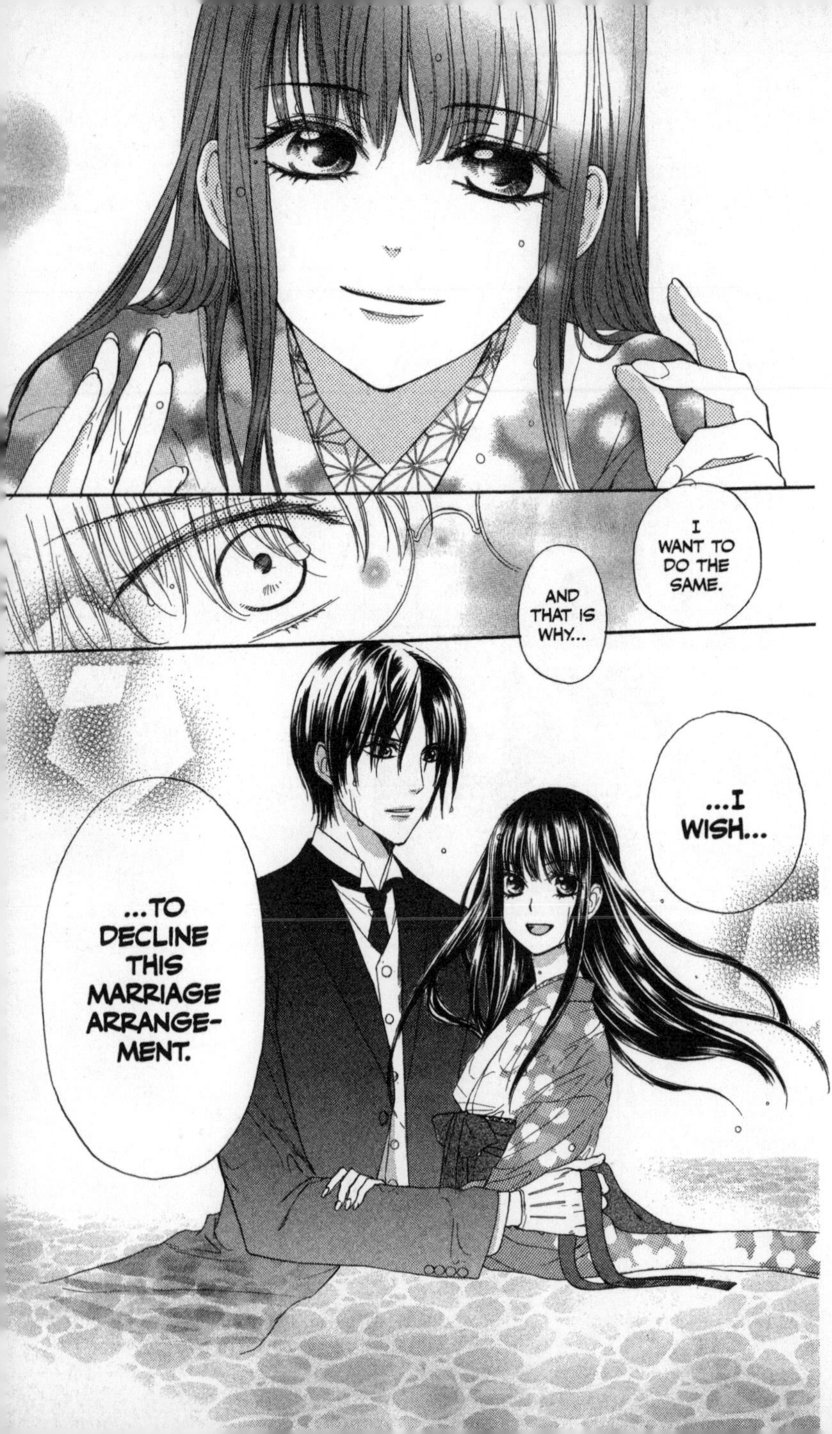
I WANT TO DO THE SAME.
AND THAT IS WHY...
...I WISH...
...TO DECLINE THIS MARRIAGE ARRANGE-MENT.

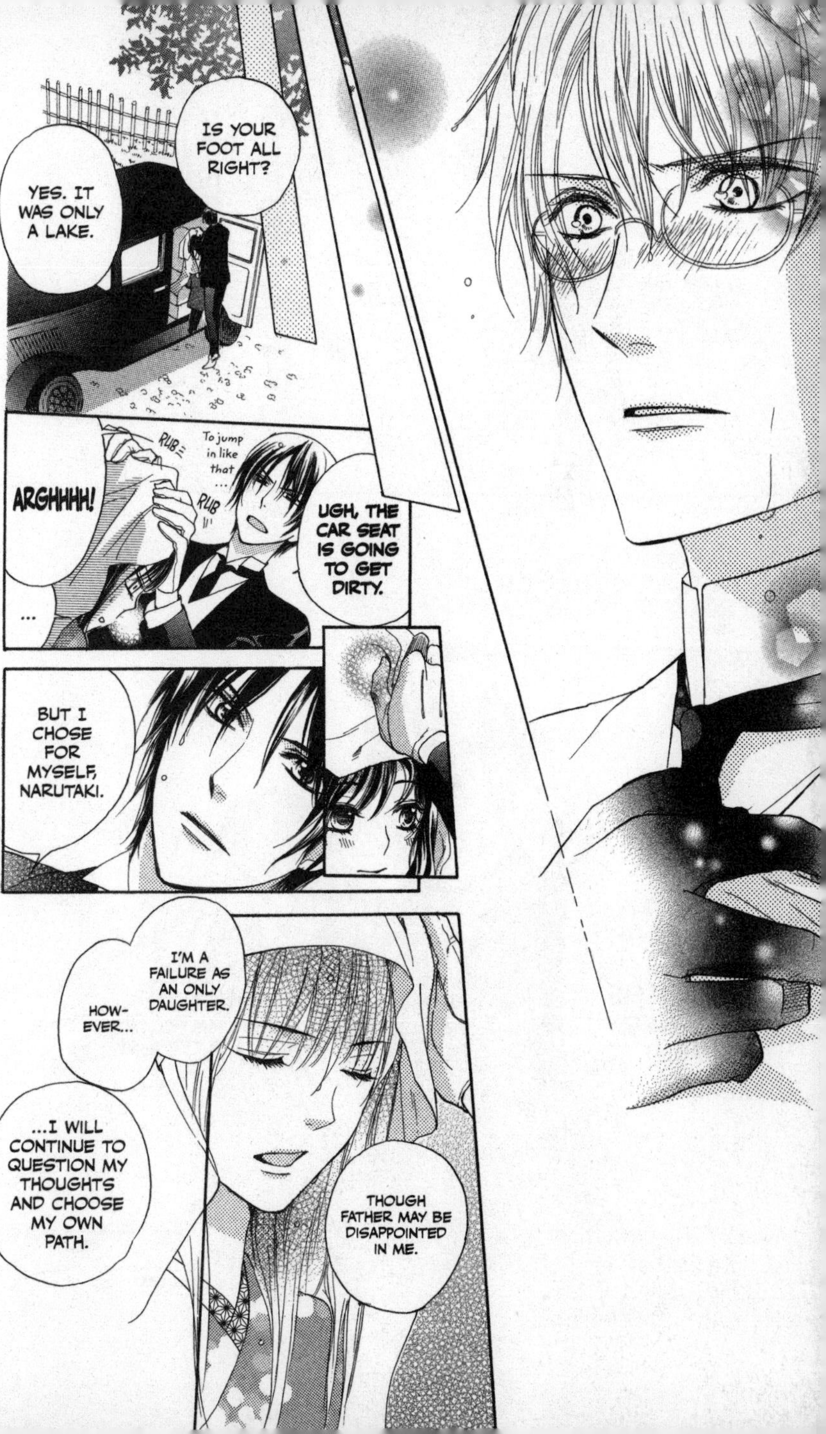
IS YOUR FOOT ALL RIGHT?
YES. IT WAS ONLY A LAKE.
UGH, THE CAR SEAT IS GOING TO GET DIRTY.
To jump in like that ...
RUB
RUB
ARGHHHH!
...
BUT I CHOSE FOR MYSELF, NARUTAKI.
I'M A FAILURE AS AN ONLY DAUGHTER.
HOW-EVER...
THOUGH FATHER MAY BE DISAPPOINTED IN ME.
...I WILL CONTINUE TO QUESTION MY THOUGHTS AND CHOOSE MY OWN PATH.

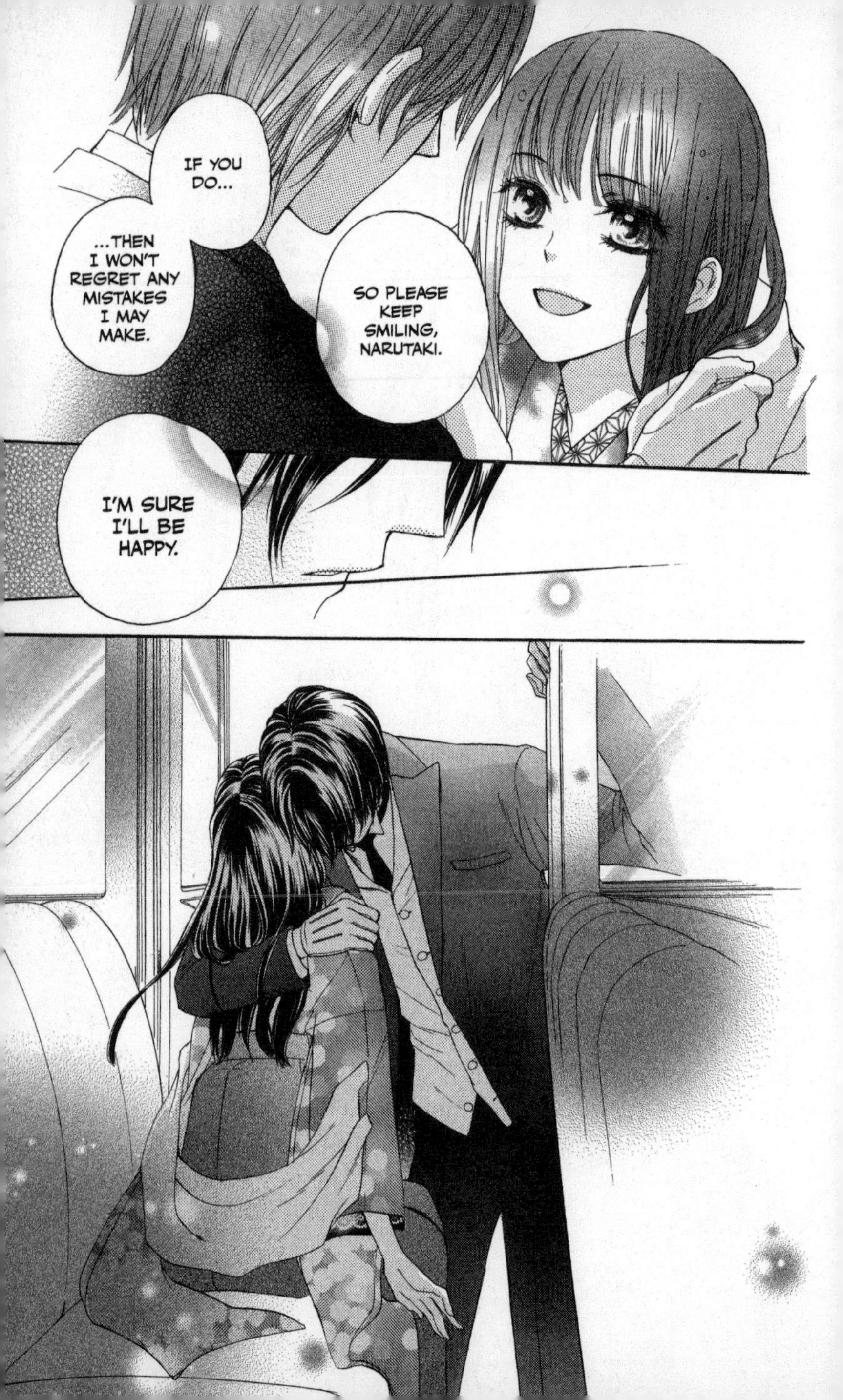
SO PLEASE KEEP SMILING, NARUTAKI.
IF YOU DO...
...THEN I WON'T REGRET ANY MISTAKES I MAY MAKE.
I'M SURE I'LL BE HAPPY.

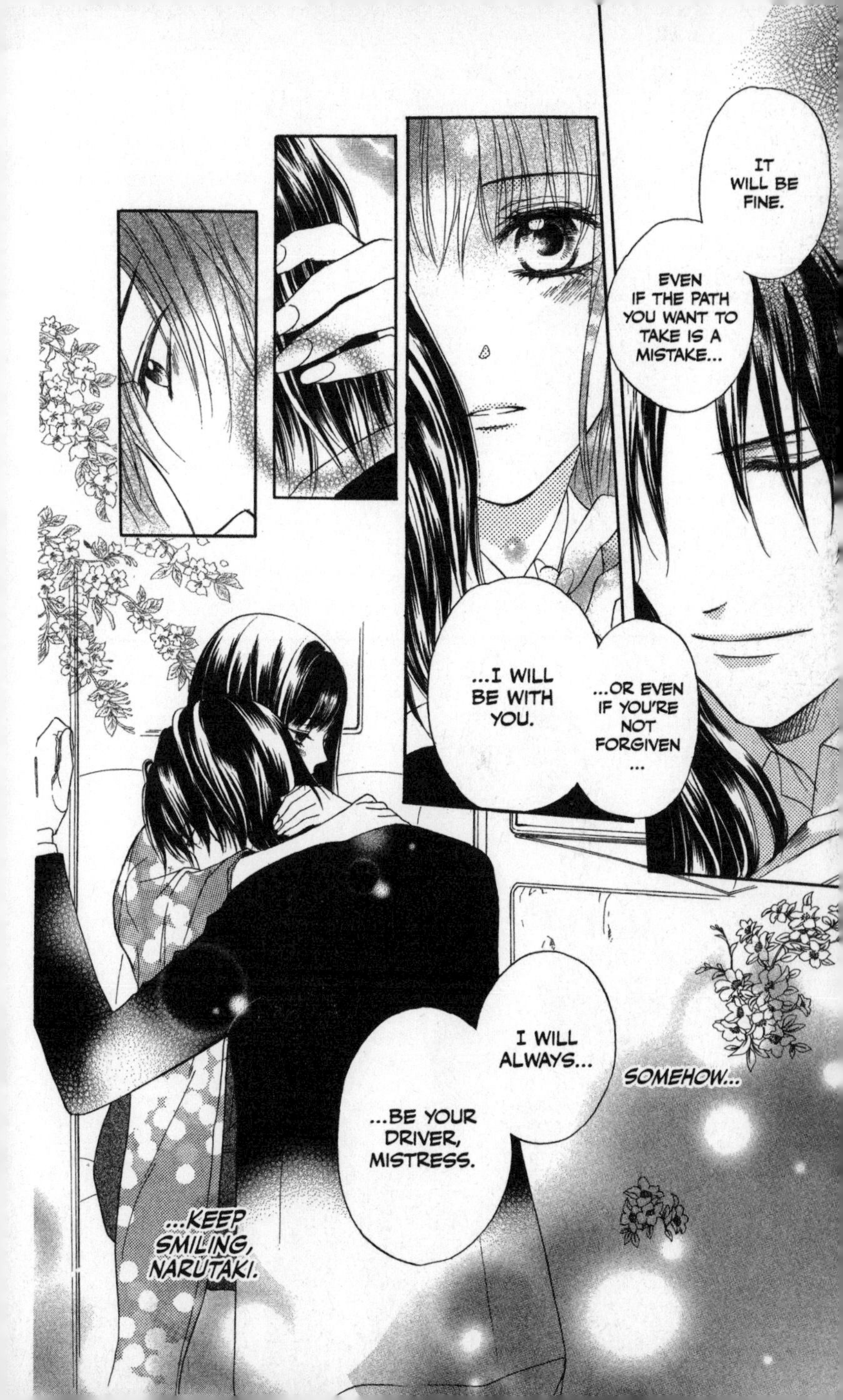
IT WILL BE FINE.
EVEN IF THE PATH YOU WANT TO TAKE IS A MISTAKE...
...OR EVEN IF YOU'RE NOT FORGIVEN...
...I WILL BE WITH YOU.
I WILL ALWAYS...
...BE YOUR DRIVER, MISTRESS.
SOMEHOW...
...KEEP SMILING, NARUTAKI.

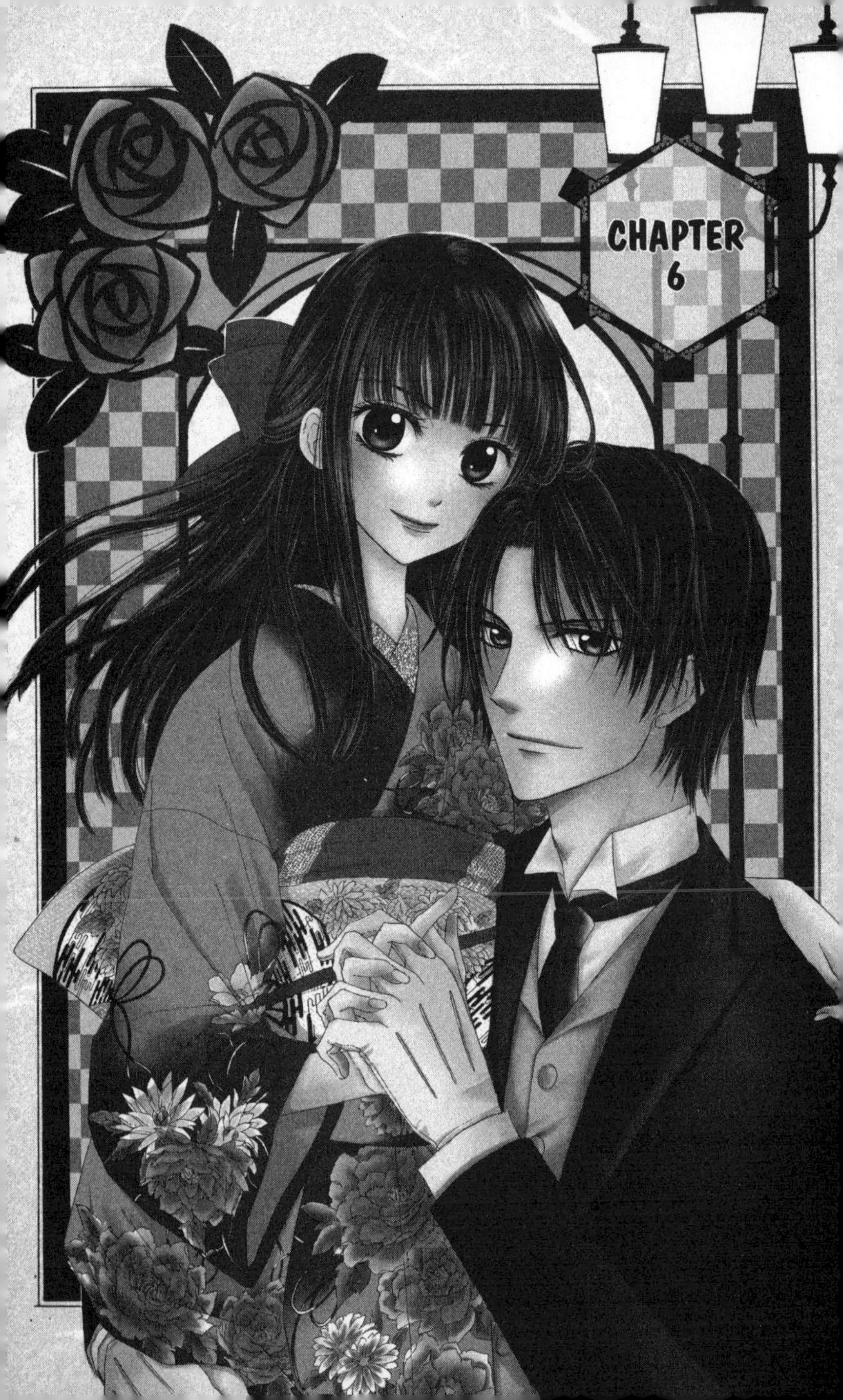
CHAPTER 6

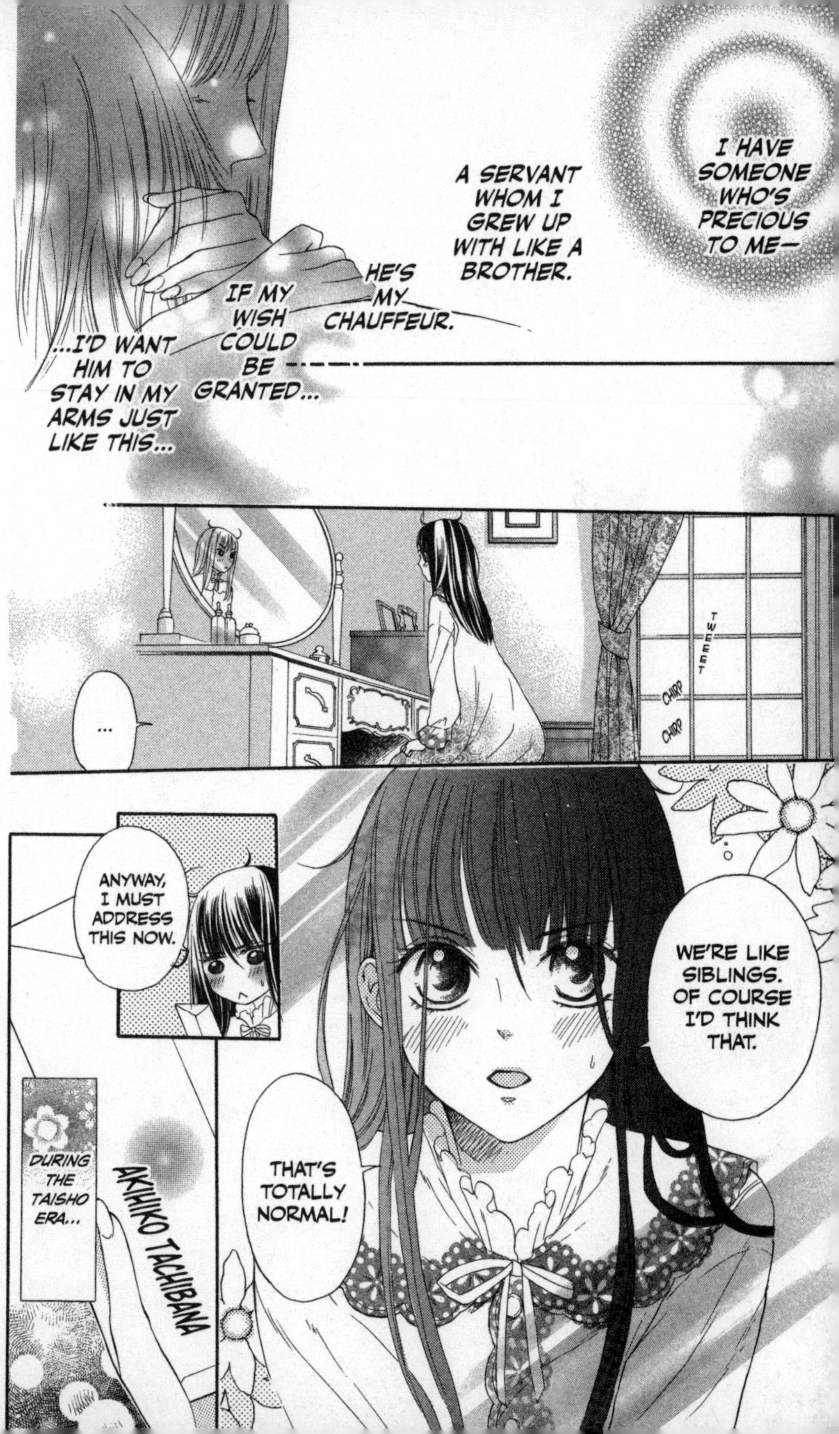
I HAVE SOMEONE WHO'S PRECIOUS TO ME—
A SERVANT WHOM I GREW UP WITH LIKE A BROTHER.
HE'S MY CHAUFFEUR.
IF MY WISH COULD BE GRANTED...
...I'D WANT HIM TO STAY IN MY ARMS JUST LIKE THIS...
TWEEET
CHIRP
CHIRP
...
WE'RE LIKE SIBLINGS. OF COURSE I'D THINK THAT.
THAT'S TOTALLY NORMAL!
ANYWAY, I MUST ADDRESS THIS NOW.
DURING THE TAISHO ERA...
AKIHIKO TACHIBANA

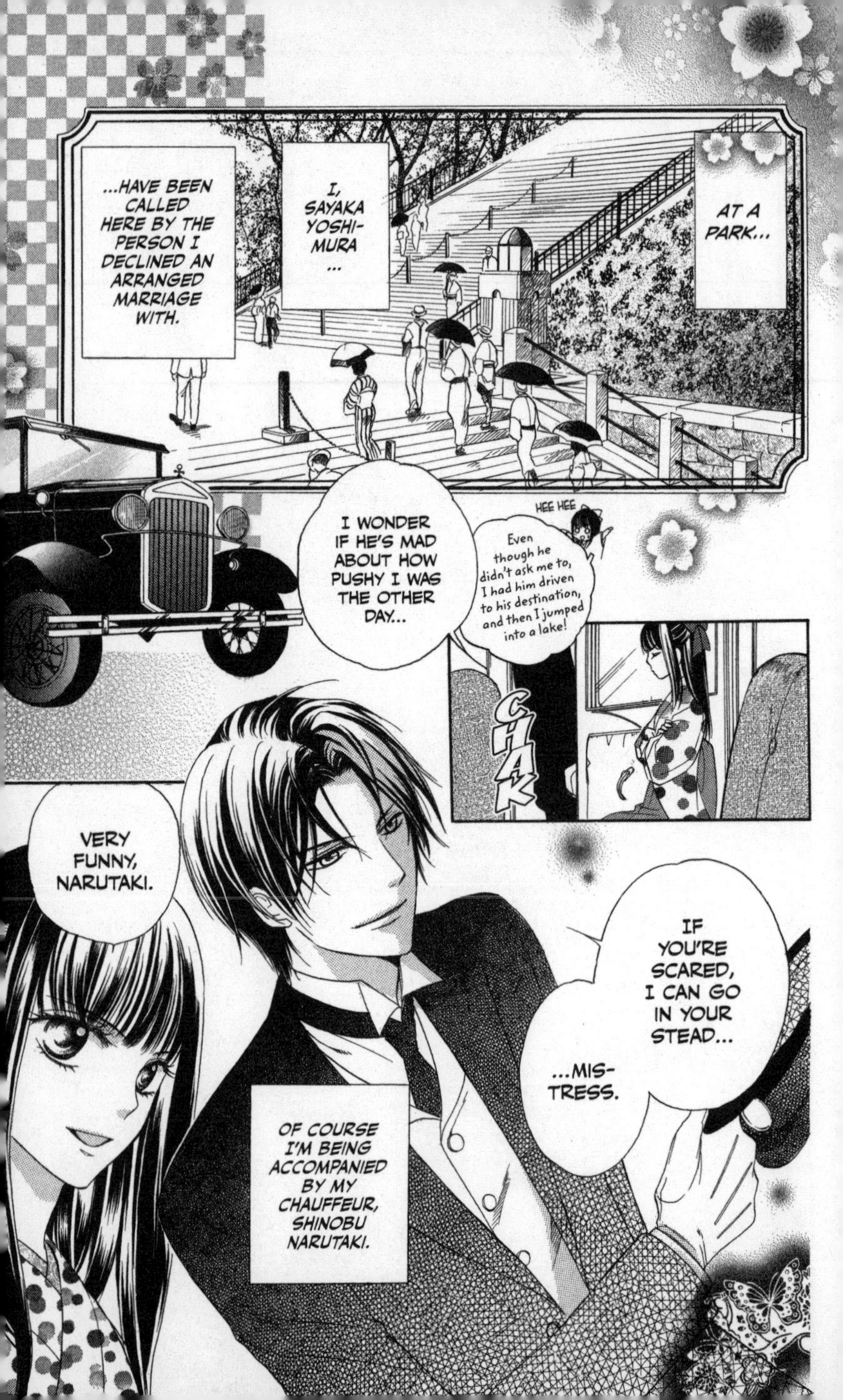
AT A PARK...
I, SAYAKA YOSHIMURA...
...HAVE BEEN CALLED HERE BY THE PERSON I DECLINED AN ARRANGED MARRIAGE WITH.
I WONDER IF HE'S MAD ABOUT HOW PUSHY I WAS THE OTHER DAY...
Even though he didn't ask me to, I had him driven to his destination, and then I jumped into a lake!
HEE HEE
CHAK
IF YOU'RE SCARED, I CAN GO IN YOUR STEAD...
...MISTRESS.
VERY FUNNY, NARUTAKI.
OF COURSE I'M BEING ACCOMPANIED BY MY CHAUFFEUR, SHINOBU NARUTAKI.

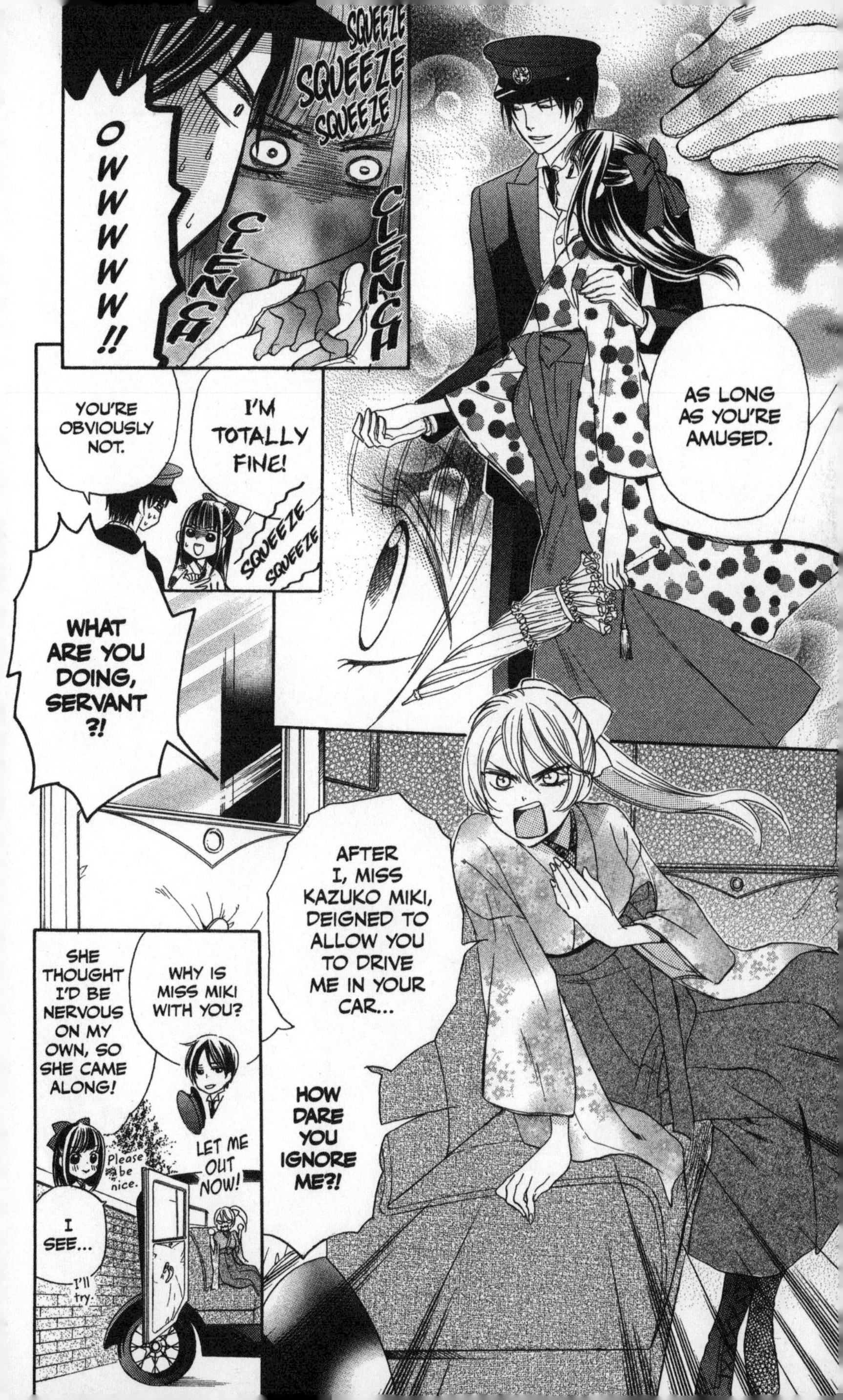
AS LONG AS YOU'RE AMUSED.
SQUEEZE
SQUEEZE
SQUEEZE
OWWWWWWW!!
CLENCH
CLENCH
I'M TOTALLY FINE!
YOU'RE OBVIOUSLY NOT.
SQUEEZE
SQUEEZE
WHAT ARE YOU DOING, SERVANT?!
AFTER I, MISS KAZUKO MIKI, DEIGNED TO ALLOW YOU TO DRIVE ME IN YOUR CAR...
HOW DARE YOU IGNORE ME?!
WHY IS MISS MIKI WITH YOU?
SHE THOUGHT I'D BE NERVOUS ON MY OWN, SO SHE CAME ALONG!
LET ME OUT NOW!
Please be nice.
I SEE...
I'll try.

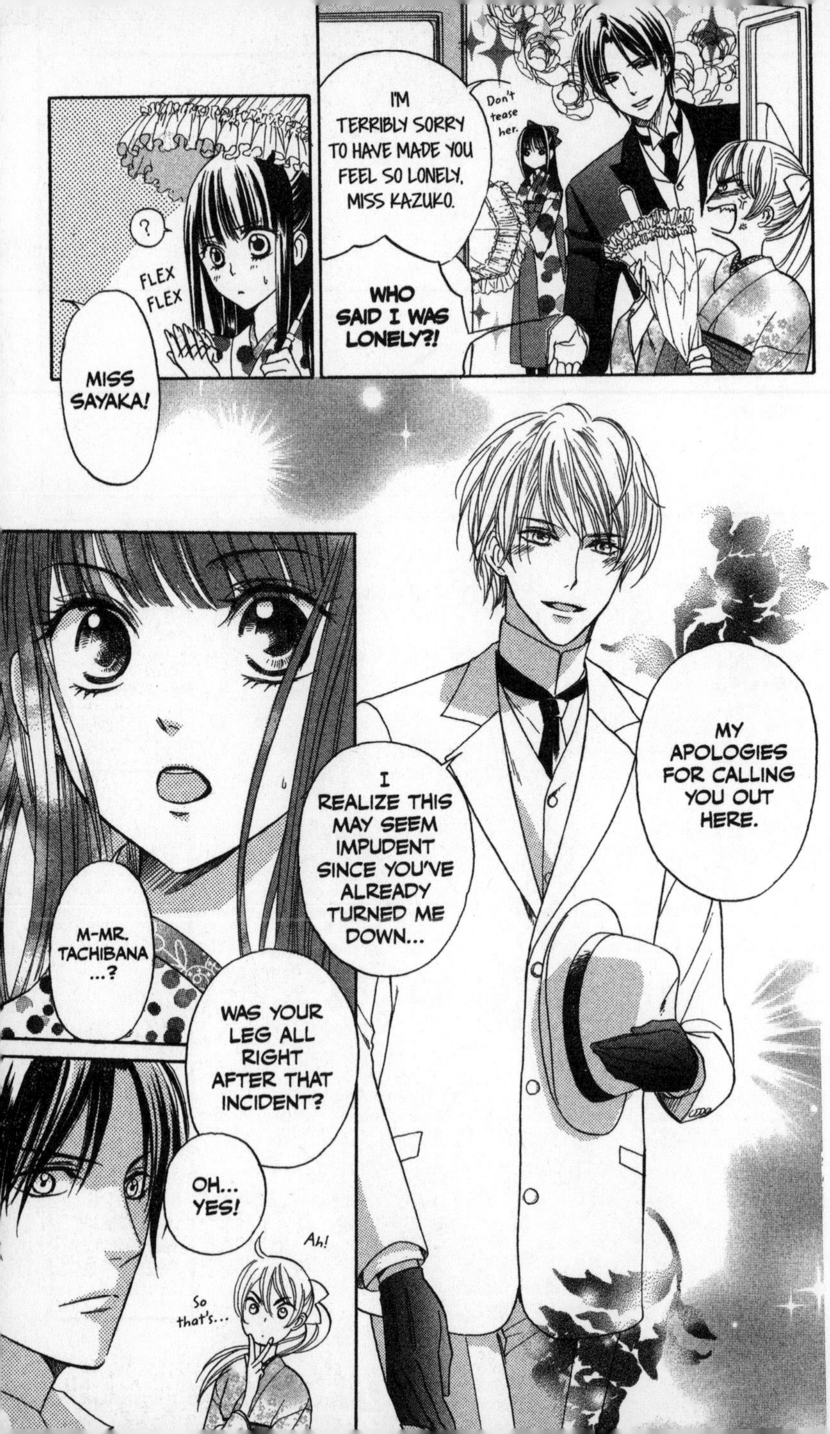
I'M TERRIBLY SORRY TO HAVE MADE YOU FEEL SO LONELY, MISS KAZUKO.
WHO SAID I WAS LONELY?!
Don't tease her.
?
FLEX FLEX
MISS SAYAKA!
MY APOLOGIES FOR CALLING YOU OUT HERE.
I REALIZE THIS MAY SEEM IMPUDENT SINCE YOU'VE ALREADY TURNED ME DOWN...
M-MR. TACHIBANA ...?
WAS YOUR LEG ALL RIGHT AFTER THAT INCIDENT?
OH... YES!
Ah!
So that's...

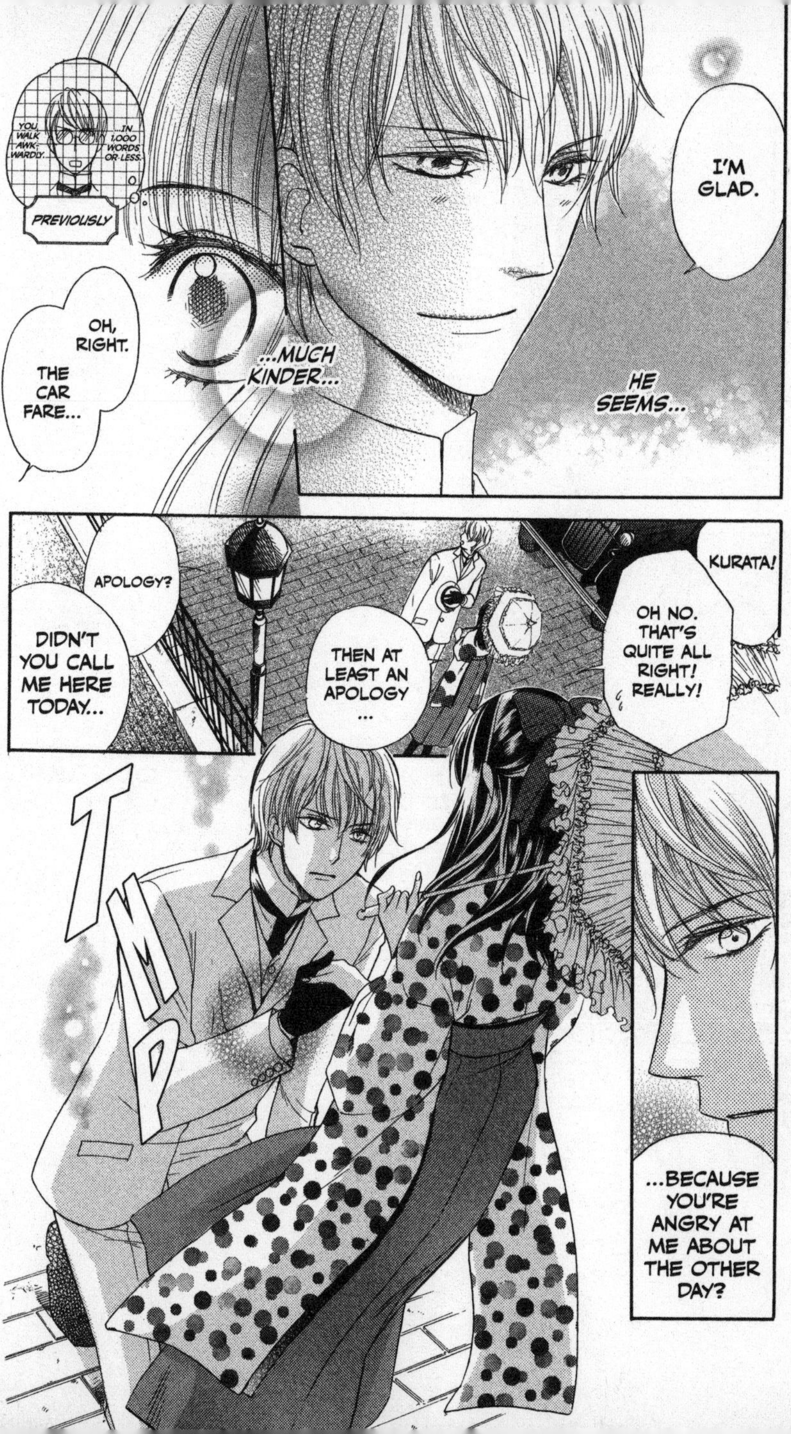

I'M GLAD.
HE SEEMS...
...MUCH KINDER...
PREVIOUSLY
YOU WALK AWK-WARDLY.
...IN 1,000 WORDS OR LESS.
OH, RIGHT.
THE CAR FARE...
KURATA!
OH NO. THAT'S QUITE ALL RIGHT! REALLY!
THEN AT LEAST AN APOLOGY ...
APOLOGY?
DIDN'T YOU CALL ME HERE TODAY...
...BECAUSE YOU'RE ANGRY AT ME ABOUT THE OTHER DAY?
TMP

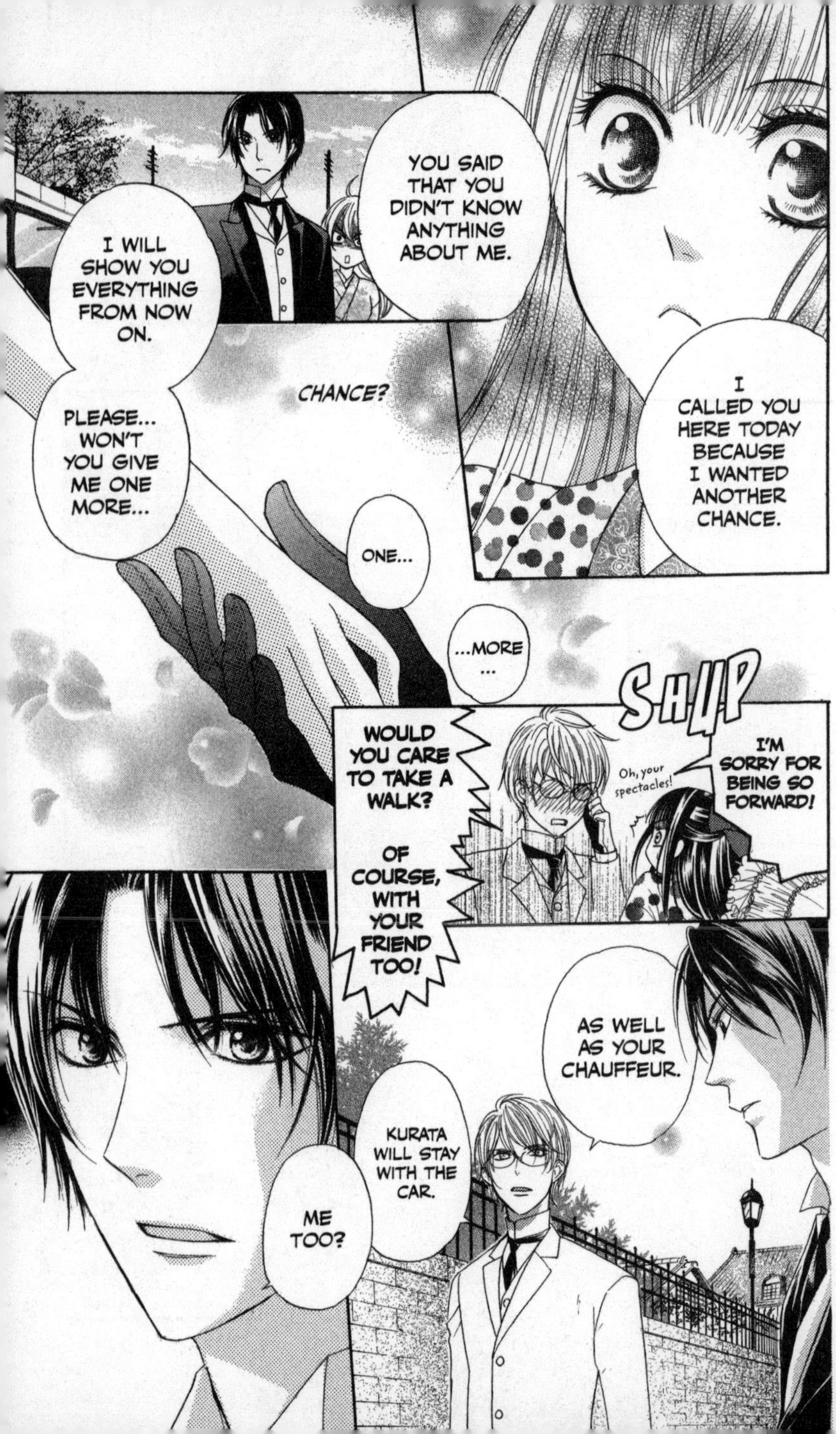
YOU SAID THAT YOU DIDN'T KNOW ANYTHING ABOUT ME.
I CALLED YOU HERE TODAY BECAUSE I WANTED ANOTHER CHANCE.
CHANCE?
I WILL SHOW YOU EVERYTHING FROM NOW ON.
PLEASE... WON'T YOU GIVE ME ONE MORE...
ONE...
...MORE ...
SHUP
I'M SORRY FOR BEING SO FORWARD!
Oh, your spectacles!
WOULD YOU CARE TO TAKE A WALK?
OF COURSE, WITH YOUR FRIEND TOO!
AS WELL AS YOUR CHAUFFEUR.
KURATA WILL STAY WITH THE CAR.
ME TOO?

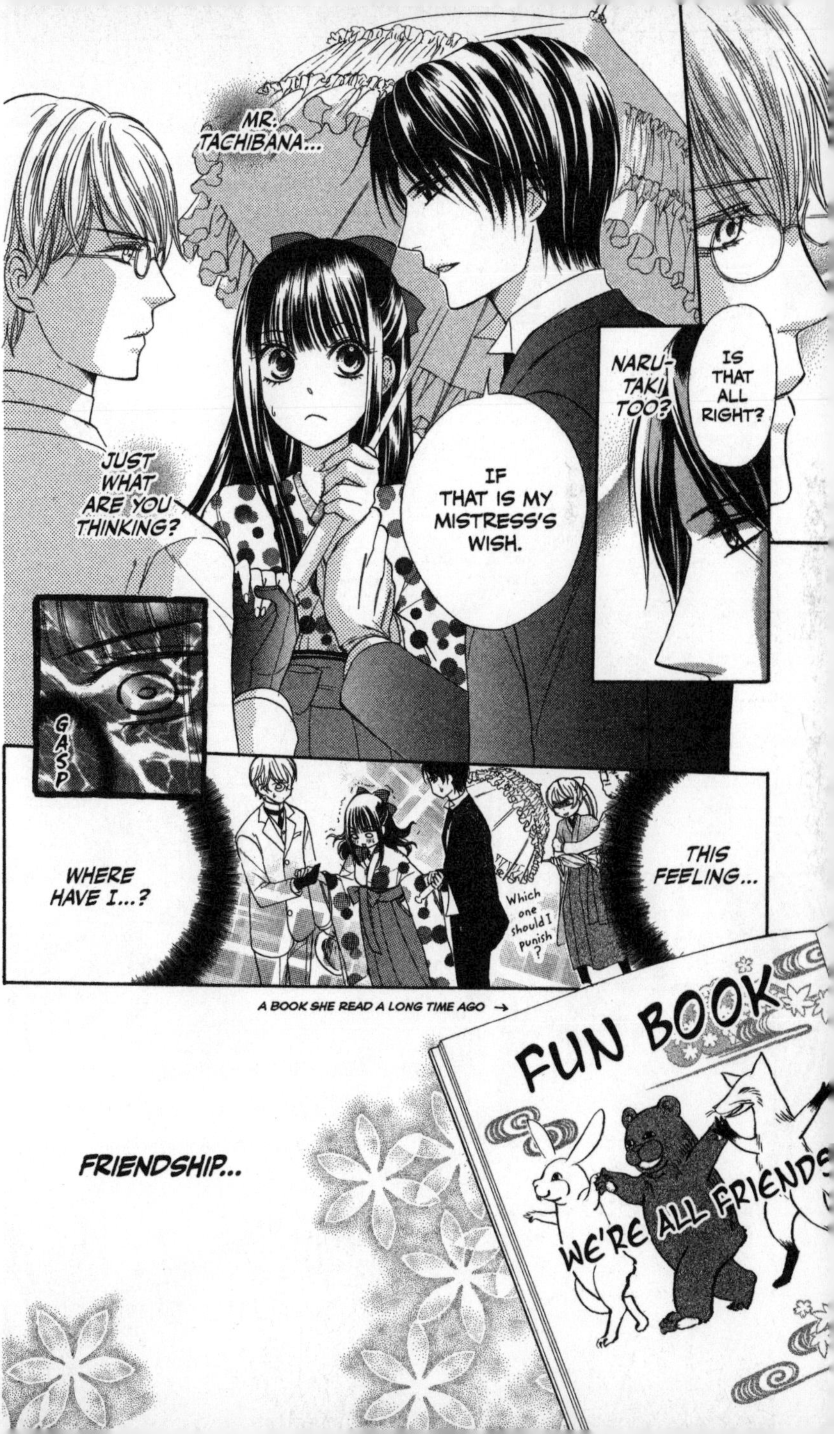
IS THAT ALL RIGHT?
NARU-TAKI TOO?
MR. TACHIBANA...
IF THAT IS MY MISTRESS'S WISH.
JUST WHAT ARE YOU THINKING?
GASP
THIS FEELING...
Which one should I punish?
WHERE HAVE I...?
A BOOK SHE READ A LONG TIME AGO →
FUN BOOK
WE'RE ALL FRIENDS
FRIENDSHIP...

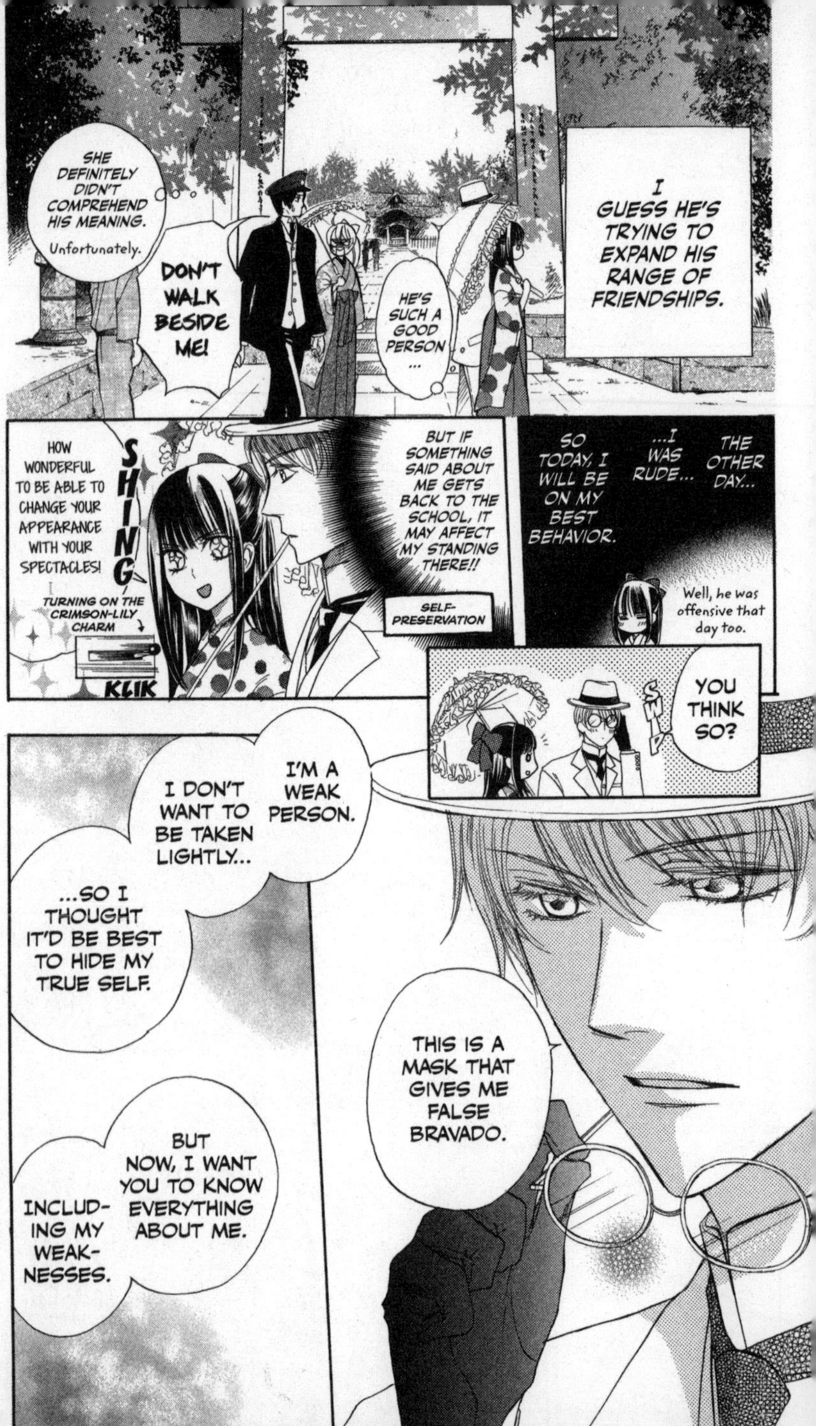
I GUESS HE'S TRYING TO EXPAND HIS RANGE OF FRIENDSHIPS.
HE'S SUCH A GOOD PERSON...
DON'T WALK BESIDE ME!
SHE DEFINITELY DIDN'T COMPREHEND HIS MEANING.
Unfortunately.
THE OTHER DAY...
...I WAS RUDE...
SO TODAY, I WILL BE ON MY BEST BEHAVIOR.
Well, he was offensive that day too.
BUT IF SOMETHING SAID ABOUT ME GETS BACK TO THE SCHOOL, IT MAY AFFECT MY STANDING THERE!!
SELF-PRESERVATION
SHING
HOW WONDERFUL TO BE ABLE TO CHANGE YOUR APPEARANCE WITH YOUR SPECTACLES!
TURNING ON THE CRIMSON-LILY CHARM
KLIK
YOU THINK SO?
SWIP
THIS IS A MASK THAT GIVES ME FALSE BRAVADO.
I'M A WEAK PERSON.
I DON'T WANT TO BE TAKEN LIGHTLY...
...SO I THOUGHT IT'D BE BEST TO HIDE MY TRUE SELF.
BUT NOW, I WANT YOU TO KNOW EVERYTHING ABOUT ME.
INCLUDING MY WEAK-NESSES.

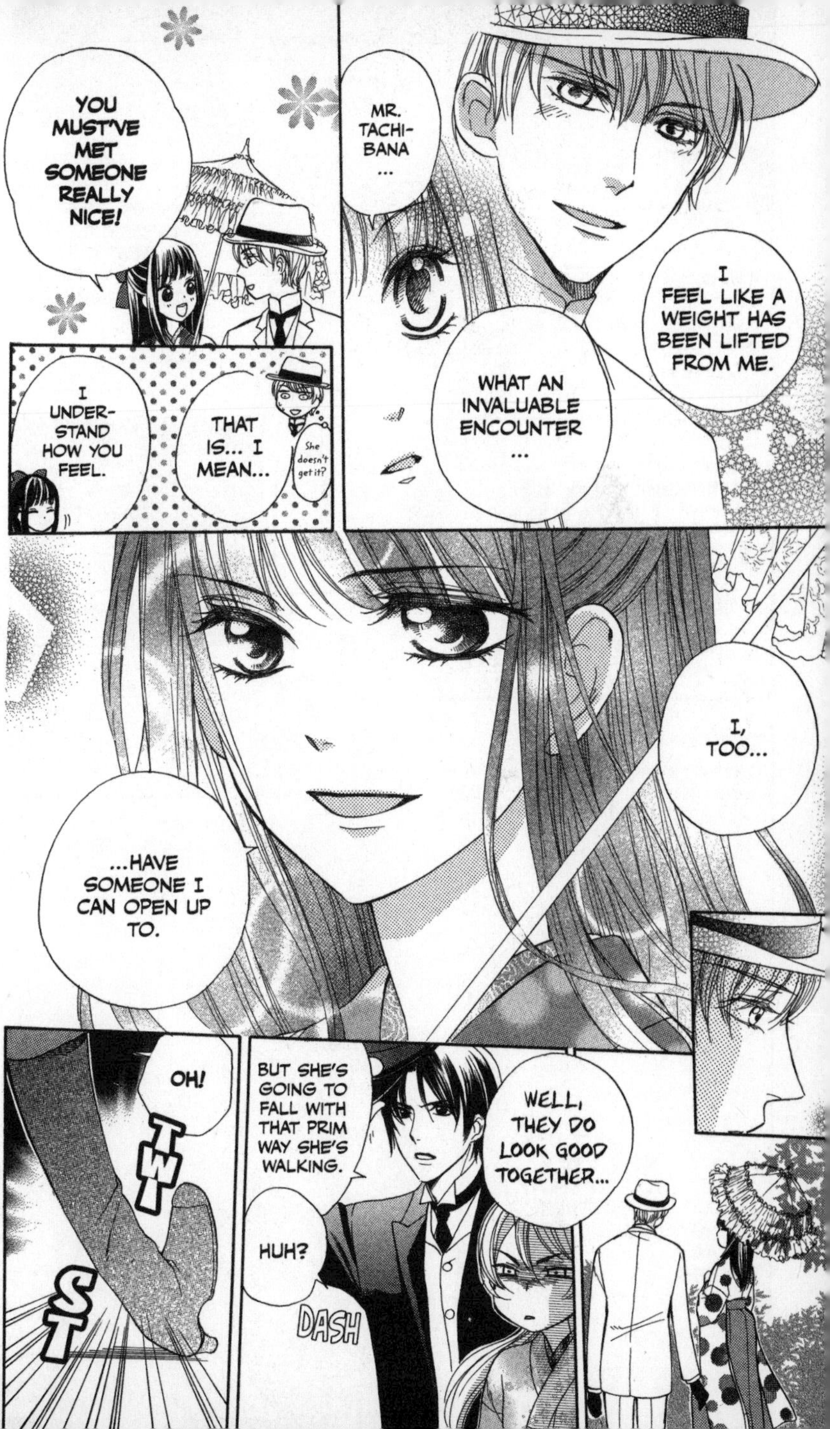
MR. TACHIBANA...
I FEEL LIKE A WEIGHT HAS BEEN LIFTED FROM ME.
WHAT AN INVALUABLE ENCOUNTER...
YOU MUST'VE MET SOMEONE REALLY NICE!
THAT IS... I MEAN...
She doesn't get it?
I UNDERSTAND HOW YOU FEEL.
I, TOO...
...HAVE SOMEONE I CAN OPEN UP TO.
WELL, THEY DO LOOK GOOD TOGETHER...
BUT SHE'S GOING TO FALL WITH THAT PRIM WAY SHE'S WALKING.
HUH?
DASH
OH!
TWIST

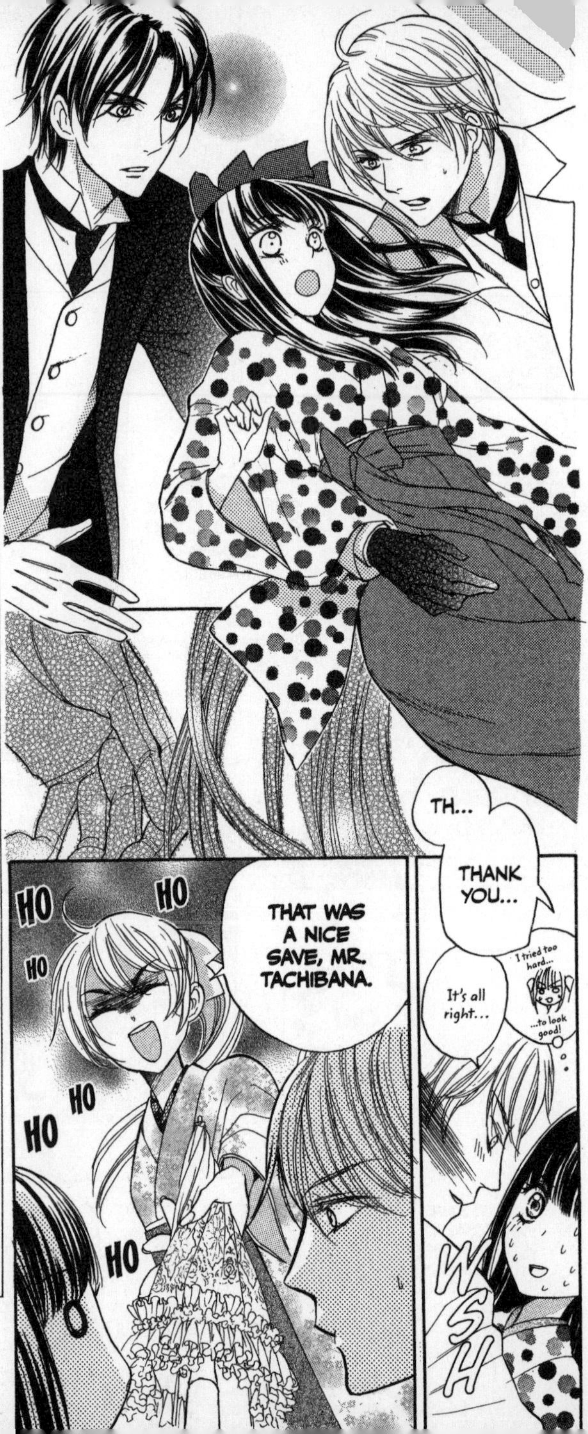
TH...
THANK YOU...
It's all right...
I tried too hard...
...to look good!
WSH
THAT WAS A NICE SAVE, MR. TACHIBANA.
HO
HO
HO
HO
HO
HO

CHAPTER 6

Mr. Tachibana changed so much it was as if he had been abducted by aliens. Even though I like men in glasses, I think he didn't really need them. They're also a pain to draw...

The park was based on Ueno Park, but I've never been there. So I don't even know if there actually is a lake where you can ride boats there. It'd be embarrassing if I was wrong, so I didn't say it was Ueno. Though there are even more embarrassing mistakes I've made...

This was my first time getting a color page, so I was happy about that.

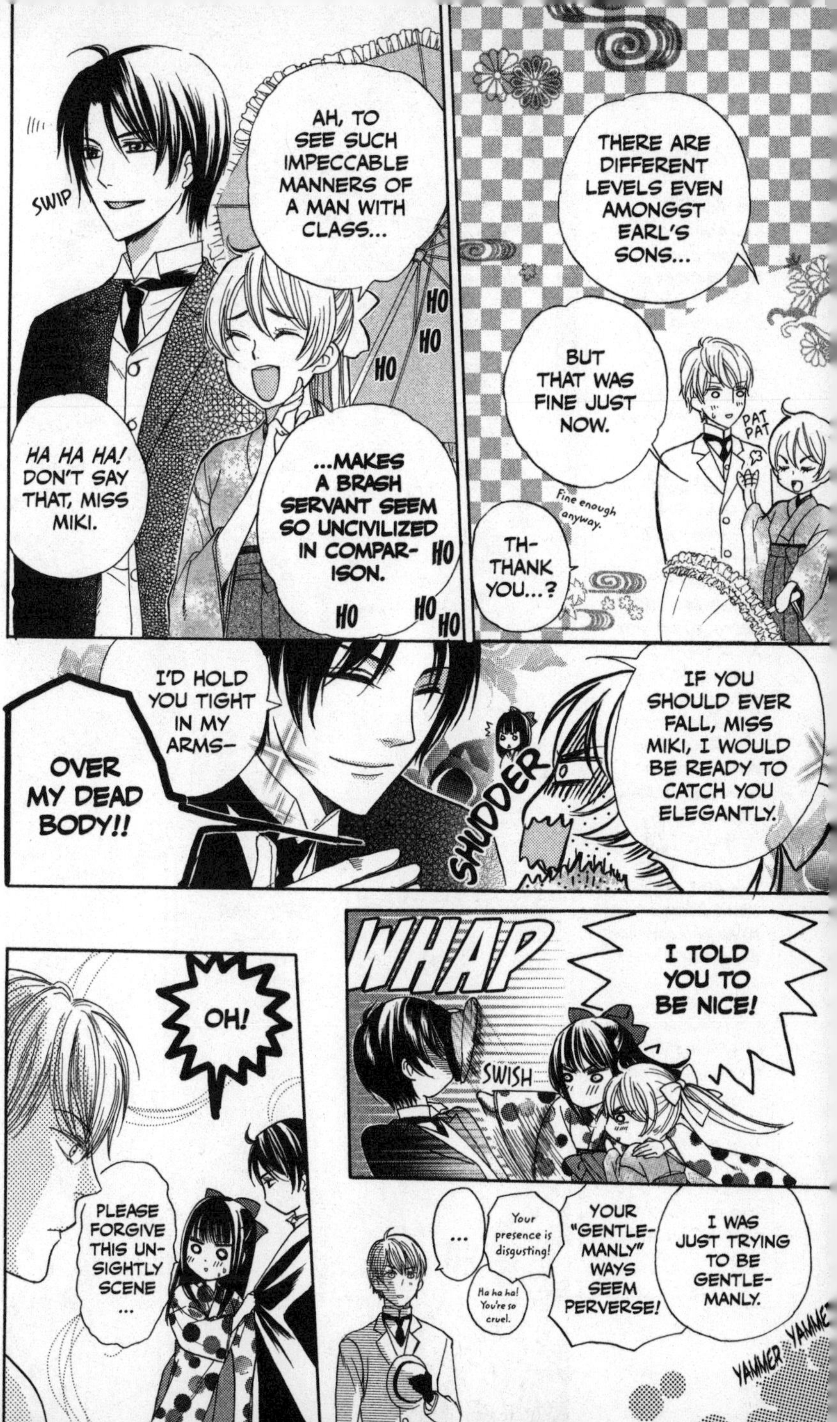
THERE ARE DIFFERENT LEVELS EVEN AMONGST EARL'S SONS...
BUT THAT WAS FINE JUST NOW.
PAT PAT
Fine enough anyway.
TH-THANK YOU...?
AH, TO SEE SUCH IMPECCABLE MANNERS OF A MAN WITH CLASS...
HO HO HO
...MAKES A BRASH SERVANT SEEM SO UNCIVILIZED IN COMPARISON.
HO HO HO HO
SWIP
HA HA HA! DON'T SAY THAT, MISS MIKI.
IF YOU SHOULD EVER FALL, MISS MIKI, I WOULD BE READY TO CATCH YOU ELEGANTLY.
SHUDDER
I'D HOLD YOU TIGHT IN MY ARMS–
OVER MY DEAD BODY!!
WHAP
I TOLD YOU TO BE NICE!
SWISH
I WAS JUST TRYING TO BE GENTLEMANLY.
YOUR "GENTLEMANLY" WAYS SEEM PERVERSE!
Your presence is disgusting!
Ha ha ha! You're so cruel.
...
YAMMER YAMMER
OH!
PLEASE FORGIVE THIS UNSIGHTLY SCENE...

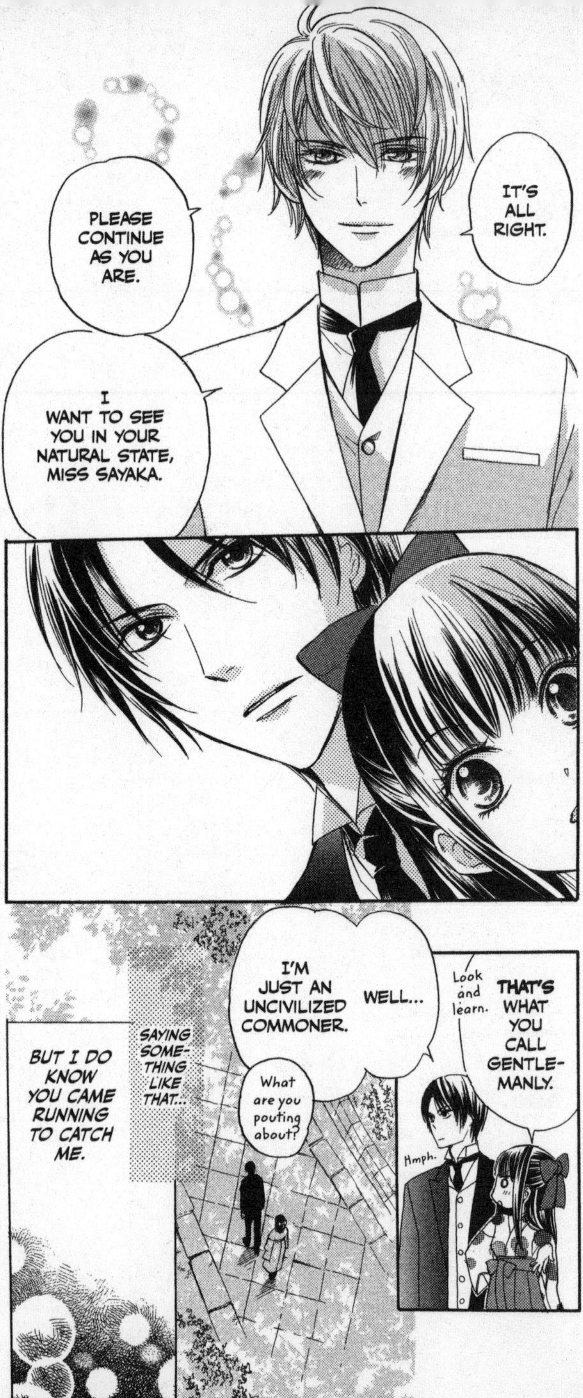
IT'S ALL RIGHT.
PLEASE CONTINUE AS YOU ARE.
I WANT TO SEE YOU IN YOUR NATURAL STATE, MISS SAYAKA.
THAT'S WHAT YOU CALL GENTLE-MANLY.
Look and learn.
Hmph.
WELL...
I'M JUST AN UNCIVILIZED COMMONER.
What are you pouting about?
SAYING SOME-THING LIKE THAT...
BUT I DO KNOW YOU CAME RUNNING TO CATCH ME.

ABOUT NARUTAKI

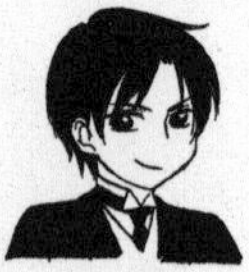

Shinobu Narutaki. He's a 22-year-old personal chauffeur. I don't think he acts like a 22-year-old or even a Taisho-era boy. I thought I'd make him the dedicated type, but ever since he was whipped in the second chapter, he's been going down the path of a masochist.

Since it's called **The Heiress and the Chauffeur**, it was easy to move him about in the story. However, out of all the characters, he had the most corrections for his face. It was fun to include a handsome man, but it was also hard.

I wanted to use a beautiful but unfortunate café barmaid to nurse his wounded heart, but there wasn't anywhere I could include it. It was probably best (and less complicated) to keep him devoted to Sayaka.

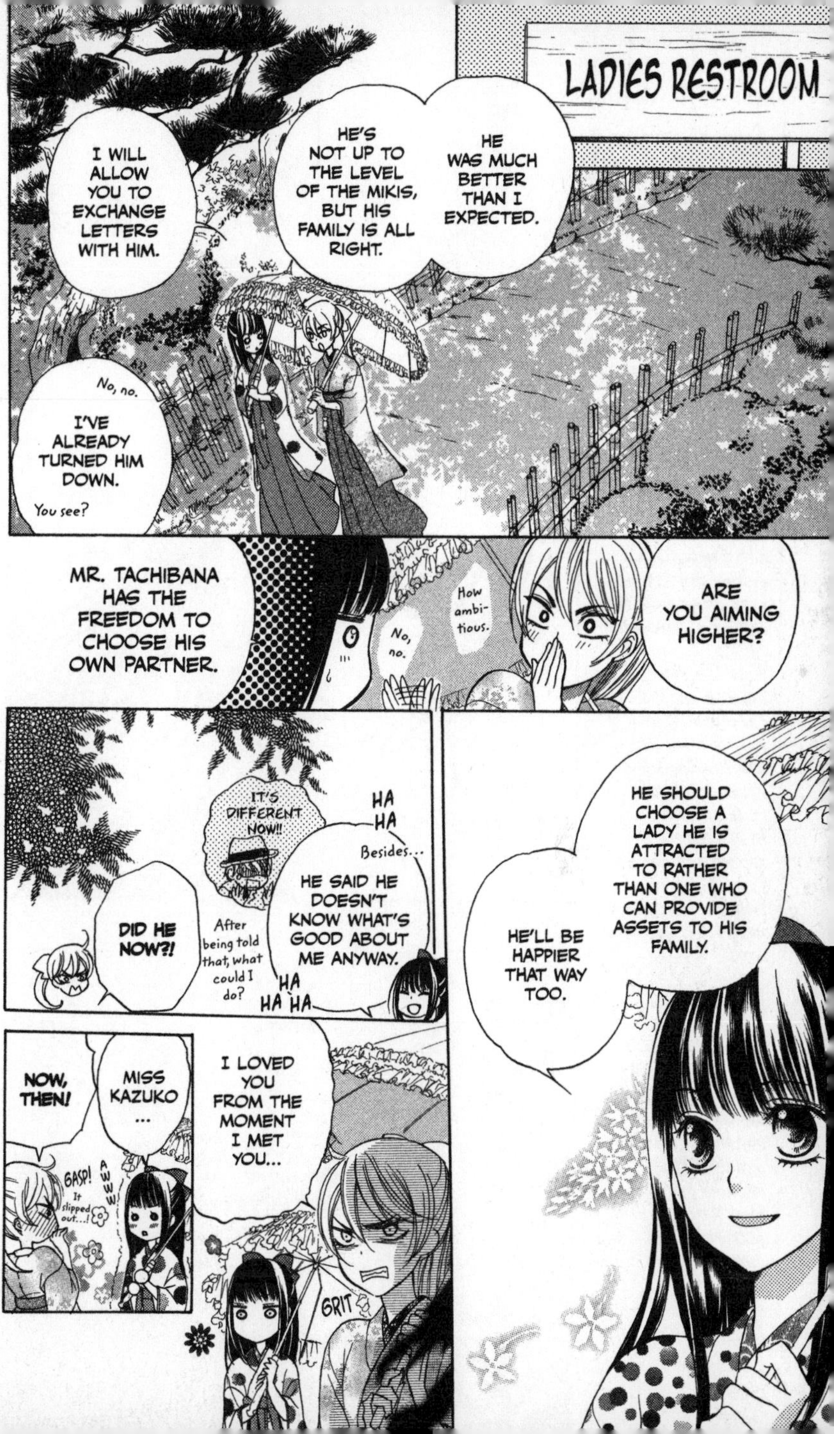
LADIES RESTROOM
HE WAS MUCH BETTER THAN I EXPECTED.
HE'S NOT UP TO THE LEVEL OF THE MIKIS, BUT HIS FAMILY IS ALL RIGHT.
I WILL ALLOW YOU TO EXCHANGE LETTERS WITH HIM.
No, no.
I'VE ALREADY TURNED HIM DOWN.
You see?
ARE YOU AIMING HIGHER?
How ambitious.
No, no.
MR. TACHIBANA HAS THE FREEDOM TO CHOOSE HIS OWN PARTNER.
HE SHOULD CHOOSE A LADY HE IS ATTRACTED TO RATHER THAN ONE WHO CAN PROVIDE ASSETS TO HIS FAMILY.
HE'LL BE HAPPIER THAT WAY TOO.
HA HA
Besides...
HE SAID HE DOESN'T KNOW WHAT'S GOOD ABOUT ME ANYWAY.
IT'S DIFFERENT NOW!!
HA HA HA
After being told that, what could I do?
DID HE NOW?!
I LOVED YOU FROM THE MOMENT I MET YOU...
GRIT
MISS KAZUKO...
AWWW
GASP! It slipped out...!
NOW, THEN!

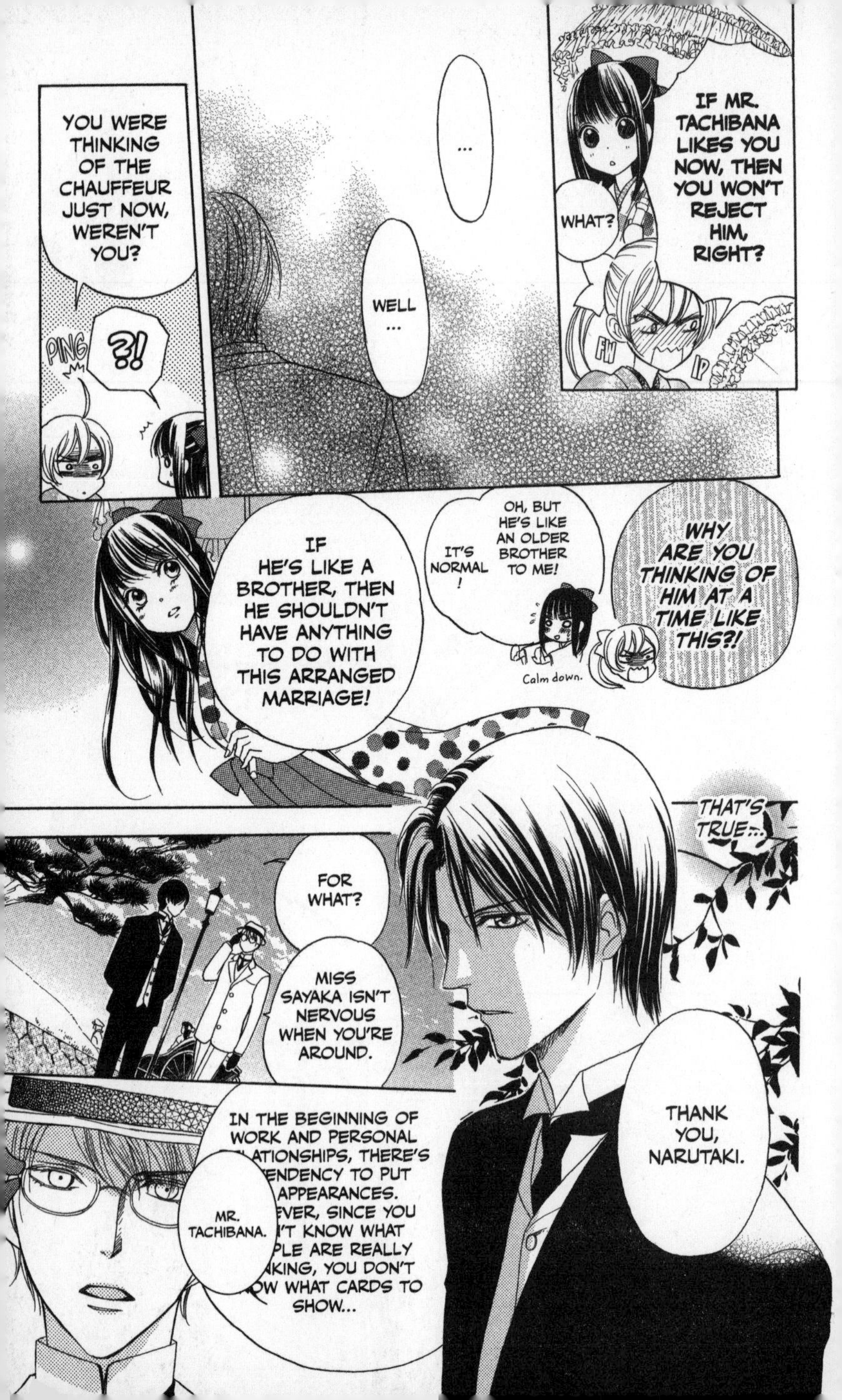
IF MR. TACHIBANA LIKES YOU NOW, THEN YOU WON'T REJECT HIM, RIGHT?
WHAT?
FWIP
...
WELL ...
YOU WERE THINKING OF THE CHAUFFEUR JUST NOW, WEREN'T YOU?
PING
?!
WHY ARE YOU THINKING OF HIM AT A TIME LIKE THIS?!
OH, BUT HE'S LIKE AN OLDER BROTHER TO ME!
IT'S NORMAL!
Calm down.
IF HE'S LIKE A BROTHER, THEN HE SHOULDN'T HAVE ANYTHING TO DO WITH THIS ARRANGED MARRIAGE!
THAT'S TRUE...
THANK YOU, NARUTAKI.
FOR WHAT?
MISS SAYAKA ISN'T NERVOUS WHEN YOU'RE AROUND.
IN THE BEGINNING OF WORK AND PERSONAL ATIONSHIPS, THERE'S ENDENCY TO PUT APPEARANCES. EVER, SINCE YOU 'T KNOW WHAT PLE ARE REALLY KING, YOU DON'T OW WHAT CARDS TO SHOW...
MR. TACHIBANA.

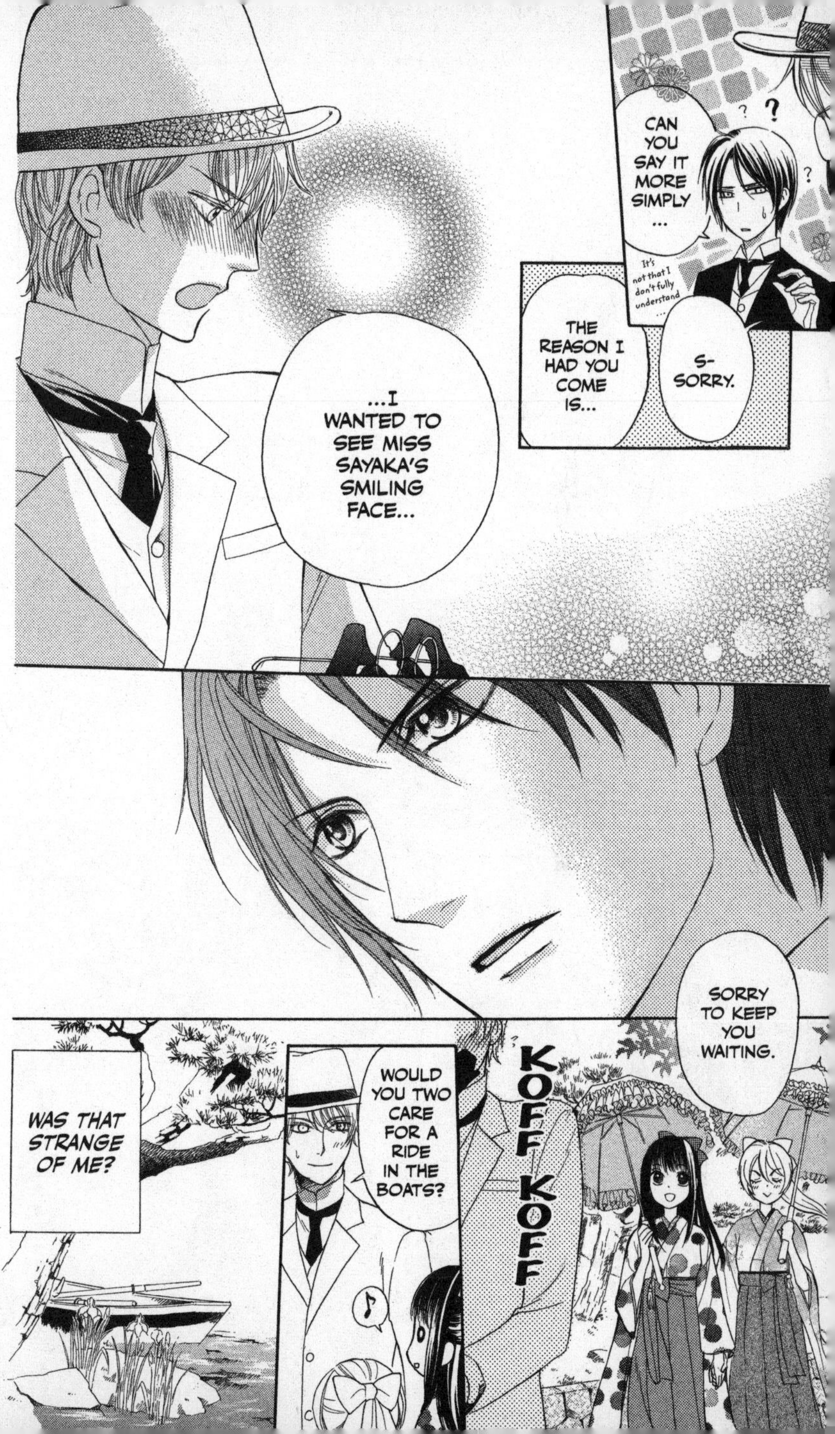

CAN YOU SAY IT MORE SIMPLY...
It's not that I don't fully understand...
S-SORRY.
THE REASON I HAD YOU COME IS...
...I WANTED TO SEE MISS SAYAKA'S SMILING FACE...
SORRY TO KEEP YOU WAITING.
KOFF KOFF
WOULD YOU TWO CARE FOR A RIDE IN THE BOATS?
WAS THAT STRANGE OF ME?

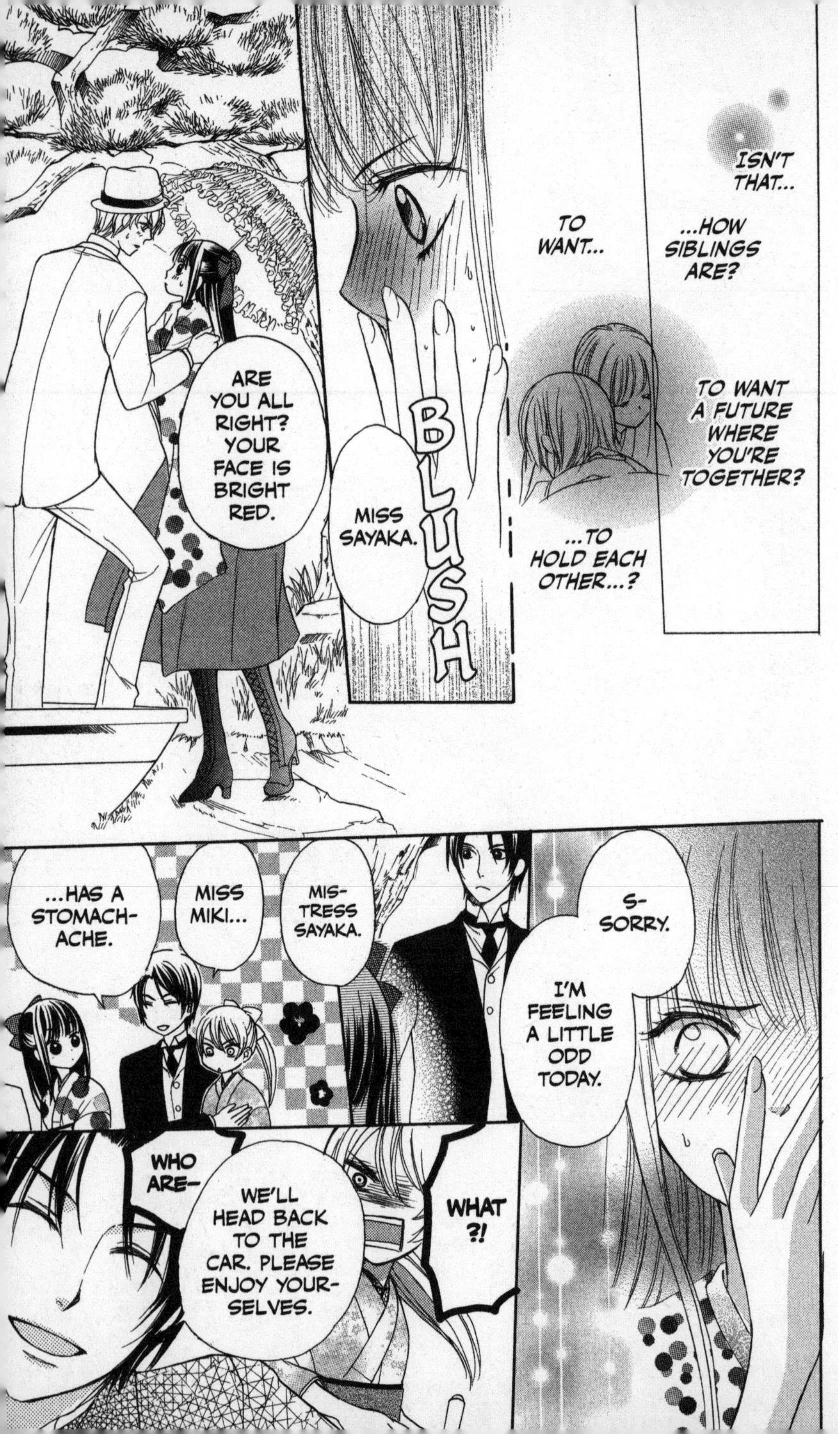

ISN'T THAT...
...HOW SIBLINGS ARE?
TO WANT...
TO WANT A FUTURE WHERE YOU'RE TOGETHER?
...TO HOLD EACH OTHER...?
BLUSH
MISS SAYAKA.
ARE YOU ALL RIGHT? YOUR FACE IS BRIGHT RED.
S-SORRY.
I'M FEELING A LITTLE ODD TODAY.
MIS-TRESS SAYAKA.
MISS MIKI...
...HAS A STOMACH-ACHE.
WHAT?!
WE'LL HEAD BACK TO THE CAR. PLEASE ENJOY YOUR-SELVES.
WHO ARE-

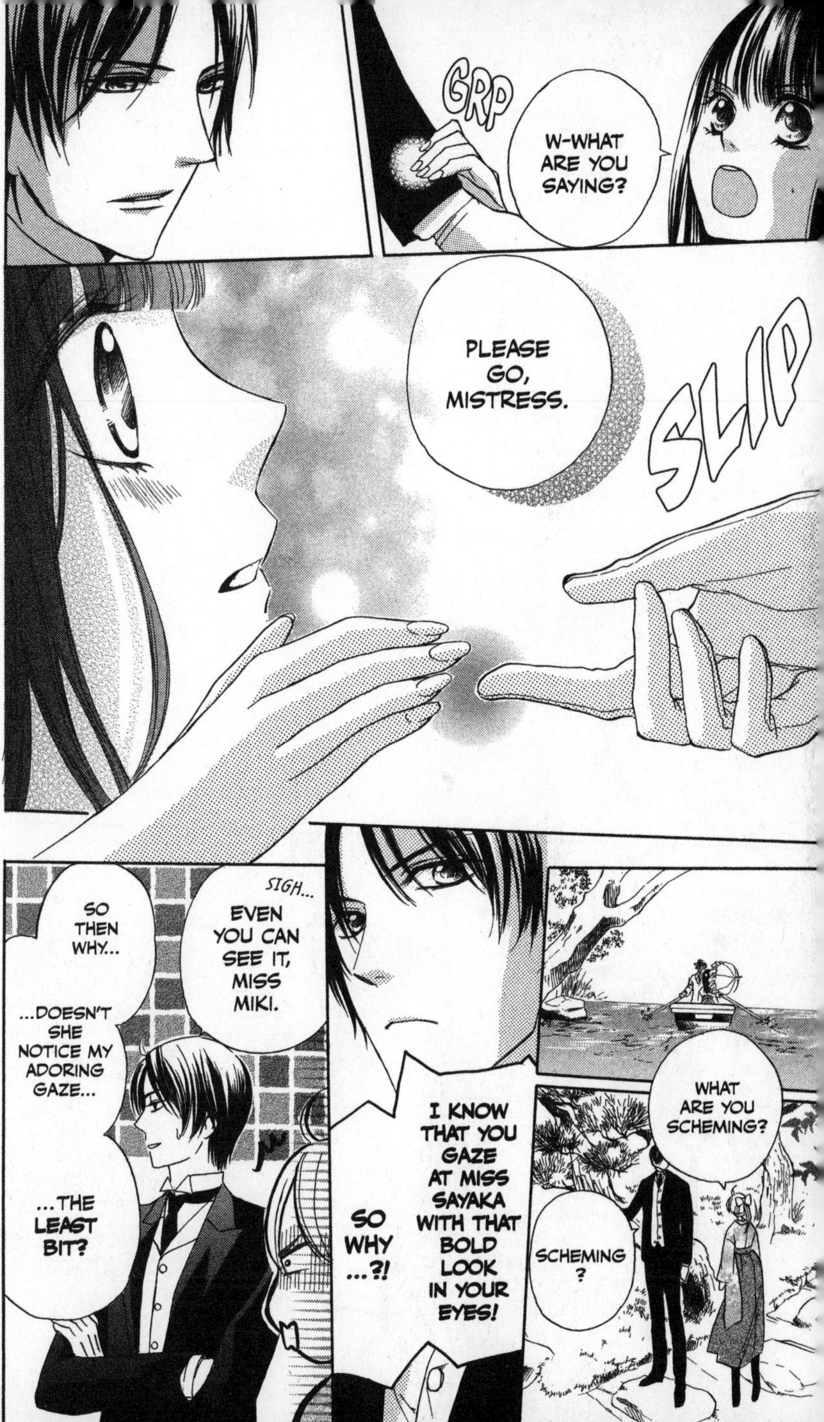
GRP
W-WHAT ARE YOU SAYING?
PLEASE GO, MISTRESS.
SLIP
WHAT ARE YOU SCHEMING?
SCHEMING?
I KNOW THAT YOU GAZE AT MISS SAYAKA WITH THAT BOLD LOOK IN YOUR EYES!
SO WHY ...?!
SIGH...
EVEN YOU CAN SEE IT, MISS MIKI.
SO THEN WHY...
...DOESN'T SHE NOTICE MY ADORING GAZE...
...THE LEAST BIT?

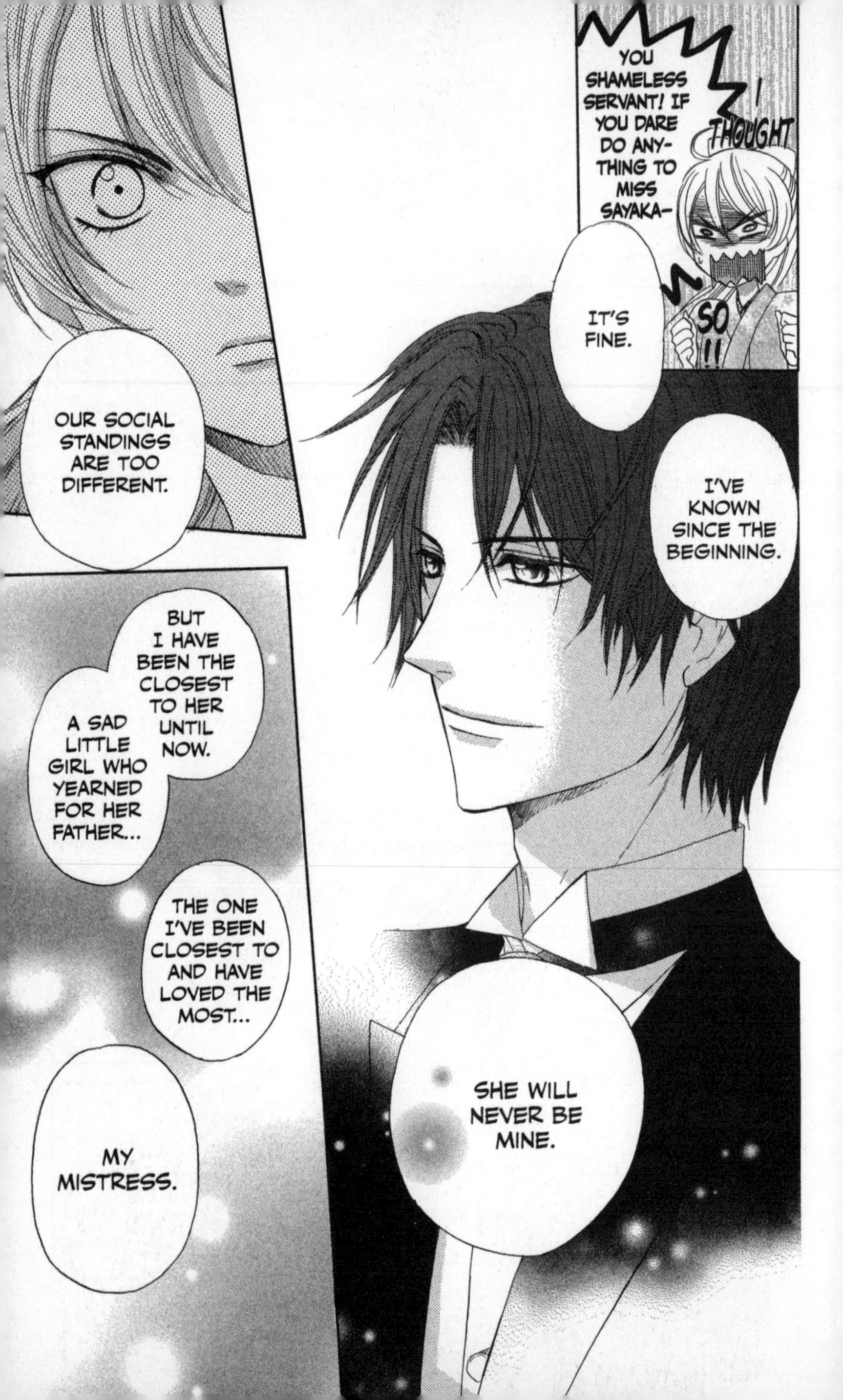
YOU SHAMELESS SERVANT! IF YOU DARE DO ANY-THING TO MISS SAYAKA-
I THOUGHT SO!!
IT'S FINE.
I'VE KNOWN SINCE THE BEGINNING.
OUR SOCIAL STANDINGS ARE TOO DIFFERENT.
BUT I HAVE BEEN THE CLOSEST TO HER UNTIL NOW.
A SAD LITTLE GIRL WHO YEARNED FOR HER FATHER...
THE ONE I'VE BEEN CLOSEST TO AND HAVE LOVED THE MOST...
MY MISTRESS.
SHE WILL NEVER BE MINE.

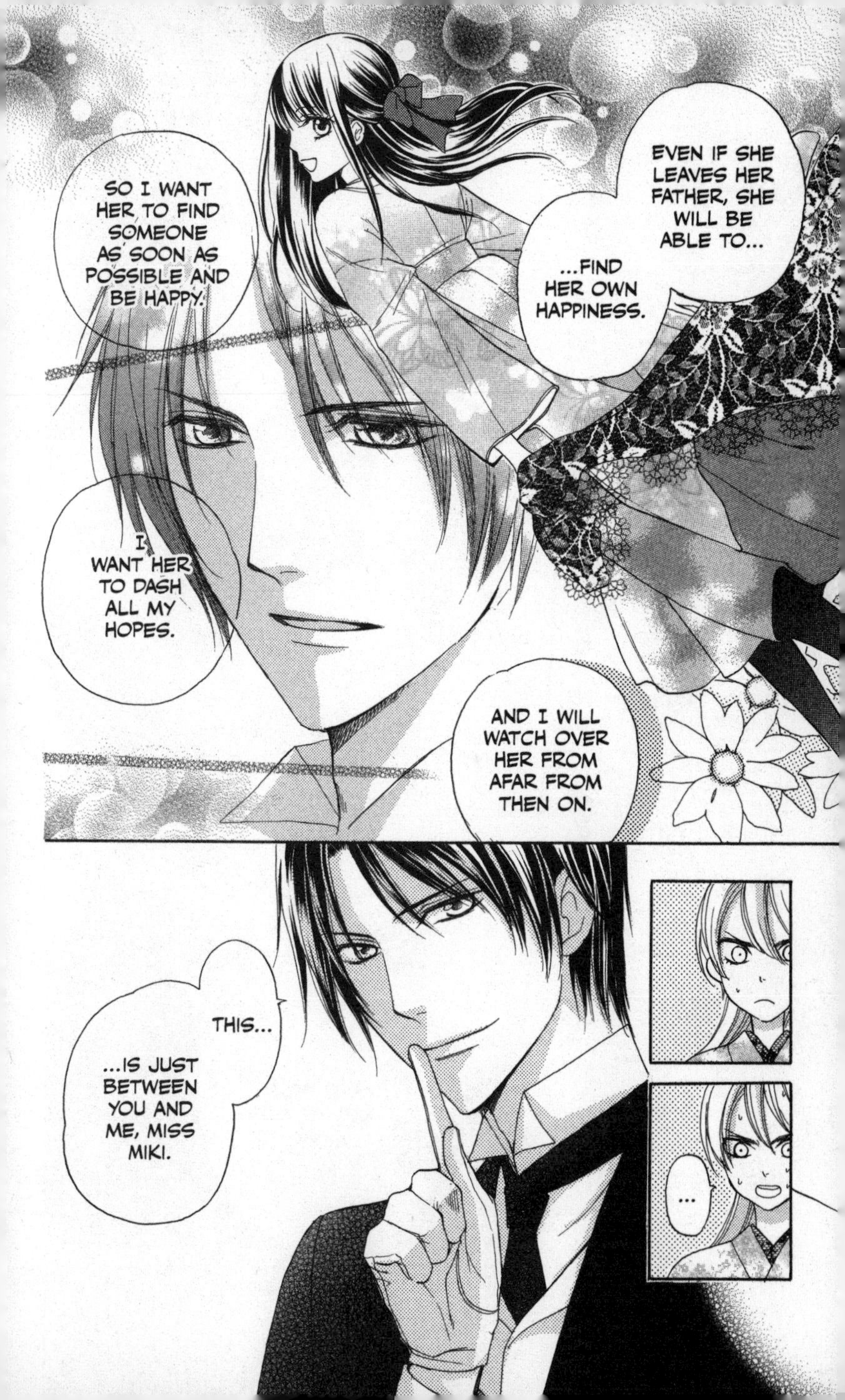
EVEN IF SHE LEAVES HER FATHER, SHE WILL BE ABLE TO...
...FIND HER OWN HAPPINESS.
SO I WANT HER TO FIND SOMEONE AS SOON AS POSSIBLE AND BE HAPPY.
I WANT HER TO DASH ALL MY HOPES.
AND I WILL WATCH OVER HER FROM AFAR FROM THEN ON.
...
THIS...
...IS JUST BETWEEN YOU AND ME, MISS MIKI.

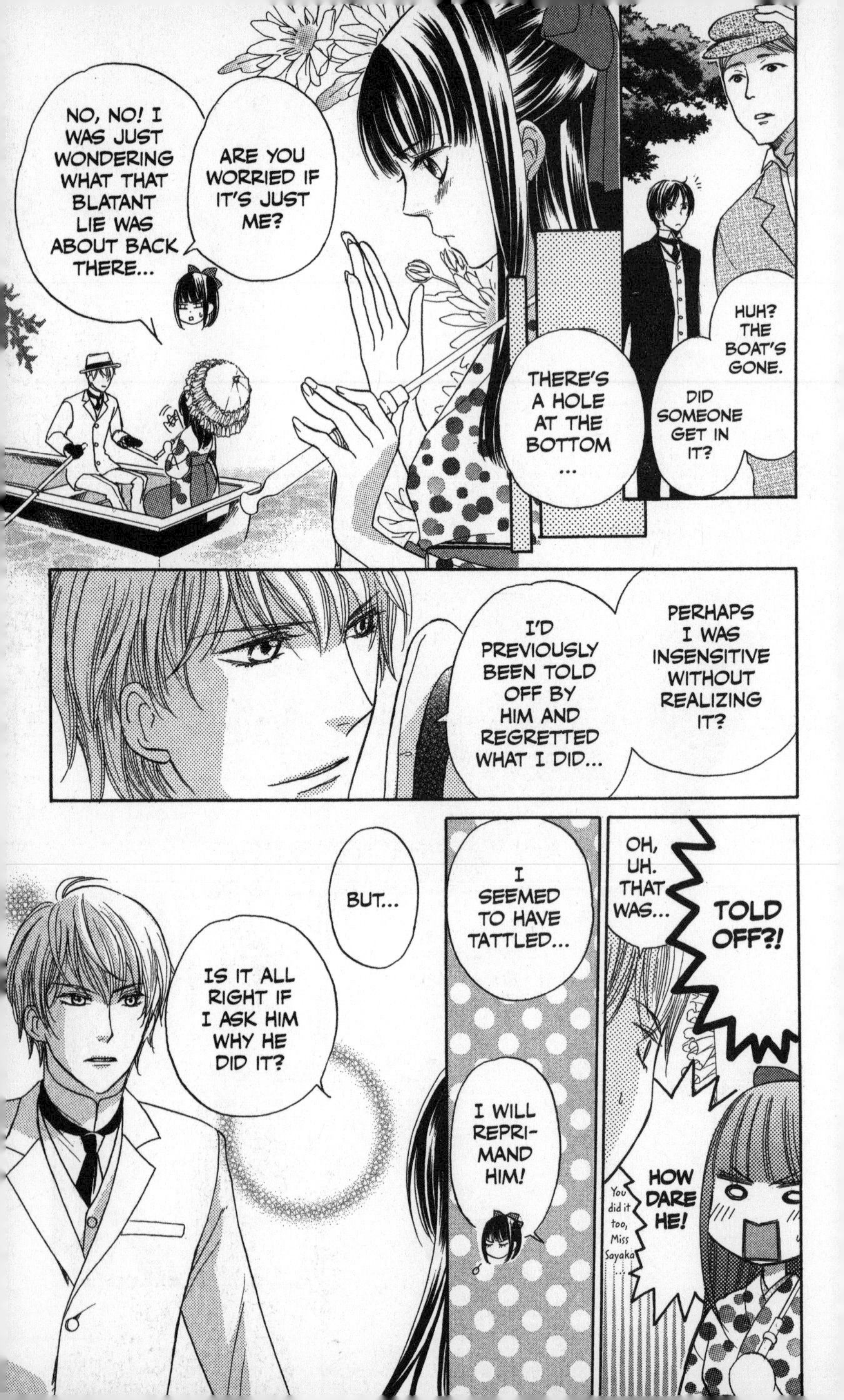
HUH? THE BOAT'S GONE.
DID SOMEONE GET IN IT?
THERE'S A HOLE AT THE BOTTOM ...
ARE YOU WORRIED IF IT'S JUST ME?
NO, NO! I WAS JUST WONDERING WHAT THAT BLATANT LIE WAS ABOUT BACK THERE...
PERHAPS I WAS INSENSITIVE WITHOUT REALIZING IT?
I'D PREVIOUSLY BEEN TOLD OFF BY HIM AND REGRETTED WHAT I DID...
OH, UH. THAT WAS...
TOLD OFF?!
HOW DARE HE!
You did it too, Miss Sayaka...
I SEEMED TO HAVE TATTLED...
I WILL REPRIMAND HIM!
BUT...
IS IT ALL RIGHT IF I ASK HIM WHY HE DID IT?

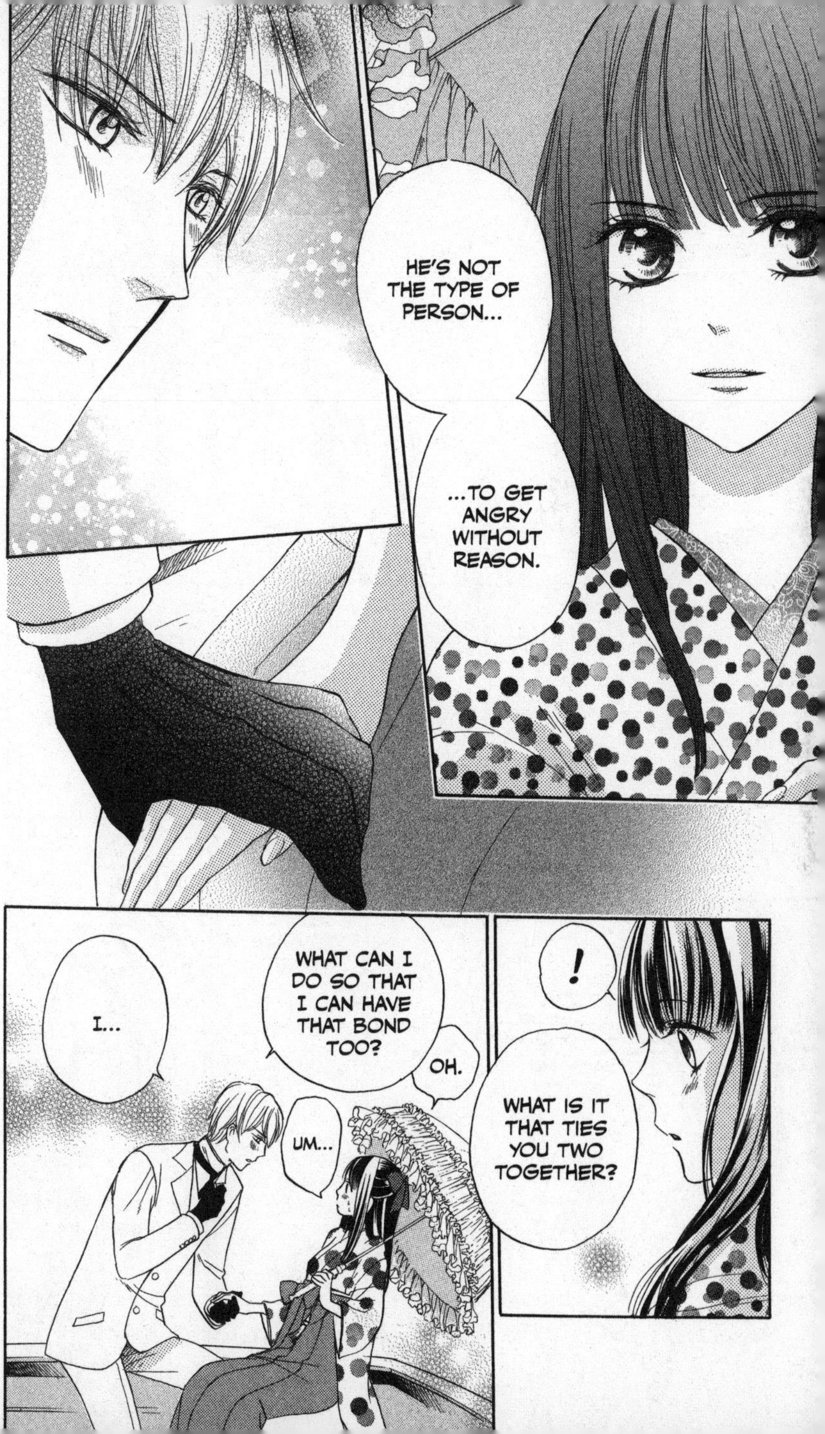
HE'S NOT THE TYPE OF PERSON...
...TO GET ANGRY WITHOUT REASON.
!
WHAT IS IT THAT TIES YOU TWO TOGETHER?
WHAT CAN I DO SO THAT I CAN HAVE THAT BOND TOO?
OH.
UM...
I...

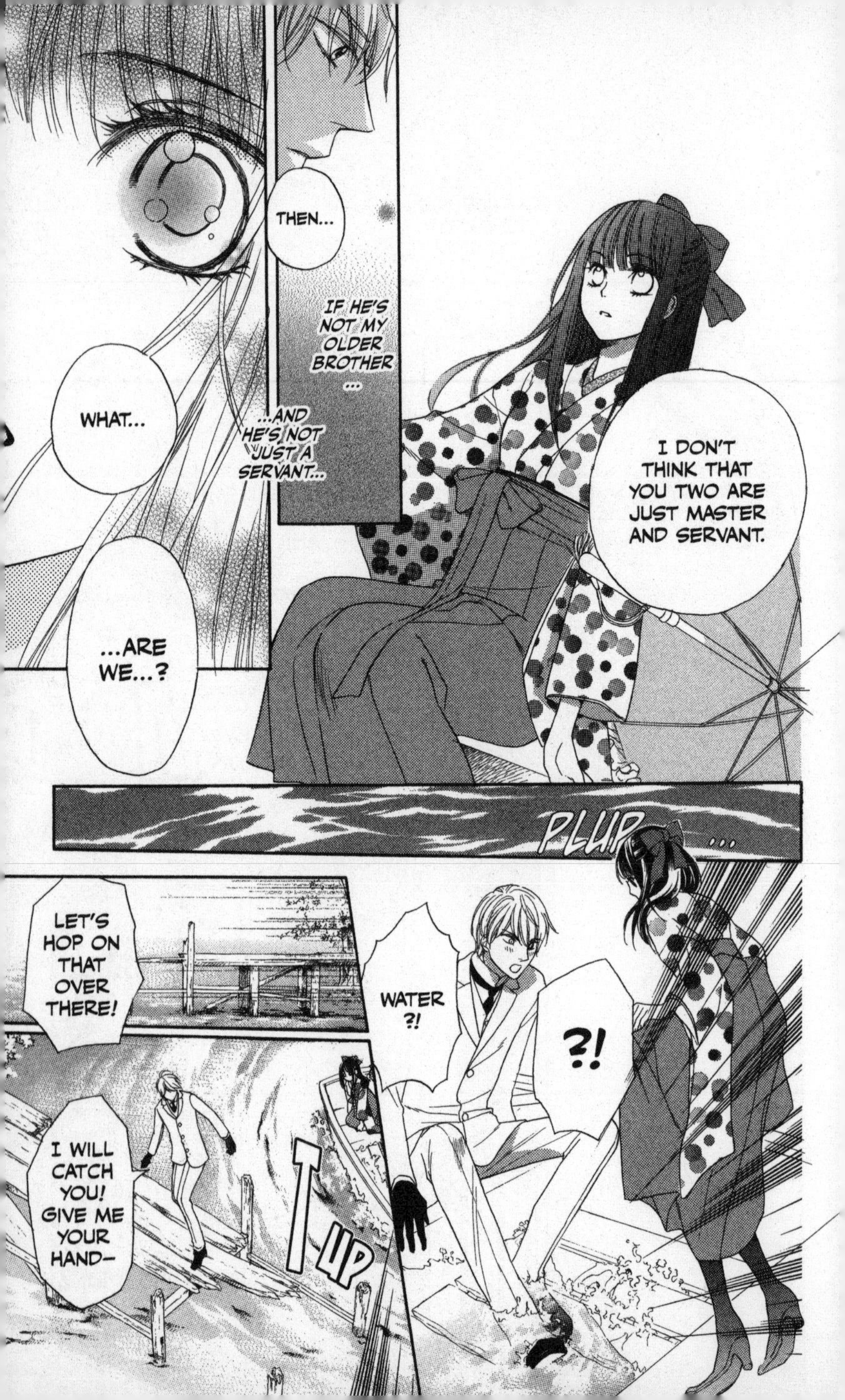
I DON'T THINK THAT YOU TWO ARE JUST MASTER AND SERVANT.
THEN...
IF HE'S NOT MY OLDER BROTHER...
...AND HE'S NOT JUST A SERVANT...
WHAT...
...ARE WE...?
PLUP...
?!
WATER?!
LET'S HOP ON THAT OVER THERE!
TUP
I WILL CATCH YOU! GIVE ME YOUR HAND—

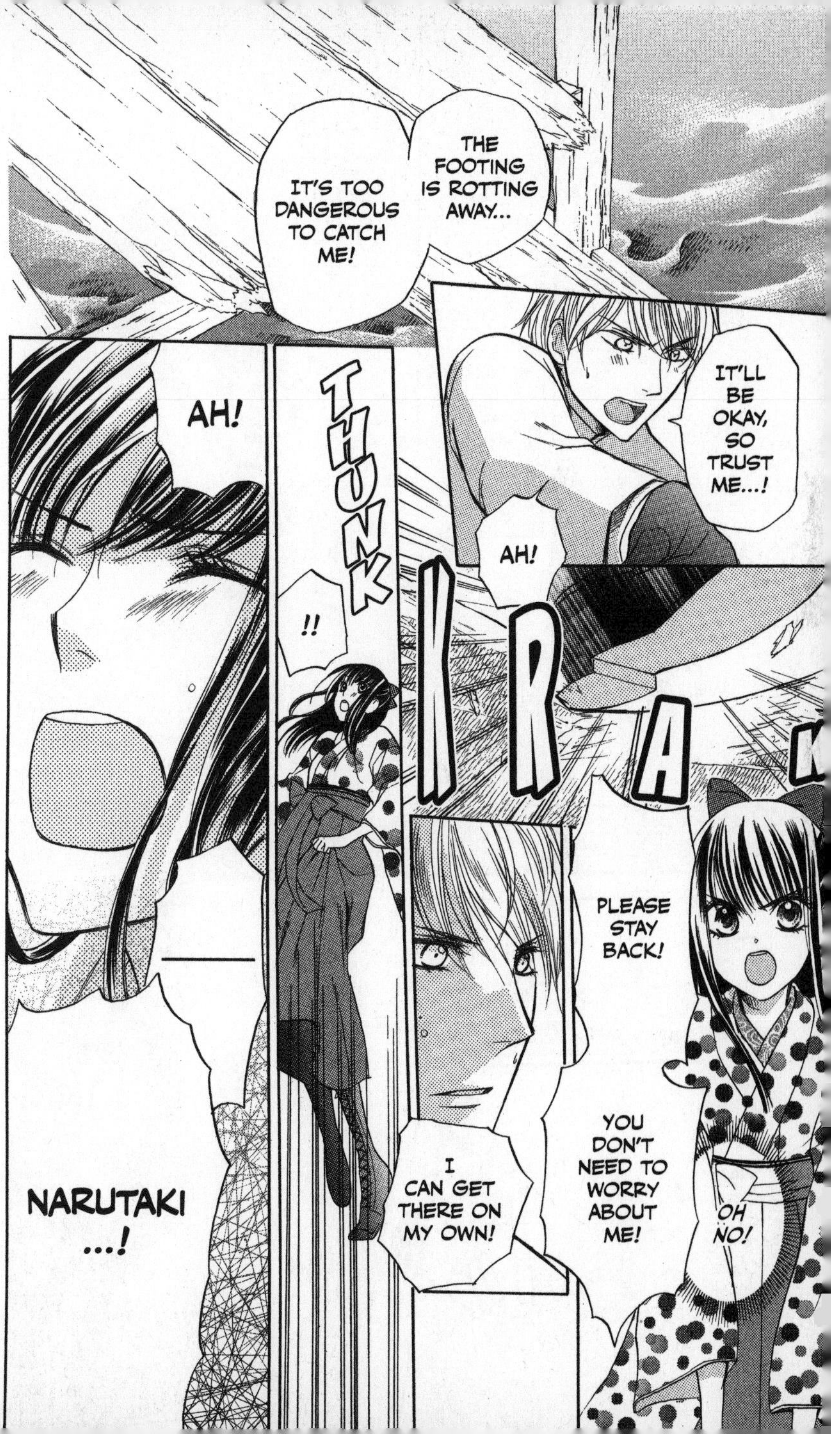
THE FOOTING IS ROTTING AWAY...
IT'S TOO DANGEROUS TO CATCH ME!
IT'LL BE OKAY, SO TRUST ME...!
AH!
KRAK
PLEASE STAY BACK!
YOU DON'T NEED TO WORRY ABOUT ME!
OH NO!
I CAN GET THERE ON MY OWN!
THUNK
!!
AH!
NARUTAKI ...!

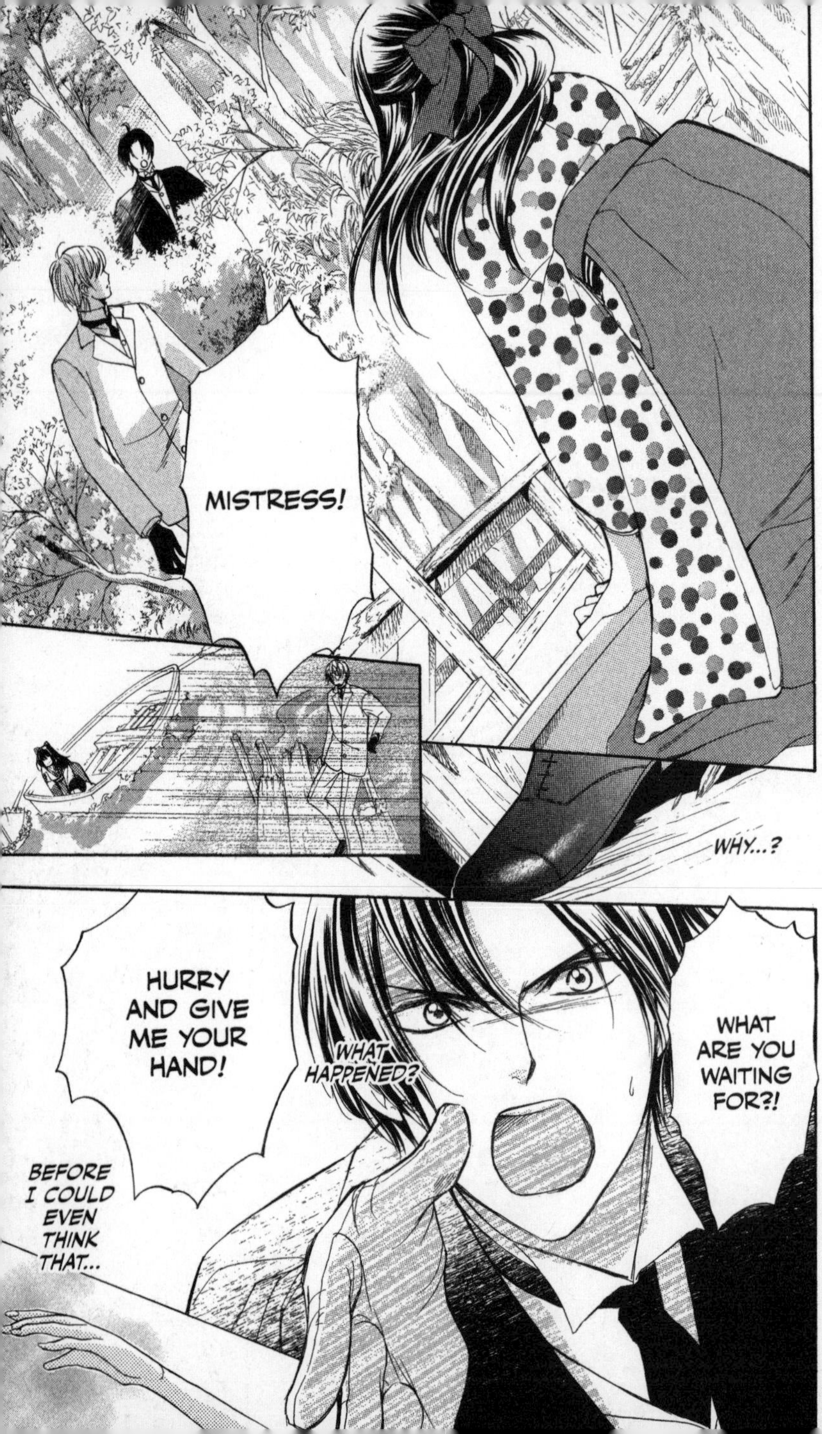
MISTRESS!
WHY...?
WHAT ARE YOU WAITING FOR?!
WHAT HAPPENED?
HURRY AND GIVE ME YOUR HAND!
BEFORE I COULD EVEN THINK THAT...

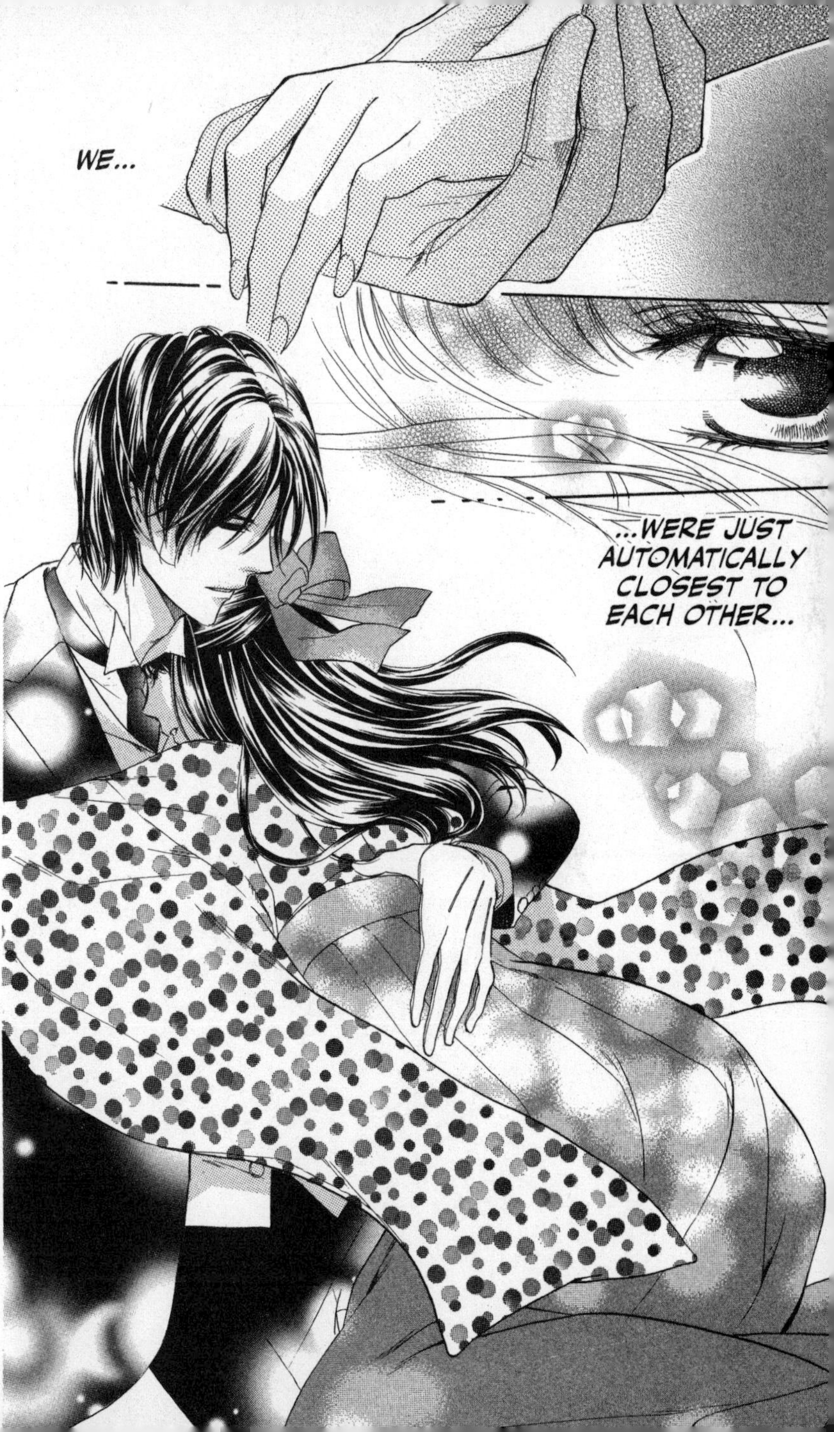
WE...
...WERE JUST AUTOMATICALLY CLOSEST TO EACH OTHER...

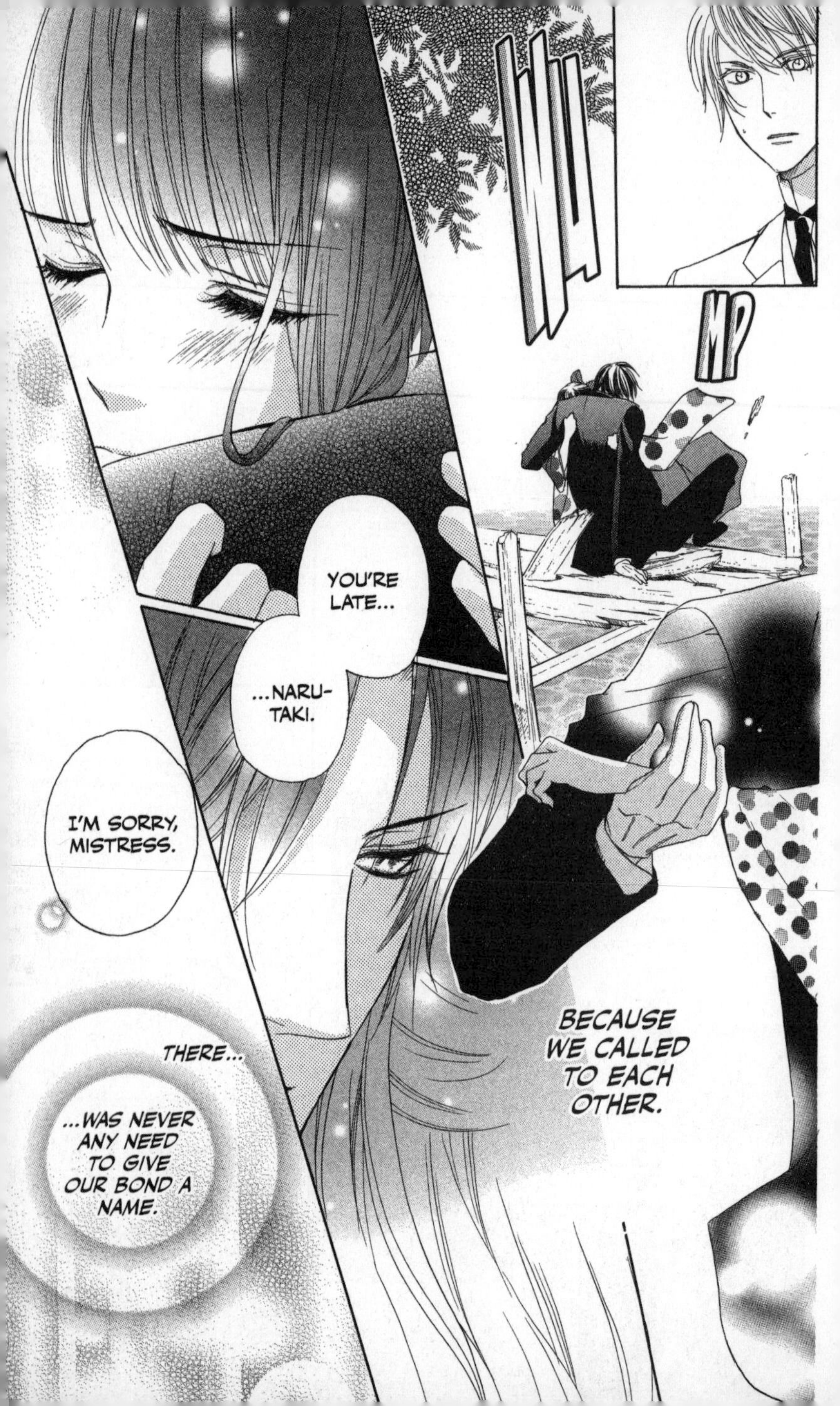
WHUMP
YOU'RE LATE...
...NARUTAKI.
I'M SORRY, MISTRESS.
BECAUSE WE CALLED TO EACH OTHER.
THERE...
...WAS NEVER ANY NEED TO GIVE OUR BOND A NAME.

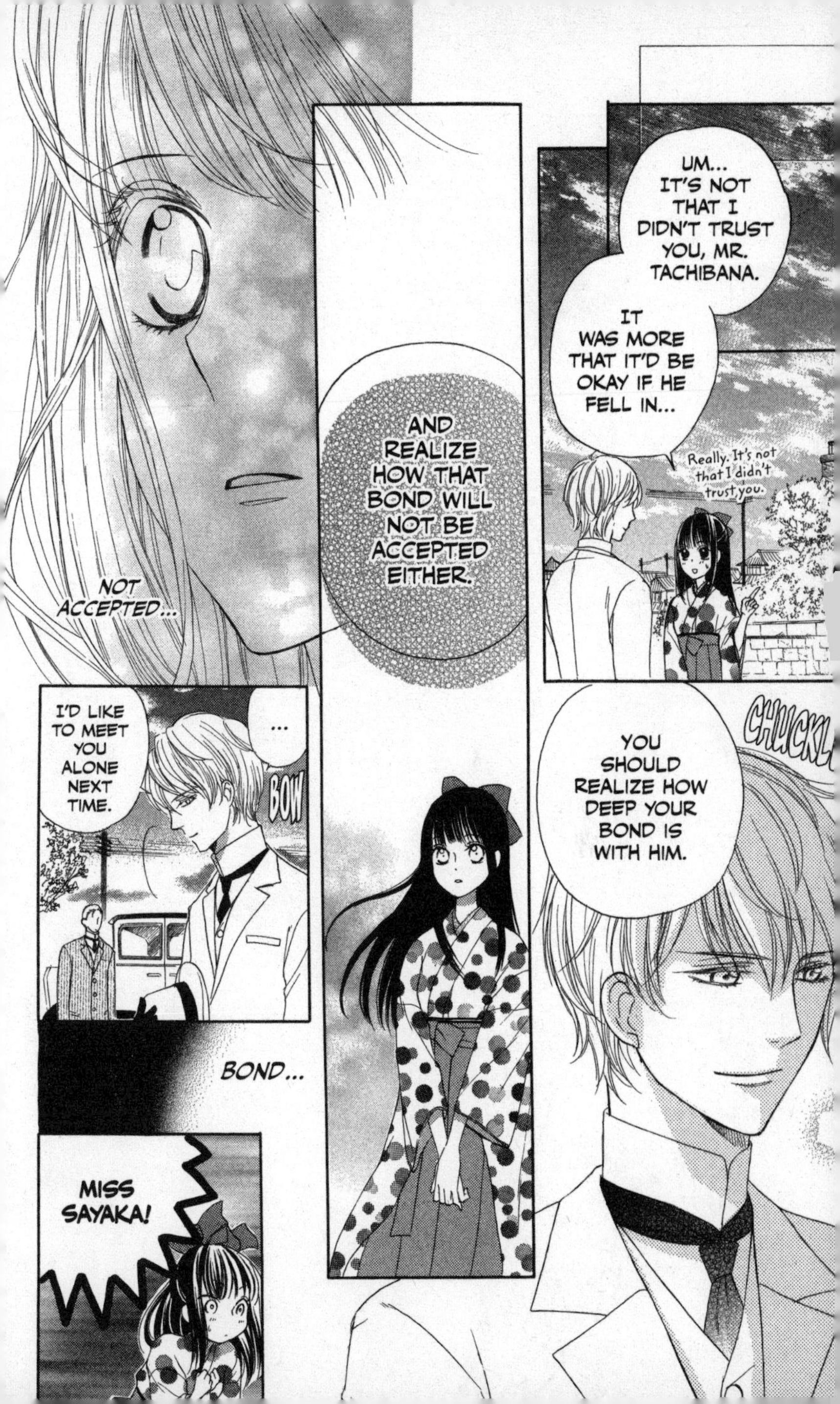
UM... IT'S NOT THAT I DIDN'T TRUST YOU, MR. TACHIBANA.
IT WAS MORE THAT IT'D BE OKAY IF HE FELL IN...
Really. It's not that I didn't trust you.
YOU SHOULD REALIZE HOW DEEP YOUR BOND IS WITH HIM.
CHUCKL
AND REALIZE HOW THAT BOND WILL NOT BE ACCEPTED EITHER.
NOT ACCEPTED...
...
BOW
I'D LIKE TO MEET YOU ALONE NEXT TIME.
BOND...
MISS SAYAKA!

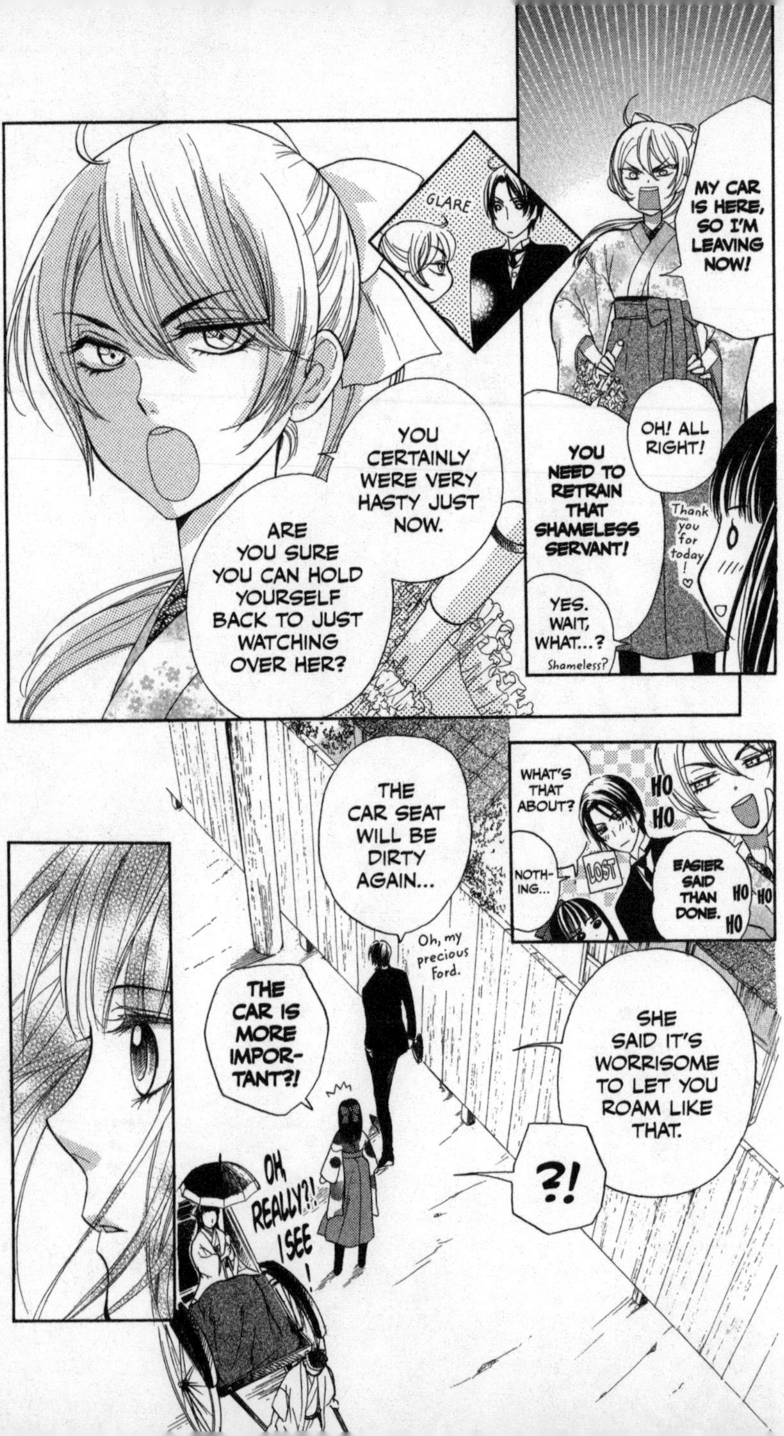
MY CAR IS HERE, SO I'M LEAVING NOW!
OH! ALL RIGHT!
Thank you for today! ♡
YOU NEED TO RETRAIN THAT SHAMELESS SERVANT!
YES. WAIT, WHAT...?
Shameless?
GLARE
YOU CERTAINLY WERE VERY HASTY JUST NOW.
ARE YOU SURE YOU CAN HOLD YOURSELF BACK TO JUST WATCHING OVER HER?
HO HO
EASIER SAID THAN DONE.
HO HO HO HO
WHAT'S THAT ABOUT?
NOTHING...
LOST
SHE SAID IT'S WORRISOME TO LET YOU ROAM LIKE THAT.
?!
THE CAR SEAT WILL BE DIRTY AGAIN...
Oh, my precious Ford.
THE CAR IS MORE IMPORTANT?!
OH, REALLY?! I SEE!

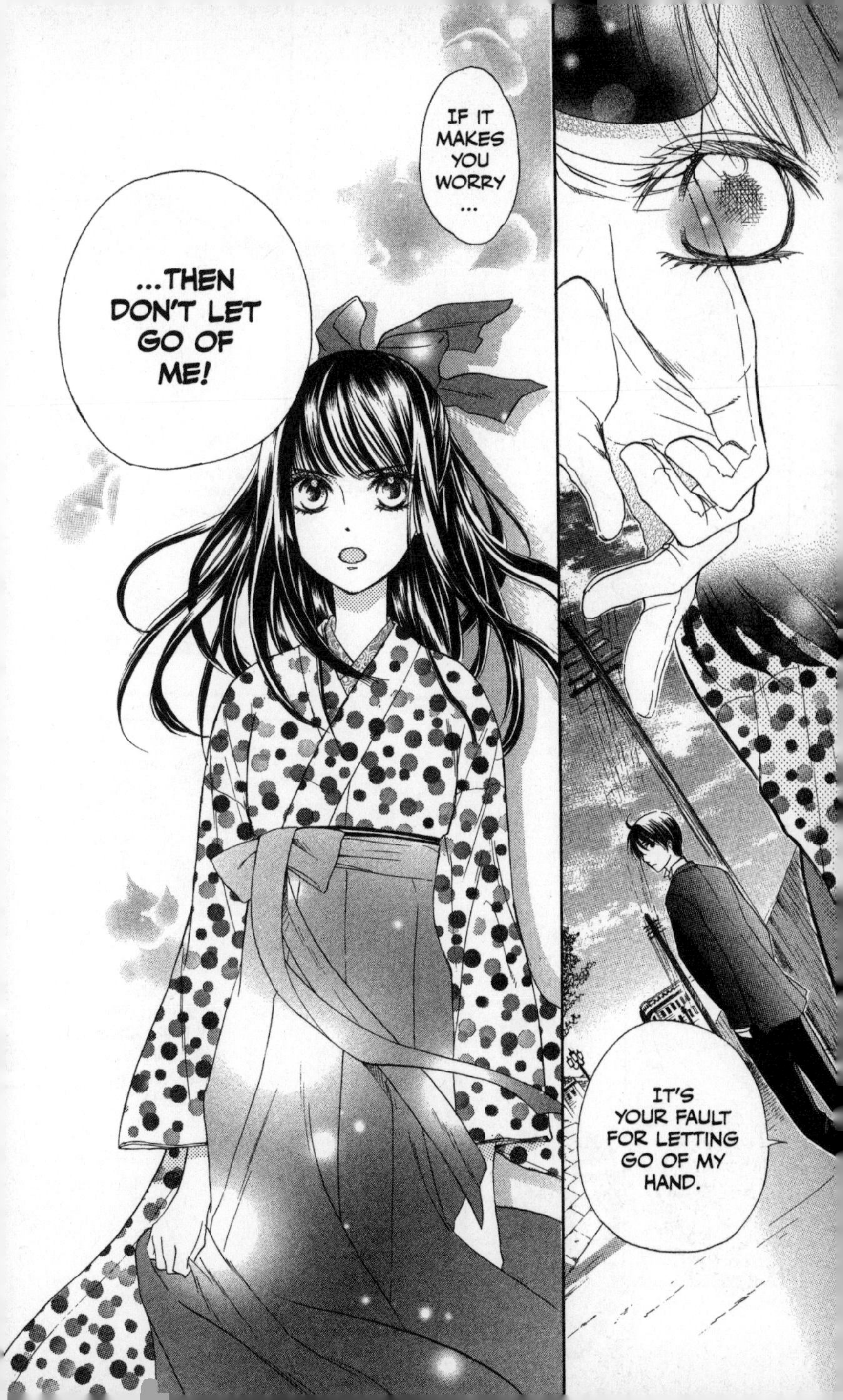
IT'S YOUR FAULT FOR LETTING GO OF MY HAND.
IF IT MAKES YOU WORRY ...
...THEN DON'T LET GO OF ME!

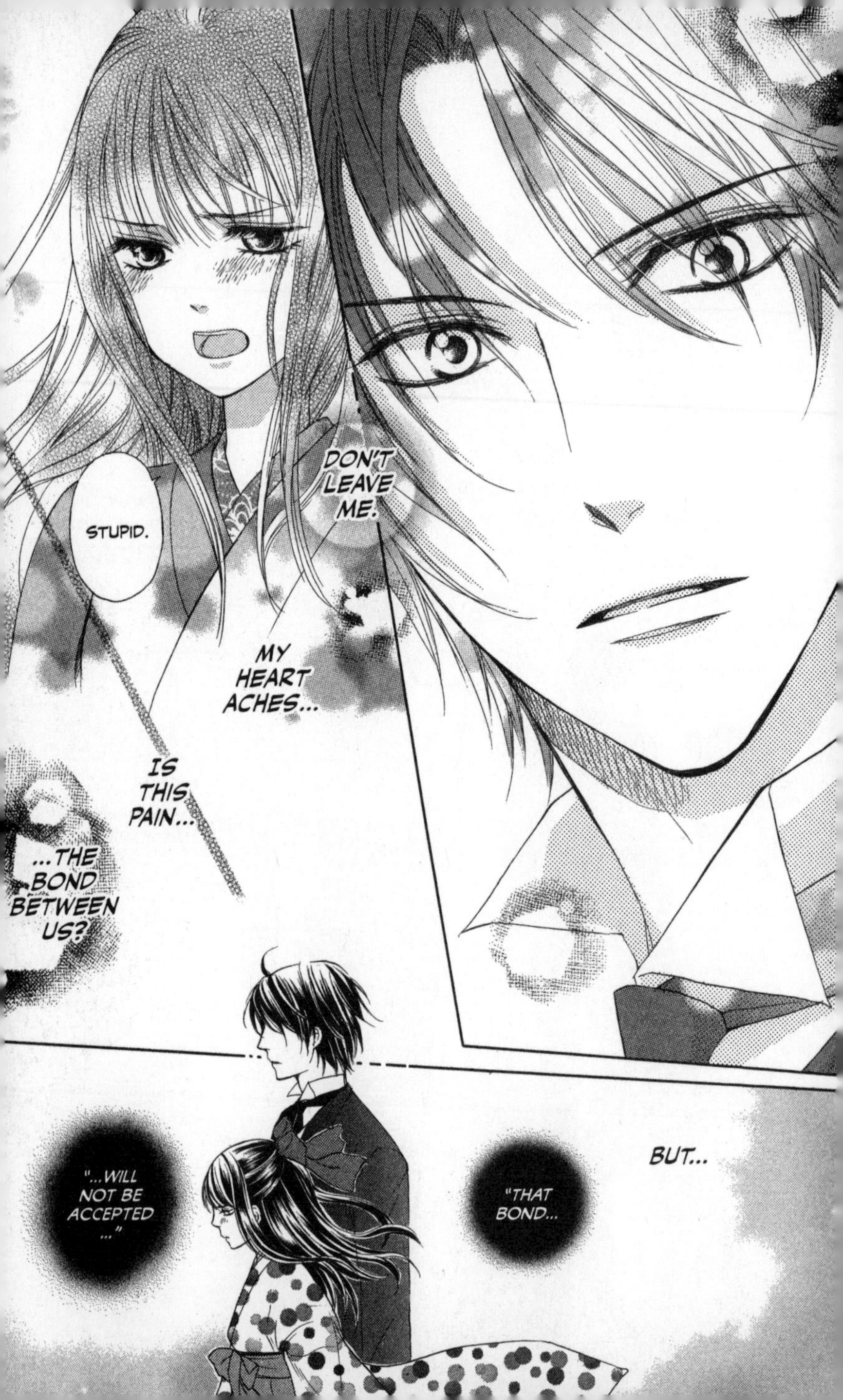
DON'T LEAVE ME.
STUPID.
MY HEART ACHES...
IS THIS PAIN...
...THE BOND BETWEEN US?
BUT...
"THAT BOND...
"...WILL NOT BE ACCEPTED ..."

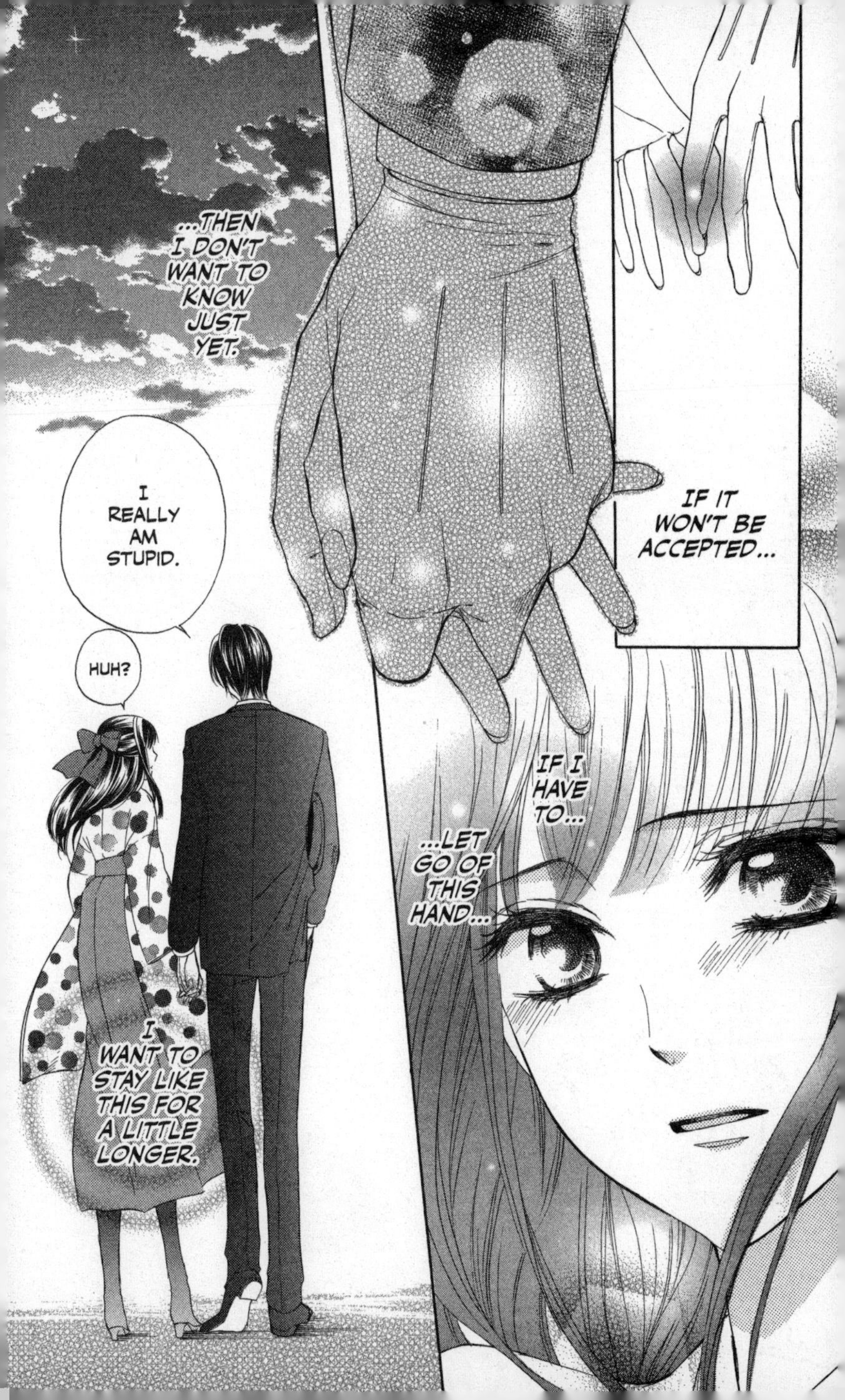
IF IT WON'T BE ACCEPTED...
IF I HAVE TO...
...LET GO OF THIS HAND...
...THEN I DON'T WANT TO KNOW JUST YET.
I REALLY AM STUPID.
HUH?
I WANT TO STAY LIKE THIS FOR A LITTLE LONGER.

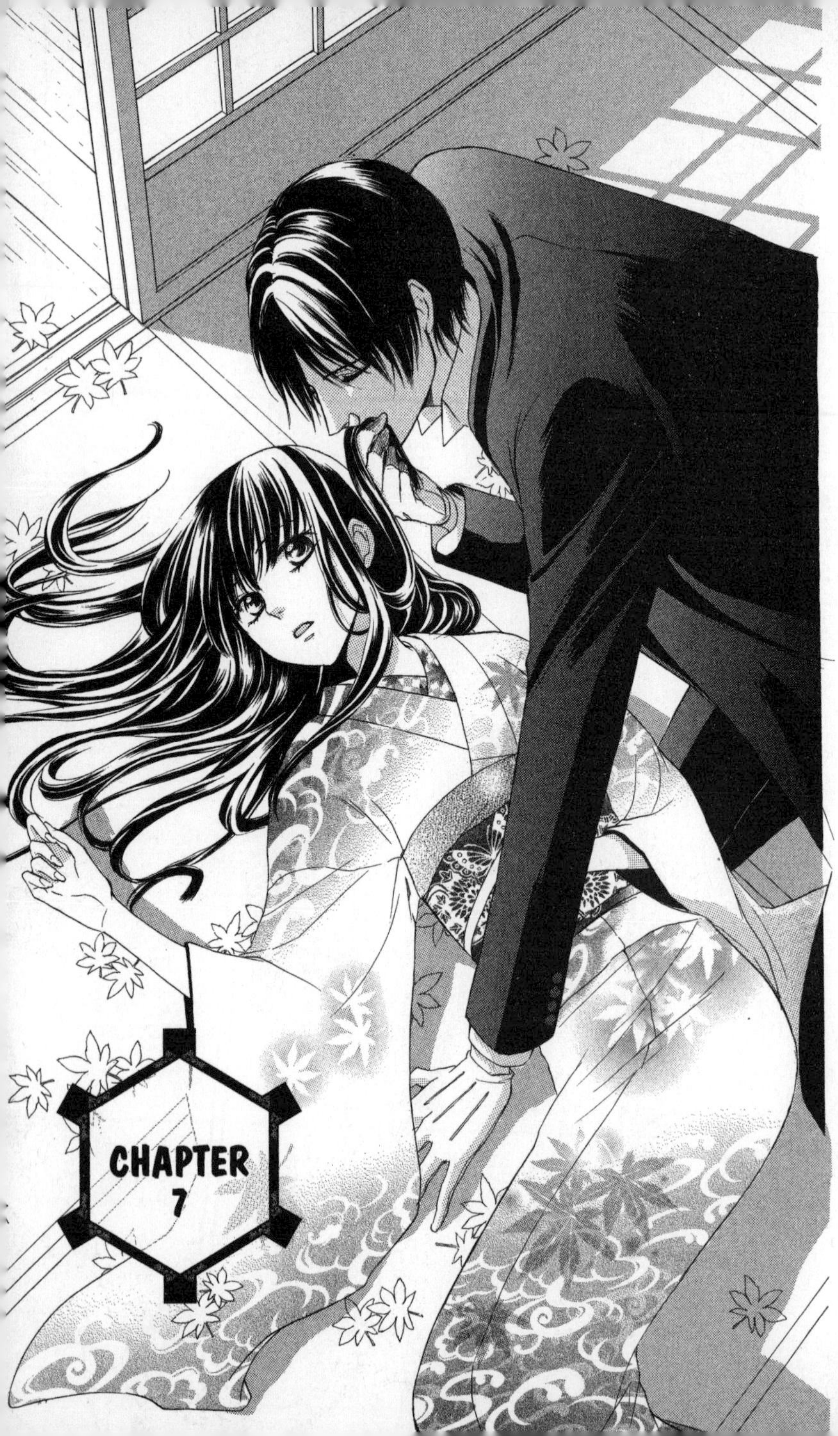
CHAPTER 7

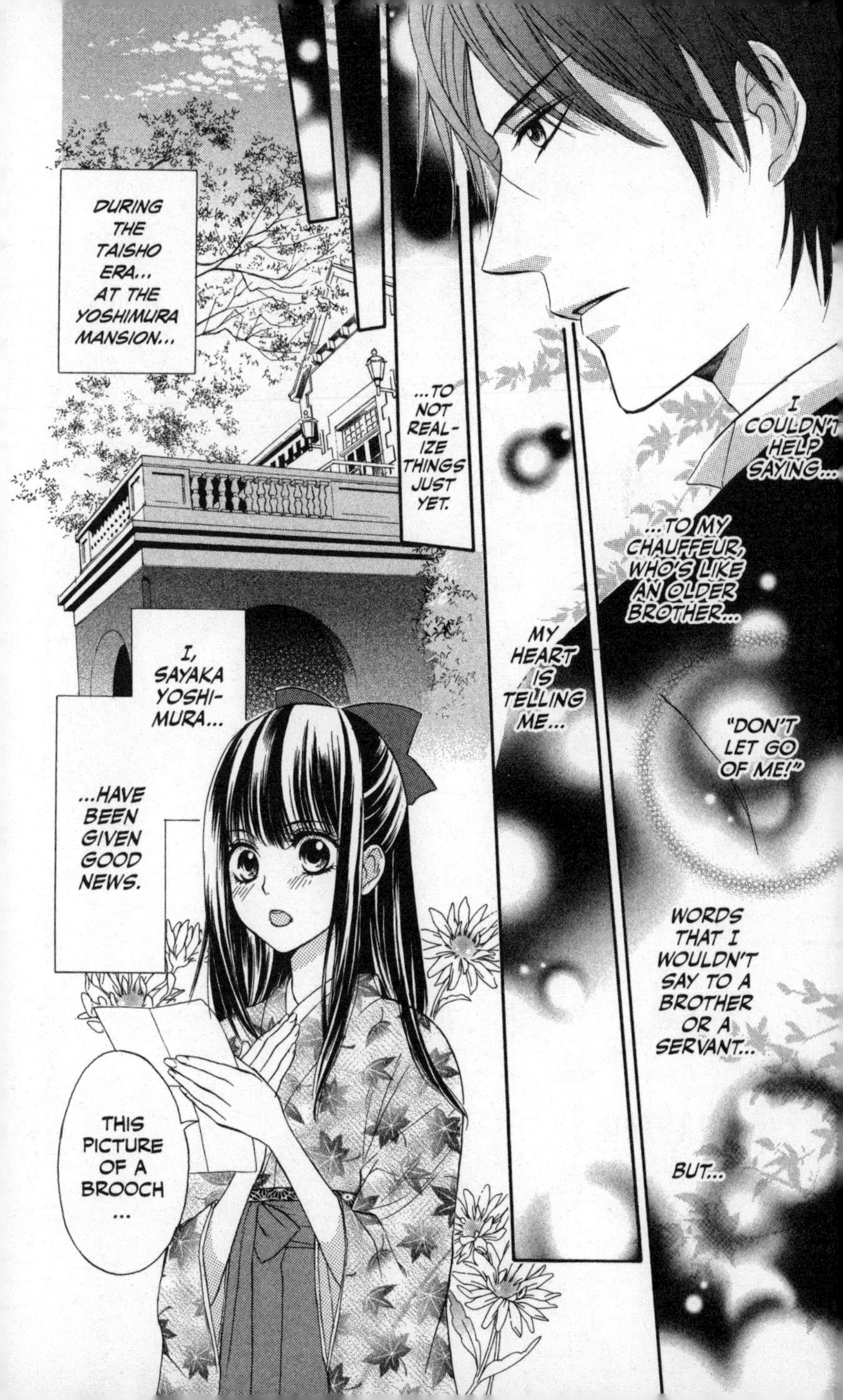
I COULDN'T HELP SAYING...
...TO MY CHAUFFEUR, WHO'S LIKE AN OLDER BROTHER...
"DON'T LET GO OF ME!"
WORDS THAT I WOULDN'T SAY TO A BROTHER OR A SERVANT...
BUT...
MY HEART IS TELLING ME...
...TO NOT REALIZE THINGS JUST YET.
DURING THE TAISHO ERA... AT THE YOSHIMURA MANSION...
I, SAYAKA YOSHIMURA...
...HAVE BEEN GIVEN GOOD NEWS.
THIS PICTURE OF A BROOCH ...

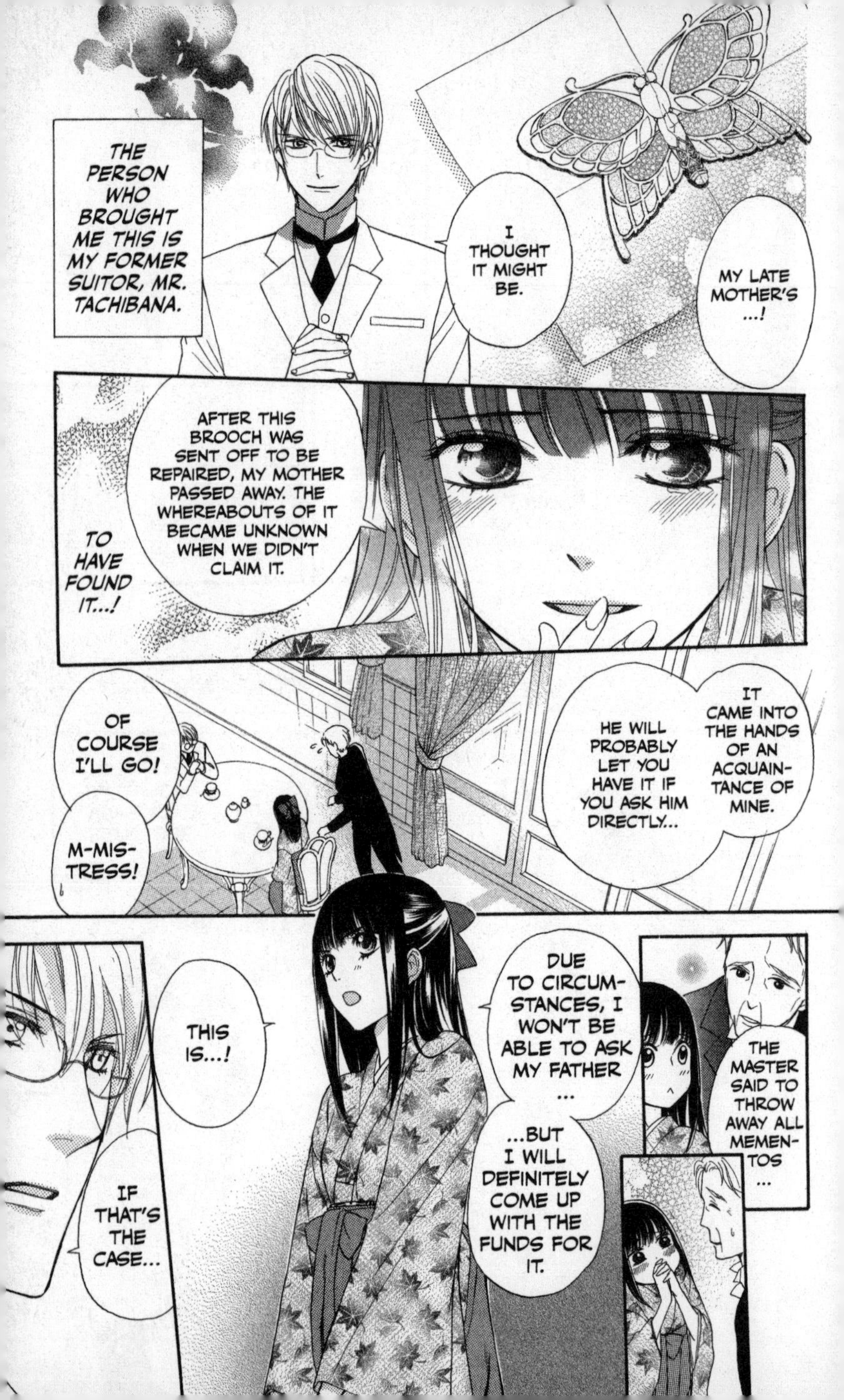
MY LATE MOTHER'S ...!
I THOUGHT IT MIGHT BE.
THE PERSON WHO BROUGHT ME THIS IS MY FORMER SUITOR, MR. TACHIBANA.
AFTER THIS BROOCH WAS SENT OFF TO BE REPAIRED, MY MOTHER PASSED AWAY. THE WHEREABOUTS OF IT BECAME UNKNOWN WHEN WE DIDN'T CLAIM IT.
TO HAVE FOUND IT...!
IT CAME INTO THE HANDS OF AN ACQUAIN-TANCE OF MINE.
HE WILL PROBABLY LET YOU HAVE IT IF YOU ASK HIM DIRECTLY...
OF COURSE I'LL GO!
M-MIS-TRESS!
THE MASTER SAID TO THROW AWAY ALL MEMEN-TOS ...
DUE TO CIRCUM-STANCES, I WON'T BE ABLE TO ASK MY FATHER ...
...BUT I WILL DEFINITELY COME UP WITH THE FUNDS FOR IT.
THIS IS...!
IF THAT'S THE CASE...

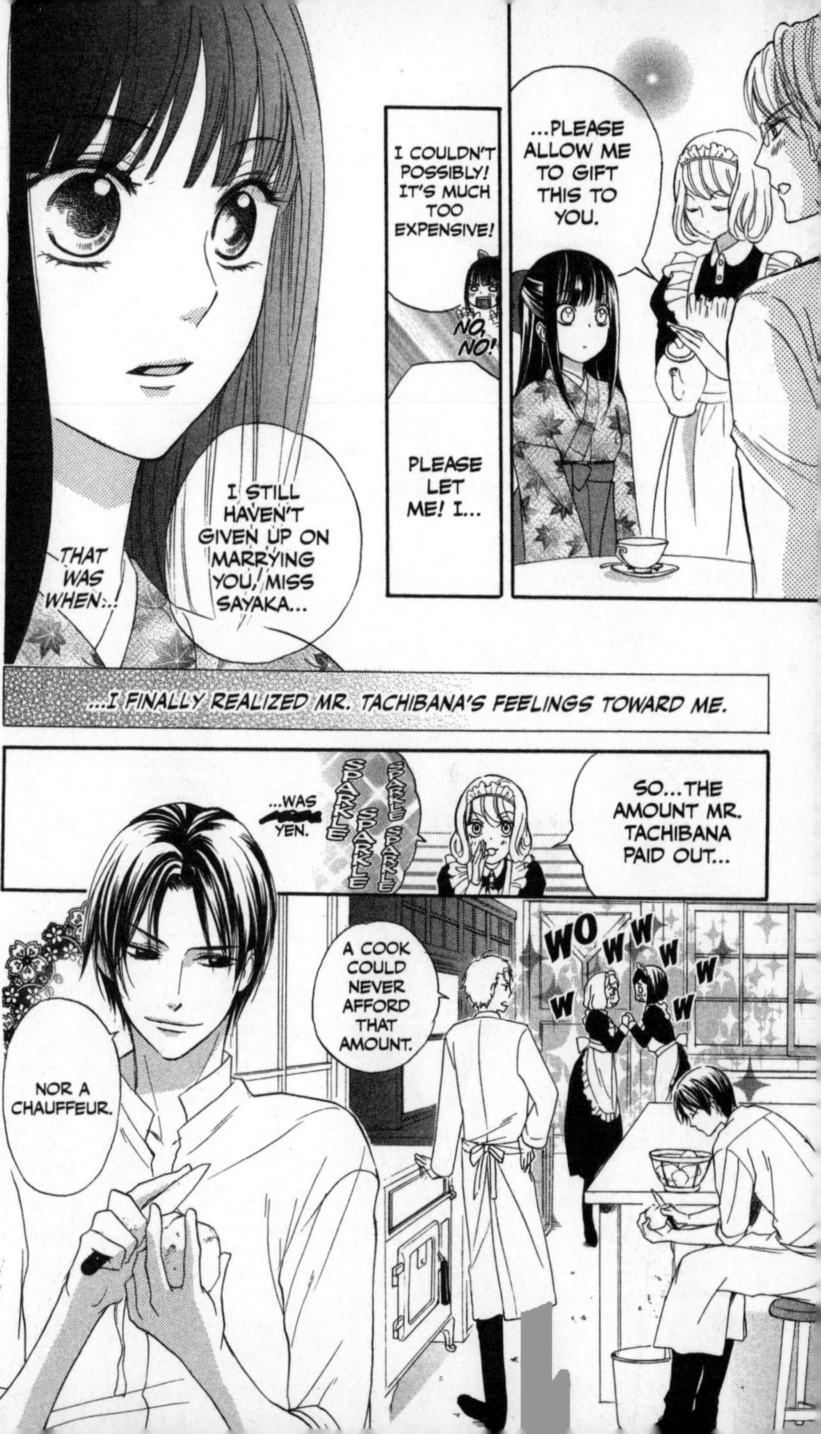
...PLEASE ALLOW ME TO GIFT THIS TO YOU.
I COULDN'T POSSIBLY! IT'S MUCH TOO EXPENSIVE!
NO, NO!
PLEASE LET ME! I...
I STILL HAVEN'T GIVEN UP ON MARRYING YOU, MISS SAYAKA...
THAT WAS WHEN...
...I FINALLY REALIZED MR. TACHIBANA'S FEELINGS TOWARD ME.
SO...THE AMOUNT MR. TACHIBANA PAID OUT...
SPARKLE SPARKLE
SPARKLE SPARKLE
...WAS YEN.
WOWWWWWW
A COOK COULD NEVER AFFORD THAT AMOUNT.
NOR A CHAUFFEUR.

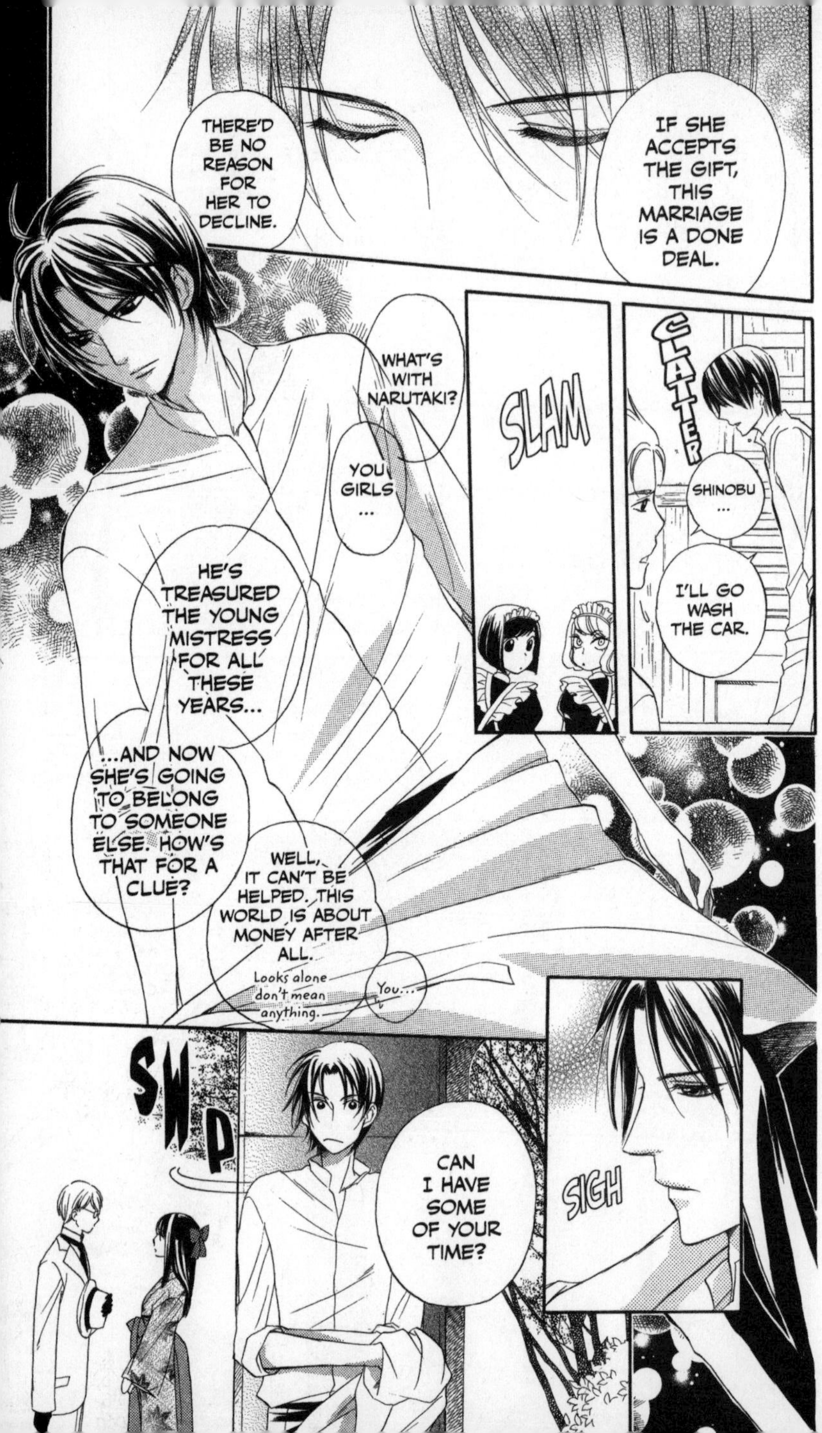
IF SHE ACCEPTS THE GIFT, THIS MARRIAGE IS A DONE DEAL.
THERE'D BE NO REASON FOR HER TO DECLINE.
CLATTER
SHINOBU...
I'LL GO WASH THE CAR.
SLAM
WHAT'S WITH NARUTAKI?
YOU GIRLS...
HE'S TREASURED THE YOUNG MISTRESS FOR ALL THESE YEARS...
...AND NOW SHE'S GOING TO BELONG TO SOMEONE ELSE. HOW'S THAT FOR A CLUE?
WELL, IT CAN'T BE HELPED. THIS WORLD IS ABOUT MONEY AFTER ALL.
Looks alone don't mean anything.
You...
SIGH
CAN I HAVE SOME OF YOUR TIME?
SWP

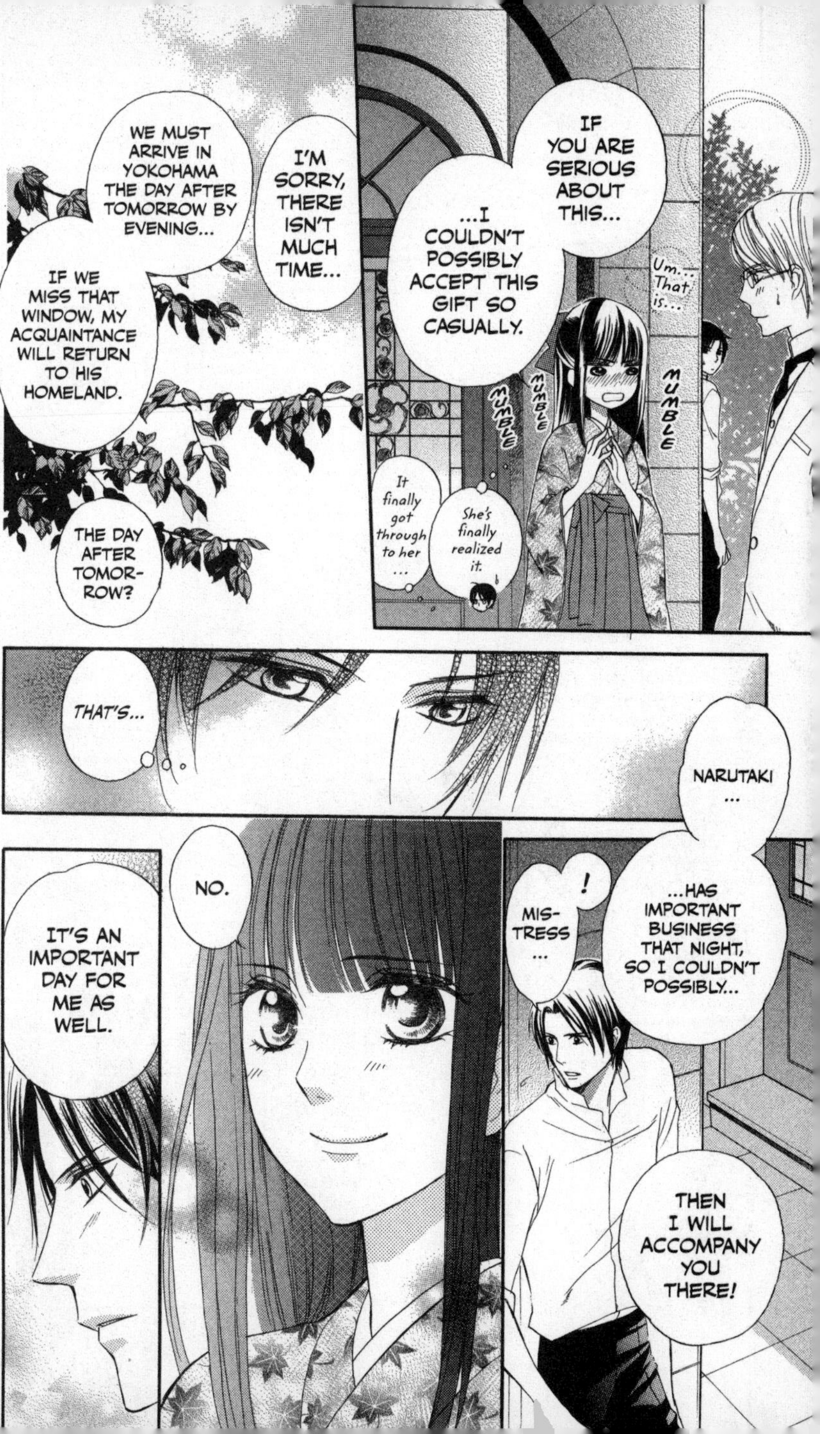
IF YOU ARE SERIOUS ABOUT THIS...
...I COULDN'T POSSIBLY ACCEPT THIS GIFT SO CASUALLY.
Um... That is...
MUMBLE
MUMBLE
MUMBLE
She's finally realized it.
It finally got through to her...
I'M SORRY, THERE ISN'T MUCH TIME...
WE MUST ARRIVE IN YOKOHAMA THE DAY AFTER TOMORROW BY EVENING...
IF WE MISS THAT WINDOW, MY ACQUAINTANCE WILL RETURN TO HIS HOMELAND.
THE DAY AFTER TOMOR-ROW?
THAT'S...
NARUTAKI...
...HAS IMPORTANT BUSINESS THAT NIGHT, SO I COULDN'T POSSIBLY...
!
MIS-TRESS...
THEN I WILL ACCOMPANY YOU THERE!
NO.
IT'S AN IMPORTANT DAY FOR ME AS WELL.

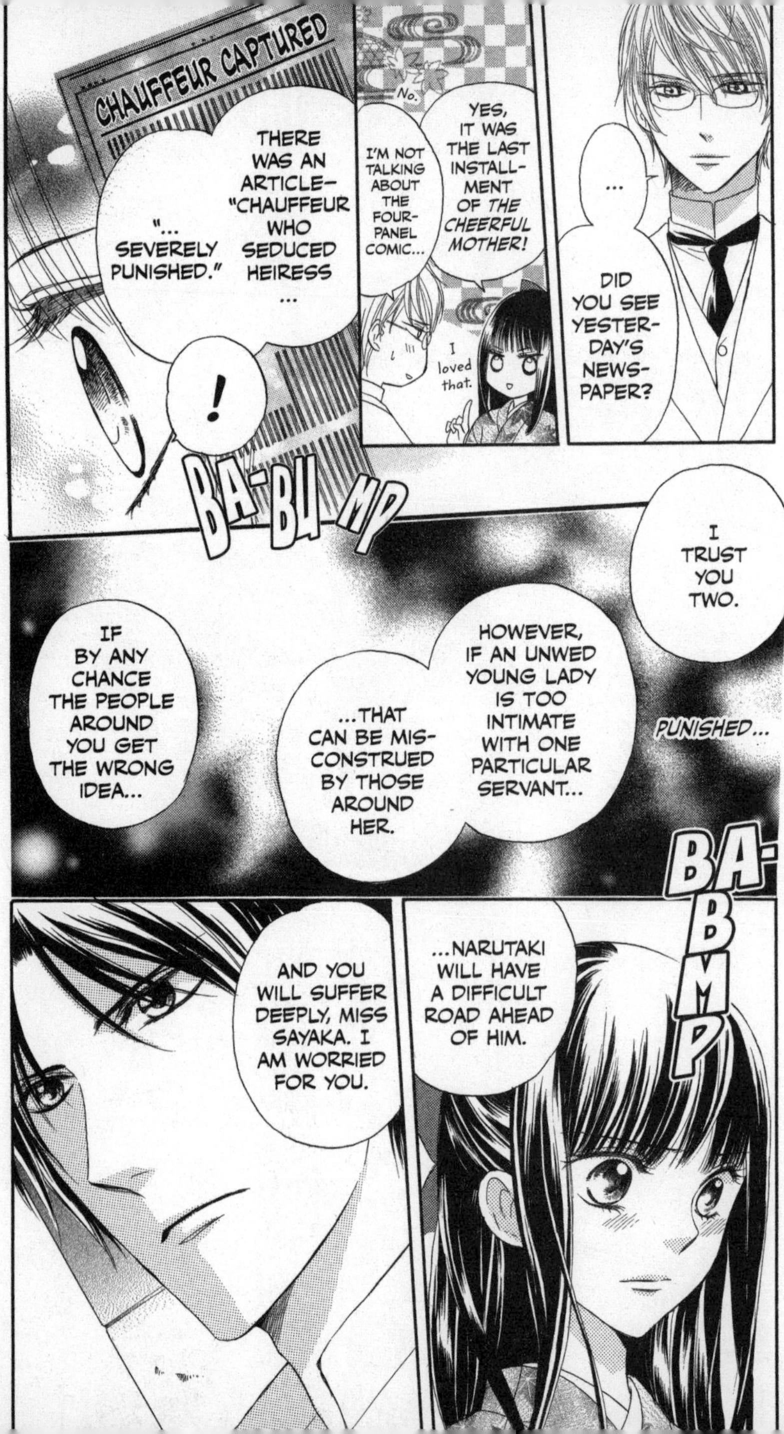
...
DID YOU SEE YESTERDAY'S NEWSPAPER?
YES, IT WAS THE LAST INSTALLMENT OF THE CHEERFUL MOTHER!
I loved that.
No.
I'M NOT TALKING ABOUT THE FOUR-PANEL COMIC...
CHAUFFEUR CAPTURED
THERE WAS AN ARTICLE—"CHAUFFEUR WHO SEDUCED HEIRESS ...
"... SEVERELY PUNISHED."
!
BA-BUMP
I TRUST YOU TWO.
PUNISHED...
HOWEVER, IF AN UNWED YOUNG LADY IS TOO INTIMATE WITH ONE PARTICULAR SERVANT...
...THAT CAN BE MISCONSTRUED BY THOSE AROUND HER.
IF BY ANY CHANCE THE PEOPLE AROUND YOU GET THE WRONG IDEA...
BA-BUMP
...NARUTAKI WILL HAVE A DIFFICULT ROAD AHEAD OF HIM.
AND YOU WILL SUFFER DEEPLY, MISS SAYAKA. I AM WORRIED FOR YOU.

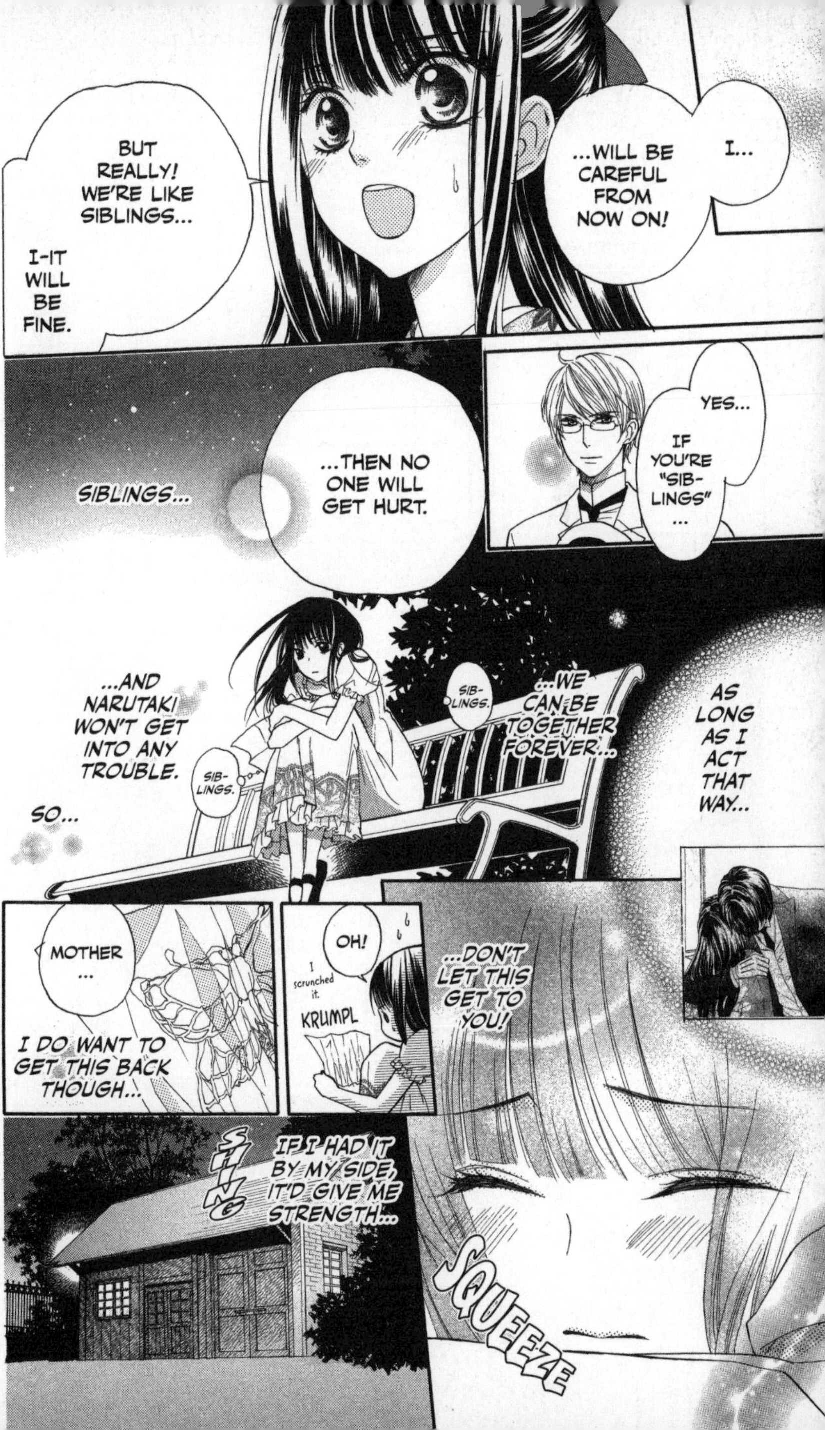
I...
...WILL BE CAREFUL FROM NOW ON!
BUT REALLY! WE'RE LIKE SIBLINGS...
I-IT WILL BE FINE.
YES...
IF YOU'RE "SIBLINGS"...
...THEN NO ONE WILL GET HURT.
SIBLINGS...
AS LONG AS I ACT THAT WAY...
...WE CAN BE TOGETHER FOREVER...
SIB-LINGS.
SIB-LINGS.
...AND NARUTAKI WON'T GET INTO ANY TROUBLE.
SO...
...DON'T LET THIS GET TO YOU!
SQUEEZE
OH!
I scrunched it.
KRUMPL
MOTHER...
I DO WANT TO GET THIS BACK THOUGH...
SHING
IF I HAD IT BY MY SIDE, IT'D GIVE ME STRENGTH...

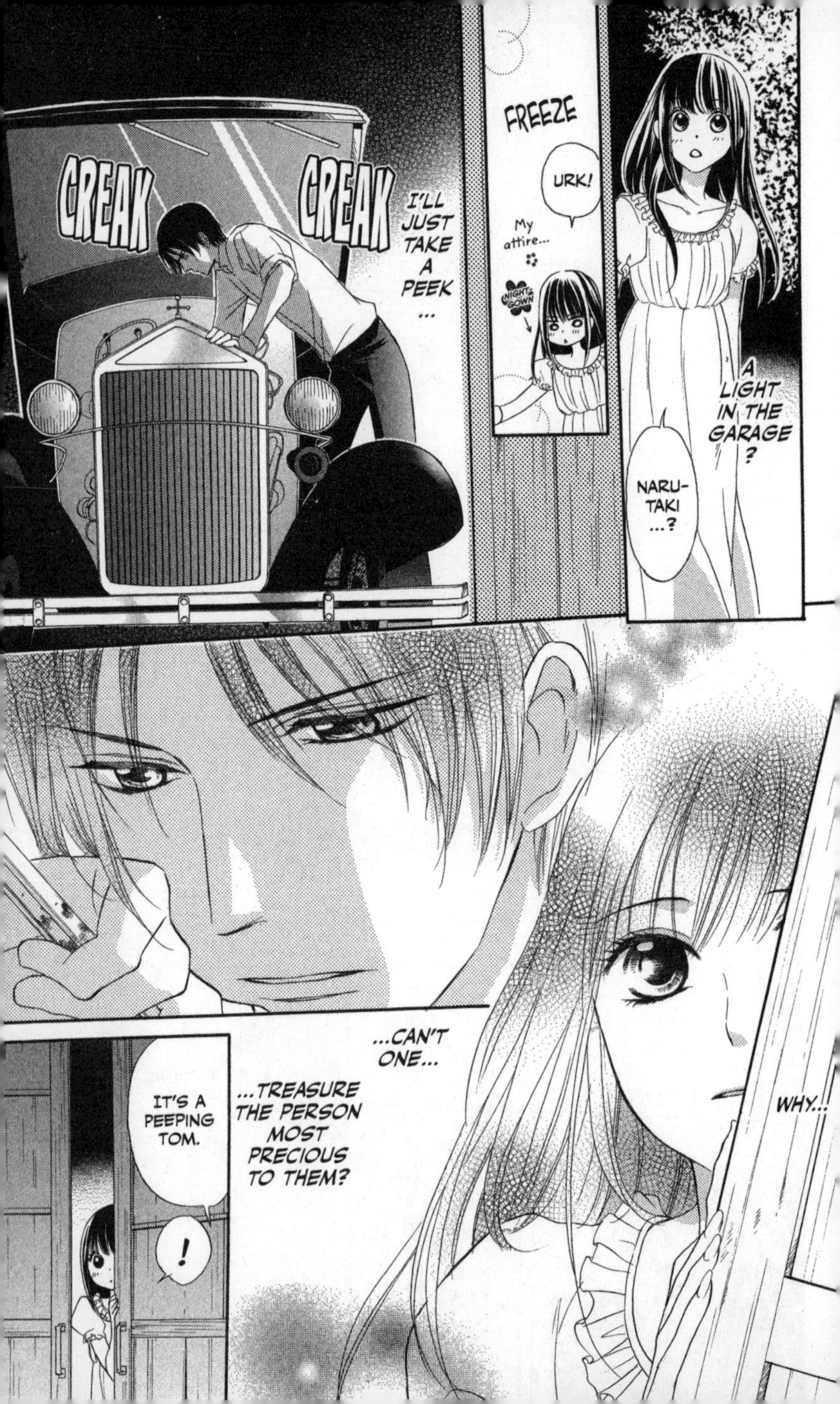
A LIGHT IN THE GARAGE?
NARU-TAKI ...?
FREEZE
URK!
My attire...
NIGHT-GOWN
CREAK
CREAK
I'LL JUST TAKE A PEEK ...
WHY...
...CAN'T ONE...
...TREASURE THE PERSON MOST PRECIOUS TO THEM?
IT'S A PEEPING TOM.
!

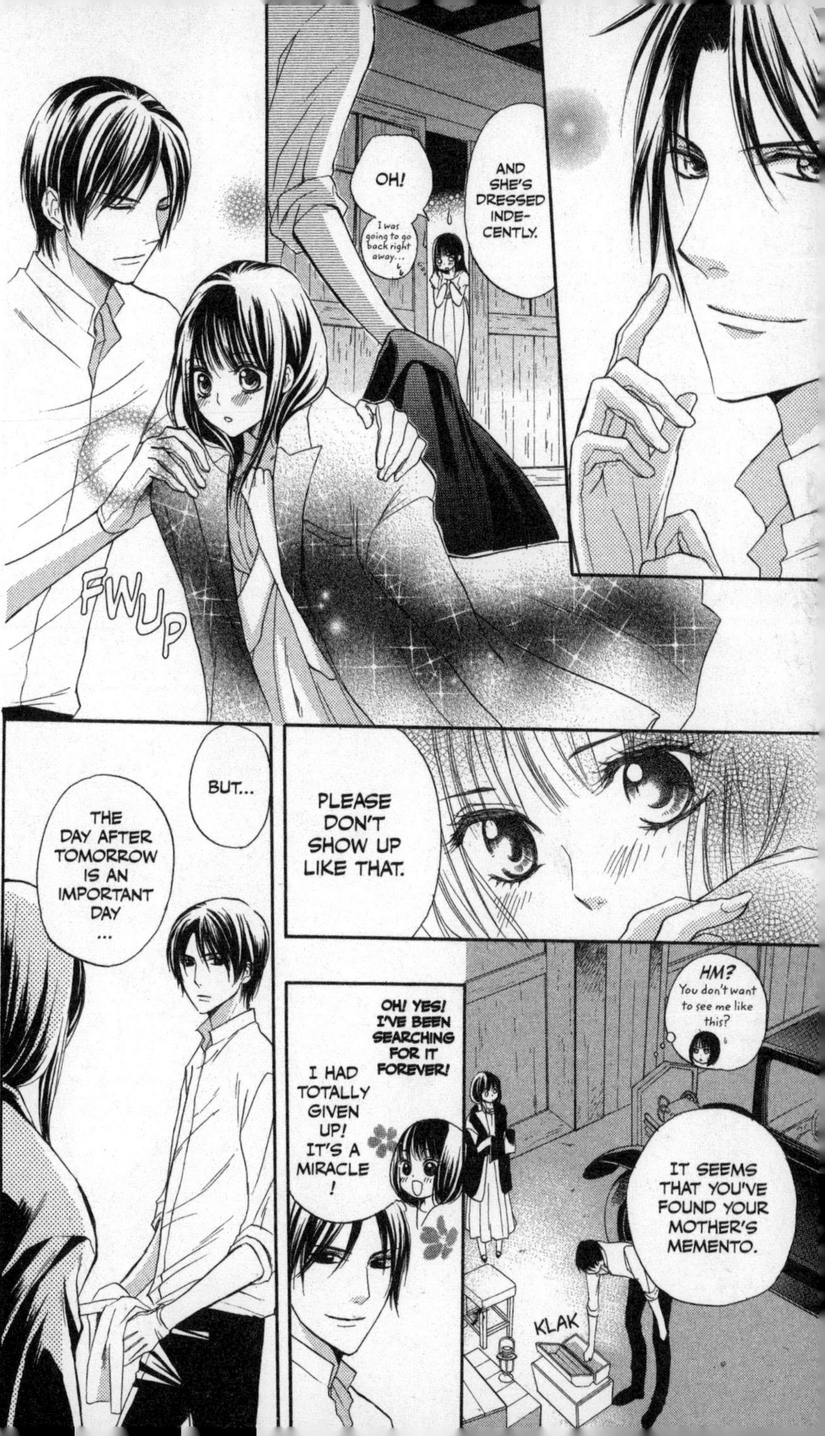
AND SHE'S DRESSED INDE-CENTLY.
OH!
I was going to go back right away...
FWUP
PLEASE DON'T SHOW UP LIKE THAT.
HM? You don't want to see me like this?
IT SEEMS THAT YOU'VE FOUND YOUR MOTHER'S MEMENTO.
KLAK
OH! YES! I'VE BEEN SEARCHING FOR IT FOREVER!
I HAD TOTALLY GIVEN UP! IT'S A MIRACLE!
BUT...
THE DAY AFTER TOMORROW IS AN IMPORTANT DAY ...

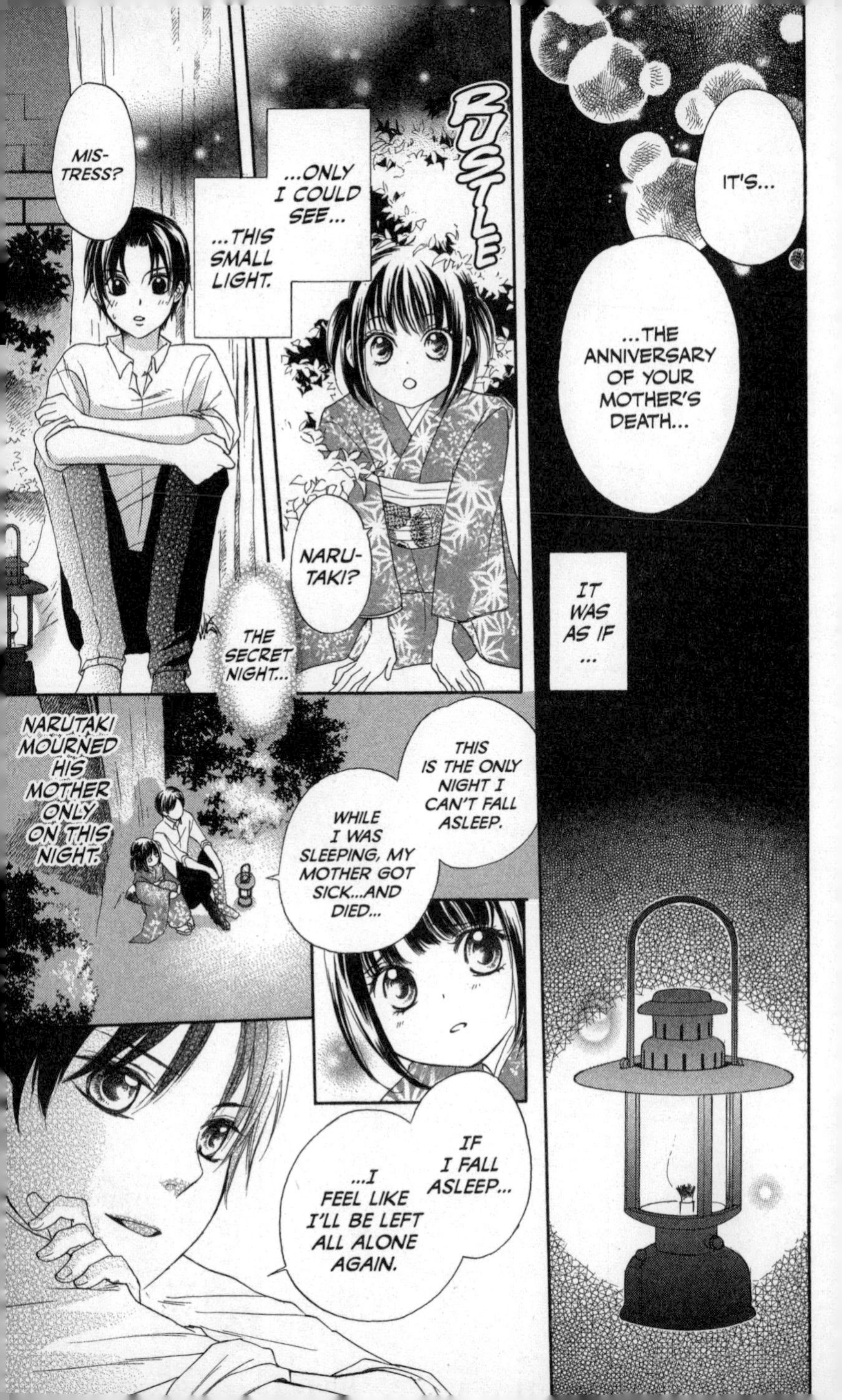
IT'S...
...THE ANNIVERSARY OF YOUR MOTHER'S DEATH...
RUSTLE
NARU-TAKI?
MIS-TRESS?
...ONLY I COULD SEE...
...THIS SMALL LIGHT.
THE SECRET NIGHT...
IT WAS AS IF ...
THIS IS THE ONLY NIGHT I CAN'T FALL ASLEEP.
WHILE I WAS SLEEPING, MY MOTHER GOT SICK...AND DIED...
NARUTAKI MOURNED HIS MOTHER ONLY ON THIS NIGHT.
IF I FALL ASLEEP...
...I FEEL LIKE I'LL BE LEFT ALL ALONE AGAIN.

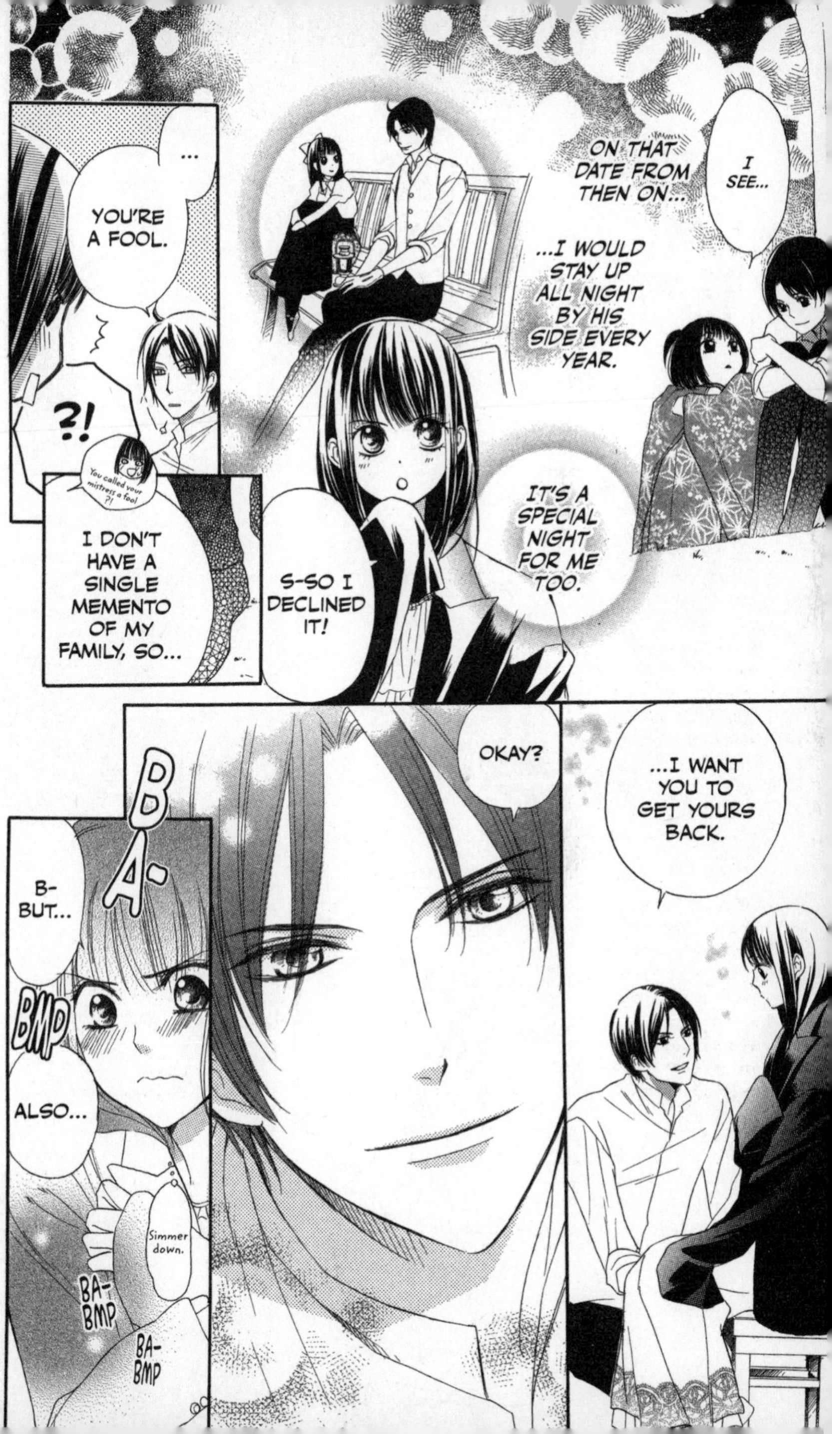
I SEE...
ON THAT DATE FROM THEN ON...
...I WOULD STAY UP ALL NIGHT BY HIS SIDE EVERY YEAR.
IT'S A SPECIAL NIGHT FOR ME TOO.
S-SO I DECLINED IT!
...
YOU'RE A FOOL.
?!
You called your mistress a fool?!
I DON'T HAVE A SINGLE MEMENTO OF MY FAMILY, SO...
...I WANT YOU TO GET YOURS BACK.
OKAY?
BA-
B-BUT...
BMP
ALSO...
Simmer down.
BA-BMP
BA-BMP

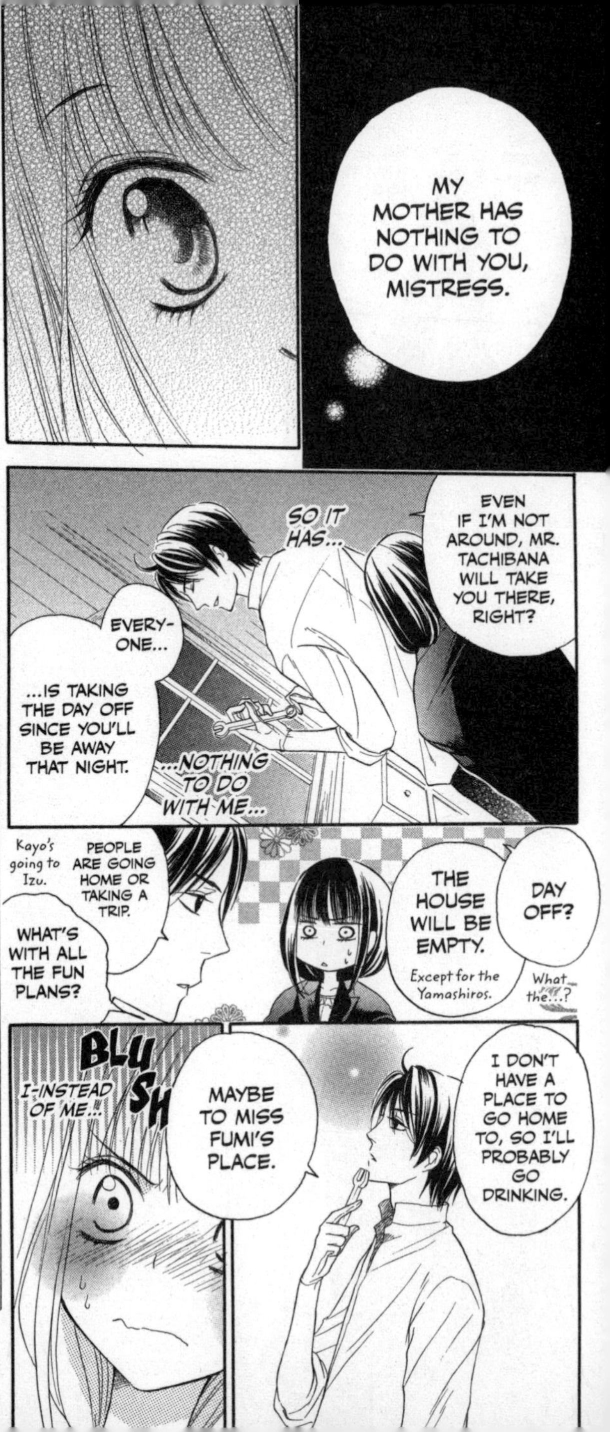
MY MOTHER HAS NOTHING TO DO WITH YOU, MISTRESS.
EVEN IF I'M NOT AROUND, MR. TACHIBANA WILL TAKE YOU THERE, RIGHT?
SO IT HAS...
EVERY-ONE...
...IS TAKING THE DAY OFF SINCE YOU'LL BE AWAY THAT NIGHT.
...NOTHING TO DO WITH ME...
DAY OFF?
What the...?
THE HOUSE WILL BE EMPTY.
Except for the Yamashiros.
PEOPLE ARE GOING HOME OR TAKING A TRIP.
Kayo's going to Izu.
WHAT'S WITH ALL THE FUN PLANS?
I DON'T HAVE A PLACE TO GO HOME TO, SO I'LL PROBABLY GO DRINKING.
MAYBE TO MISS FUMI'S PLACE.
BLUSH
I-INSTEAD OF ME...

CHAPTER 7

I had a hard time with the script because I needed to start wrapping up the series from this chapter on. I should've had Sayaka realize her feelings a lot sooner. I realized how important the pacing is in a serialized story.

In all my rewrites, I had wanted to include why Narutaki likes sweets, the backstory of the girl with glasses at school, etc., but that stuff would have gotten in the way of the main plot, so I had to eliminate them. I was sad that I couldn't include them.

At first, I was drawing the last few pages timidly, but it got so fun that I was coming up with ideas on how to approach things more boldly. This is what shojo manga is all about!

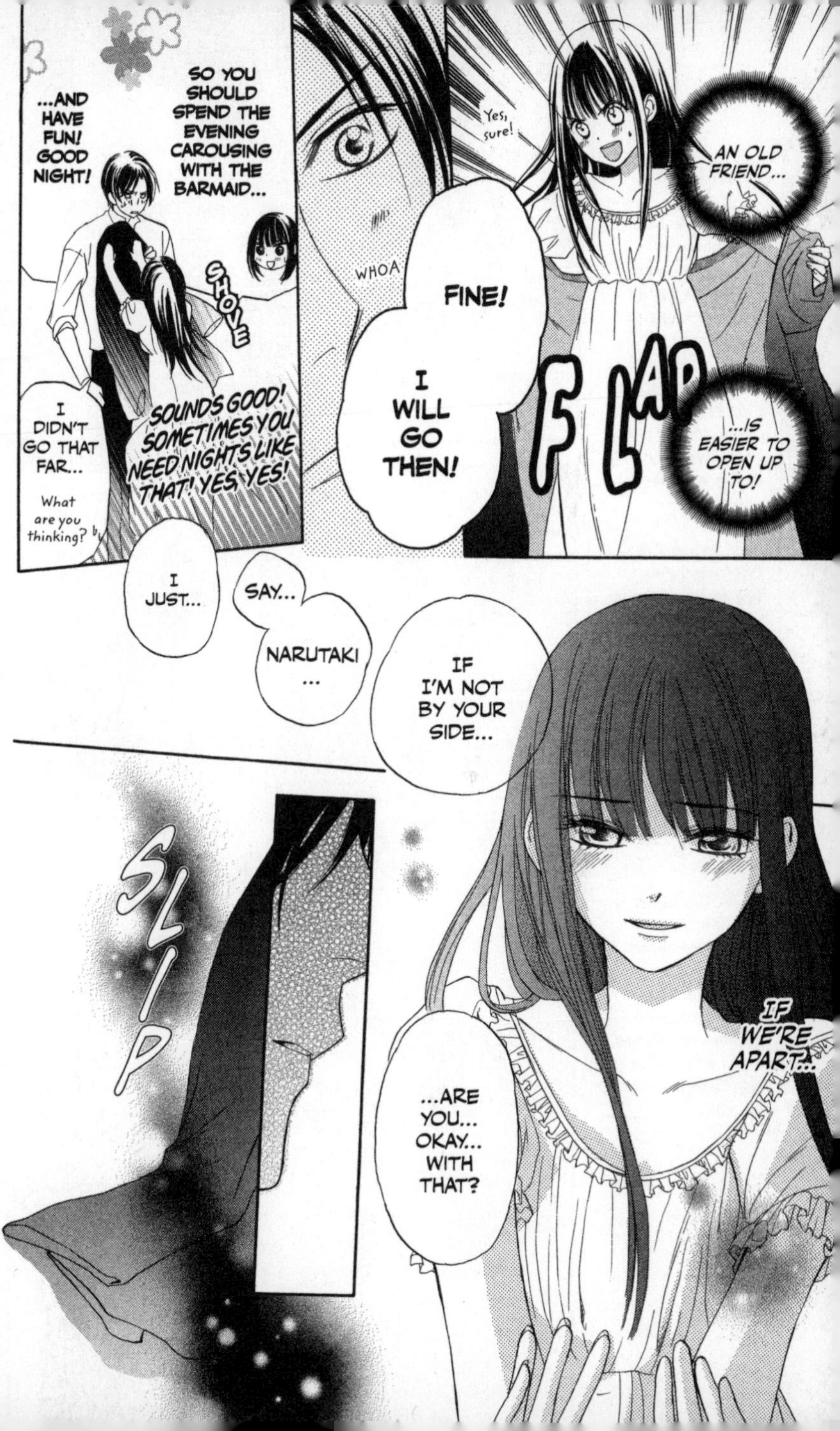
AN OLD FRIEND...
...IS EASIER TO OPEN UP TO!
Yes, sure!
FLAP
WHOA
FINE!
I WILL GO THEN!
SO YOU SHOULD SPEND THE EVENING CAROUSING WITH THE BARMAID...
...AND HAVE FUN! GOOD NIGHT!
SHOVE
SOUNDS GOOD! SOMETIMES YOU NEED NIGHTS LIKE THAT! YES, YES!
I DIDN'T GO THAT FAR...
What are you thinking?
I JUST...
SAY...
NARUTAKI...
IF I'M NOT BY YOUR SIDE...
IF WE'RE APART...
...ARE YOU... OKAY... WITH THAT?
SLIP

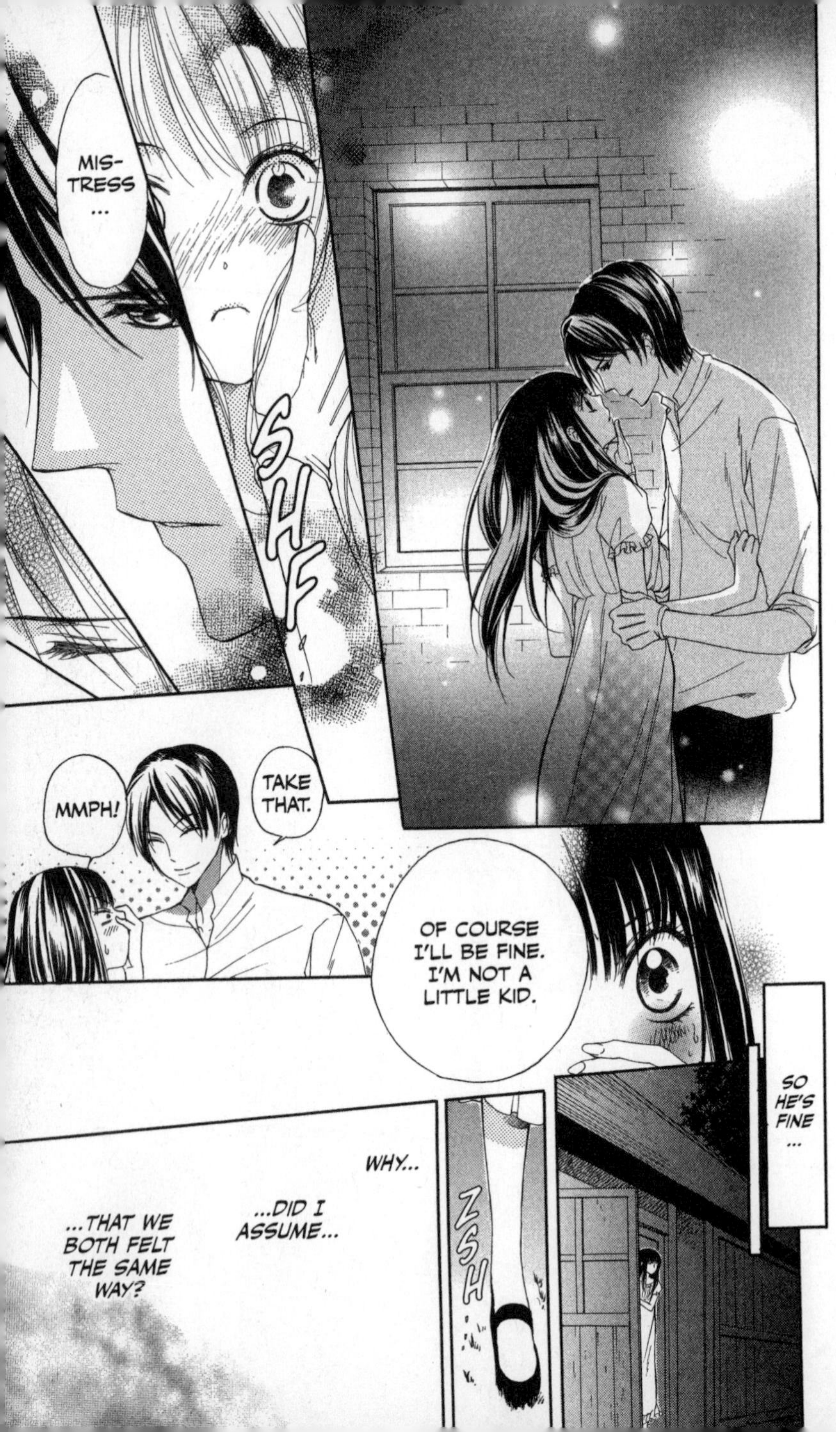

MIS-TRESS ...
SHF
OF COURSE I'LL BE FINE. I'M NOT A LITTLE KID.
TAKE THAT.
MMPH!
SO HE'S FINE ...
ZSH
WHY...
...DID I ASSUME...
...THAT WE BOTH FELT THE SAME WAY?

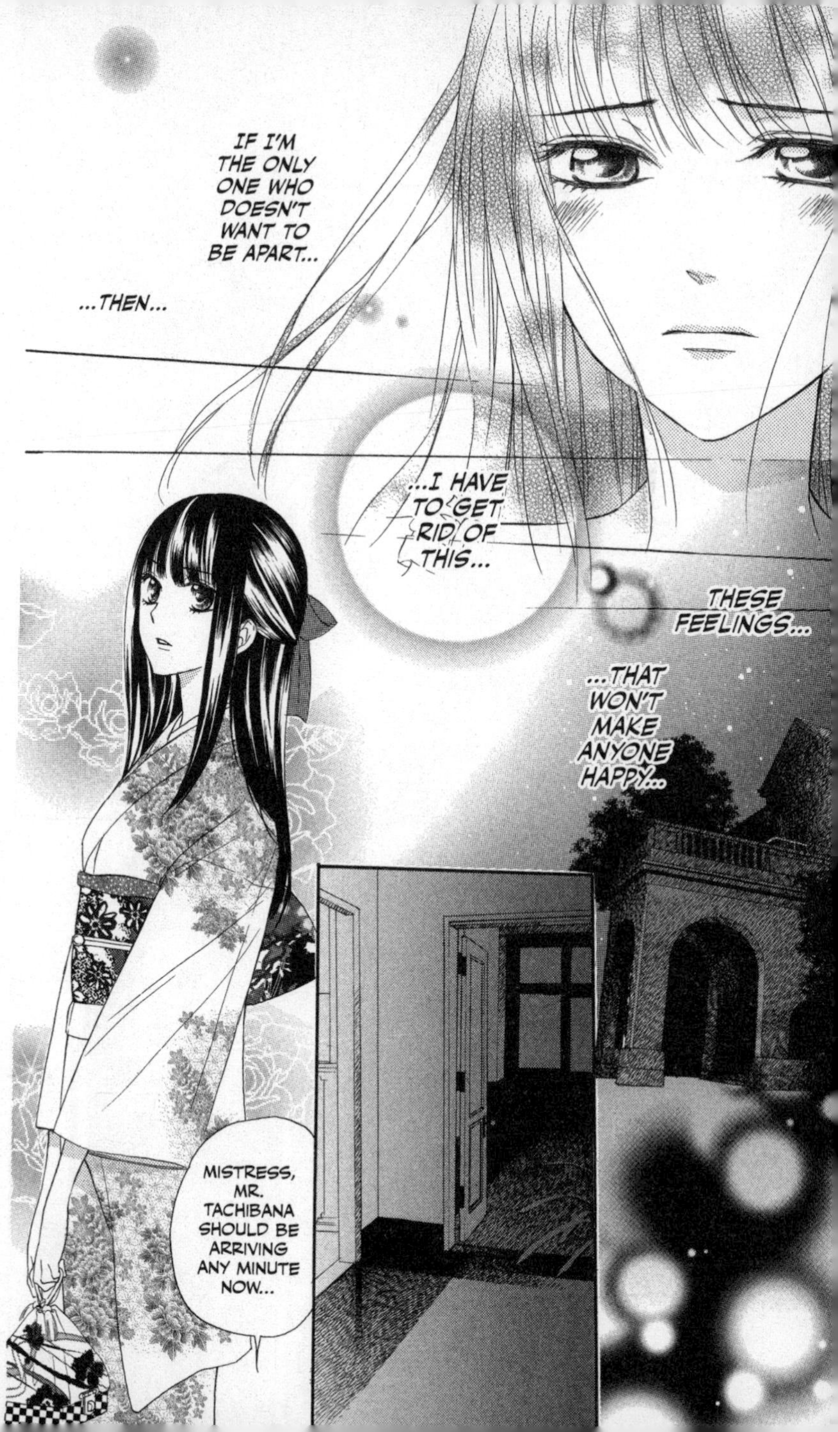
IF I'M THE ONLY ONE WHO DOESN'T WANT TO BE APART...
...THEN...
...I HAVE TO GET RID OF THIS...
THESE FEELINGS...
...THAT WON'T MAKE ANYONE HAPPY...
MISTRESS, MR. TACHIBANA SHOULD BE ARRIVING ANY MINUTE NOW...

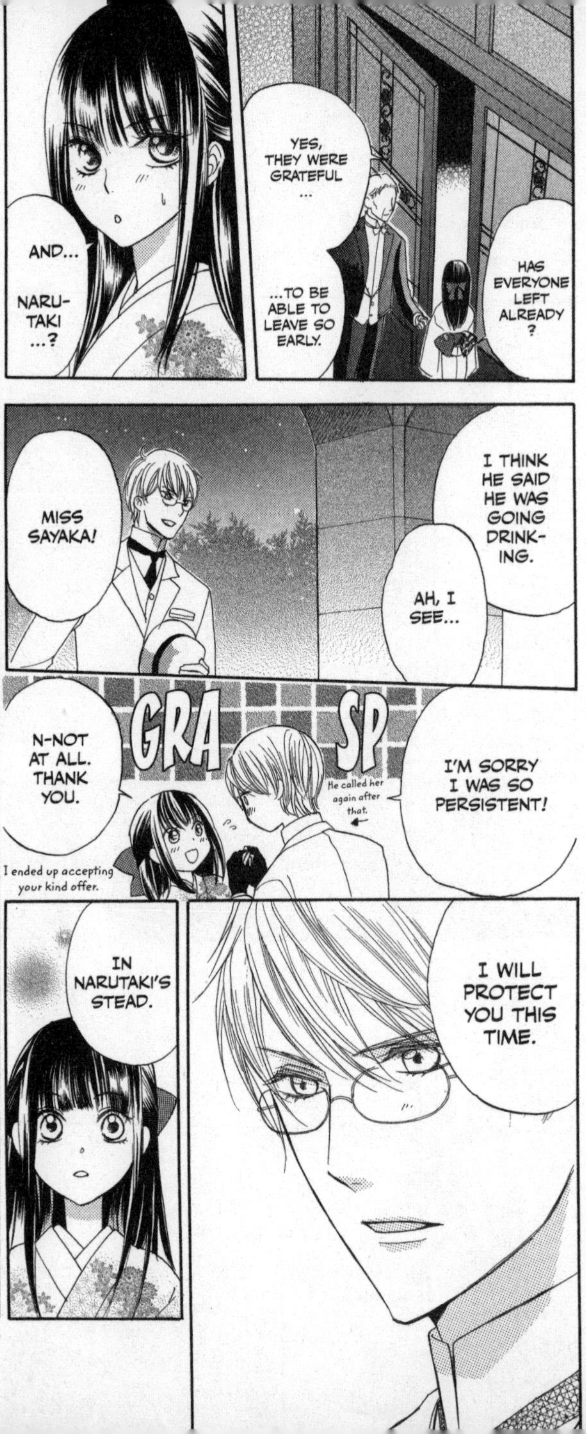
HAS EVERYONE LEFT ALREADY?
YES, THEY WERE GRATEFUL...
...TO BE ABLE TO LEAVE SO EARLY.
AND...
NARUTAKI...?
I THINK HE SAID HE WAS GOING DRINKING.
AH, I SEE...
MISS SAYAKA!
I'M SORRY I WAS SO PERSISTENT!
He called her again after that.
GRASP
N-NOT AT ALL. THANK YOU.
I ended up accepting your kind offer.
I WILL PROTECT YOU THIS TIME.
IN NARUTAKI'S STEAD.

ABOUT MISS KAZUKO

The daughter of Earl Miki. She's a 16-year-old student. I think she's an easy-to-understand, cute young lady. I initially had her play a mean character, but she ended up becoming a character who gets teased instead.

Around the fourth chapter, she suddenly became really popular. I was pleasantly surprised by it. If I were to become friends with one of the characters, it'd definitely be her.

My assistant Y-da always hand draws her kimono pattern, so she's actually the most fashionable character.

"Make Sayaka's hand drawn too," I told Y-da. But she got mad and said, "I can't draw that many!"

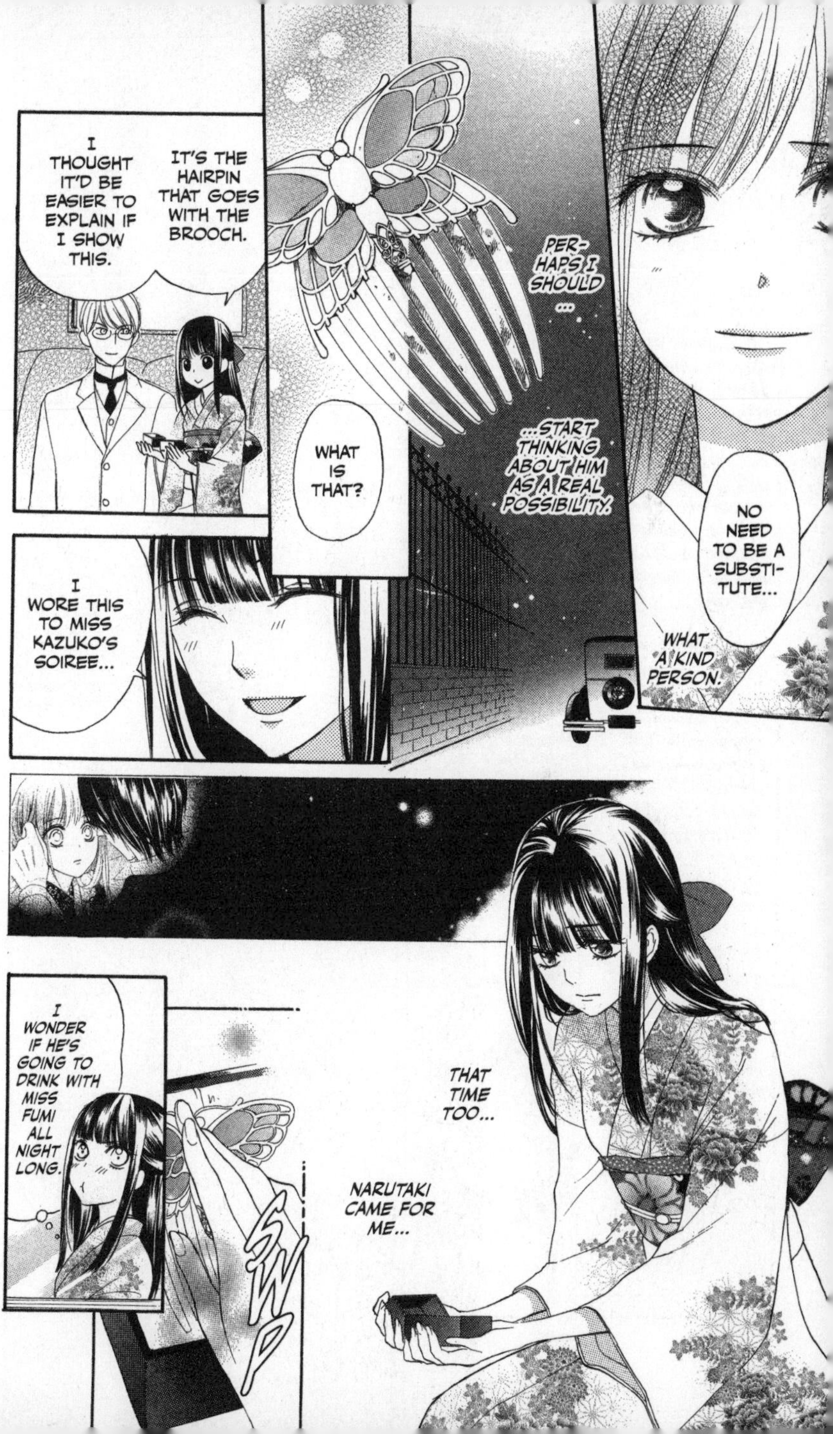
NO NEED TO BE A SUBSTITUTE...
WHAT A KIND PERSON.
PER-HAPS I SHOULD ...
...START THINKING ABOUT HIM AS A REAL POSSIBILITY.
WHAT IS THAT?
IT'S THE HAIRPIN THAT GOES WITH THE BROOCH.
I THOUGHT IT'D BE EASIER TO EXPLAIN IF I SHOW THIS.
I WORE THIS TO MISS KAZUKO'S SOIREE...
THAT TIME TOO...
NARUTAKI CAME FOR ME...
I WONDER IF HE'S GOING TO DRINK WITH MISS FUMI ALL NIGHT LONG.
SWOP

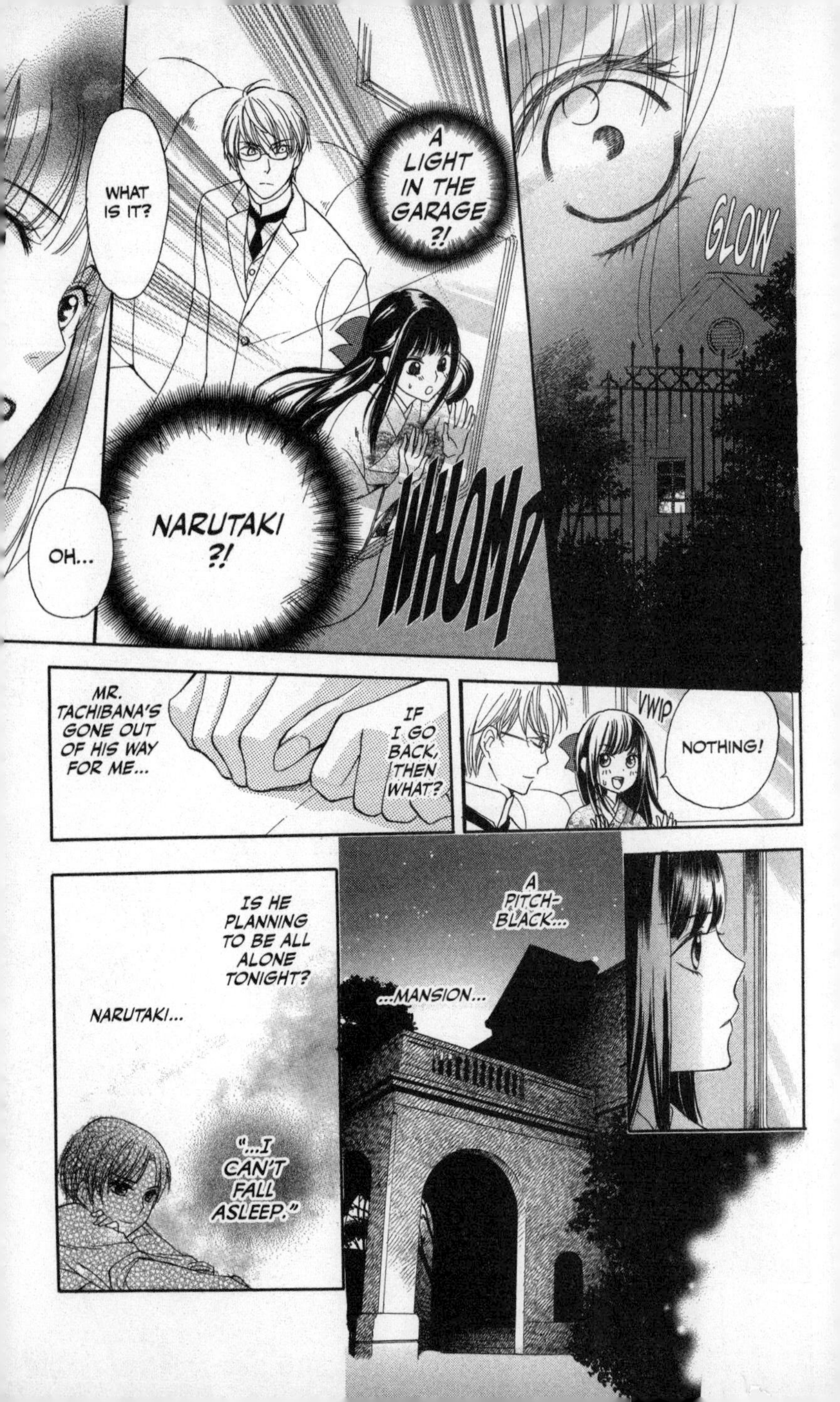
GLOW
A LIGHT IN THE GARAGE ?!
WHAT IS IT?
NARUTAKI ?!
WHOMP
OH...
VWIP
NOTHING!
IF I GO BACK, THEN WHAT?
MR. TACHIBANA'S GONE OUT OF HIS WAY FOR ME...
A PITCH-BLACK...
...MANSION...
IS HE PLANNING TO BE ALL ALONE TONIGHT?
NARUTAKI...
"...I CAN'T FALL ASLEEP."

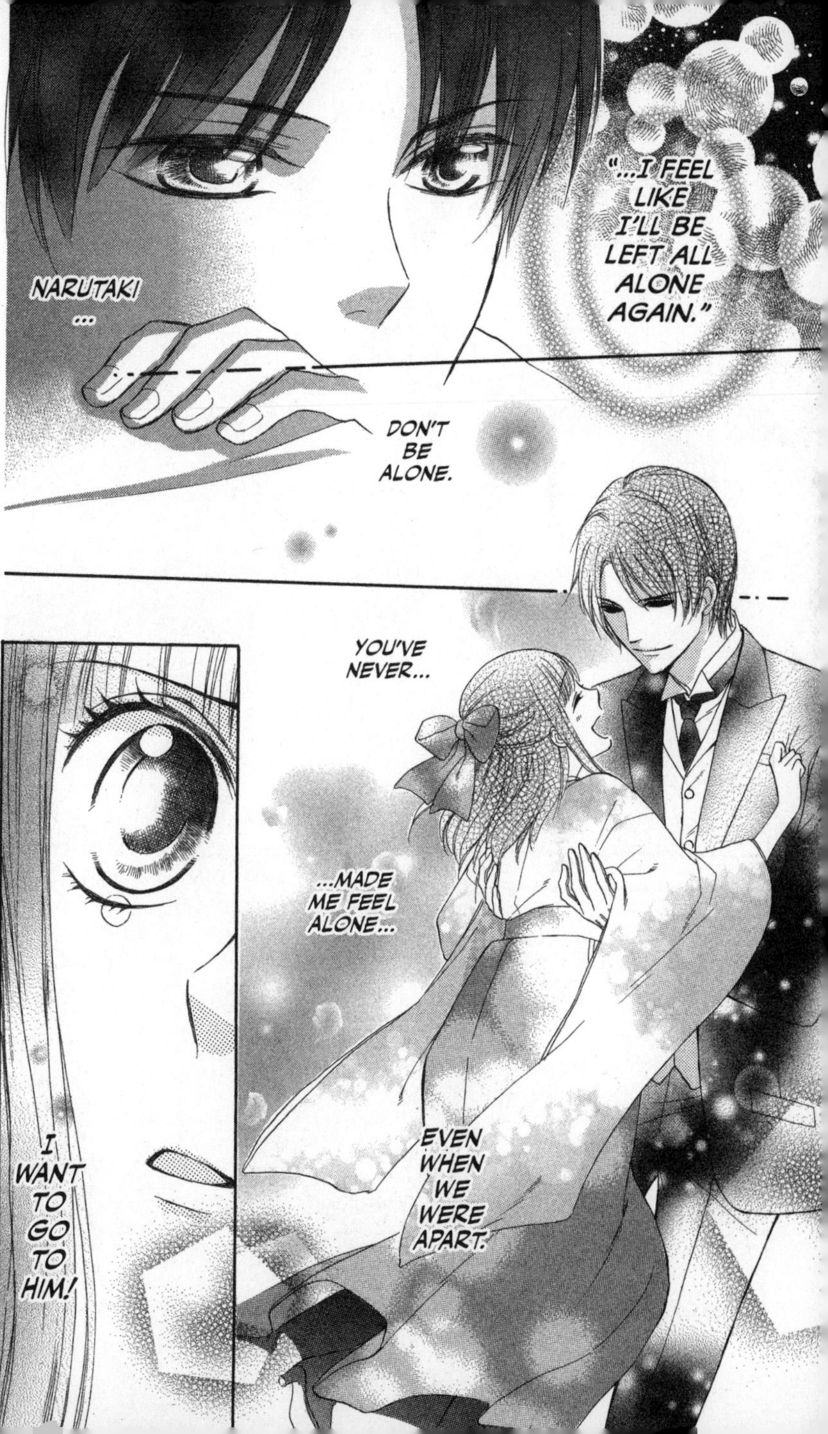
"...I FEEL LIKE I'LL BE LEFT ALL ALONE AGAIN."
NARUTAKI ...
DON'T BE ALONE.
YOU'VE NEVER...
...MADE ME FEEL ALONE...
EVEN WHEN WE WERE APART.
I WANT TO GO TO HIM!

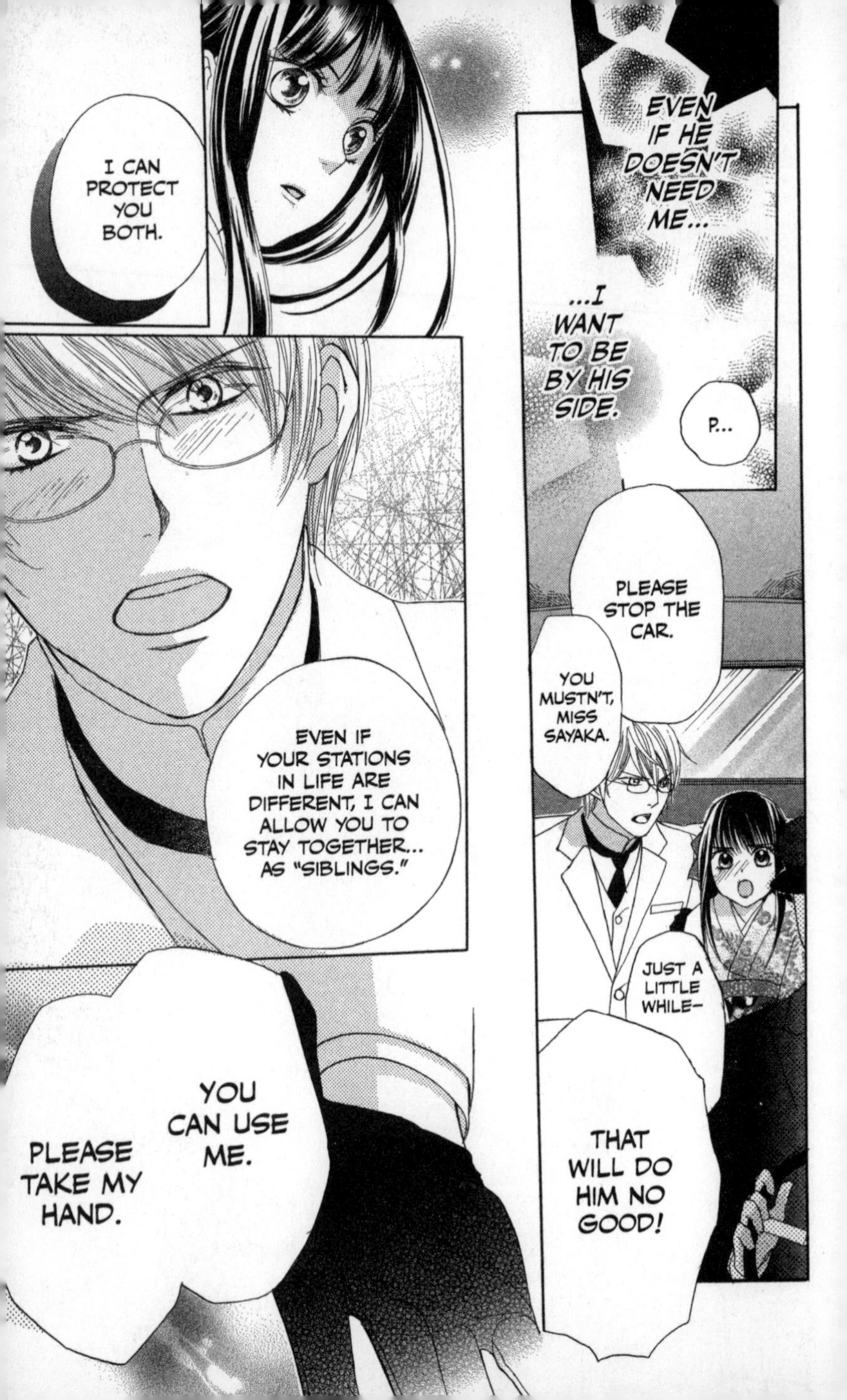
EVEN IF HE DOESN'T NEED ME...
...I WANT TO BE BY HIS SIDE.
P...
PLEASE STOP THE CAR.
YOU MUSTN'T, MISS SAYAKA.
JUST A LITTLE WHILE–
THAT WILL DO HIM NO GOOD!
I CAN PROTECT YOU BOTH.
EVEN IF YOUR STATIONS IN LIFE ARE DIFFERENT, I CAN ALLOW YOU TO STAY TOGETHER... AS "SIBLINGS."
YOU CAN USE ME.
PLEASE TAKE MY HAND.

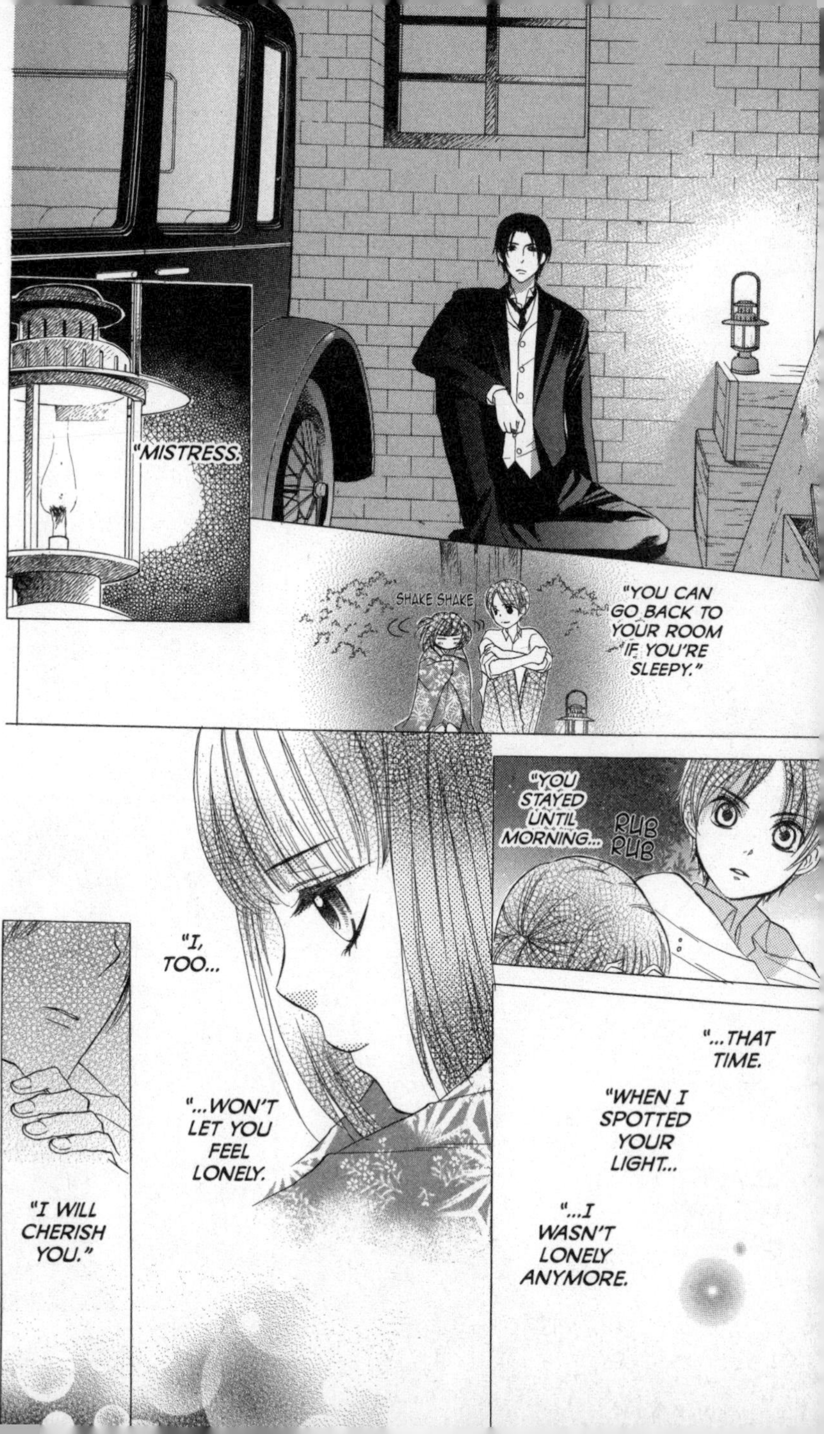
"MISTRESS.
"YOU CAN GO BACK TO YOUR ROOM IF YOU'RE SLEEPY."
SHAKE SHAKE
"YOU STAYED UNTIL MORNING...
RUB RUB
"...THAT TIME.
"WHEN I SPOTTED YOUR LIGHT...
"...I WASN'T LONELY ANYMORE.
"I, TOO...
"...WON'T LET YOU FEEL LONELY.
"I WILL CHERISH YOU."

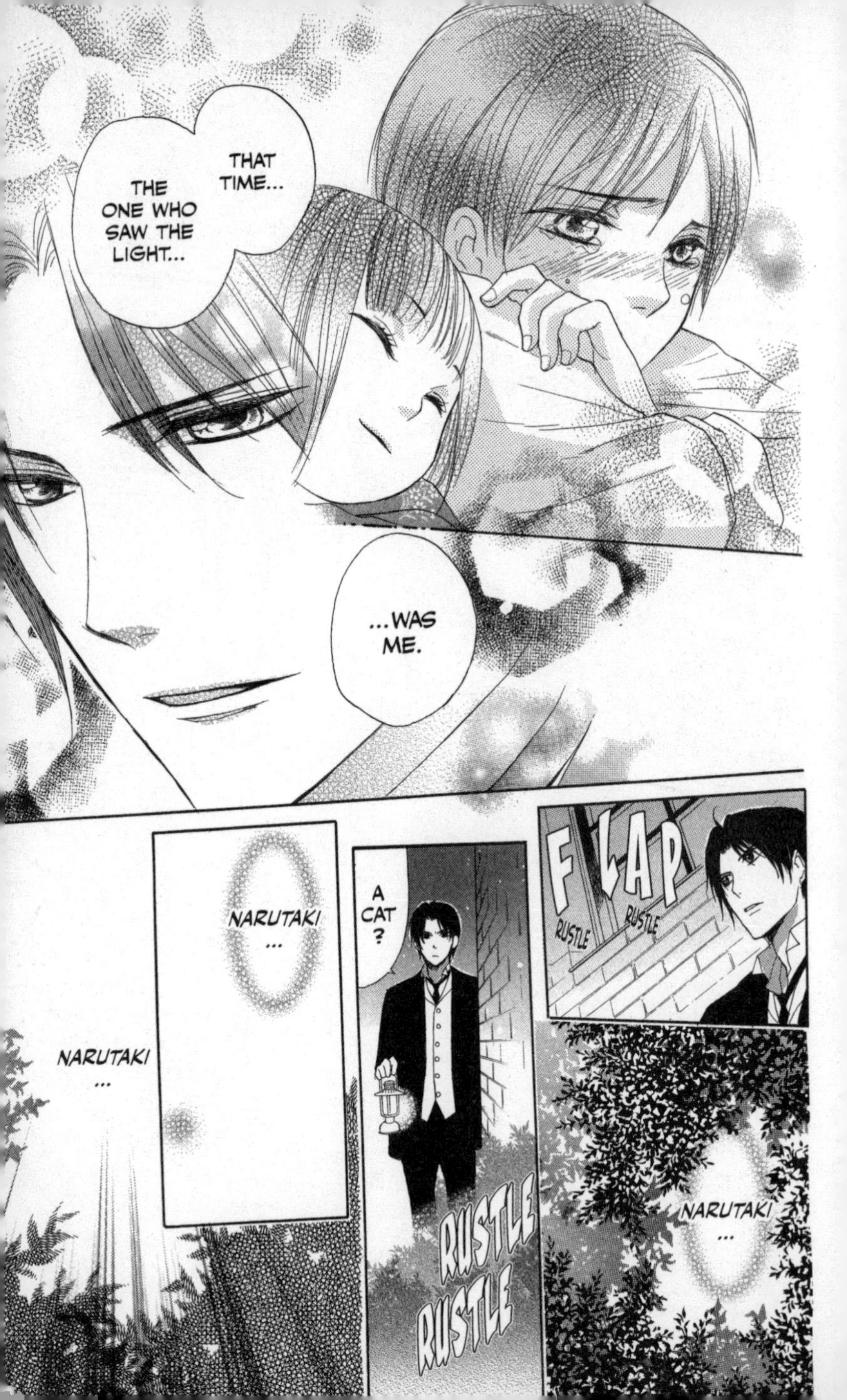
THAT TIME...
THE ONE WHO SAW THE LIGHT...
...WAS ME.
FLAP
RUSTLE
RUSTLE
NARUTAKI...
A CAT?
RUSTLE
RUSTLE
NARUTAKI...
NARUTAKI...

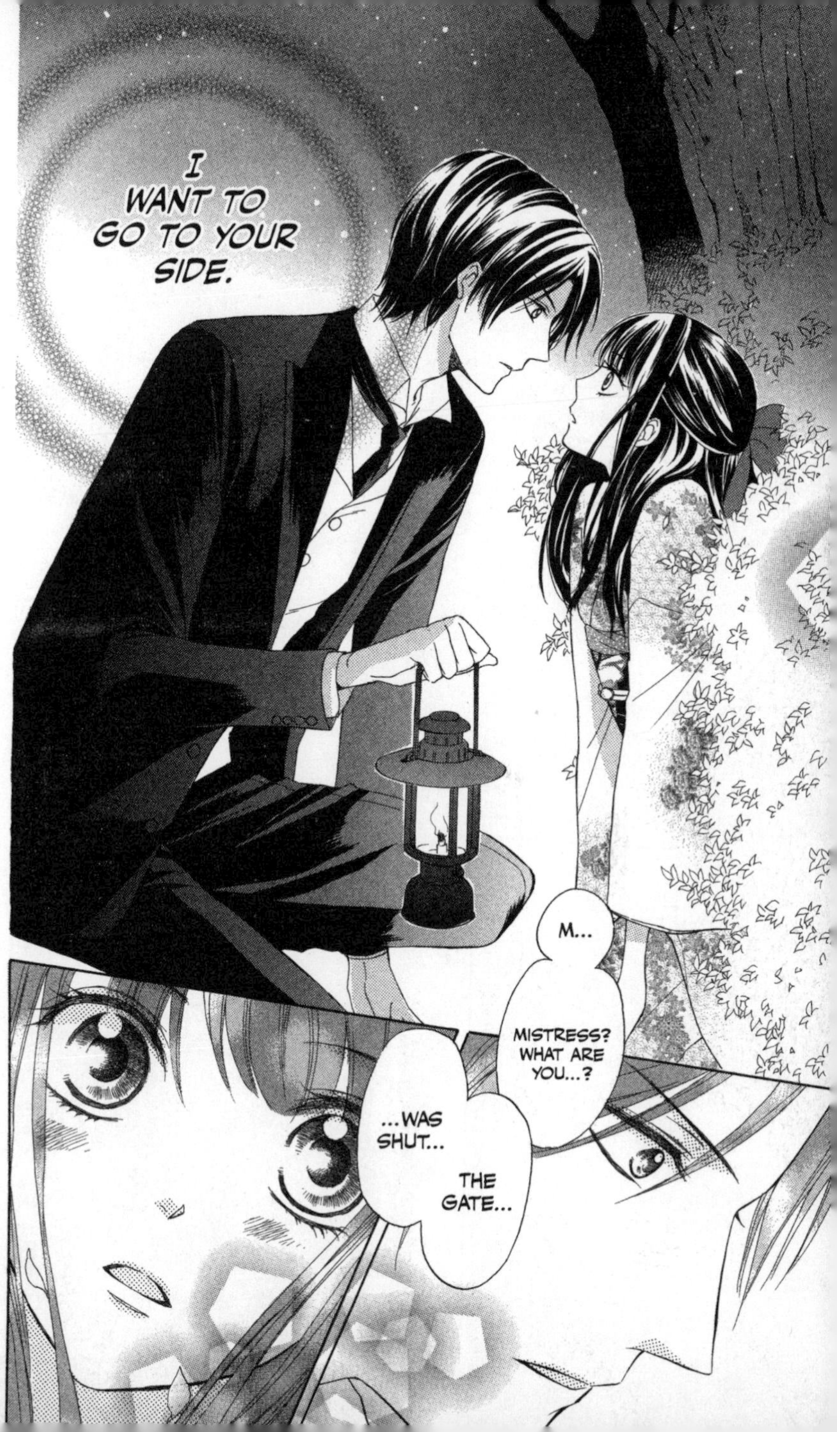
I WANT TO GO TO YOUR SIDE.
M...
MISTRESS? WHAT ARE YOU...?
THE GATE...
...WAS SHUT...

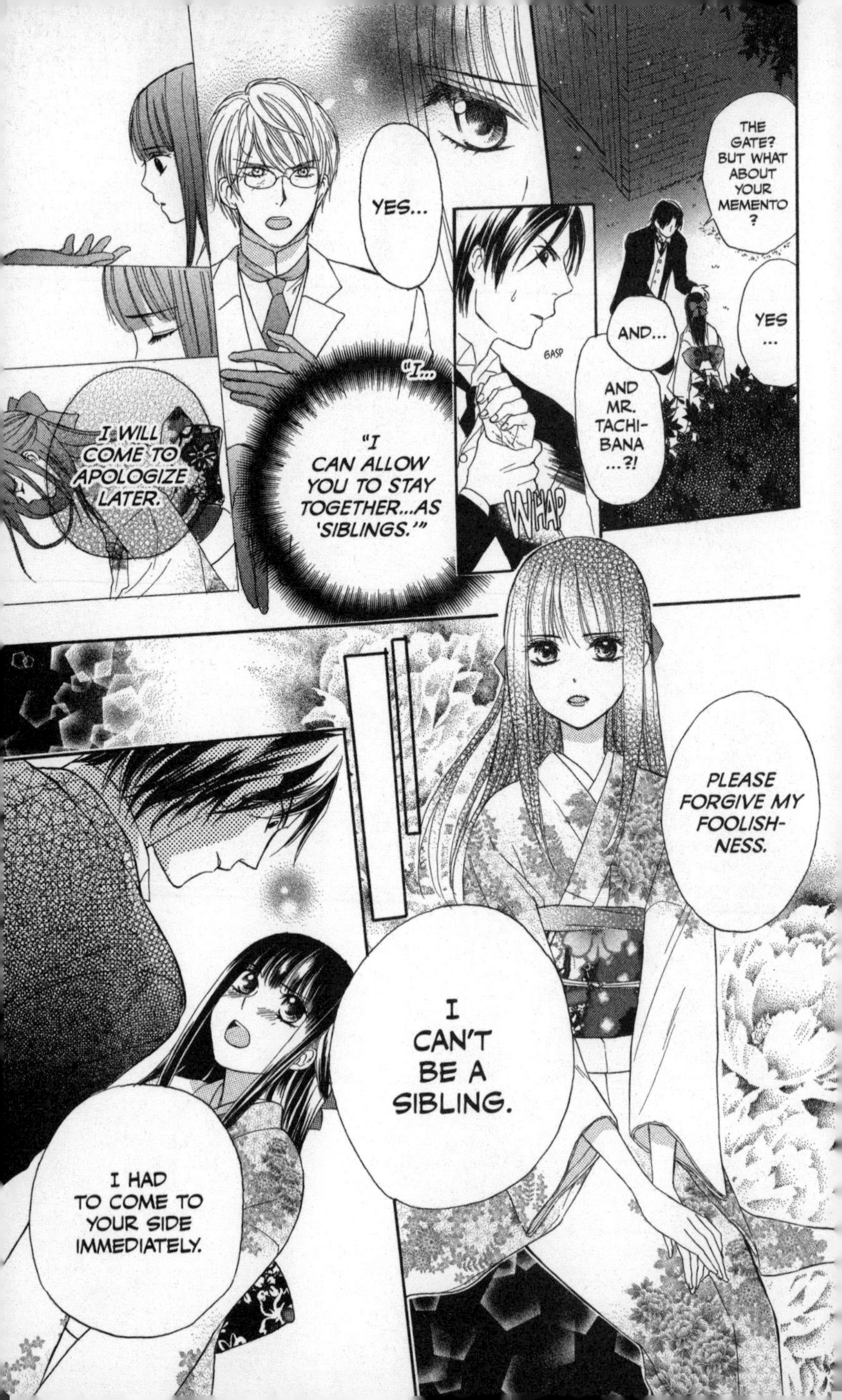
THE GATE? BUT WHAT ABOUT YOUR MEMENTO?
YES...
AND...
AND MR. TACHIBANA...?!
GASP
WHAP
YES...
"I...
"I CAN ALLOW YOU TO STAY TOGETHER...AS 'SIBLINGS.'"
I WILL COME TO APOLOGIZE LATER.
PLEASE FORGIVE MY FOOLISHNESS.
I CAN'T BE A SIBLING.
I HAD TO COME TO YOUR SIDE IMMEDIATELY.

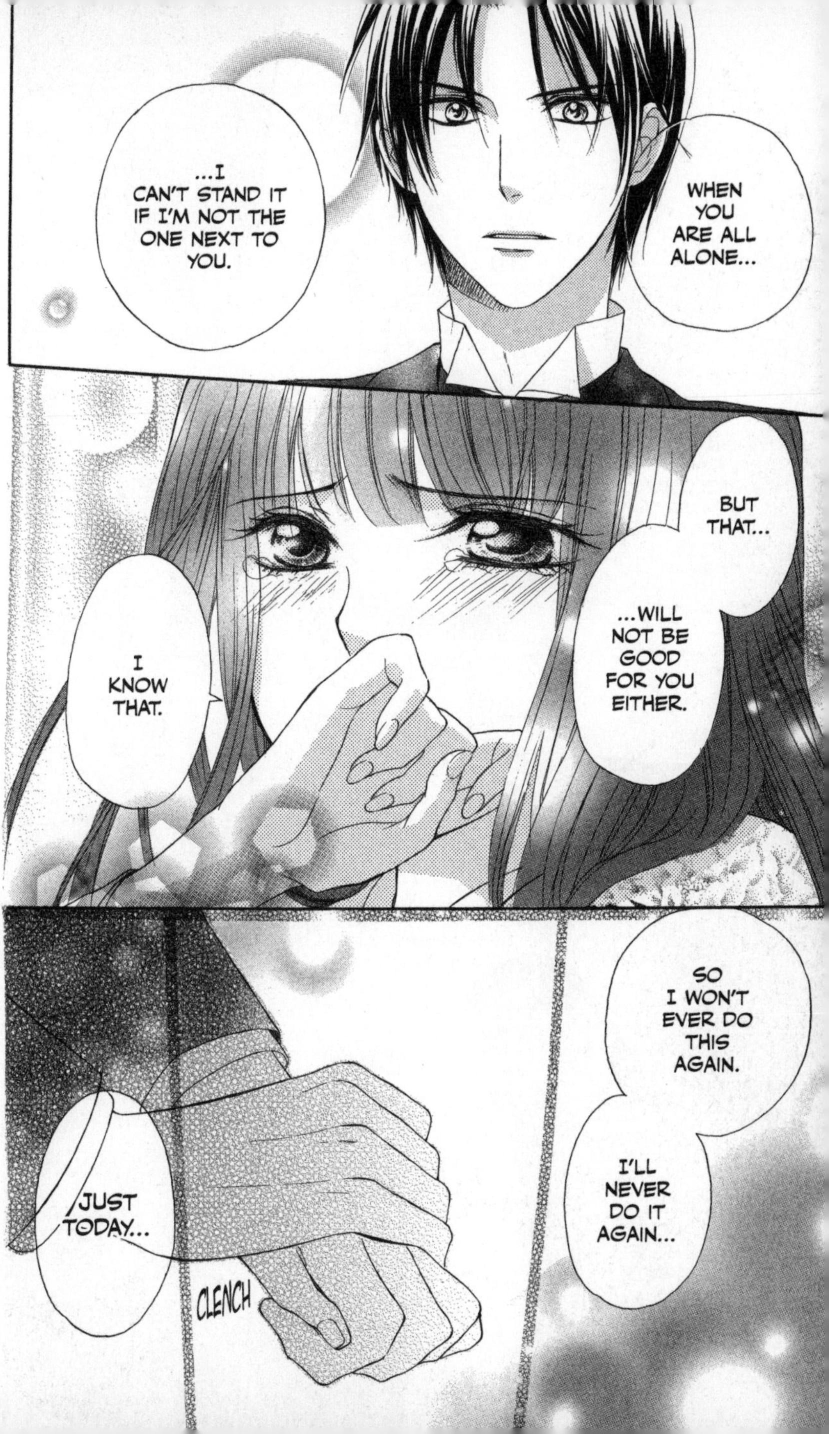
WHEN YOU ARE ALL ALONE...
...I CAN'T STAND IT IF I'M NOT THE ONE NEXT TO YOU.
BUT THAT...
...WILL NOT BE GOOD FOR YOU EITHER.
I KNOW THAT.
SO I WON'T EVER DO THIS AGAIN.
I'LL NEVER DO IT AGAIN...
CLENCH
JUST TODAY...

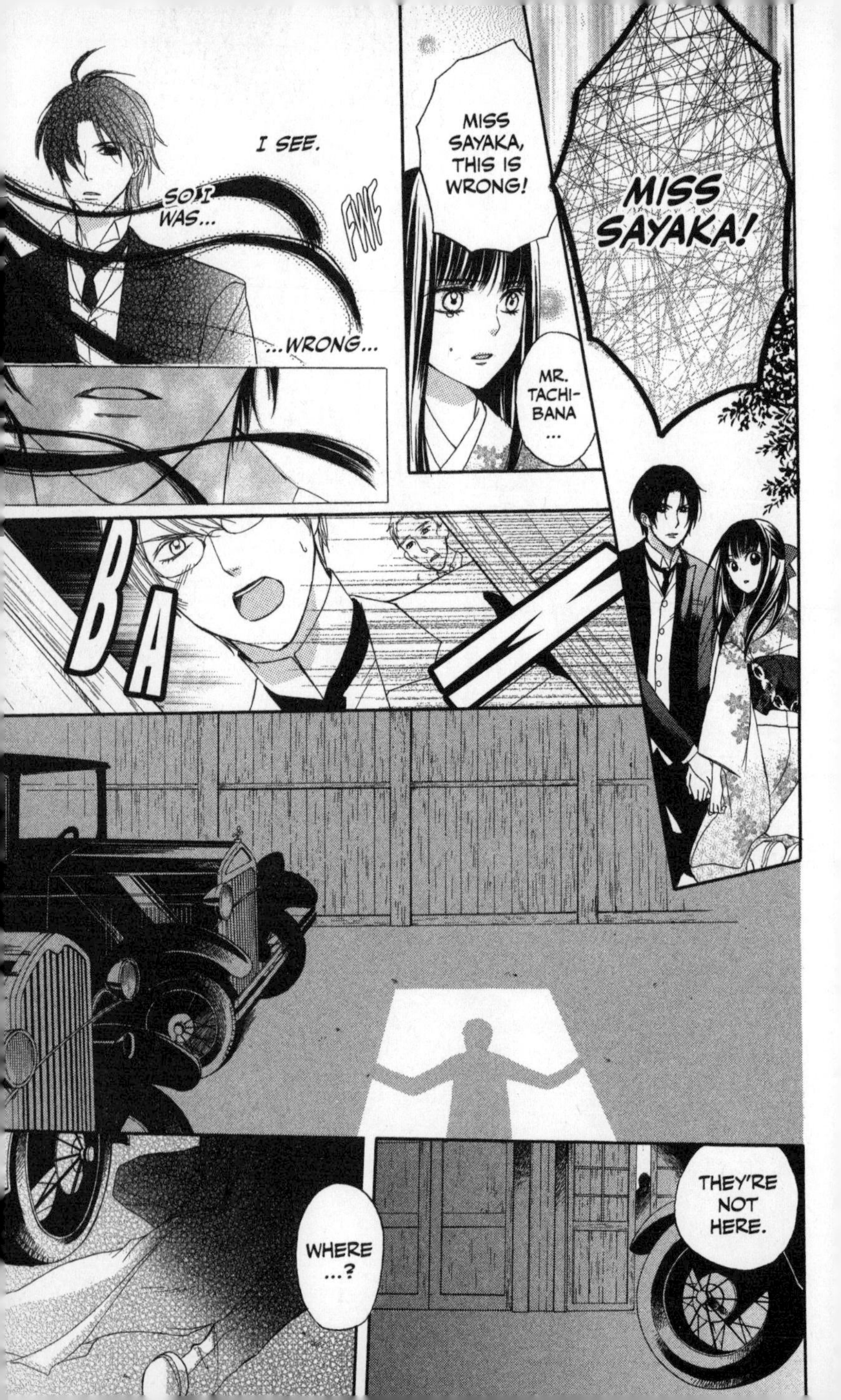
MISS SAYAKA!
MISS SAYAKA, THIS IS WRONG!
MR. TACHIBANA...
I SEE.
SO I WAS...
...WRONG...
BA
THEY'RE NOT HERE.
WHERE ...?

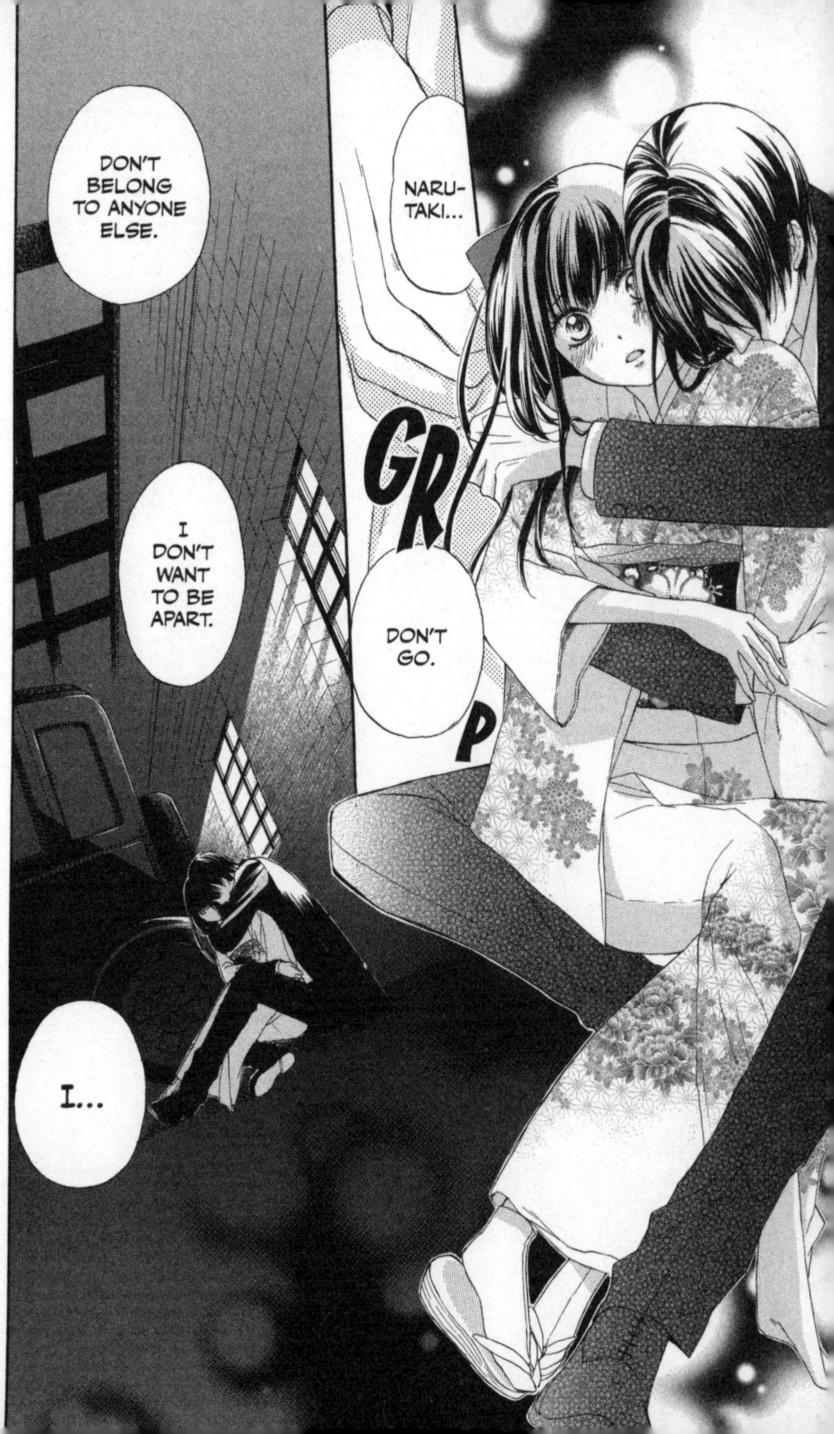
NARU-TAKI...
GRIP
DON'T GO.
DON'T BELONG TO ANYONE ELSE.
I DON'T WANT TO BE APART.
I...

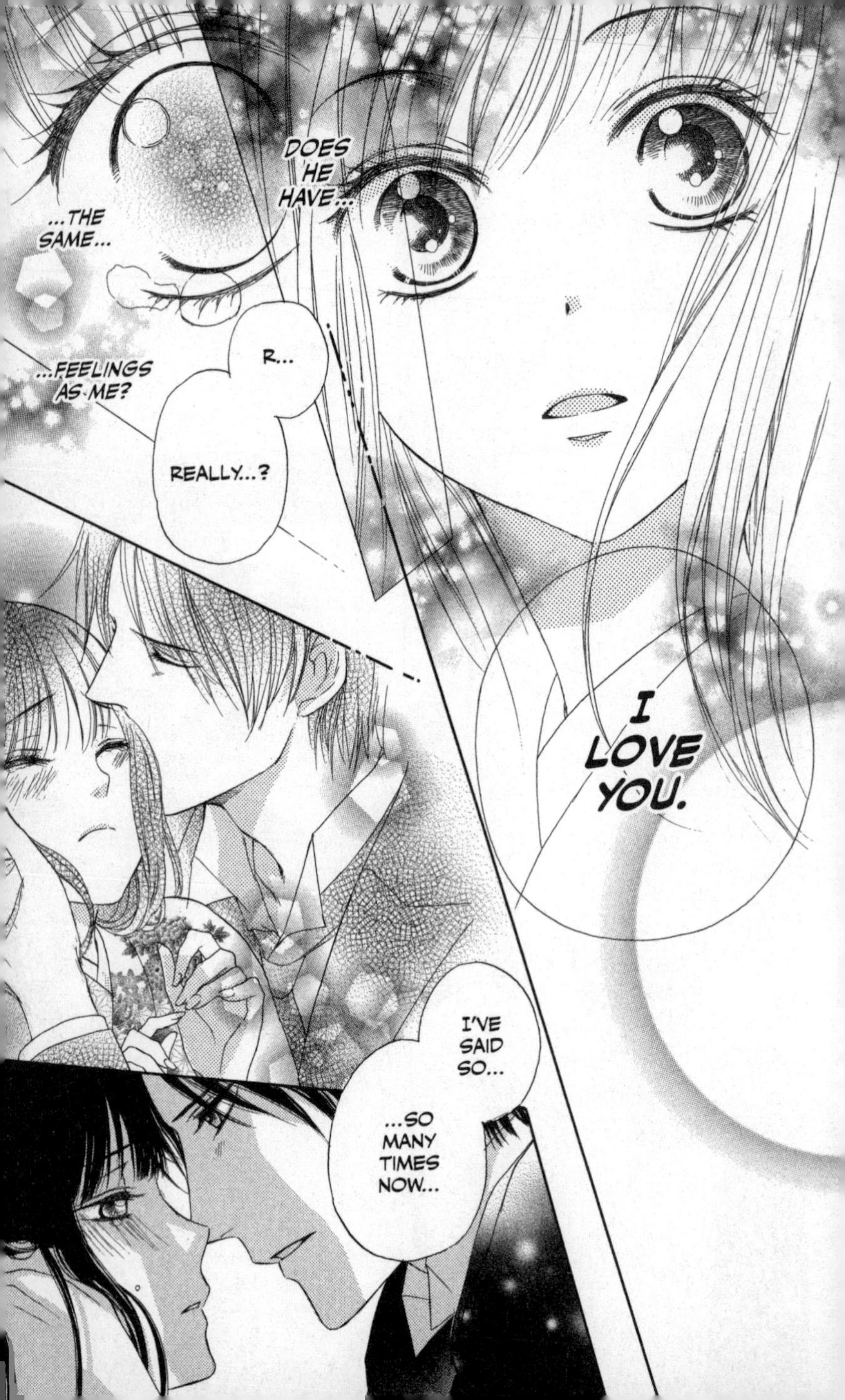
DOES HE HAVE...
...THE SAME...
...FEELINGS AS ME?
R...
REALLY...?
I LOVE YOU.
I'VE SAID SO...
...SO MANY TIMES NOW...

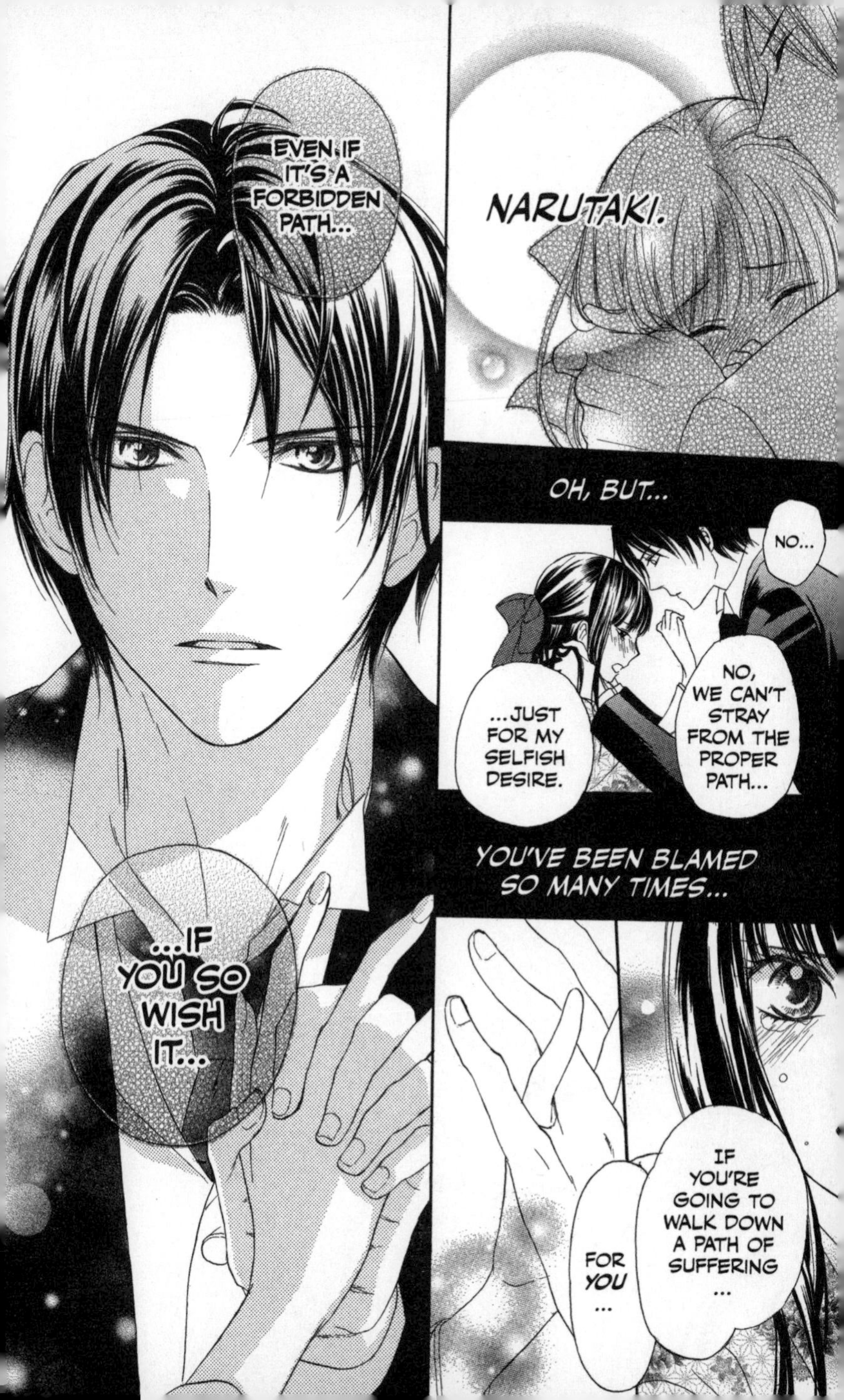
NARUTAKI.
OH, BUT...
NO...
NO, WE CAN'T STRAY FROM THE PROPER PATH...
...JUST FOR MY SELFISH DESIRE.
YOU'VE BEEN BLAMED SO MANY TIMES...
IF YOU'RE GOING TO WALK DOWN A PATH OF SUFFERING ...
FOR YOU ...
EVEN IF IT'S A FORBIDDEN PATH...
...IF YOU SO WISH IT...

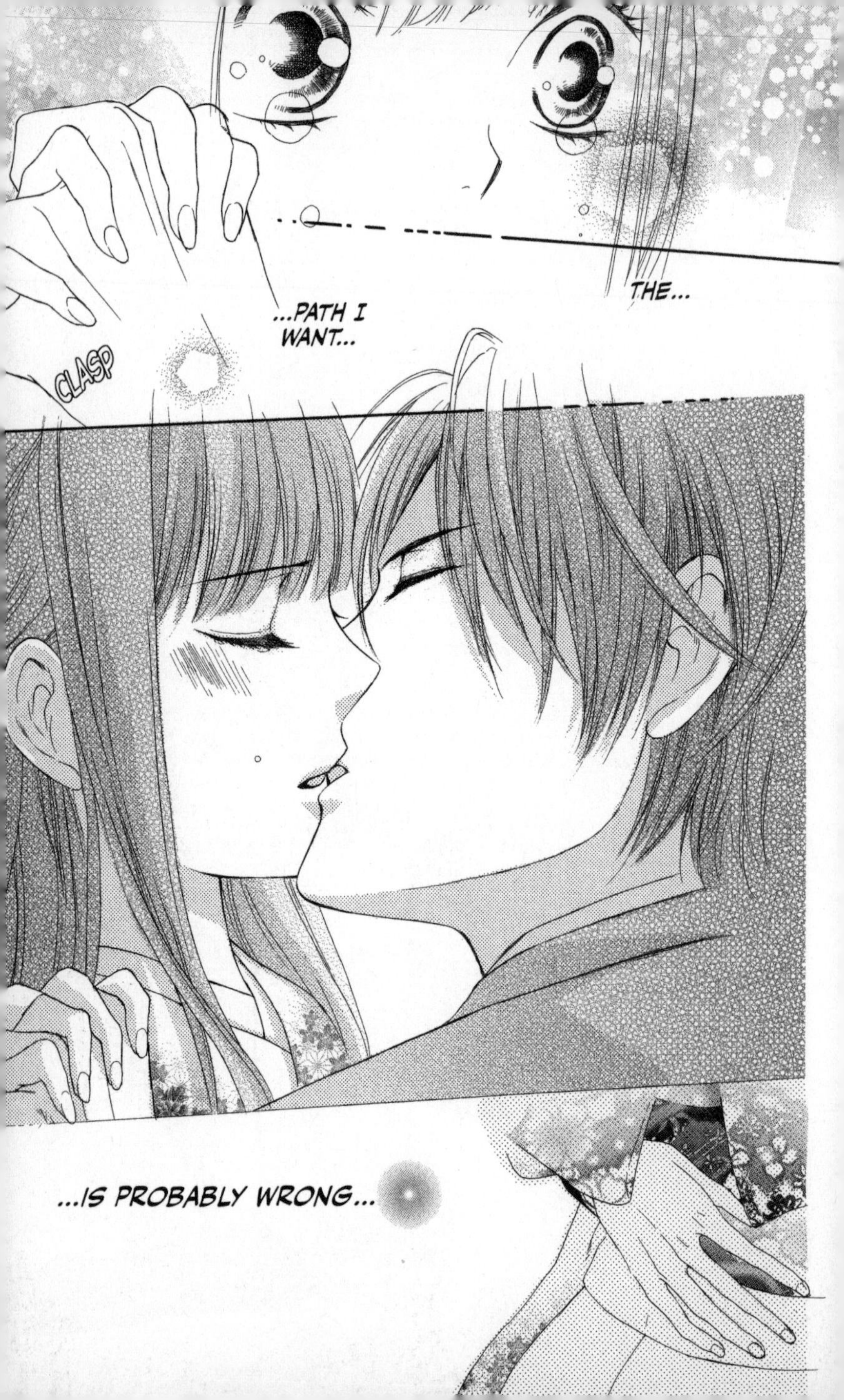
THE...
...PATH I WANT...
CLASP
...IS PROBABLY WRONG...

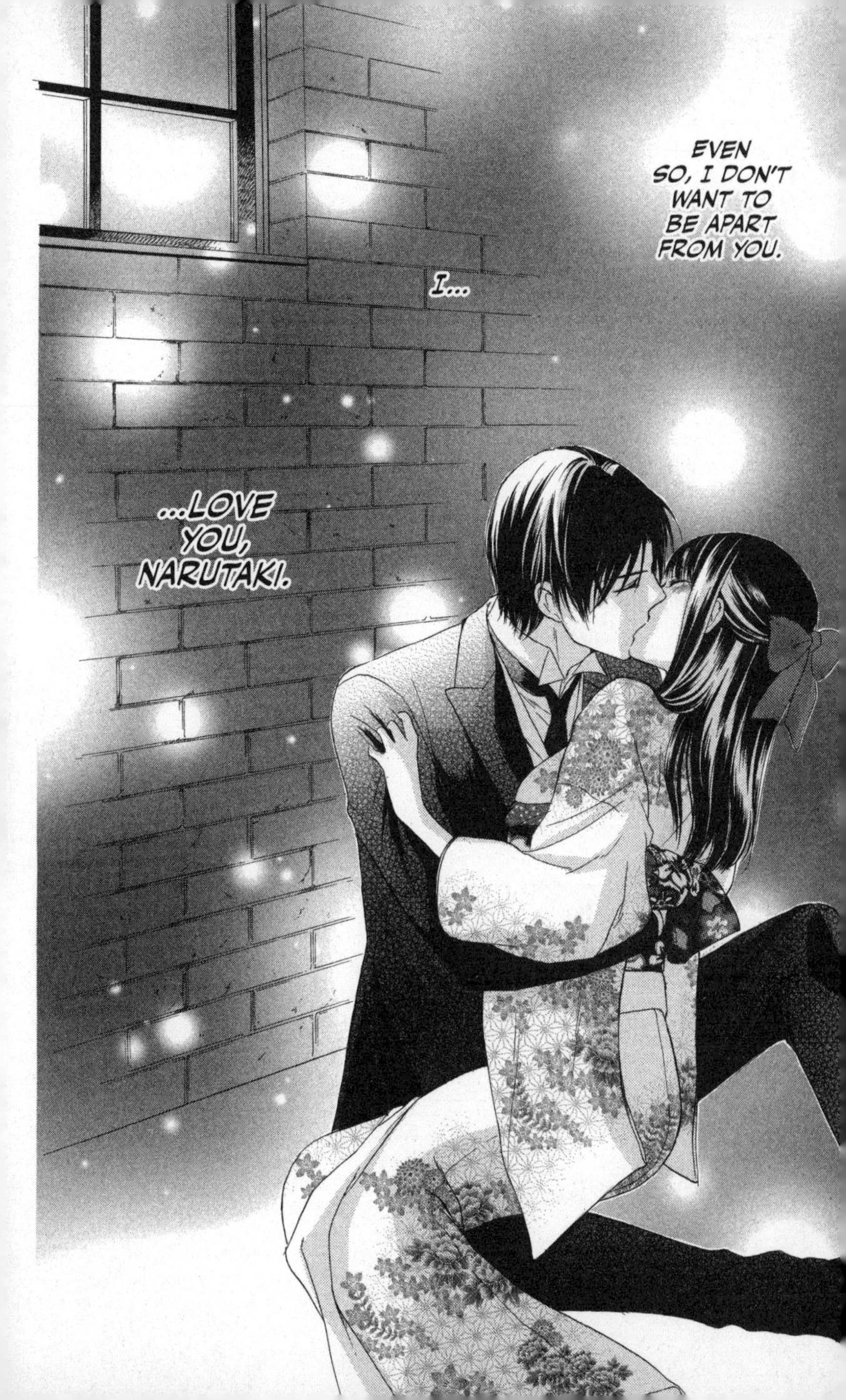
EVEN SO, I DON'T WANT TO BE APART FROM YOU.
I...
...LOVE YOU, NARUTAKI.

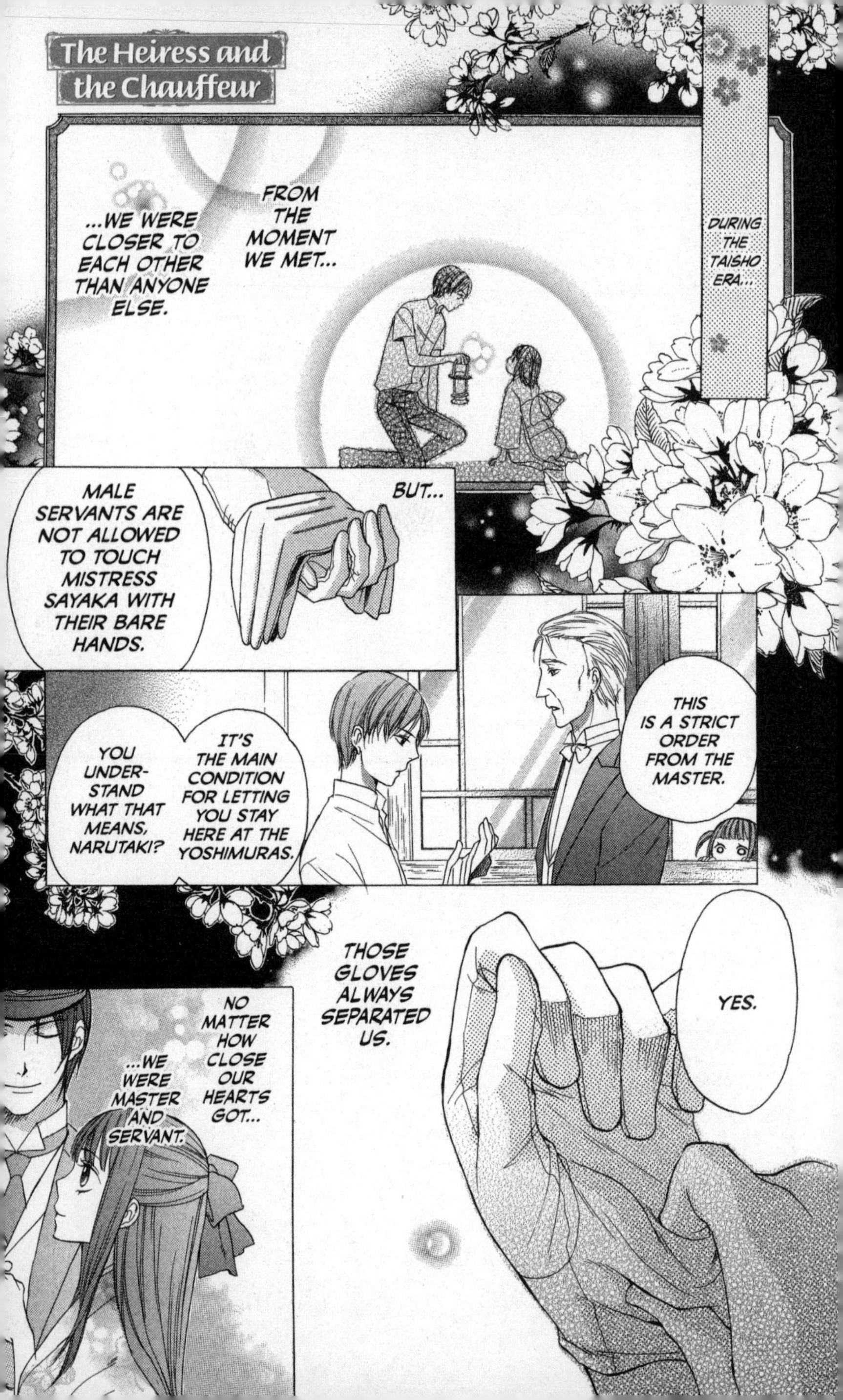
DURING THE TAISHO ERA...
FROM THE MOMENT WE MET...
...WE WERE CLOSER TO EACH OTHER THAN ANYONE ELSE.
BUT...
MALE SERVANTS ARE NOT ALLOWED TO TOUCH MISTRESS SAYAKA WITH THEIR BARE HANDS.
THIS IS A STRICT ORDER FROM THE MASTER.
IT'S THE MAIN CONDITION FOR LETTING YOU STAY HERE AT THE YOSHIMURAS.
YOU UNDER-STAND WHAT THAT MEANS, NARUTAKI?
YES.
THOSE GLOVES ALWAYS SEPARATED US.
NO MATTER HOW CLOSE OUR HEARTS GOT...
...WE WERE MASTER AND SERVANT.

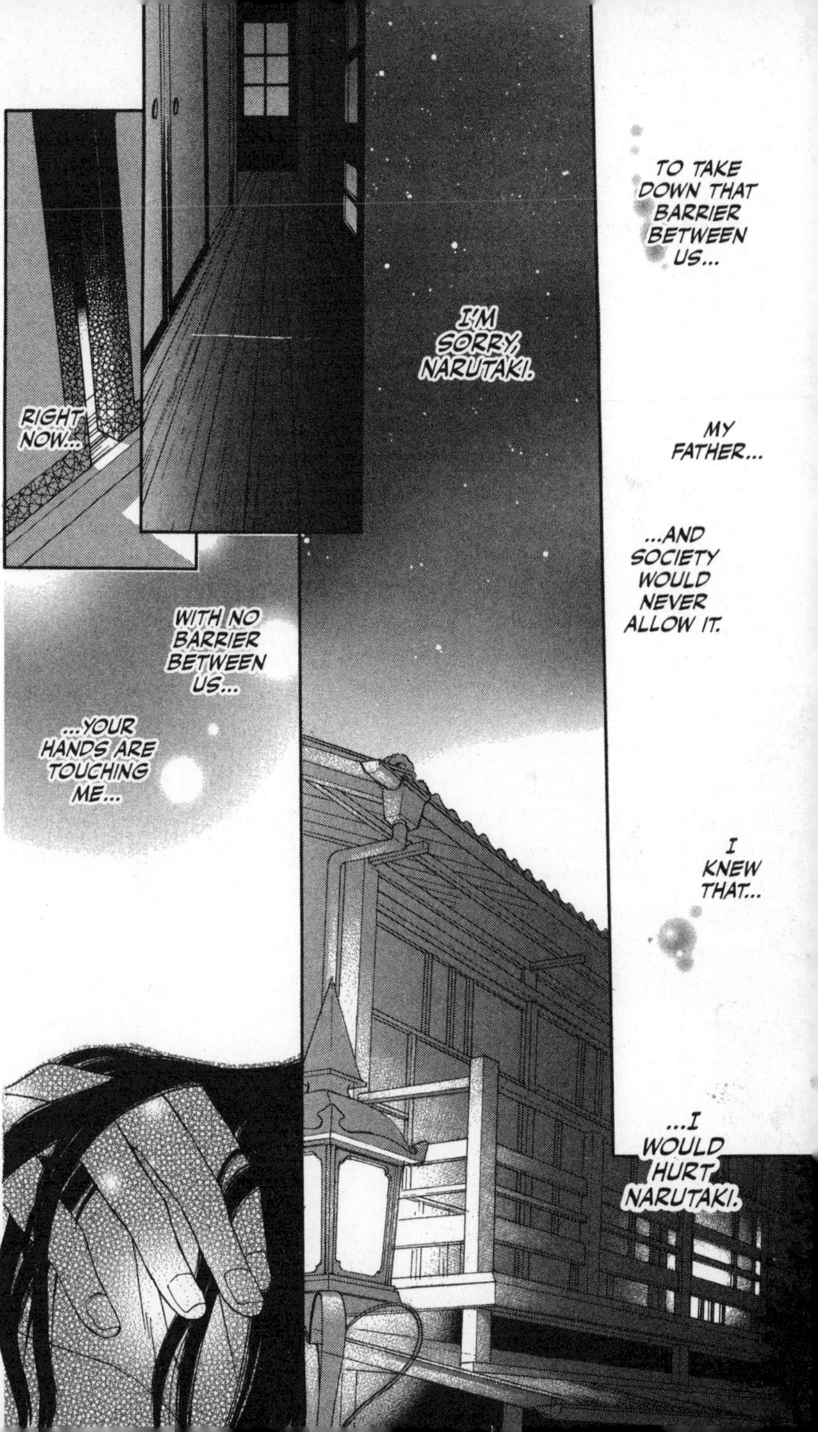
TO TAKE DOWN THAT BARRIER BETWEEN US...
MY FATHER...
...AND SOCIETY WOULD NEVER ALLOW IT.
I KNEW THAT...
...I WOULD HURT NARUTAKI.
I'M SORRY, NARUTAKI.
RIGHT NOW...
WITH NO BARRIER BETWEEN US...
...YOUR HANDS ARE TOUCHING ME...

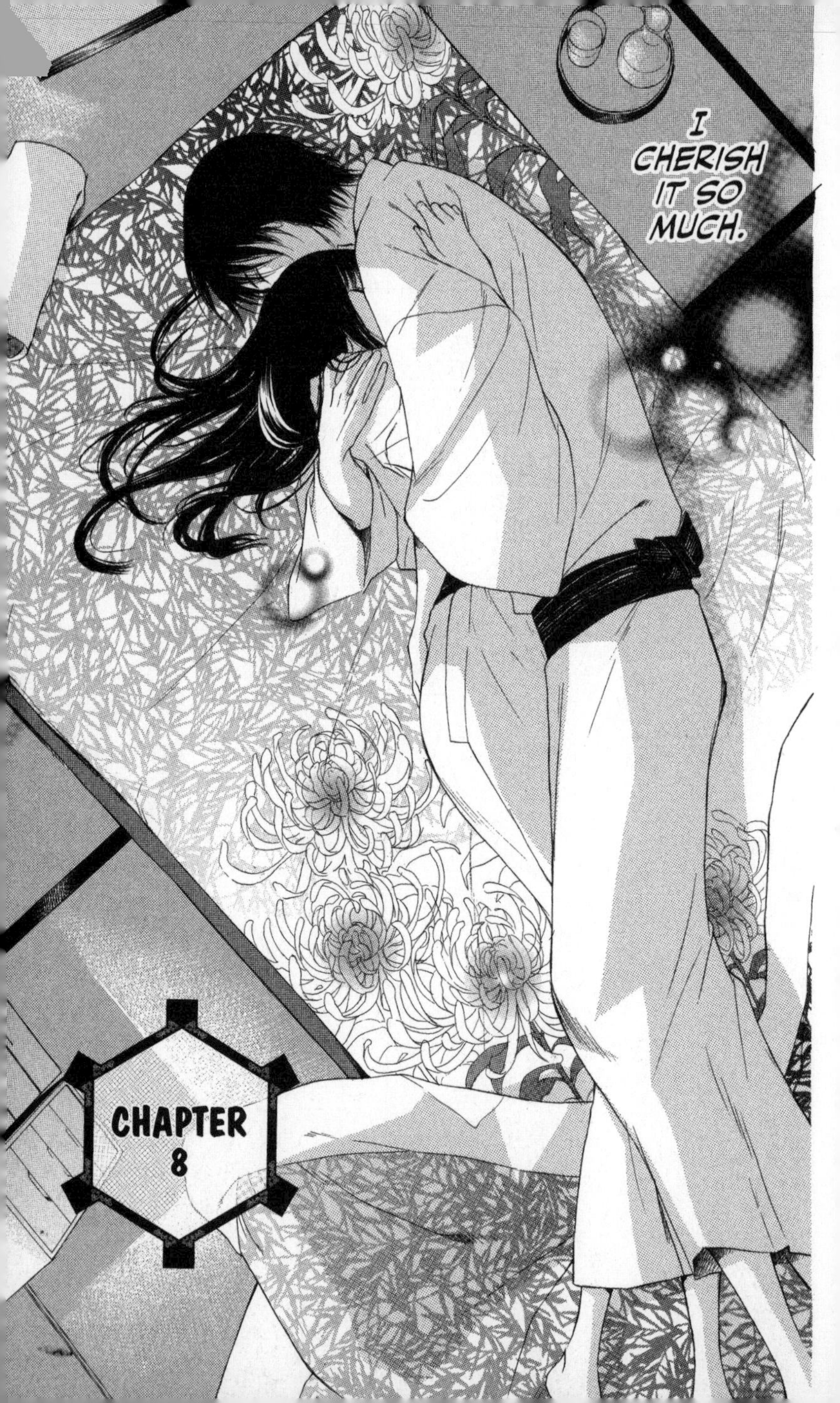
I CHERISH IT SO MUCH.
CHAPTER 8

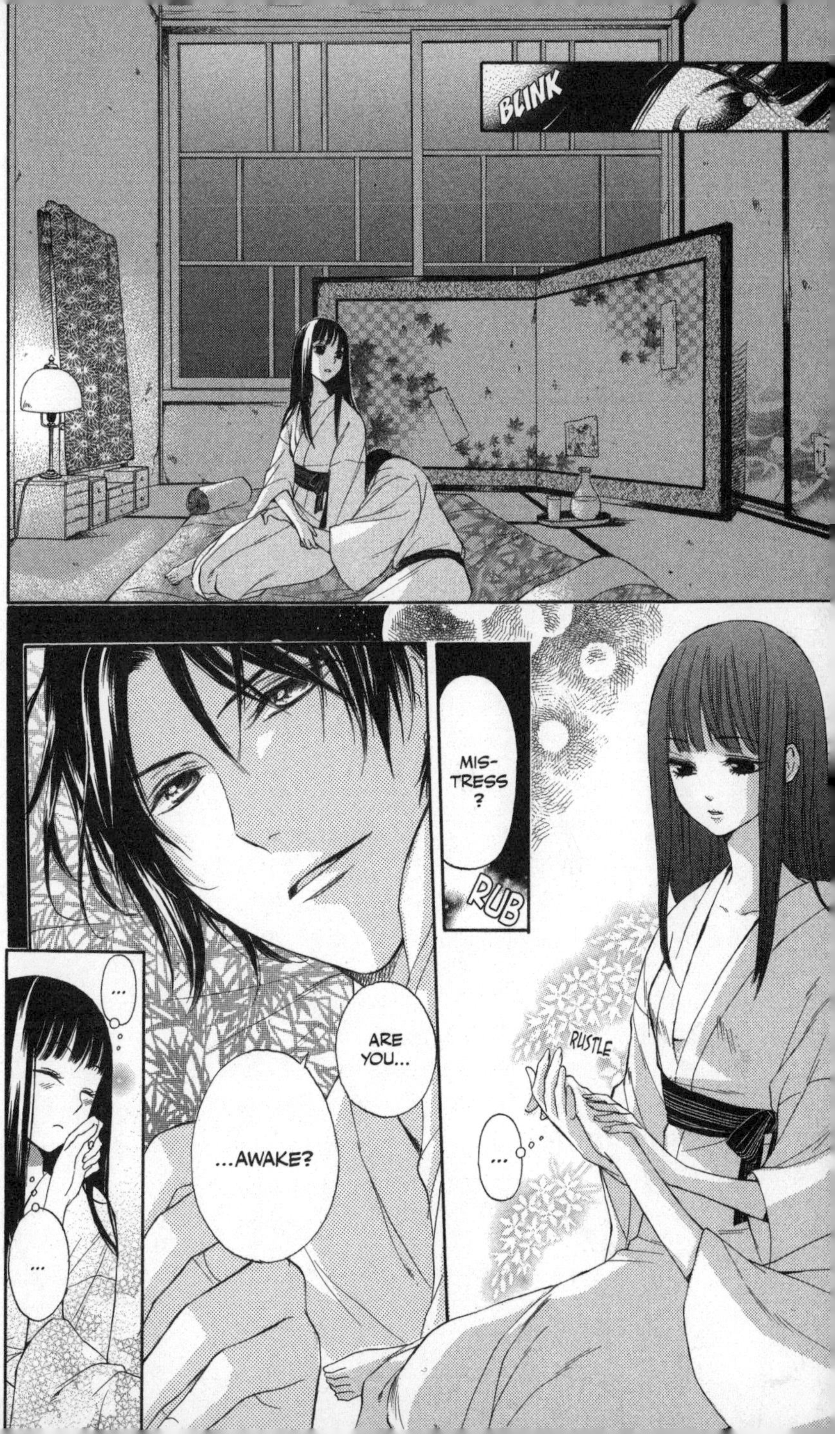
BLINK
RUSTLE
...
MIS-TRESS?
RUB
ARE YOU...
...AWAKE?
...
...

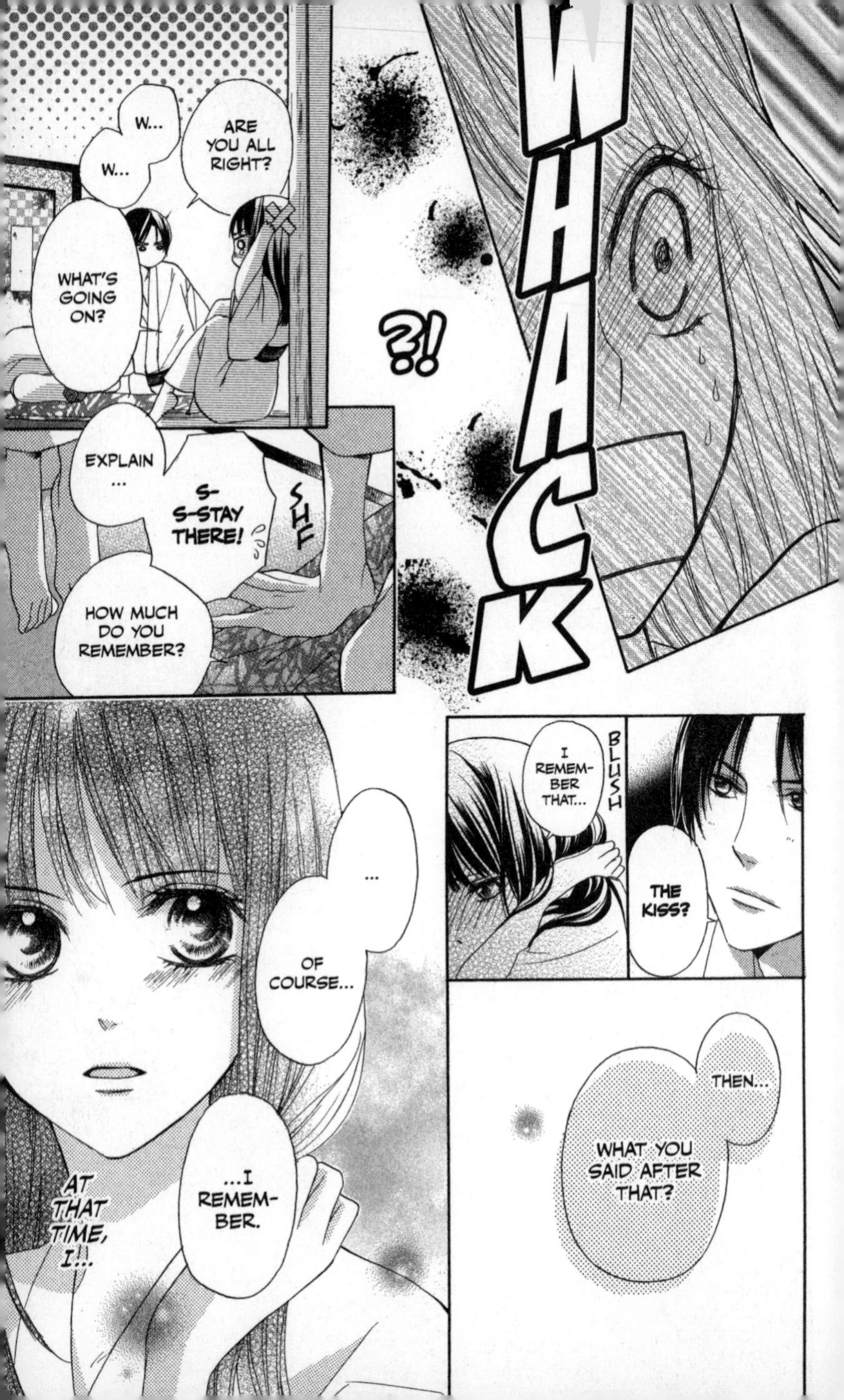
WHACK
?!
ARE YOU ALL RIGHT?
W...
W...
WHAT'S GOING ON?
SHF
S-S-STAY THERE!
EXPLAIN ...
HOW MUCH DO YOU REMEMBER?
BLUSH
I REMEMBER THAT...
THE KISS?
THEN...
WHAT YOU SAID AFTER THAT?
...
OF COURSE...
...I REMEMBER.
AT THAT TIME, I...

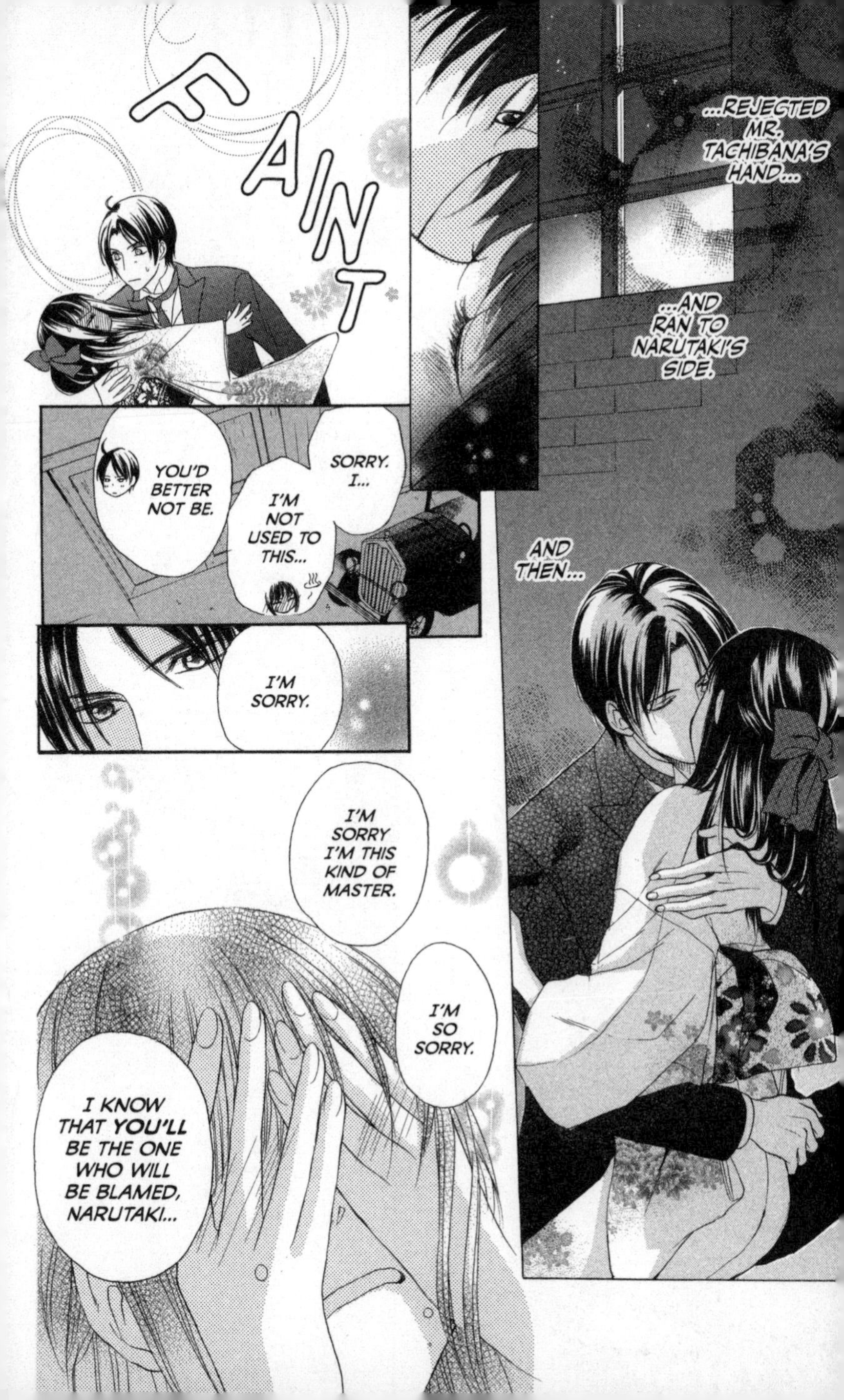
...REJECTED MR. TACHIBANA'S HAND...
...AND RAN TO NARUTAKI'S SIDE.
FAINT
AND THEN...
SORRY. I...
I'M NOT USED TO THIS...
YOU'D BETTER NOT BE.
I'M SORRY.
I'M SORRY I'M THIS KIND OF MASTER.
I'M SO SORRY.
I KNOW THAT **YOU'LL** BE THE ONE WHO WILL BE BLAMED, NARUTAKI...

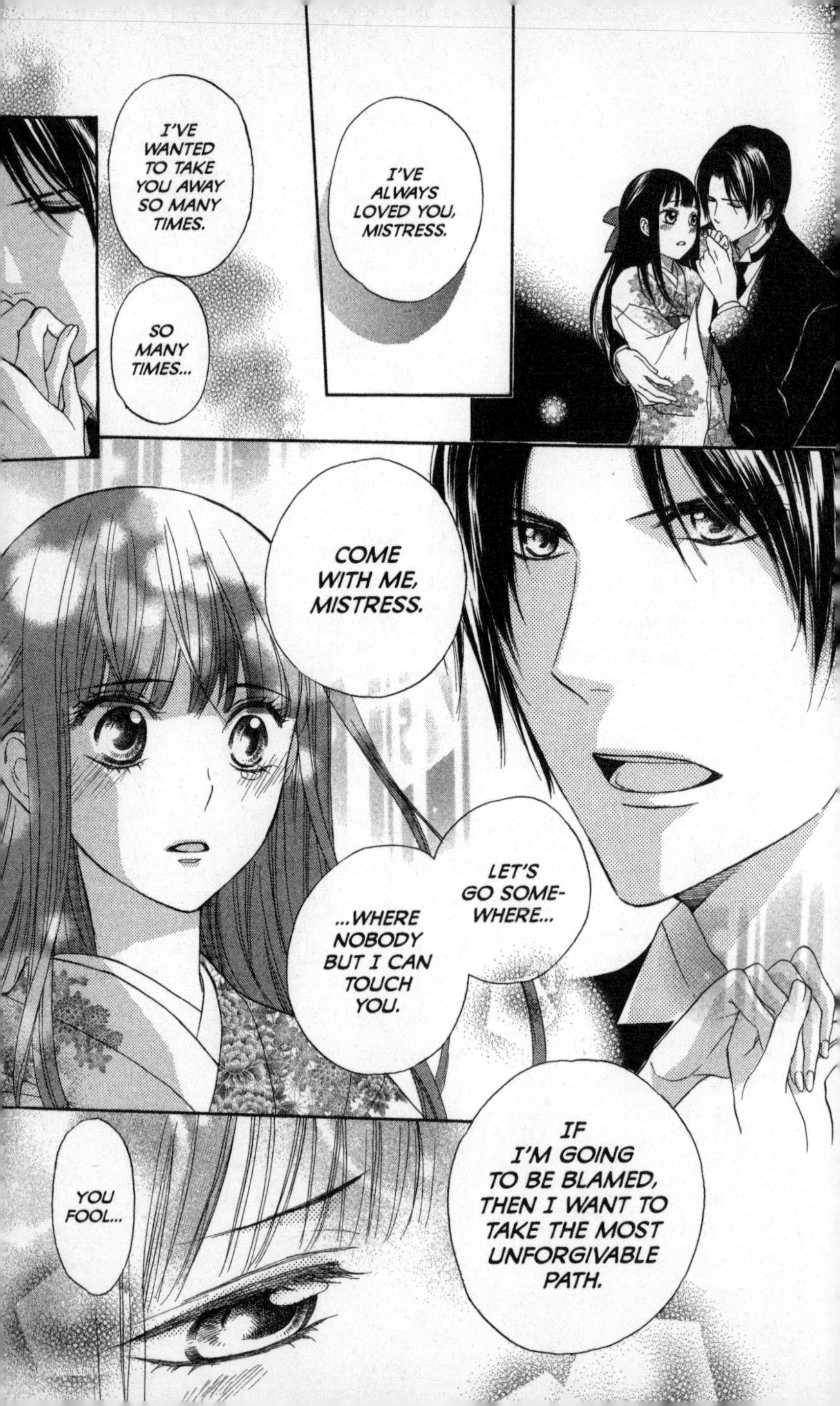
I'VE ALWAYS LOVED YOU, MISTRESS.
I'VE WANTED TO TAKE YOU AWAY SO MANY TIMES.
SO MANY TIMES...
COME WITH ME, MISTRESS.
LET'S GO SOME-WHERE...
...WHERE NOBODY BUT I CAN TOUCH YOU.
IF I'M GOING TO BE BLAMED, THEN I WANT TO TAKE THE MOST UNFORGIVABLE PATH.
YOU FOOL...

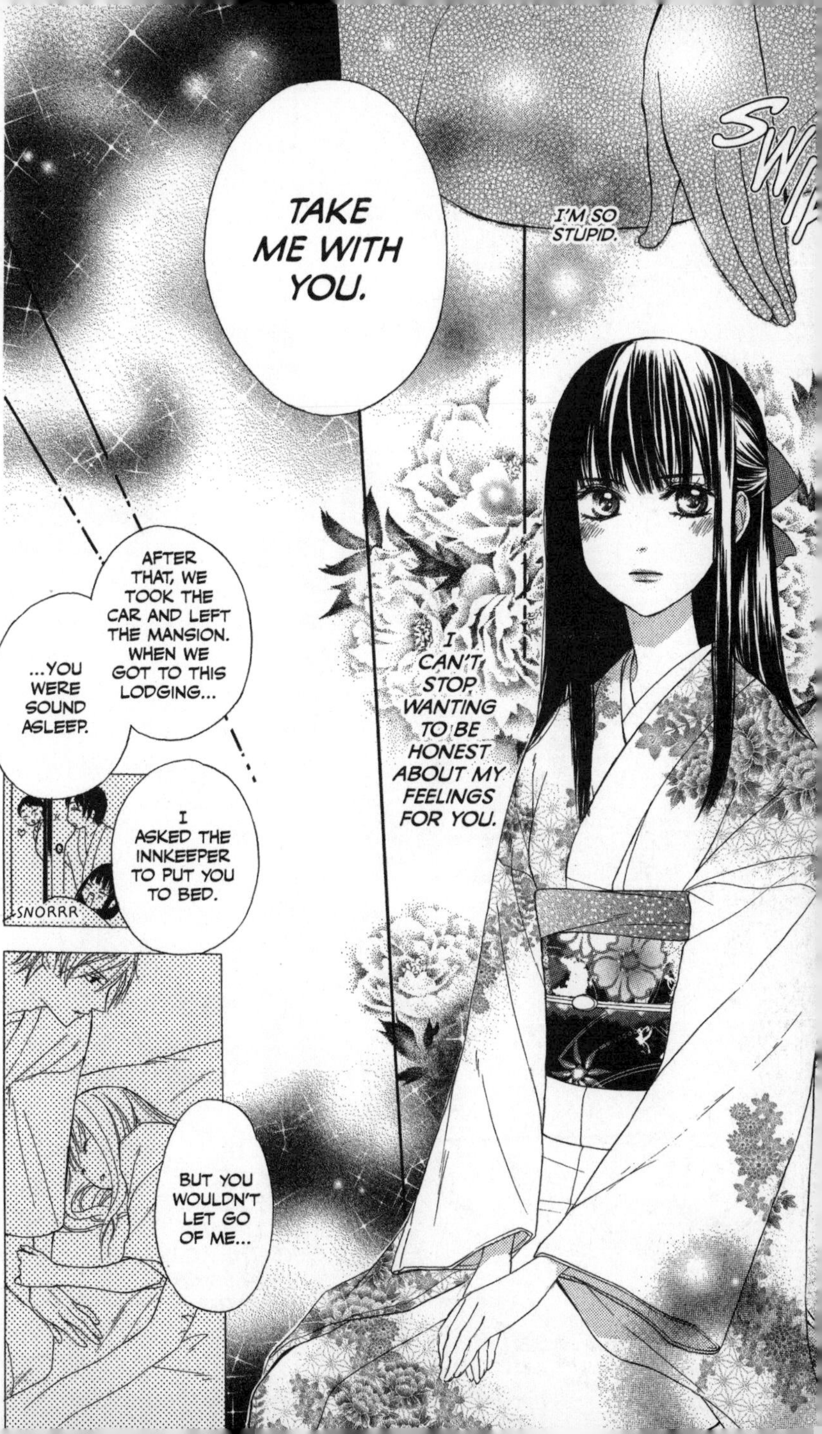
SWI
I'M SO STUPID.
TAKE ME WITH YOU.
I CAN'T STOP WANTING TO BE HONEST ABOUT MY FEELINGS FOR YOU.
AFTER THAT, WE TOOK THE CAR AND LEFT THE MANSION. WHEN WE GOT TO THIS LODGING...
...YOU WERE SOUND ASLEEP.
I ASKED THE INNKEEPER TO PUT YOU TO BED.
SNORRR
BUT YOU WOULDN'T LET GO OF ME...

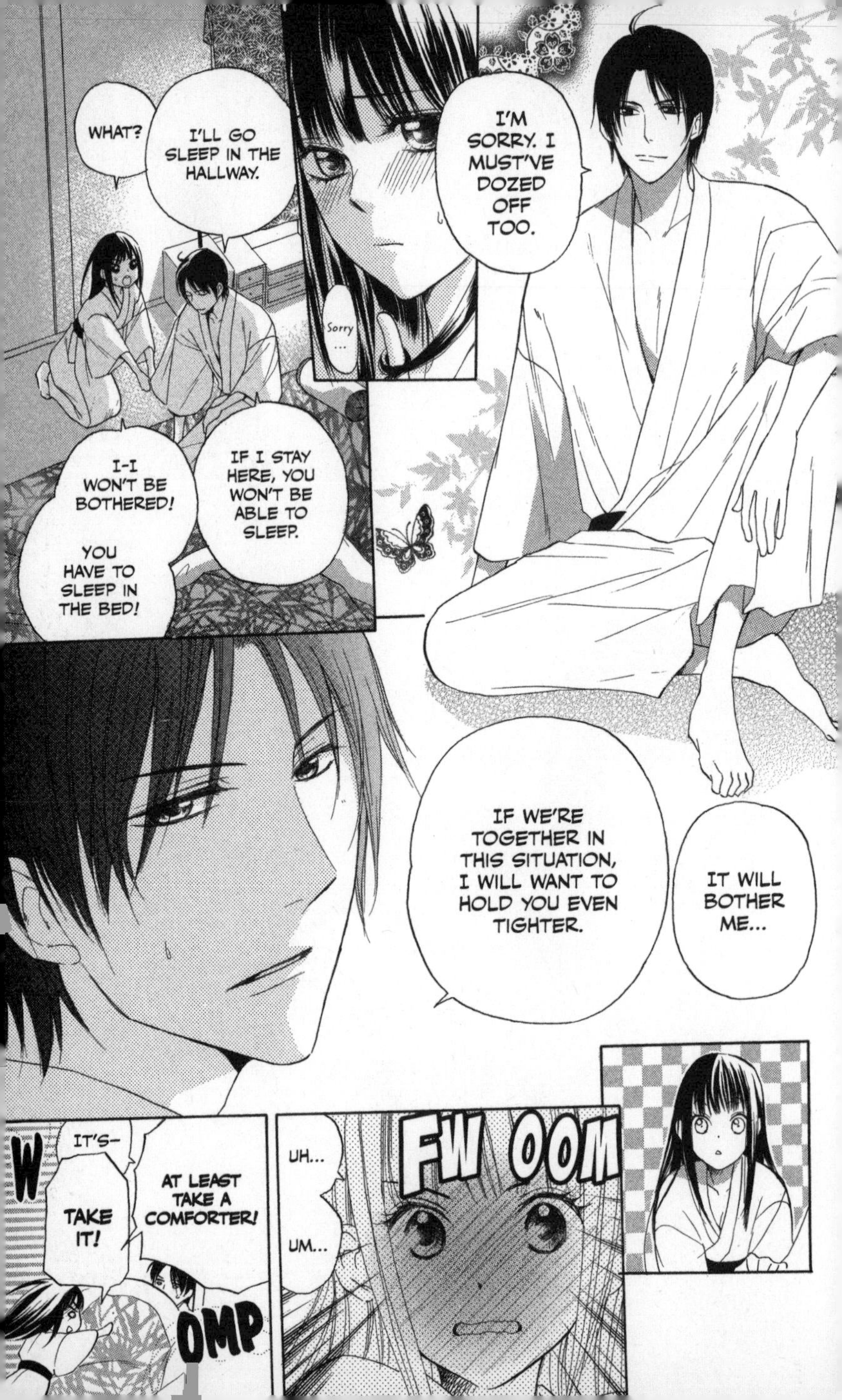
I'M SORRY. I MUST'VE DOZED OFF TOO.
Sorry...
I'LL GO SLEEP IN THE HALLWAY.
WHAT?
IF I STAY HERE, YOU WON'T BE ABLE TO SLEEP.
I-I WON'T BE BOTHERED!
YOU HAVE TO SLEEP IN THE BED!
IT WILL BOTHER ME...
IF WE'RE TOGETHER IN THIS SITUATION, I WILL WANT TO HOLD YOU EVEN TIGHTER.
FW OOM
UH...
UM...
AT LEAST TAKE A COMFORTER!
IT'S—
TAKE IT!
W
OMP

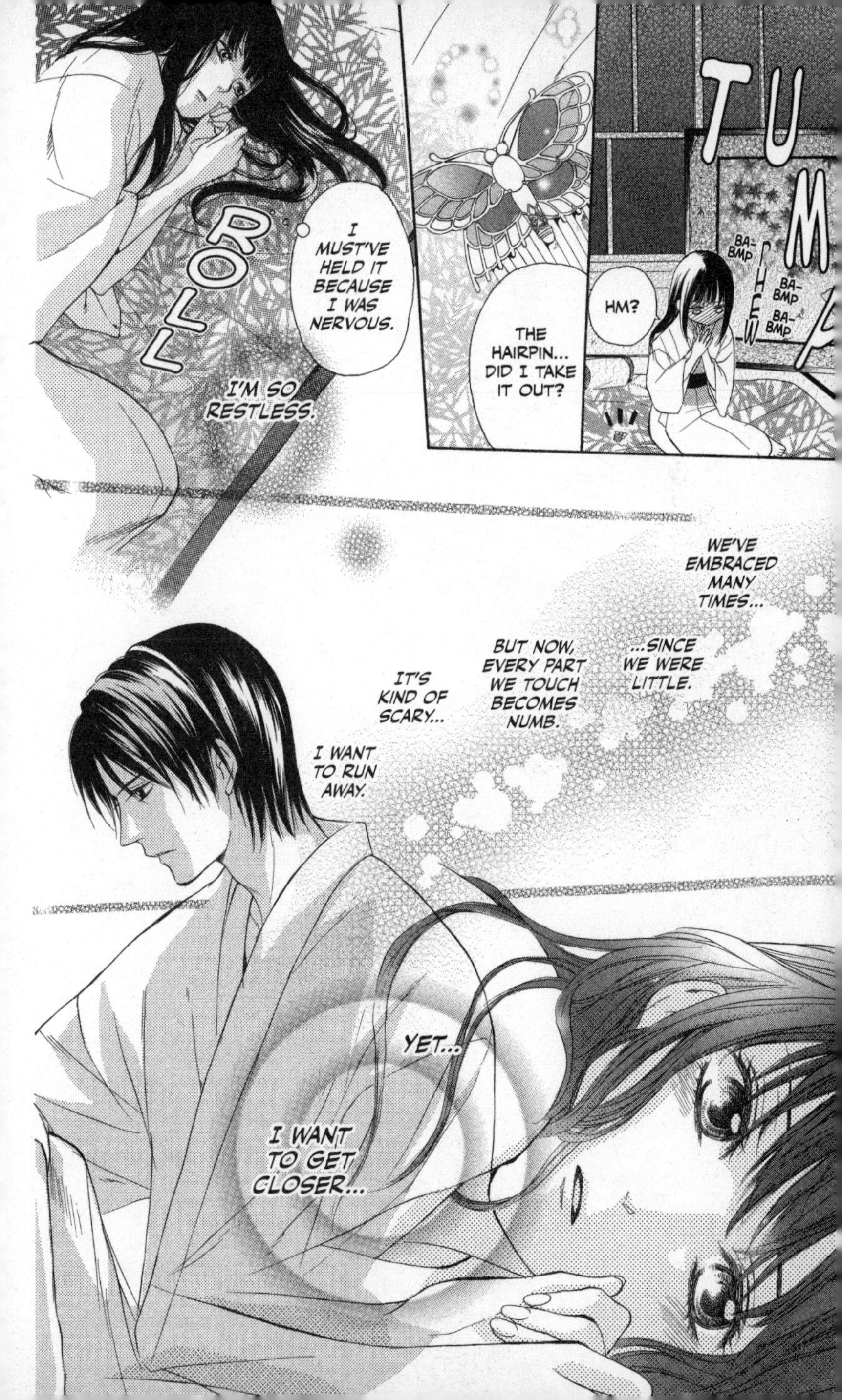
TUMP
BA-BMP
BA-BMP
BA-BMP
PHEW
HM?
THE HAIRPIN... DID I TAKE IT OUT?
I MUST'VE HELD IT BECAUSE I WAS NERVOUS.
ROLL
I'M SO RESTLESS.
WE'VE EMBRACED MANY TIMES...
...SINCE WE WERE LITTLE.
BUT NOW, EVERY PART WE TOUCH BECOMES NUMB.
IT'S KIND OF SCARY...
I WANT TO RUN AWAY.
YET...
I WANT TO GET CLOSER...

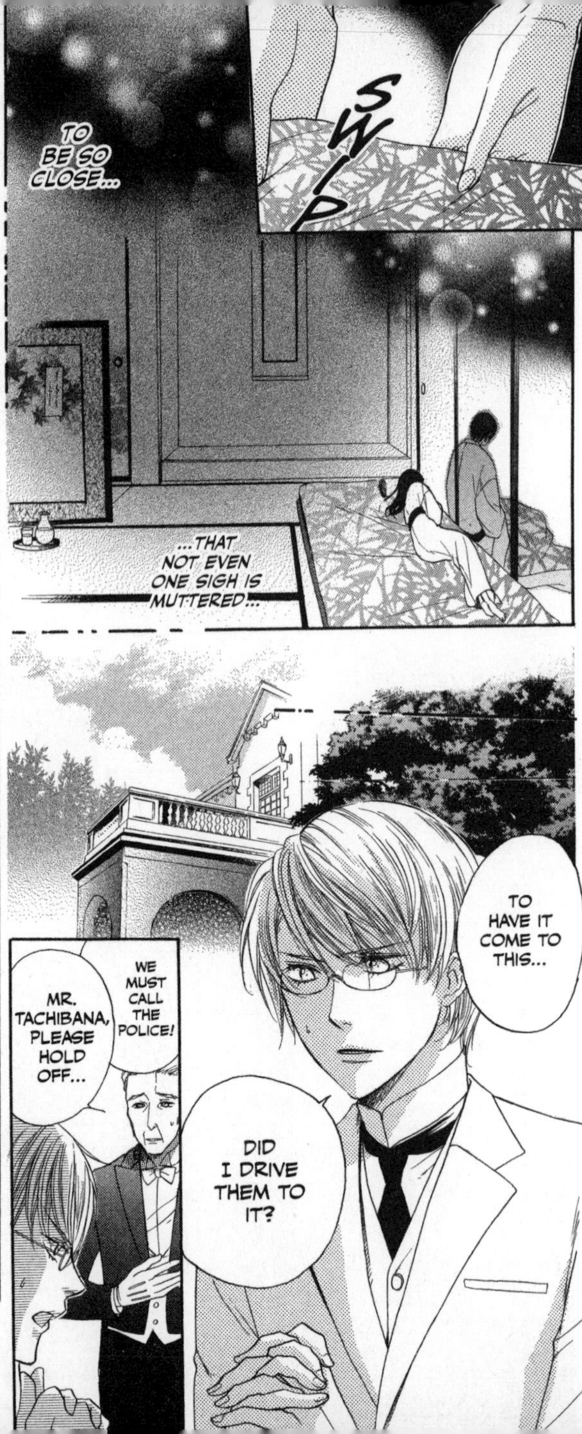
SWIP
TO BE SO CLOSE...
...THAT NOT EVEN ONE SIGH IS MUTTERED...
TO HAVE IT COME TO THIS...
DID I DRIVE THEM TO IT?
WE MUST CALL THE POLICE!
MR. TACHIBANA, PLEASE HOLD OFF...

CHAPTER 8

I had fun drawing this one. If they were going to run off and elope, I really wanted them to stay at a cheap, on-the-outskirts-of-town type of inn. I'm so happy that I was able to include this.

I always feel that I have to show a poised Sayaka being challenged about something, but for this chapter I wanted to show her mature as a woman. I wanted her to accept the feelings from the one she loves and to respond to that.

Once Narutaki got the affirmative, he was all over Sayaka. Later, I got a letter from an elementary school girl saying, "That was a little too much. (Laugh)" I'm a little remorseful...

But it sure was fun.

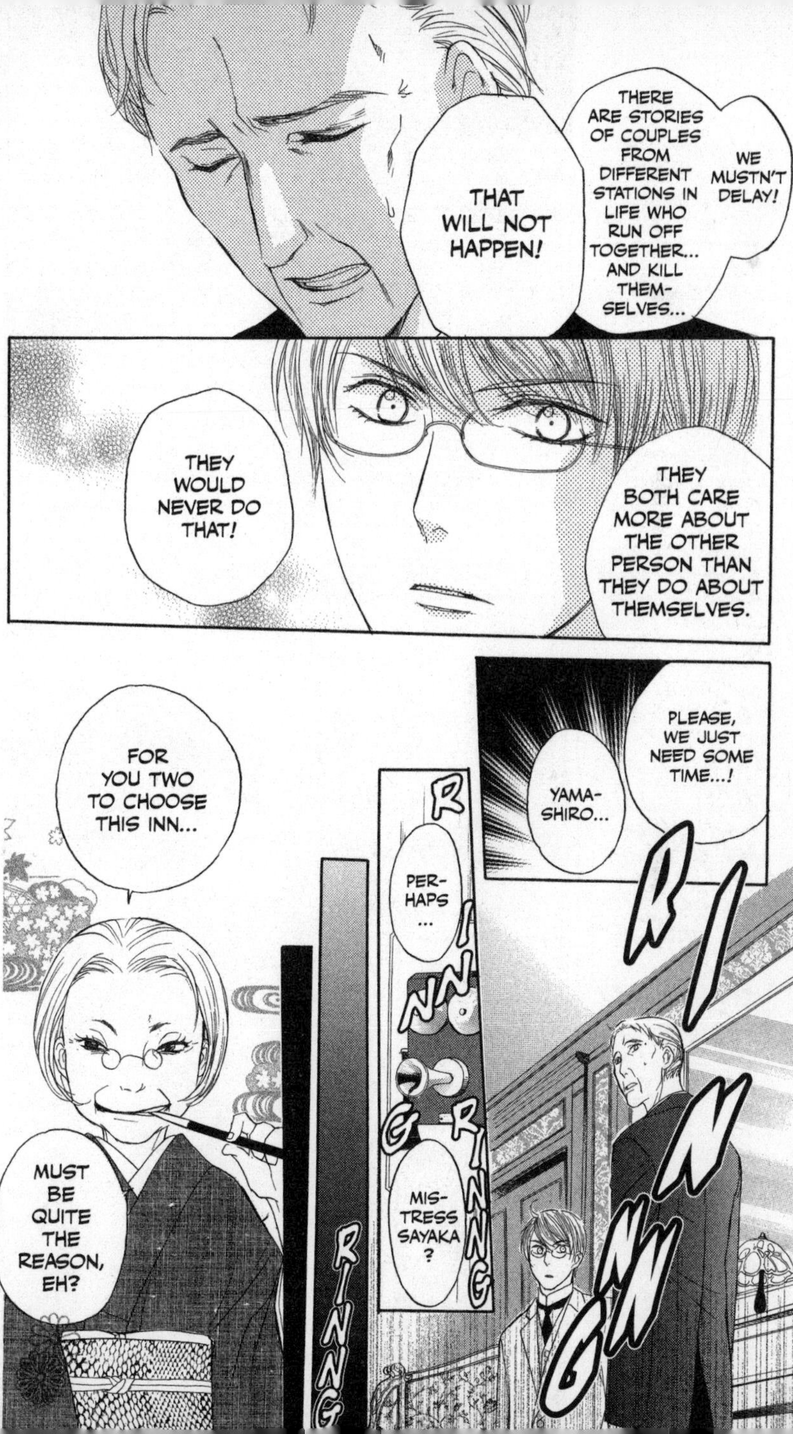
WE MUSTN'T DELAY!
THERE ARE STORIES OF COUPLES FROM DIFFERENT STATIONS IN LIFE WHO RUN OFF TOGETHER... AND KILL THEM-SELVES...
THAT WILL NOT HAPPEN!
THEY WOULD NEVER DO THAT!
THEY BOTH CARE MORE ABOUT THE OTHER PERSON THAN THEY DO ABOUT THEMSELVES.
PLEASE, WE JUST NEED SOME TIME...!
YAMA-SHIRO...
RINNNG
RINNG
PER-HAPS...
MIS-TRESS SAYAKA?
FOR YOU TWO TO CHOOSE THIS INN...
MUST BE QUITE THE REASON, EH?
RINNG

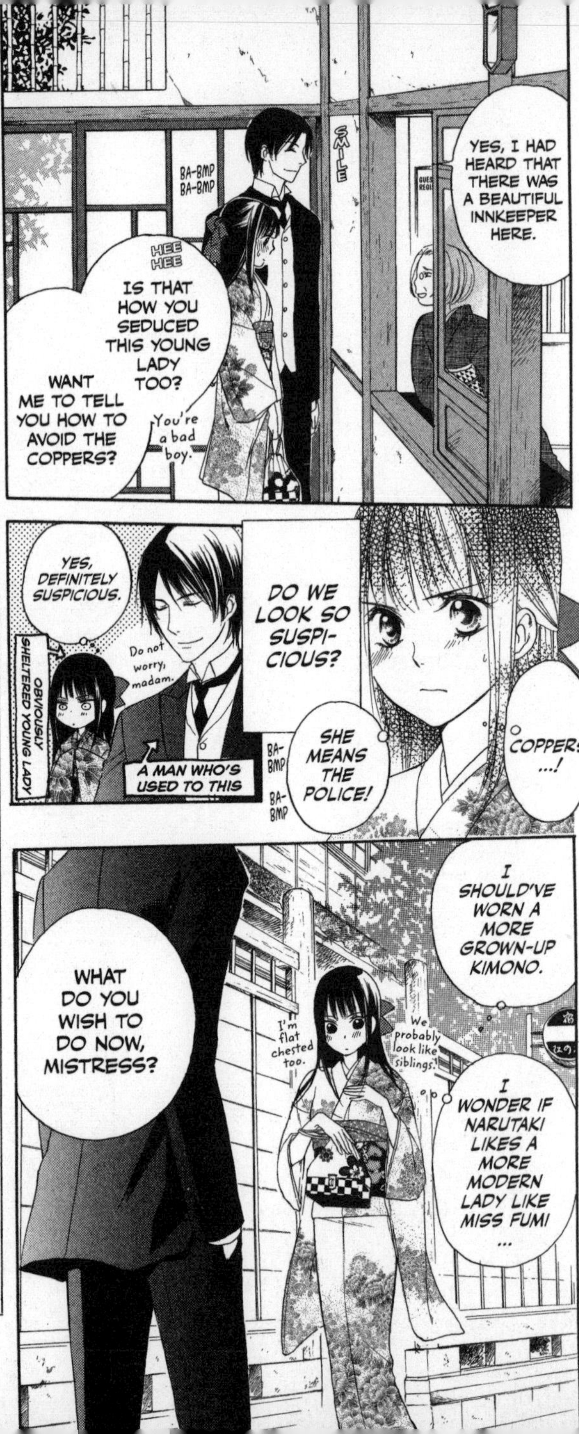
YES, I HAD HEARD THAT THERE WAS A BEAUTIFUL INNKEEPER HERE.
SMILE
BA-BMP BA-BMP
HEE HEE
IS THAT HOW YOU SEDUCED THIS YOUNG LADY TOO?
You're a bad boy.
WANT ME TO TELL YOU HOW TO AVOID THE COPPERS?
COPPERS ...!
SHE MEANS THE POLICE!
BA-BMP BA-BMP
DO WE LOOK SO SUSPI-CIOUS?
YES, DEFINITELY SUSPICIOUS.
Do not worry, madam.
A MAN WHO'S USED TO THIS
OBVIOUSLY SHELTERED YOUNG LADY
I SHOULD'VE WORN A MORE GROWN-UP KIMONO.
We probably look like siblings.
I WONDER IF NARUTAKI LIKES A MORE MODERN LADY LIKE MISS FUMI ...
I'm flat chested too.
WHAT DO YOU WISH TO DO NOW, MISTRESS?

ABOUT THE BASIS OF THIS STORY

I based this love story between an heiress and her chauffeur in the Taisho era on two particular historical incidents.

The first incident was a train suicide by a countess, Lady Kamako Yoshikawa, and her chauffeur. Only the chauffeur died in the accident, and Kamako survived. She later ran off with another chauffeur... I wonder if she had a thing for chauffeurs? I took the "Yoshi" part of the Yoshimuras from her.

The other elopement incident was Yoshiko Nabeshima, a daughter of a viscount, and her chauffeur Kinori Tada. In the end, they were able to marry and became the third-generation owners of the Tadaya Hot Spring Inn in Noto. Because they had people supporting them, her father gave in eventually. He even sent them many wedding presents. Even though they had a hard time, I like this story better since it's happier.

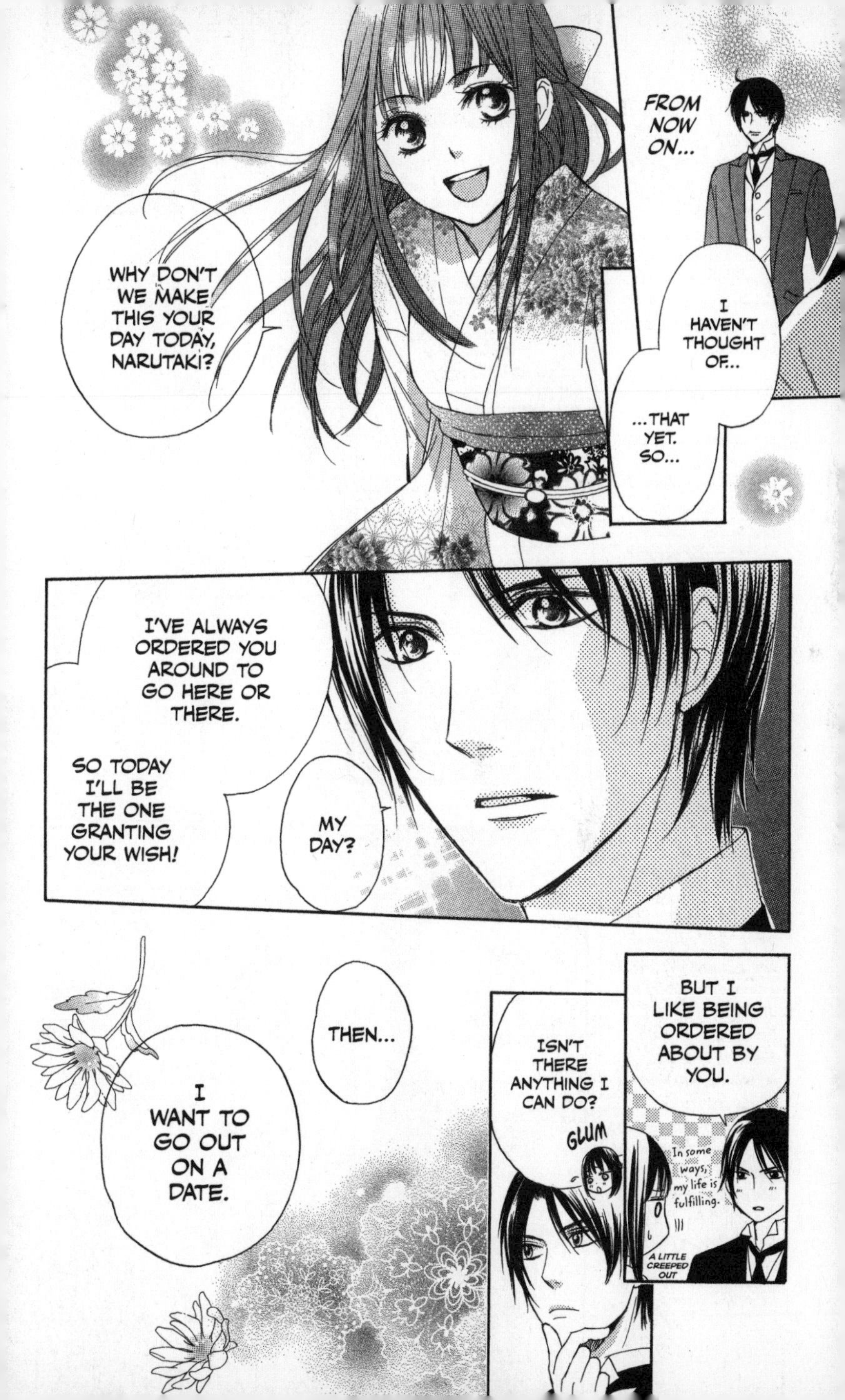
FROM NOW ON...
I HAVEN'T THOUGHT OF...
...THAT YET. SO...
WHY DON'T WE MAKE THIS YOUR DAY TODAY, NARUTAKI?
MY DAY?
I'VE ALWAYS ORDERED YOU AROUND TO GO HERE OR THERE.
SO TODAY I'LL BE THE ONE GRANTING YOUR WISH!
BUT I LIKE BEING ORDERED ABOUT BY YOU.
In some ways, my life is fulfilling.
A LITTLE CREEPED OUT
ISN'T THERE ANYTHING I CAN DO?
GLUM
THEN...
I WANT TO GO OUT ON A DATE.

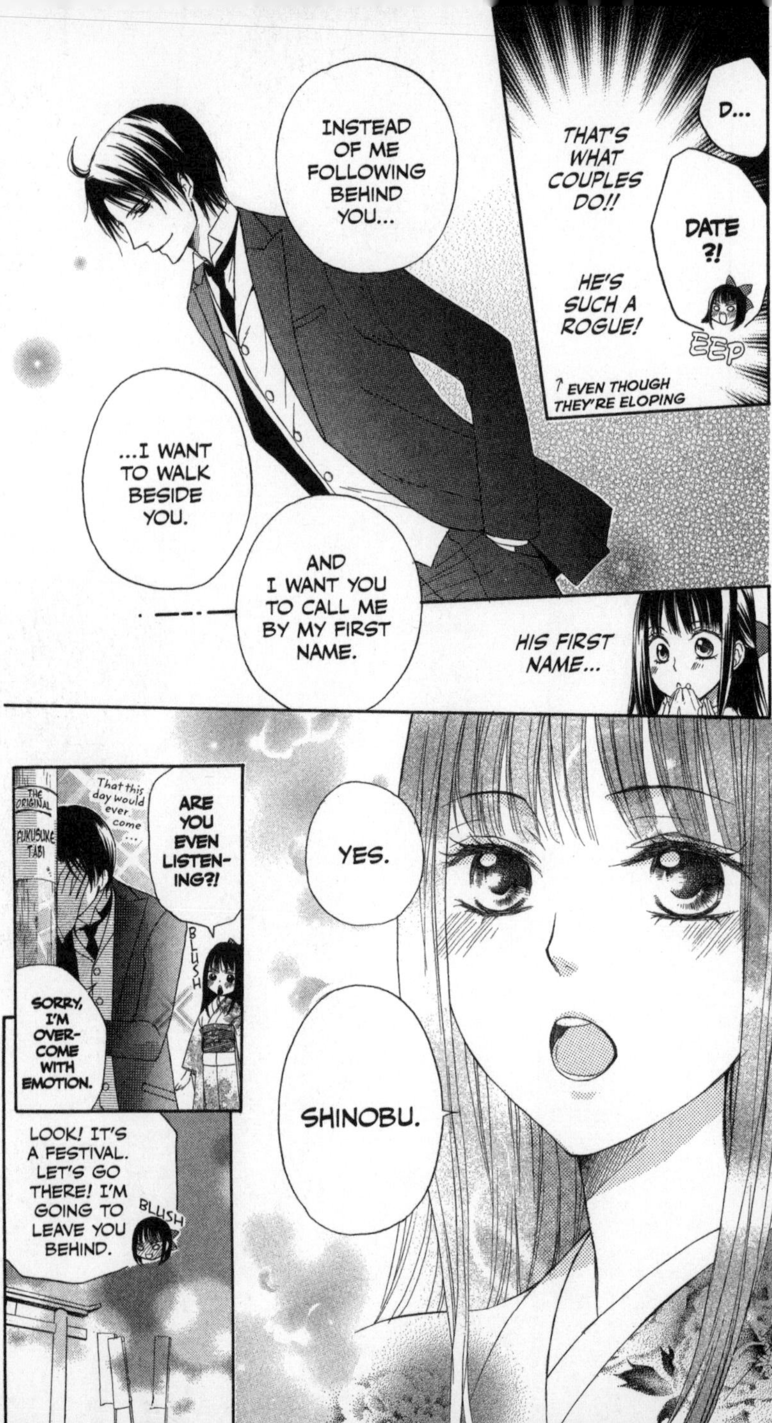
D...
THAT'S WHAT COUPLES DO!!
DATE ?!
HE'S SUCH A ROGUE!
EEP
↑ EVEN THOUGH THEY'RE ELOPING
HIS FIRST NAME...
INSTEAD OF ME FOLLOWING BEHIND YOU...
...I WANT TO WALK BESIDE YOU.
AND I WANT YOU TO CALL ME BY MY FIRST NAME.
YES.
SHINOBU.
ARE YOU EVEN LISTENING?!
That this day would ever come...
THE ORIGINAL FUKUSUKE TABI
BLUSH
SORRY, I'M OVERCOME WITH EMOTION.
LOOK! IT'S A FESTIVAL. LET'S GO THERE! I'M GOING TO LEAVE YOU BEHIND.
BLUSH

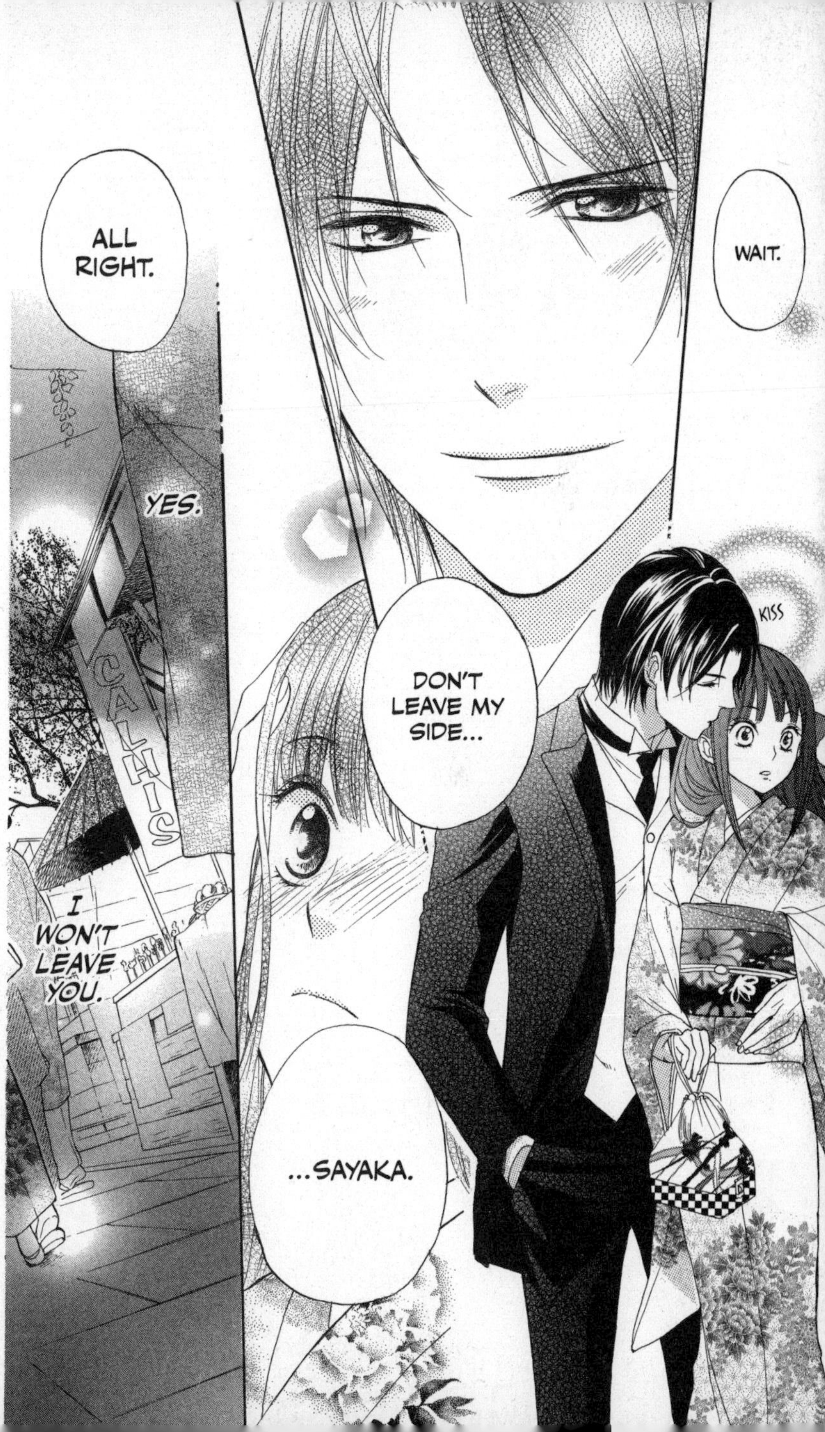
WAIT.
KISS
DON'T LEAVE MY SIDE...
...SAYAKA.
ALL RIGHT.
YES.
CALHIS
I WON'T LEAVE YOU.

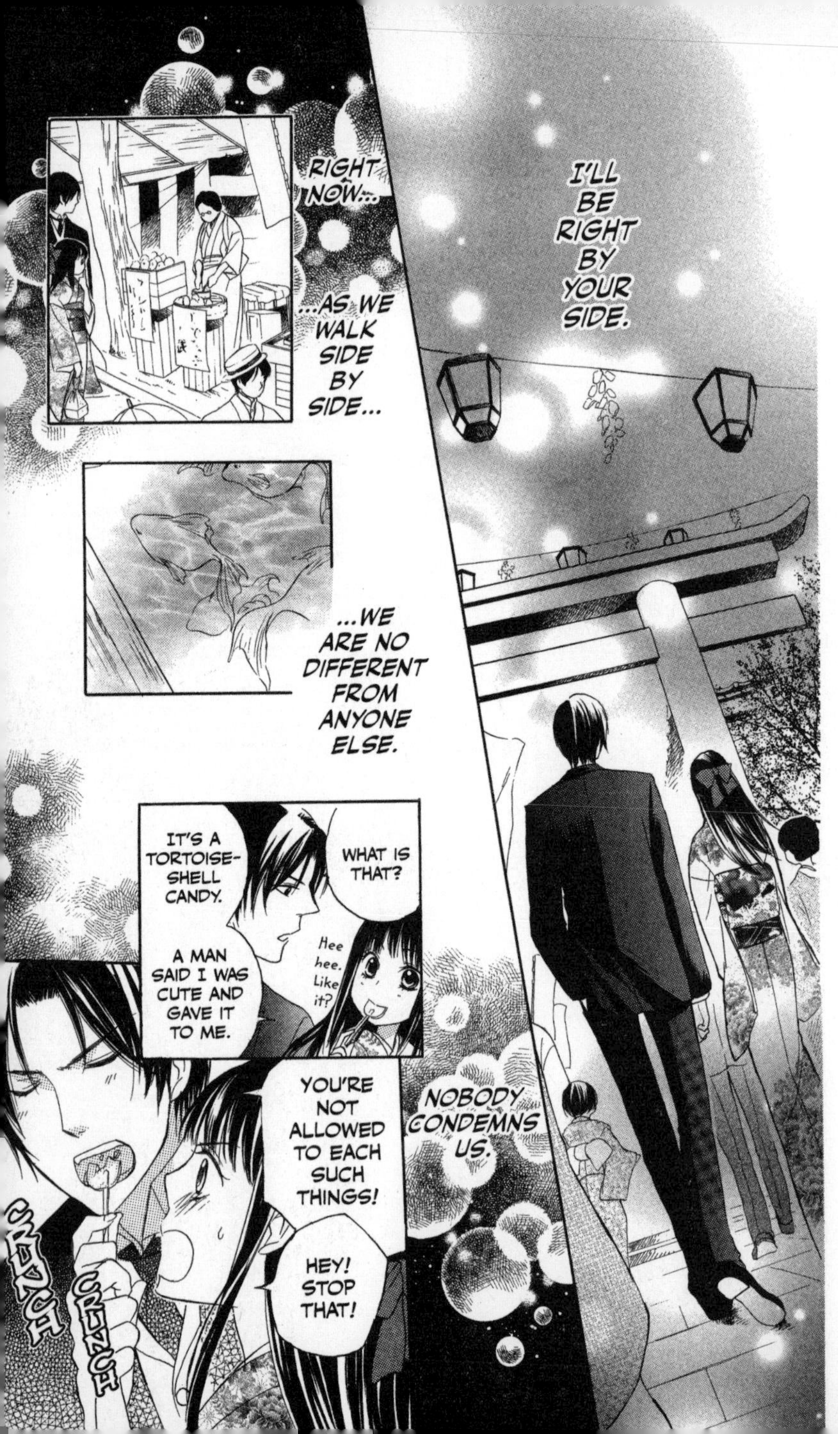
I'LL BE RIGHT BY YOUR SIDE.
NOBODY CONDEMNS US.
RIGHT NOW...
...AS WE WALK SIDE BY SIDE...
...WE ARE NO DIFFERENT FROM ANYONE ELSE.
WHAT IS THAT?
IT'S A TORTOISE-SHELL CANDY.
A MAN SAID I WAS CUTE AND GAVE IT TO ME.
Hee hee. Like it?
YOU'RE NOT ALLOWED TO EACH SUCH THINGS!
HEY! STOP THAT!
CRUNCH
CRUNCH

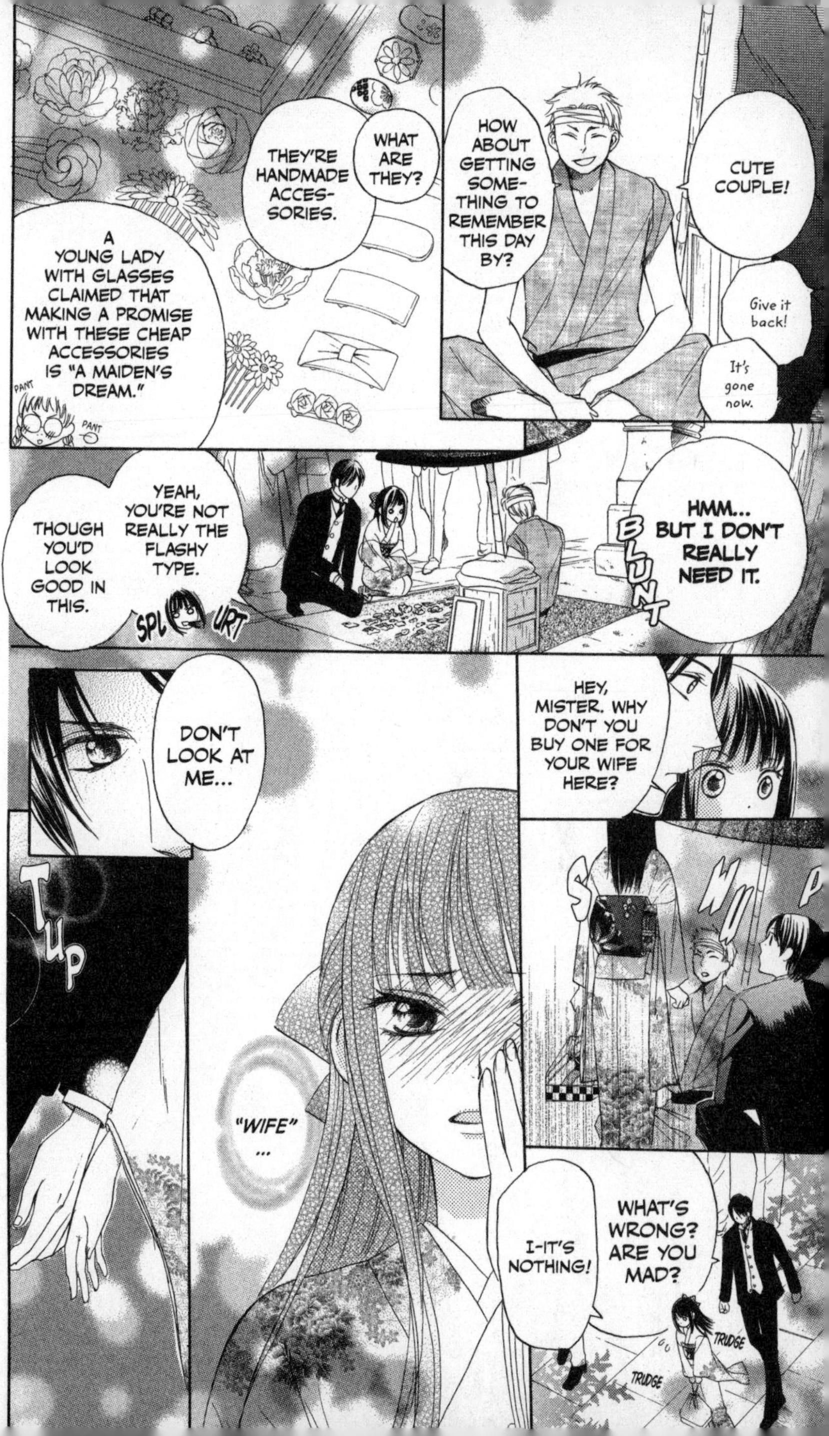
CUTE COUPLE!
HOW ABOUT GETTING SOMETHING TO REMEMBER THIS DAY BY?
Give it back!
It's gone now.
WHAT ARE THEY?
THEY'RE HANDMADE ACCESSORIES.
A YOUNG LADY WITH GLASSES CLAIMED THAT MAKING A PROMISE WITH THESE CHEAP ACCESSORIES IS "A MAIDEN'S DREAM."
PANT
PANT
HMM... BUT I DON'T REALLY NEED IT.
BLUNT
YEAH, YOU'RE NOT REALLY THE FLASHY TYPE.
THOUGH YOU'D LOOK GOOD IN THIS.
SPLURT
HEY, MISTER. WHY DON'T YOU BUY ONE FOR YOUR WIFE HERE?
DON'T LOOK AT ME...
SHWIP
WHAT'S WRONG? ARE YOU MAD?
I-IT'S NOTHING!
TRUDGE
TRUDGE
"WIFE" ...
TUP

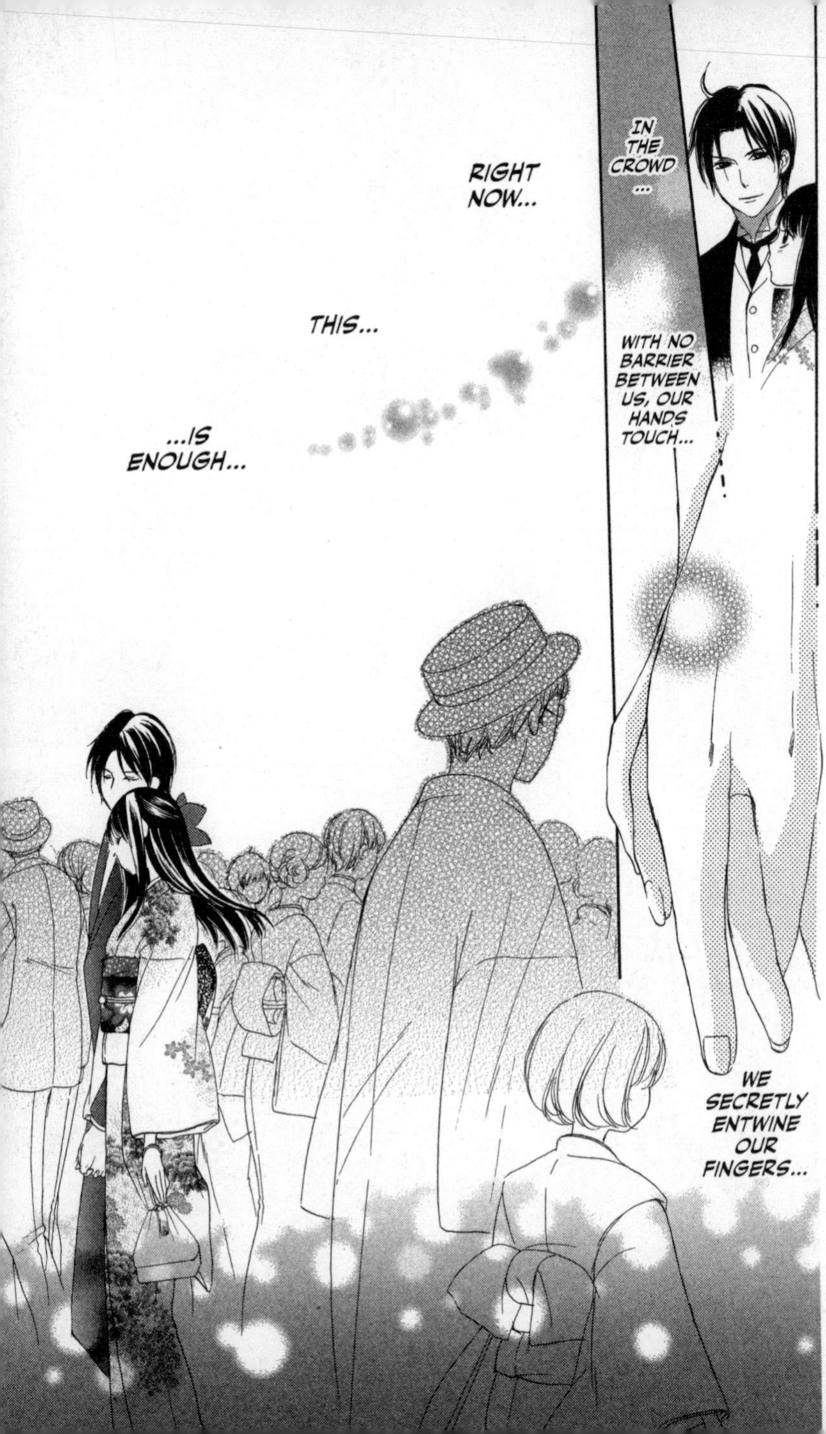
IN THE CROWD ...
WITH NO BARRIER BETWEEN US, OUR HANDS TOUCH...
WE SECRETLY ENTWINE OUR FINGERS...
RIGHT NOW...
THIS...
...IS ENOUGH...

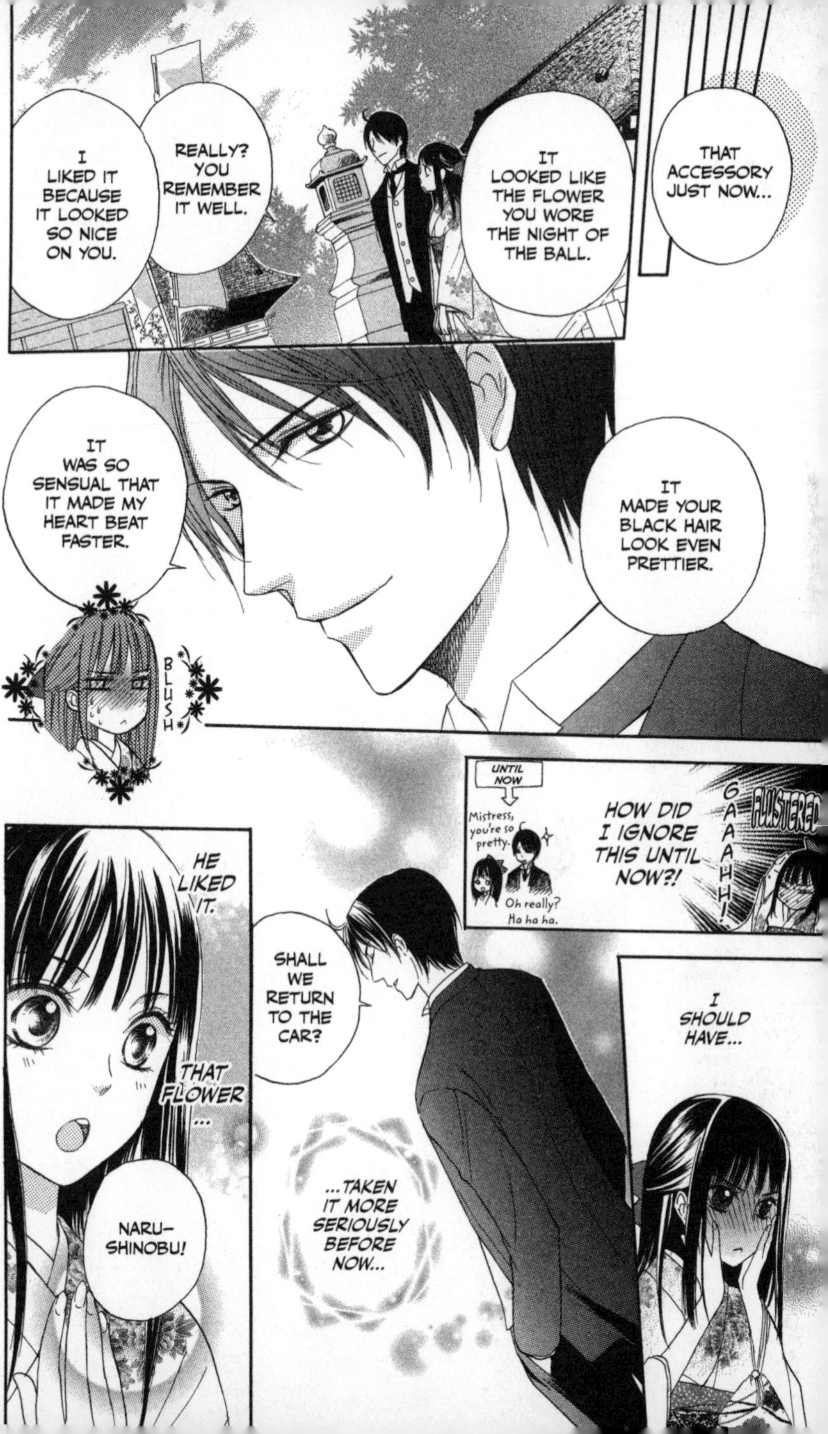
THAT ACCESSORY JUST NOW...
IT LOOKED LIKE THE FLOWER YOU WORE THE NIGHT OF THE BALL.
REALLY? YOU REMEMBER IT WELL.
I LIKED IT BECAUSE IT LOOKED SO NICE ON YOU.
IT MADE YOUR BLACK HAIR LOOK EVEN PRETTIER.
IT WAS SO SENSUAL THAT IT MADE MY HEART BEAT FASTER.
BLUSH
FLUSTERED
GAAAHH!
HOW DID I IGNORE THIS UNTIL NOW?!
UNTIL NOW
Mistress, you're so pretty.
Oh really? Ha ha ha.
I SHOULD HAVE...
...TAKEN IT MORE SERIOUSLY BEFORE NOW...
SHALL WE RETURN TO THE CAR?
HE LIKED IT.
THAT FLOWER...
NARU-SHINOBU!

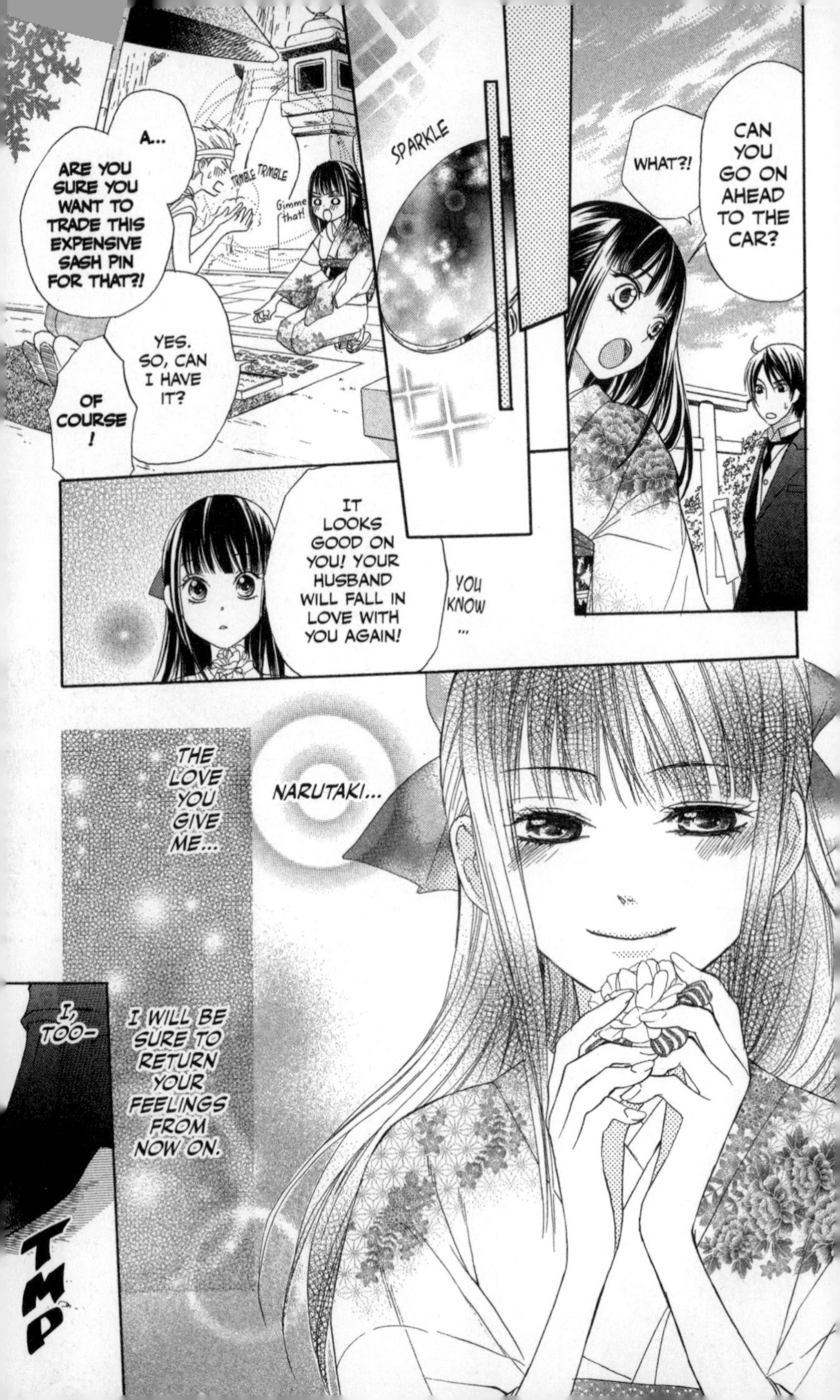
CAN YOU GO ON AHEAD TO THE CAR?
WHAT?!
SPARKLE
TRIMBLE TRIMBLE
Gimme that!
A... ARE YOU SURE YOU WANT TO TRADE THIS EXPENSIVE SASH PIN FOR THAT?!
YES. SO, CAN I HAVE IT?
OF COURSE!
YOU KNOW...
IT LOOKS GOOD ON YOU! YOUR HUSBAND WILL FALL IN LOVE WITH YOU AGAIN!
NARUTAKI...
THE LOVE YOU GIVE ME...
I WILL BE SURE TO RETURN YOUR FEELINGS FROM NOW ON.
I, TOO-
TMP

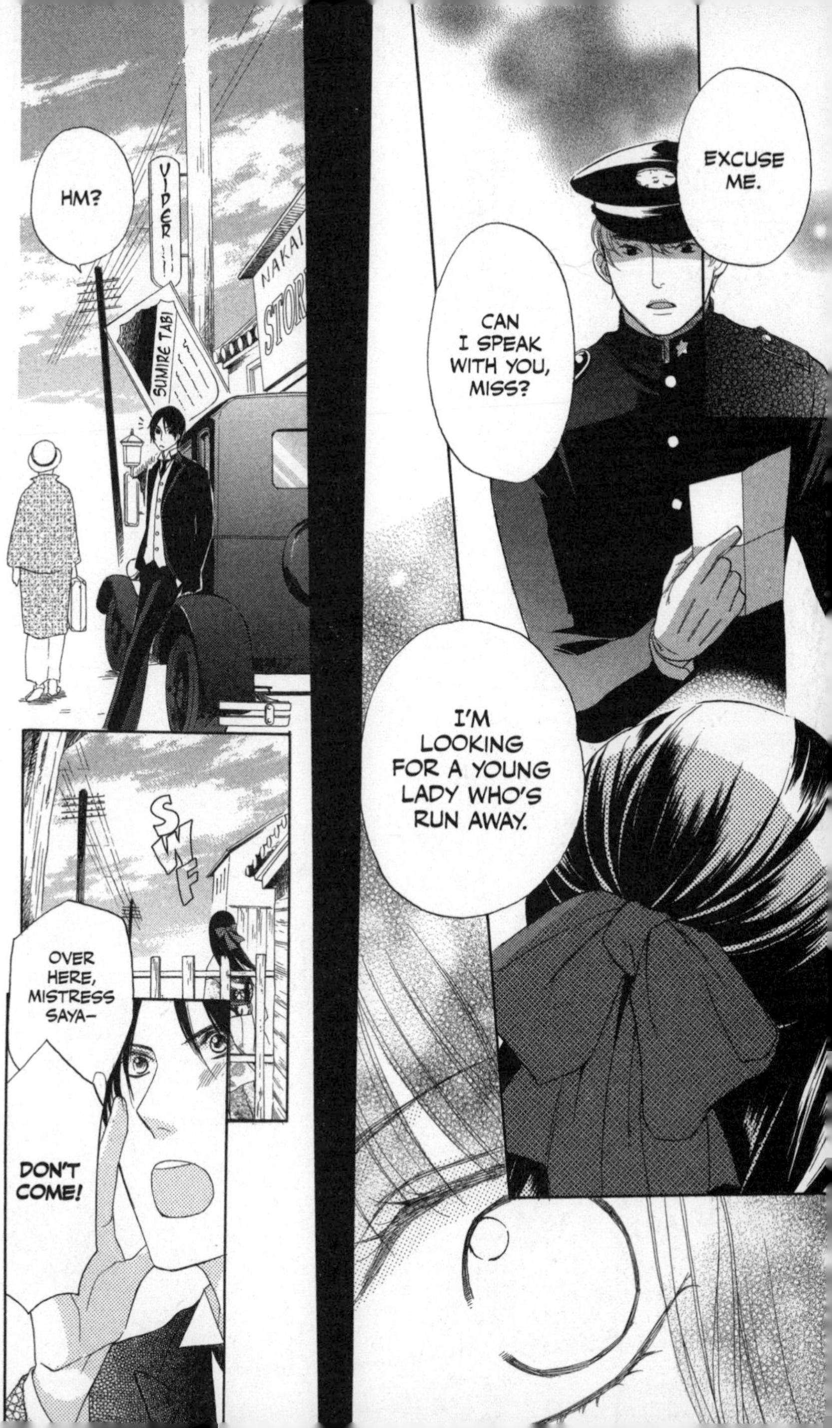
EXCUSE ME.
CAN I SPEAK WITH YOU, MISS?
I'M LOOKING FOR A YOUNG LADY WHO'S RUN AWAY.
HM?
NAKAI
SUMIRE TABI
OVER HERE, MISTRESS SAYA-
DON'T COME!

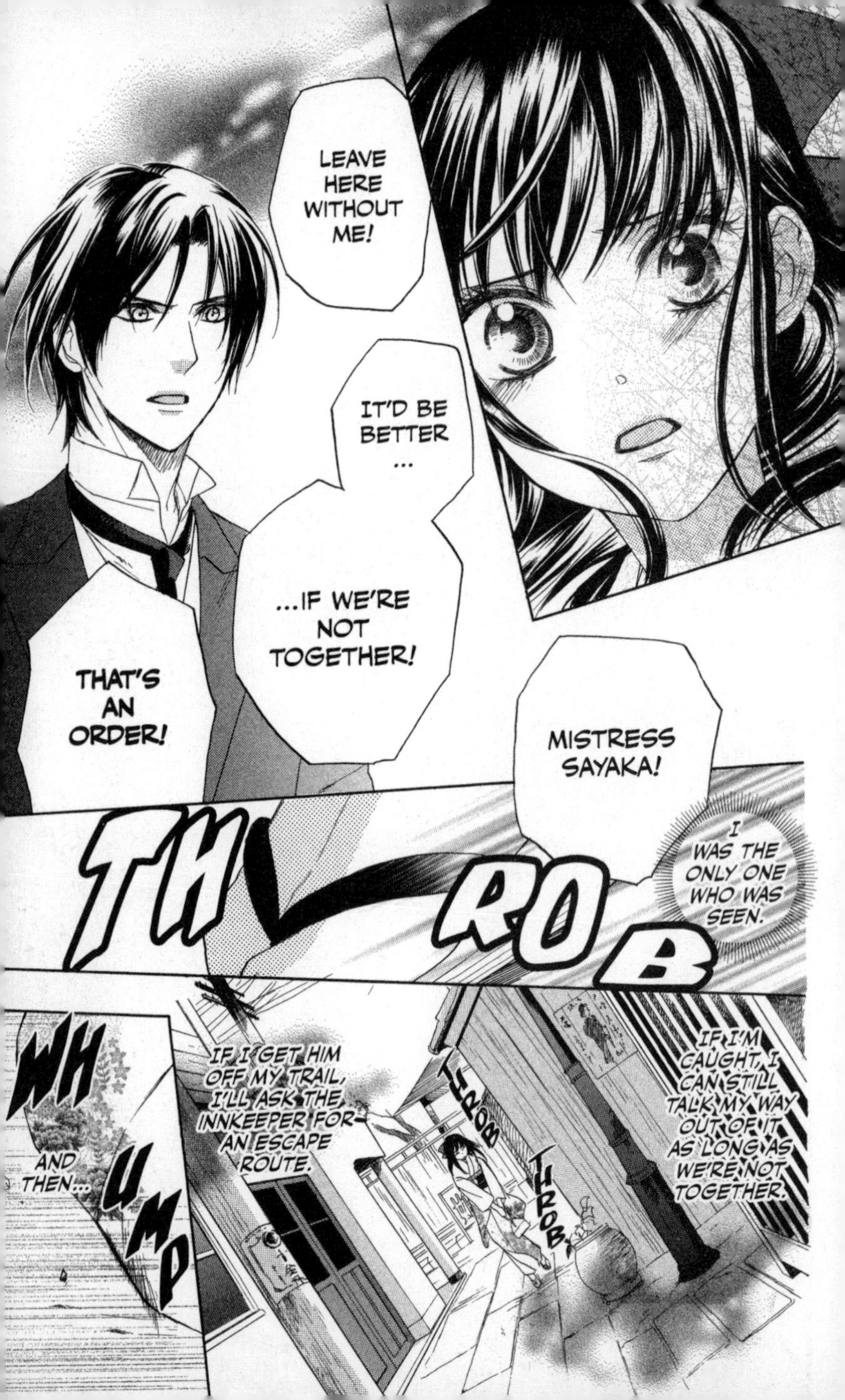
LEAVE HERE WITHOUT ME!
IT'D BE BETTER ...
...IF WE'RE NOT TOGETHER!
THAT'S AN ORDER!
I WAS THE ONLY ONE WHO WAS SEEN.
MISTRESS SAYAKA!
THROB
IF I'M CAUGHT, I CAN STILL TALK MY WAY OUT OF IT AS LONG AS WE'RE NOT TOGETHER.
THROB
THROB
IF I GET HIM OFF MY TRAIL, I'LL ASK THE INNKEEPER FOR AN ESCAPE ROUTE.
AND THEN...
WHUMP

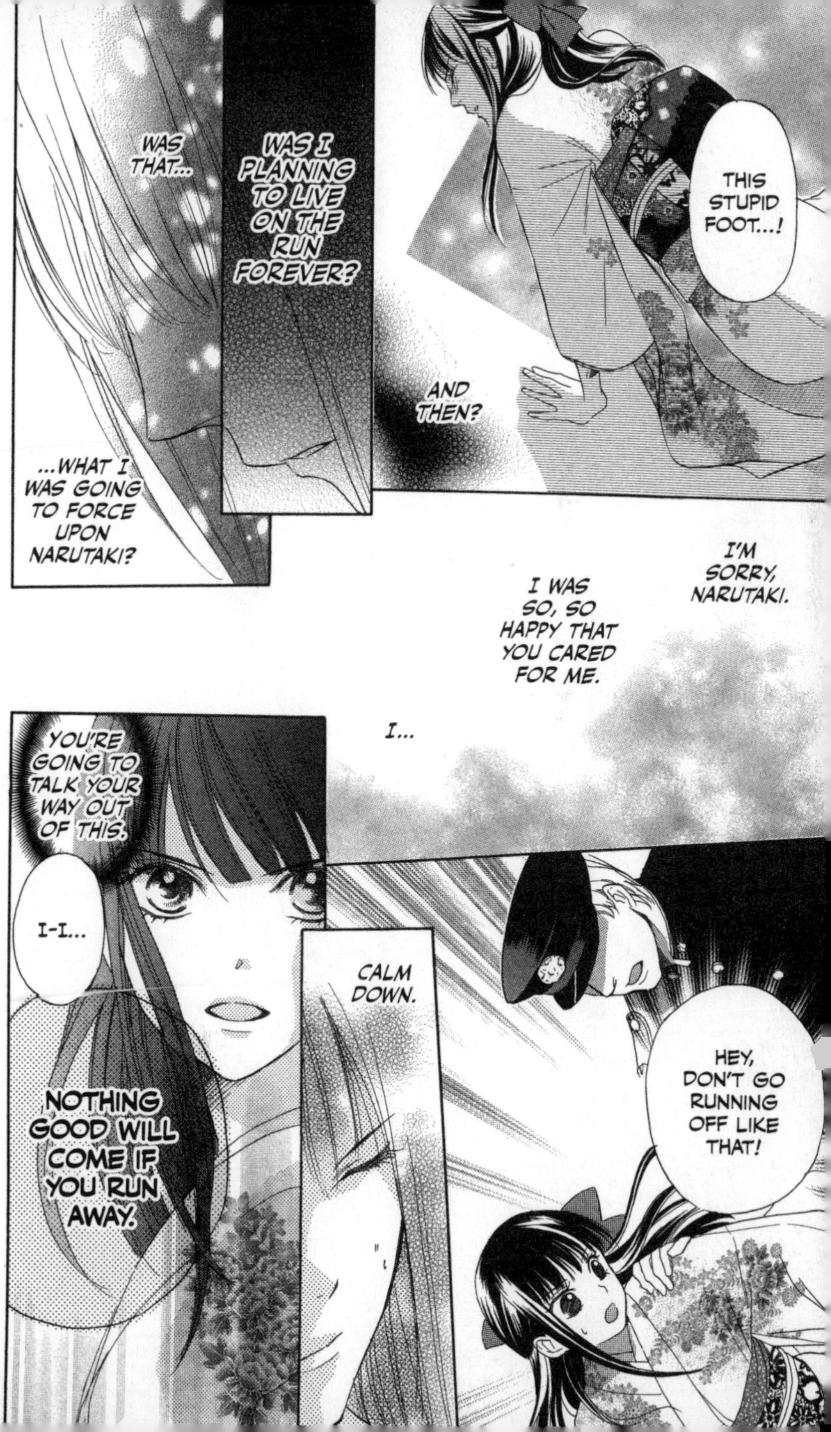
THIS STUPID FOOT...!
AND THEN?
WAS I PLANNING TO LIVE ON THE RUN FOREVER?
WAS THAT...
...WHAT I WAS GOING TO FORCE UPON NARUTAKI?
I'M SORRY, NARUTAKI.
I WAS SO, SO HAPPY THAT YOU CARED FOR ME.
I...
HEY, DON'T GO RUNNING OFF LIKE THAT!
CALM DOWN.
YOU'RE GOING TO TALK YOUR WAY OUT OF THIS.
I-I...
NOTHING GOOD WILL COME IF YOU RUN AWAY.

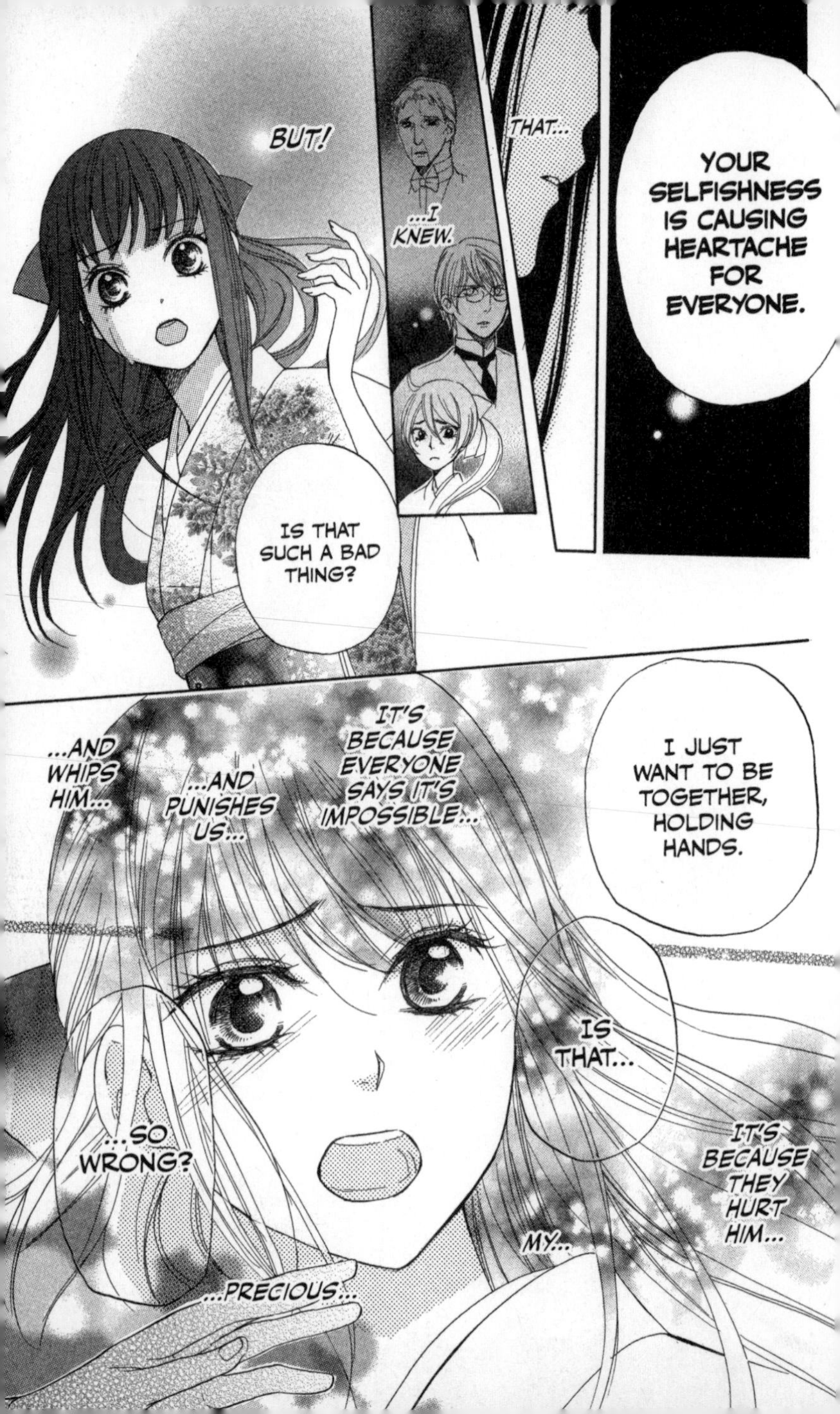
YOUR SELFISHNESS IS CAUSING HEARTACHE FOR EVERYONE.
THAT...
...I KNEW.
BUT!
IS THAT SUCH A BAD THING?
I JUST WANT TO BE TOGETHER, HOLDING HANDS.
IT'S BECAUSE EVERYONE SAYS IT'S IMPOSSIBLE...
...AND PUNISHES US...
...AND WHIPS HIM...
IS THAT...
...SO WRONG?
IT'S BECAUSE THEY HURT HIM...
MY...
...PRECIOUS...

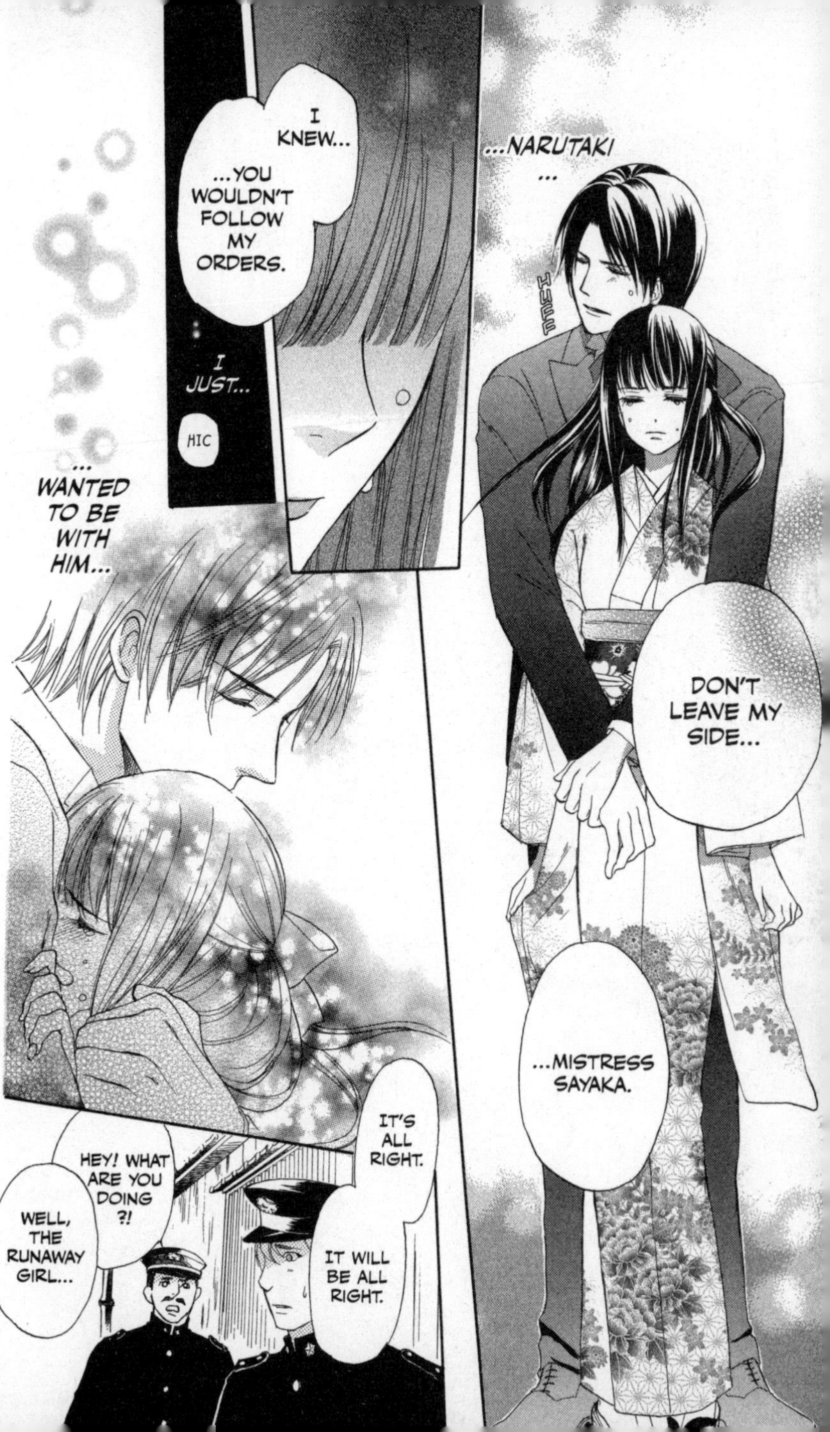
...NARUTAKI ...
DON'T LEAVE MY SIDE...
...MISTRESS SAYAKA.
I KNEW...
...YOU WOULDN'T FOLLOW MY ORDERS.
I JUST...
HIC
...WANTED TO BE WITH HIM...
IT'S ALL RIGHT.
IT WILL BE ALL RIGHT.
HEY! WHAT ARE YOU DOING ?!
WELL, THE RUNAWAY GIRL...

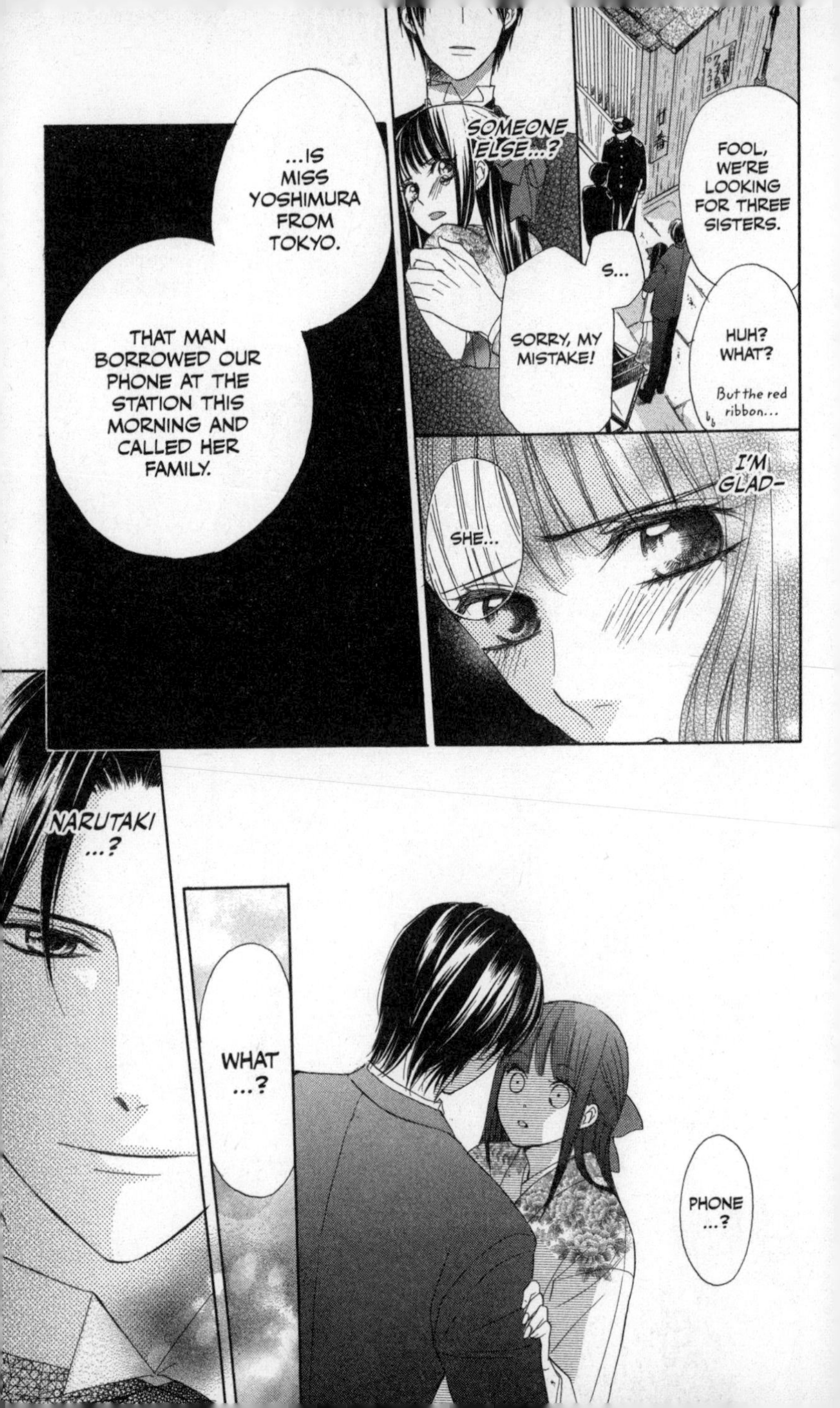
FOOL, WE'RE LOOKING FOR THREE SISTERS.
S...
SORRY, MY MISTAKE!
HUH? WHAT?
But the red ribbon...
SOMEONE ELSE...?
I'M GLAD-
SHE...
...IS MISS YOSHIMURA FROM TOKYO.
THAT MAN BORROWED OUR PHONE AT THE STATION THIS MORNING AND CALLED HER FAMILY.
PHONE ...?
NARUTAKI ...?
WHAT ...?

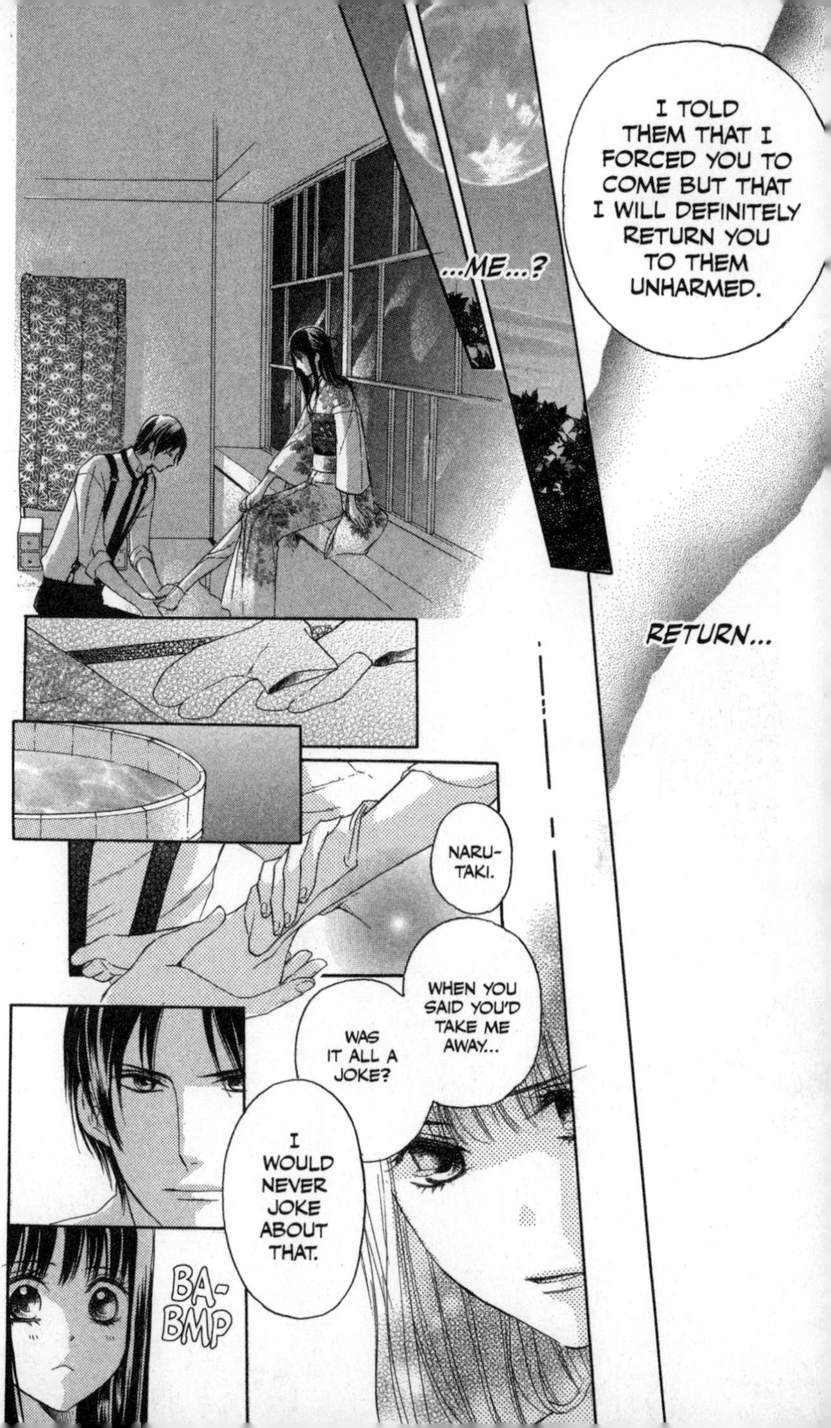

I TOLD THEM THAT I FORCED YOU TO COME BUT THAT I WILL DEFINITELY RETURN YOU TO THEM UNHARMED.
...ME...?
RETURN...
NARU-TAKI.
WHEN YOU SAID YOU'D TAKE ME AWAY...
WAS IT ALL A JOKE?
I WOULD NEVER JOKE ABOUT THAT.
BA-BMP

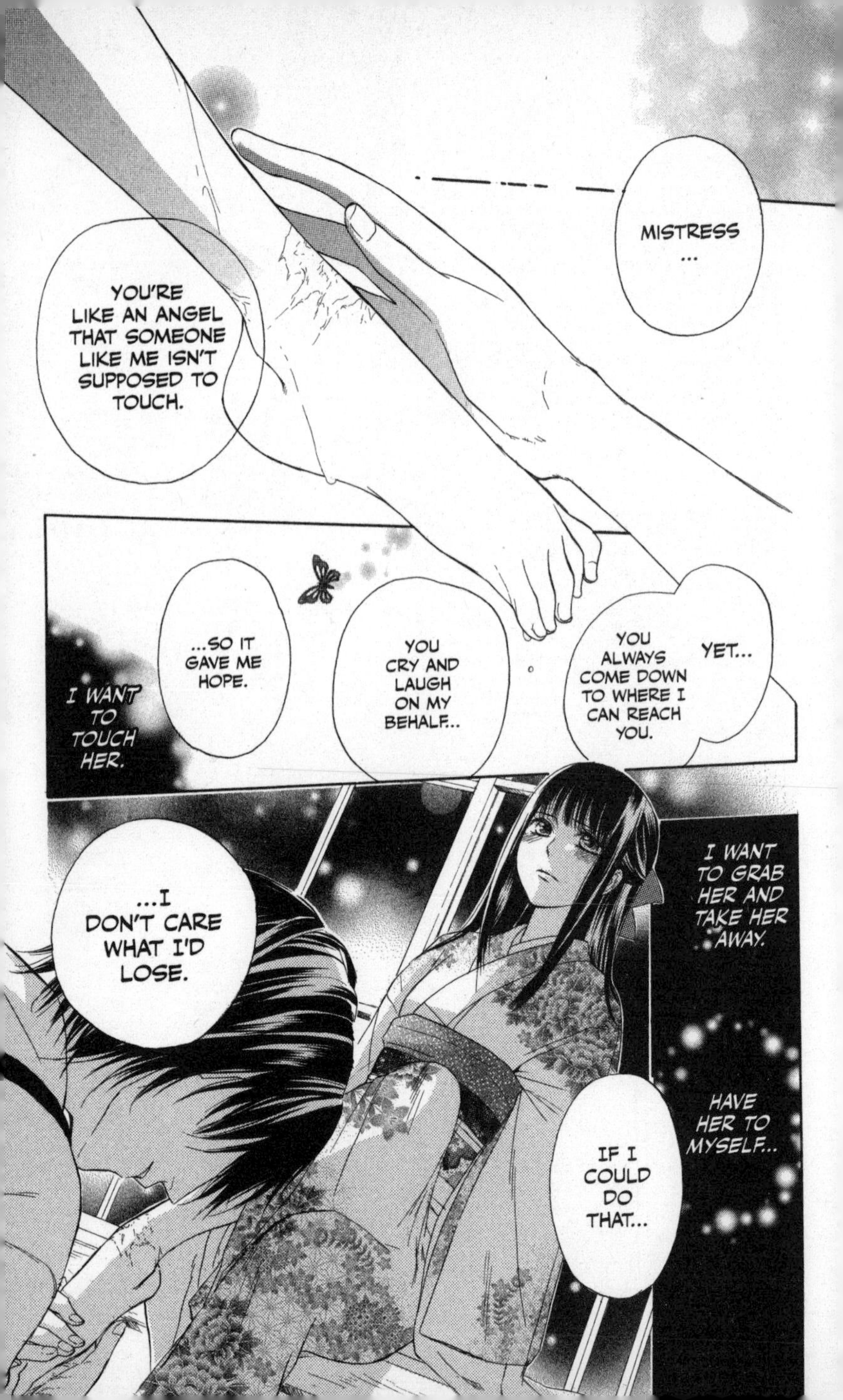
MISTRESS ...
YOU'RE LIKE AN ANGEL THAT SOMEONE LIKE ME ISN'T SUPPOSED TO TOUCH.
YET...
YOU ALWAYS COME DOWN TO WHERE I CAN REACH YOU.
YOU CRY AND LAUGH ON MY BEHALF...
...SO IT GAVE ME HOPE.
I WANT TO TOUCH HER.
I WANT TO GRAB HER AND TAKE HER AWAY.
HAVE HER TO MYSELF...
IF I COULD DO THAT...
...I DON'T CARE WHAT I'D LOSE.

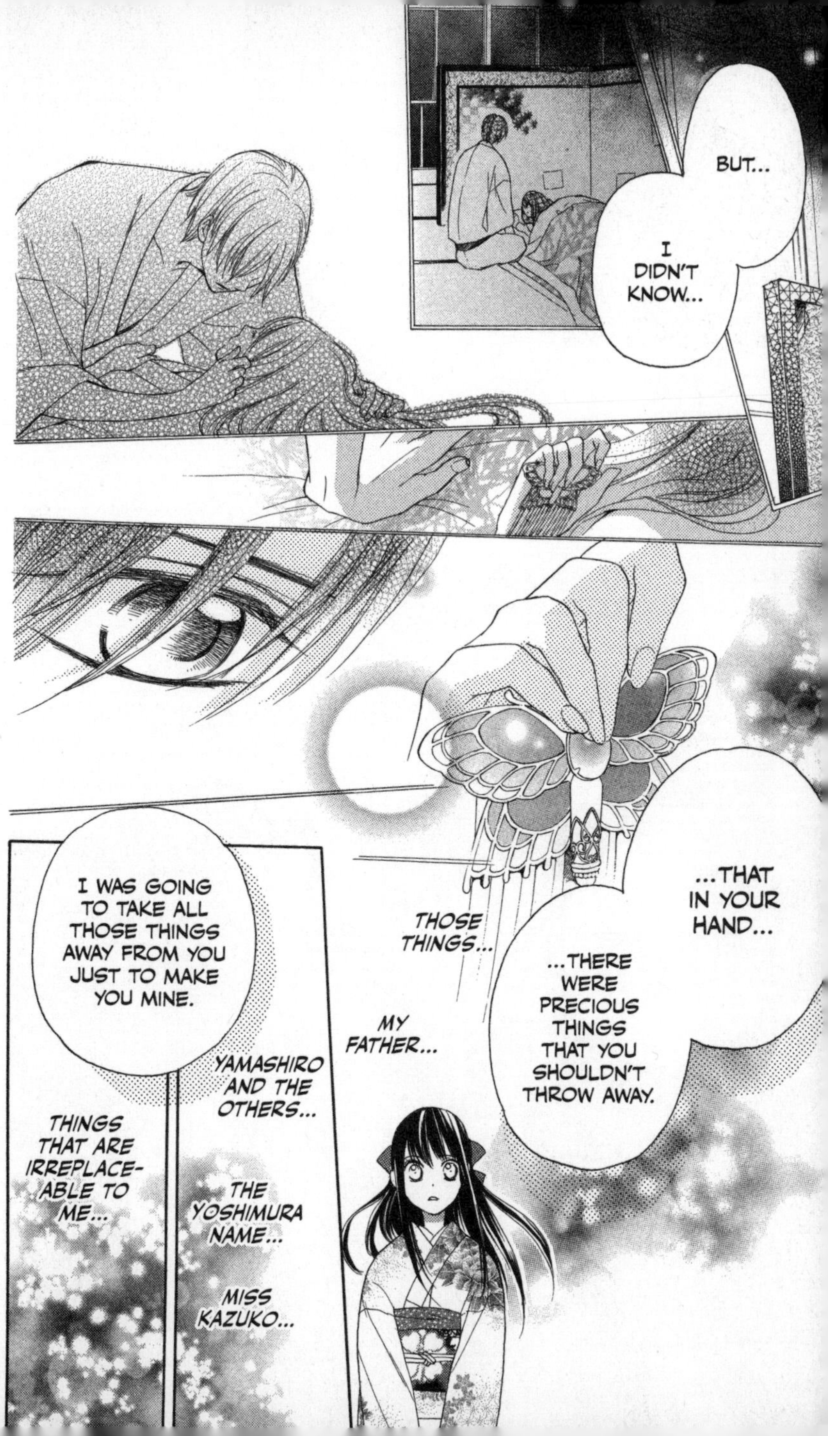
BUT...
I DIDN'T KNOW...
...THAT IN YOUR HAND...
...THERE WERE PRECIOUS THINGS THAT YOU SHOULDN'T THROW AWAY.
THOSE THINGS...
MY FATHER...
YAMASHIRO AND THE OTHERS...
THE YOSHIMURA NAME...
MISS KAZUKO...
I WAS GOING TO TAKE ALL THOSE THINGS AWAY FROM YOU JUST TO MAKE YOU MINE.
THINGS THAT ARE IRREPLACE-ABLE TO ME...

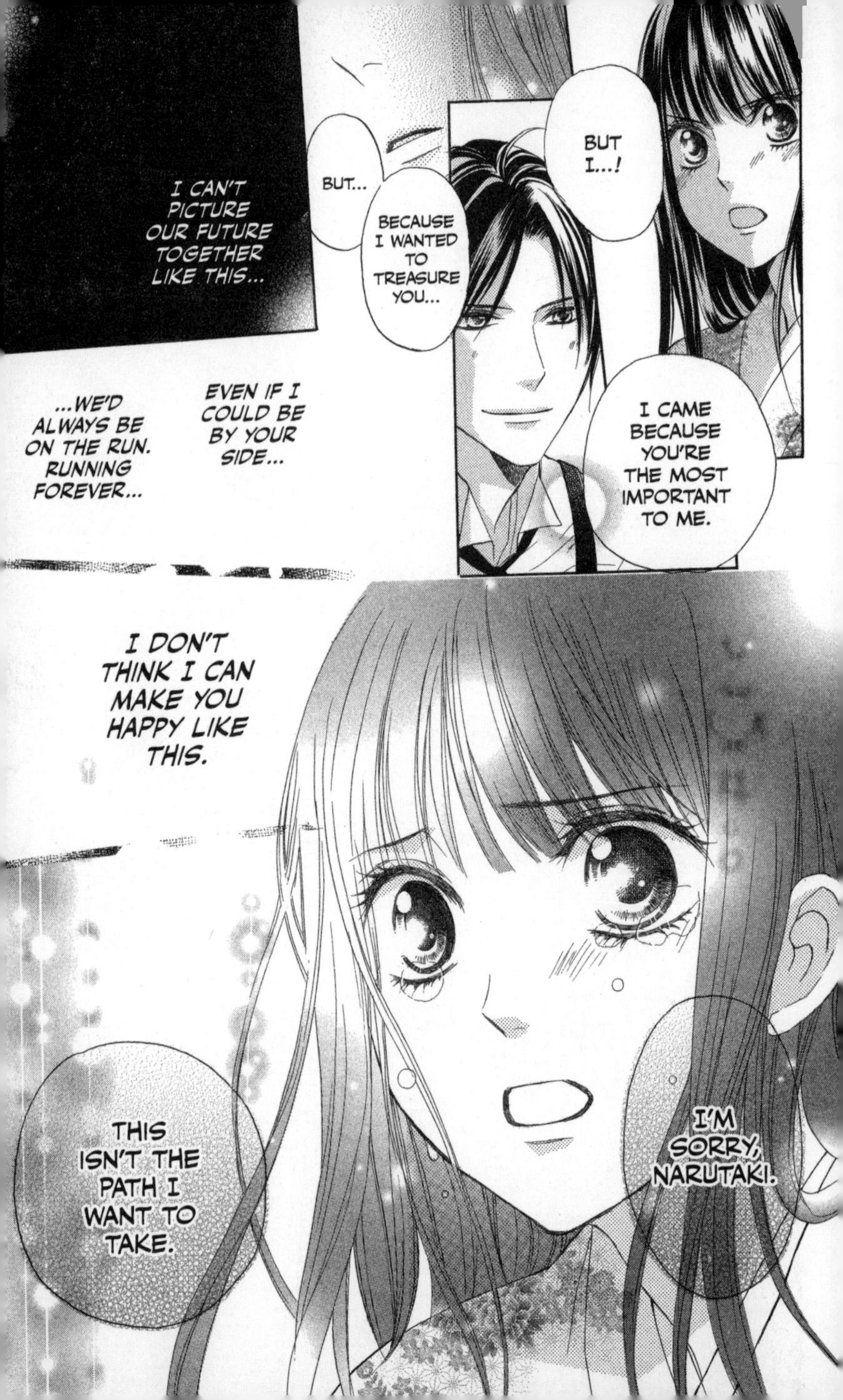
BUT I...!
I CAME BECAUSE YOU'RE THE MOST IMPORTANT TO ME.
BUT...
BECAUSE I WANTED TO TREASURE YOU...
I CAN'T PICTURE OUR FUTURE TOGETHER LIKE THIS...
EVEN IF I COULD BE BY YOUR SIDE...
...WE'D ALWAYS BE ON THE RUN. RUNNING FOREVER...
I DON'T THINK I CAN MAKE YOU HAPPY LIKE THIS.
I'M SORRY, NARUTAKI.
THIS ISN'T THE PATH I WANT TO TAKE.

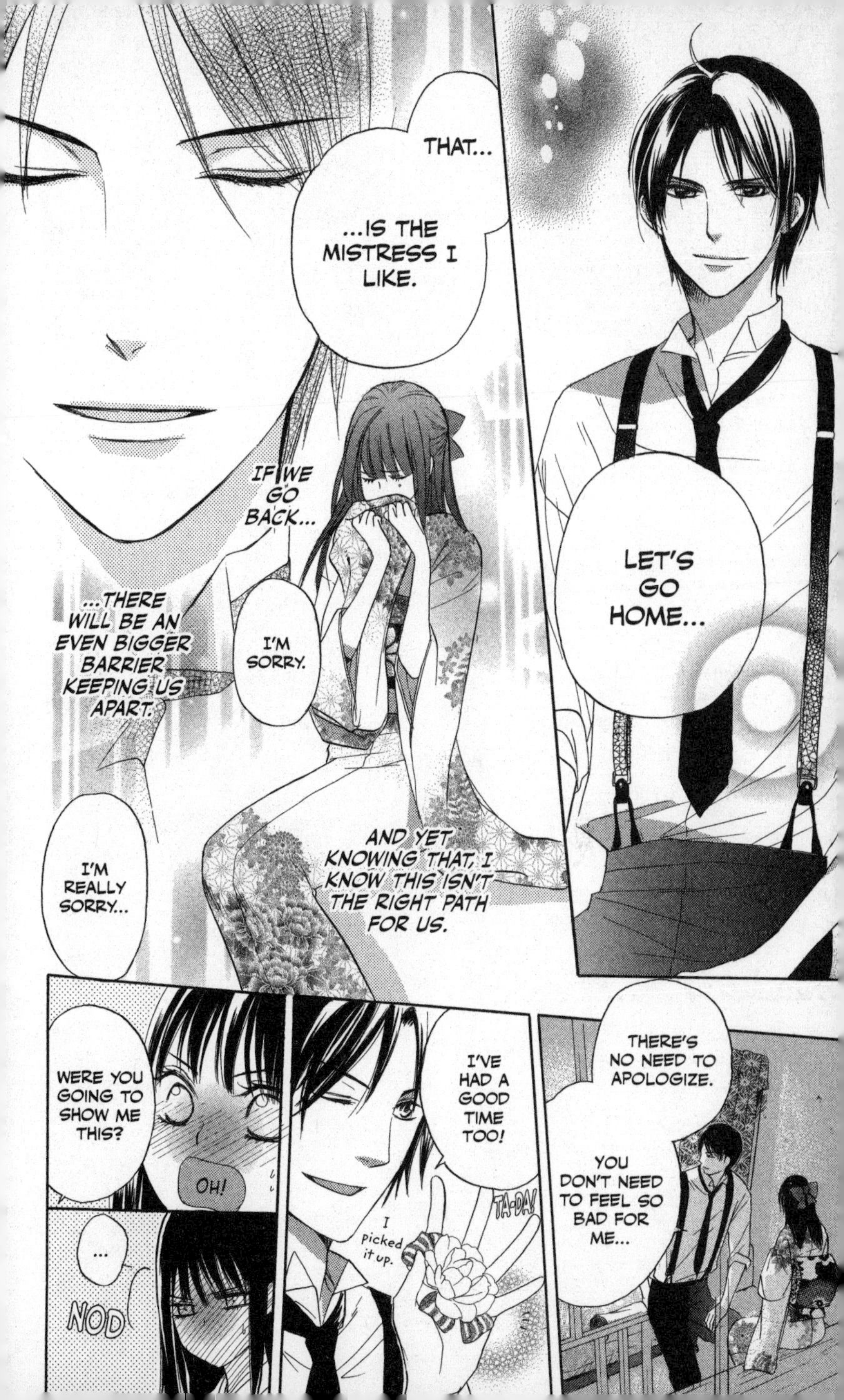
LET'S GO HOME...
THAT...
...IS THE MISTRESS I LIKE.
IF WE GO BACK...
...THERE WILL BE AN EVEN BIGGER BARRIER KEEPING US APART.
I'M SORRY.
AND YET KNOWING THAT, I KNOW THIS ISN'T THE RIGHT PATH FOR US.
I'M REALLY SORRY...
THERE'S NO NEED TO APOLOGIZE.
YOU DON'T NEED TO FEEL SO BAD FOR ME...
I'VE HAD A GOOD TIME TOO!
TA-DA!
I picked it up.
WERE YOU GOING TO SHOW ME THIS?
OH!
...
NOD

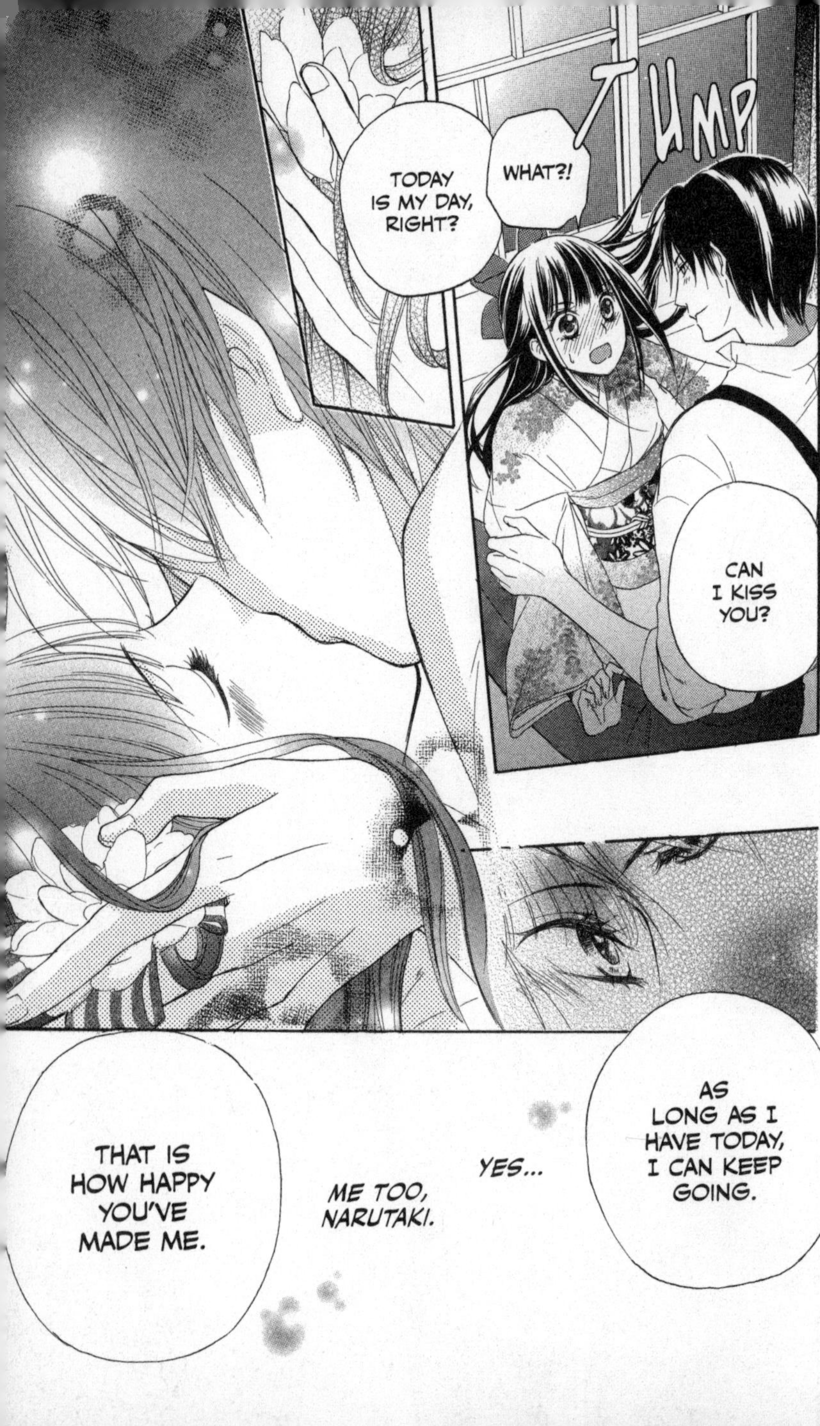
TUMP
WHAT?!
TODAY IS MY DAY, RIGHT?
CAN I KISS YOU?
AS LONG AS I HAVE TODAY, I CAN KEEP GOING.
YES...
ME TOO, NARUTAKI.
THAT IS HOW HAPPY YOU'VE MADE ME.

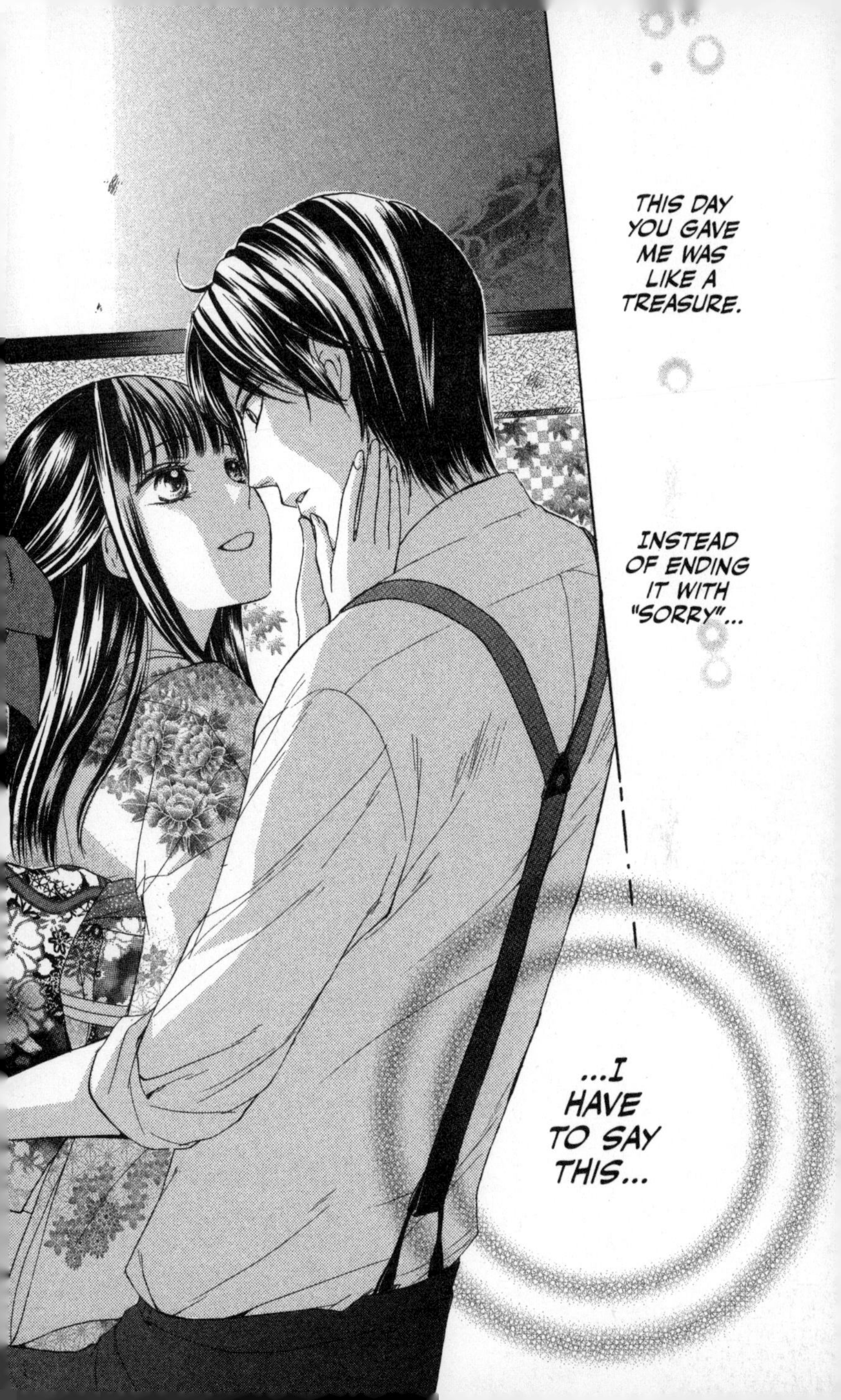
THIS DAY YOU GAVE ME WAS LIKE A TREASURE.
INSTEAD OF ENDING IT WITH "SORRY"...
...I HAVE TO SAY THIS...

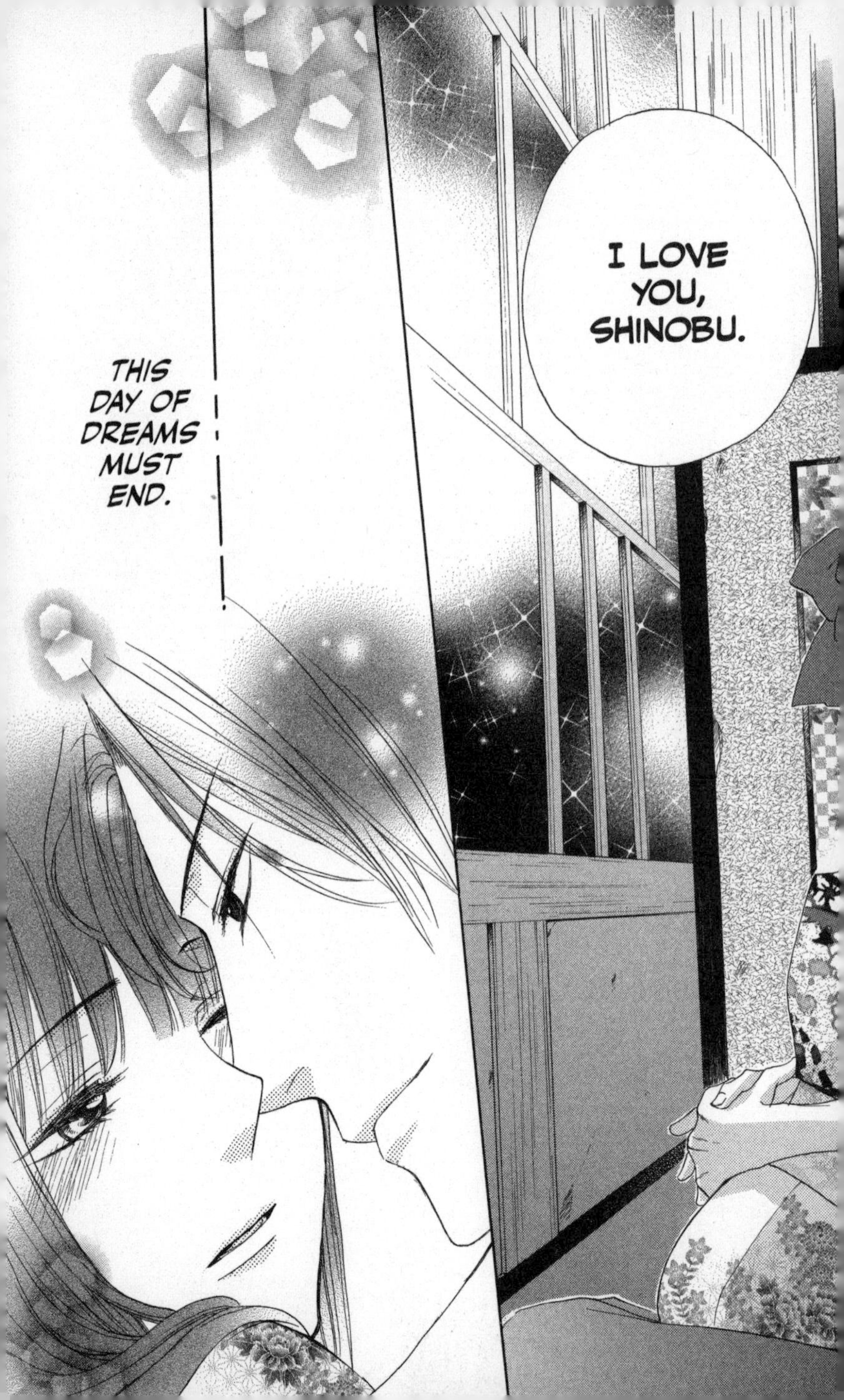
I LOVE YOU, SHINOBU.
THIS DAY OF DREAMS MUST END.

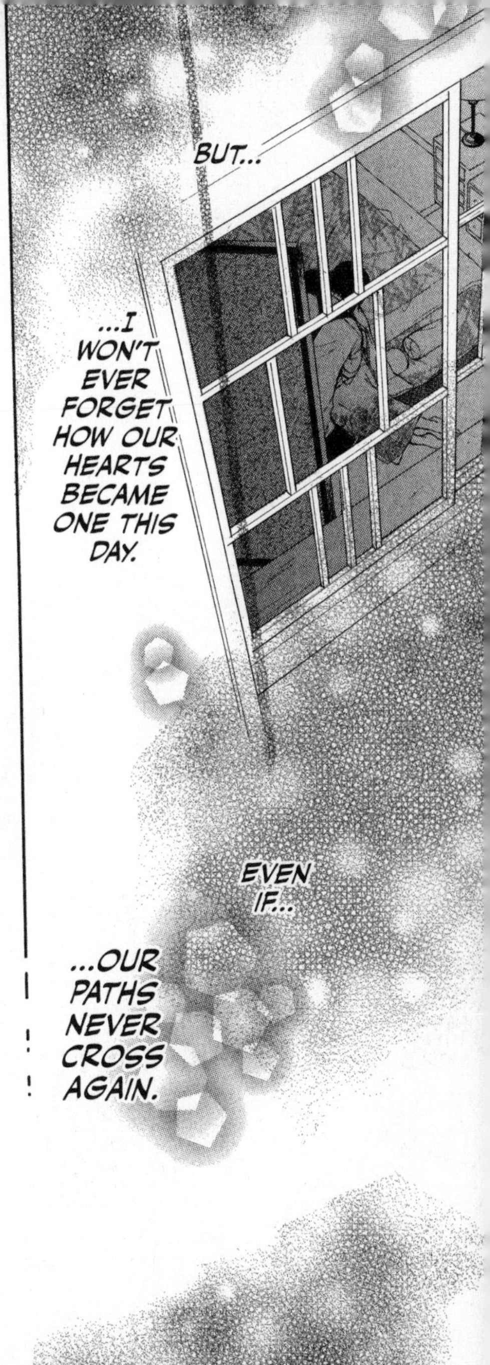
BUT...
...I WON'T EVER FORGET HOW OUR HEARTS BECAME ONE THIS DAY.
EVEN IF...
...OUR PATHS NEVER CROSS AGAIN.
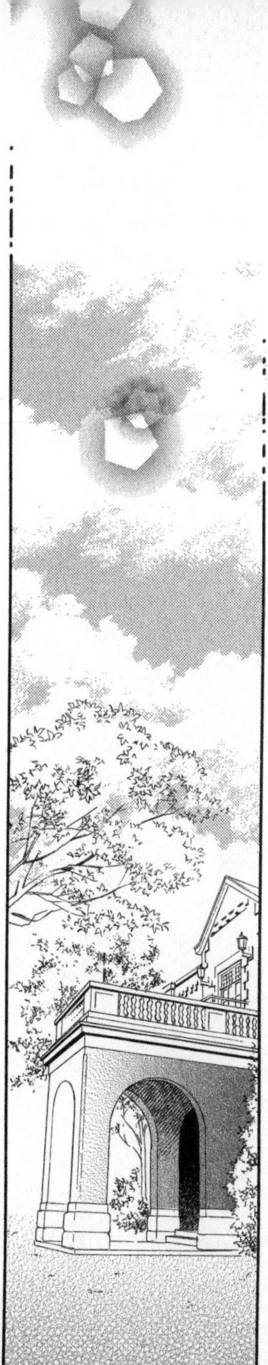

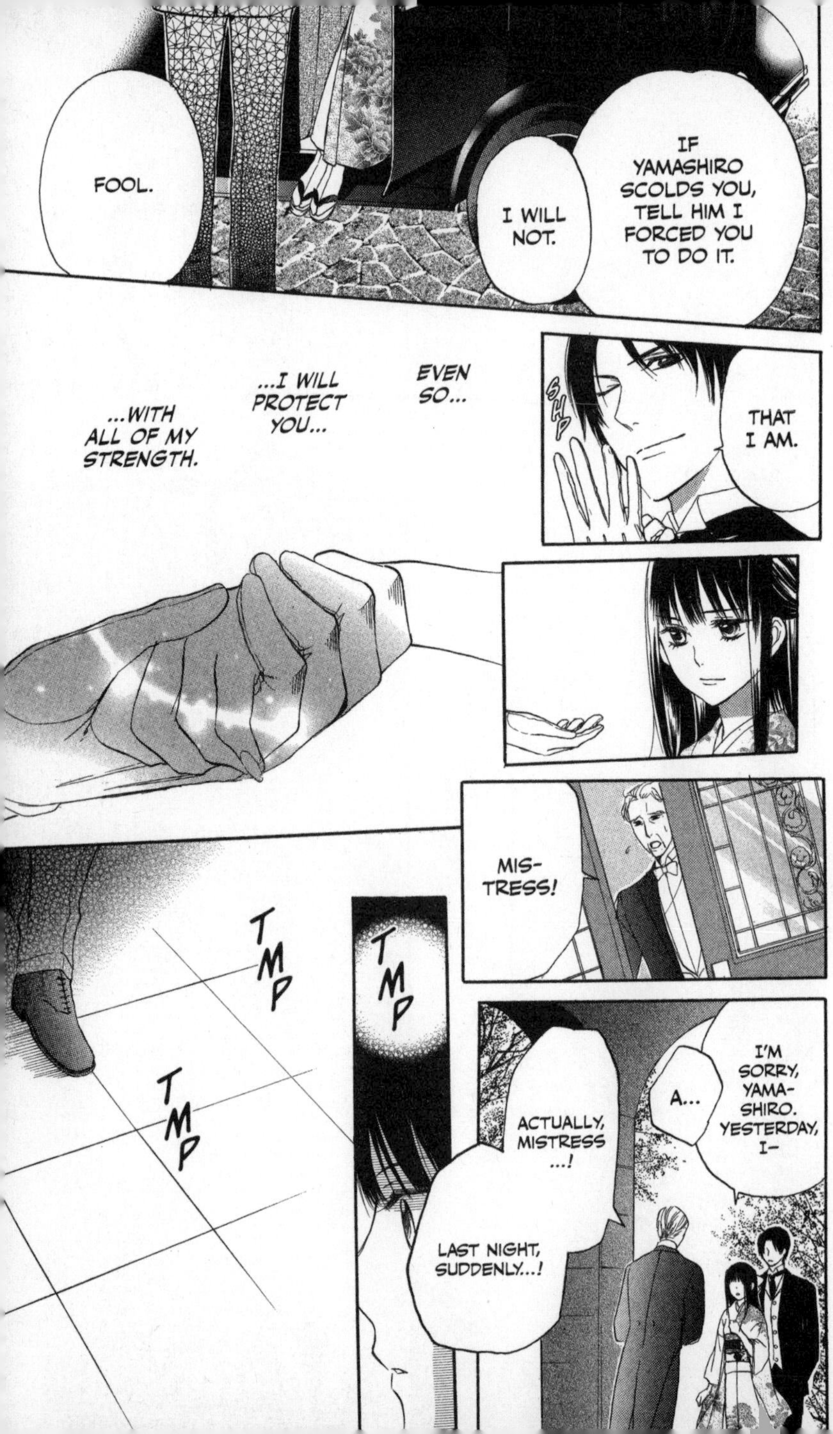
IF YAMASHIRO SCOLDS YOU, TELL HIM I FORCED YOU TO DO IT.
I WILL NOT.
FOOL.
THAT I AM.
SHP
EVEN SO...
...I WILL PROTECT YOU...
...WITH ALL OF MY STRENGTH.
MIS-TRESS!
I'M SORRY, YAMASHIRO. YESTERDAY, I—
A...
ACTUALLY, MISTRESS ...!
LAST NIGHT, SUDDENLY...!
TMP
TMP
TMP

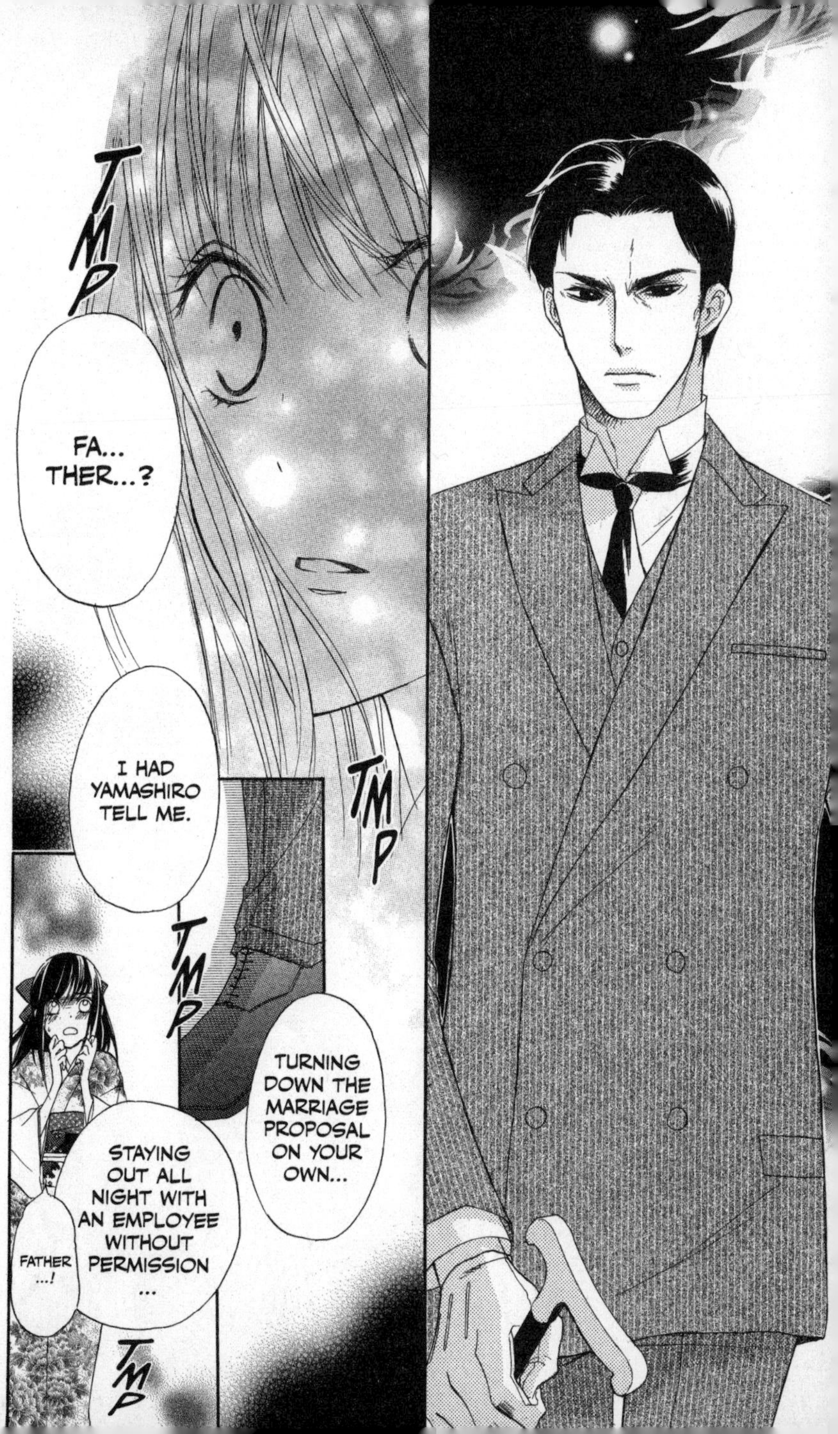

TMP
FA... THER...?
TMP
I HAD YAMASHIRO TELL ME.
TMP
TURNING DOWN THE MARRIAGE PROPOSAL ON YOUR OWN...
STAYING OUT ALL NIGHT WITH AN EMPLOYEE WITHOUT PERMISSION...
FATHER...!
TMP

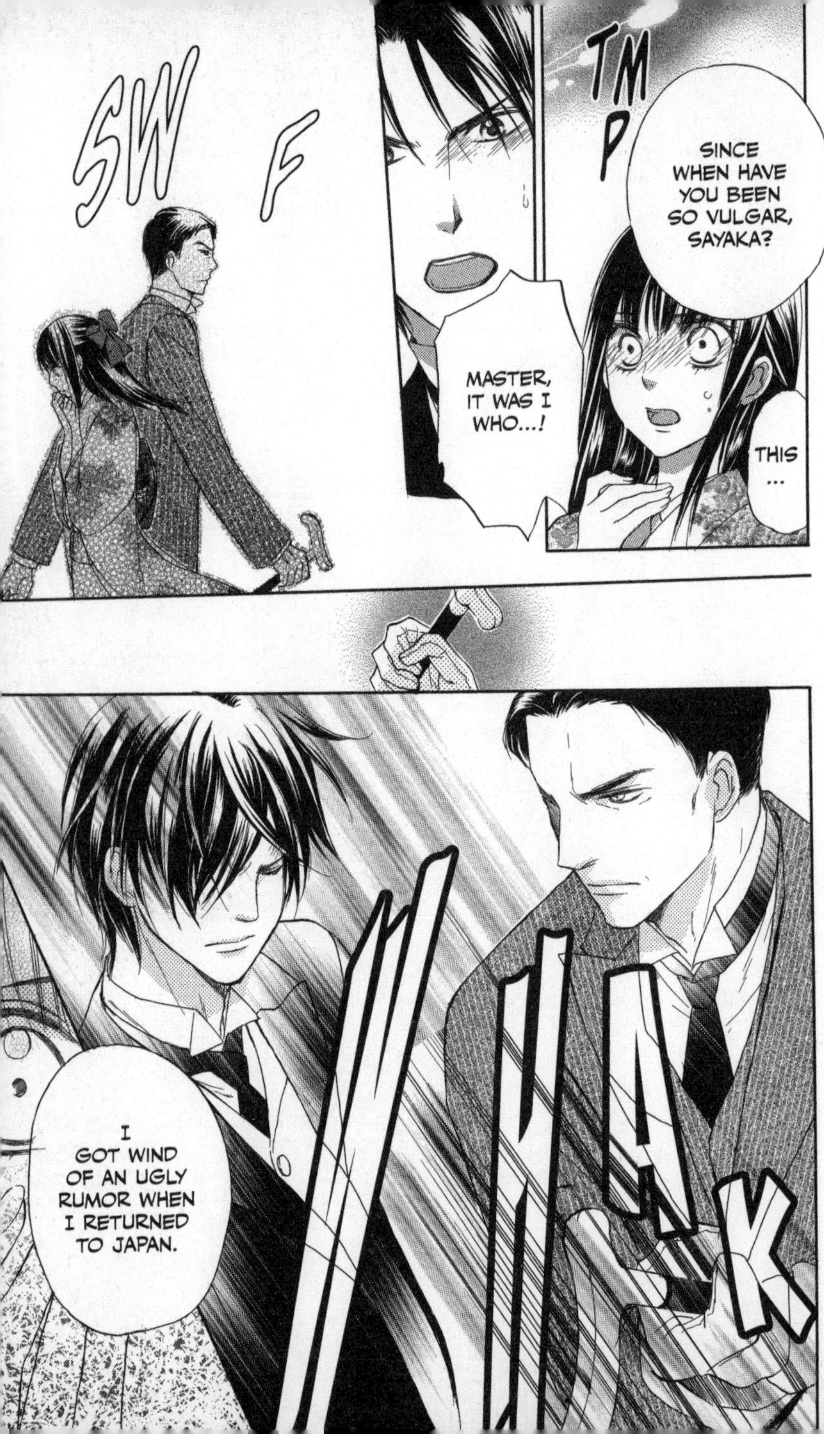
TMP
SINCE WHEN HAVE YOU BEEN SO VULGAR, SAYAKA?
THIS ...
MASTER, IT WAS I WHO...!
SWF
WHAK
I GOT WIND OF AN UGLY RUMOR WHEN I RETURNED TO JAPAN.

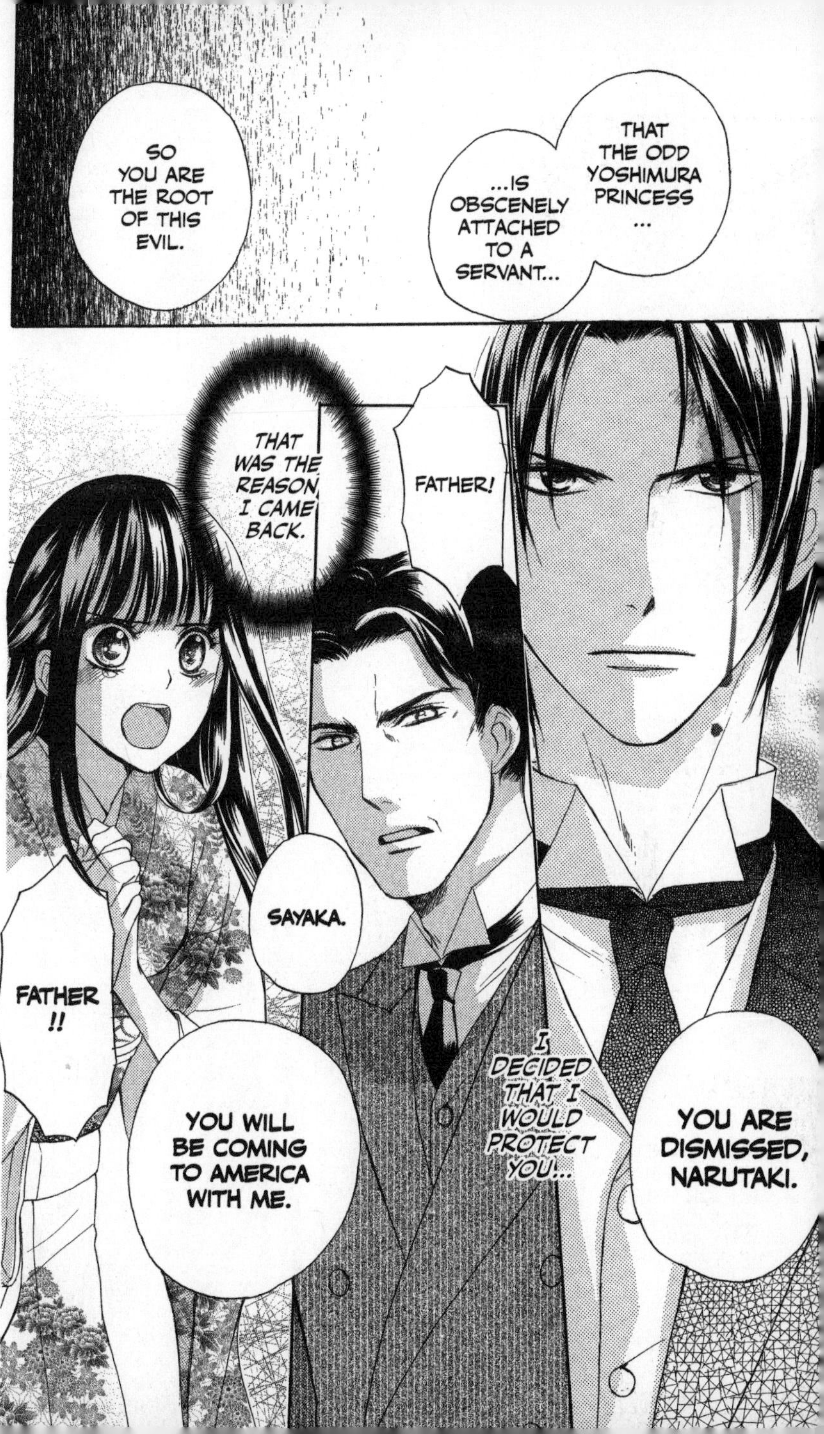
THAT THE ODD YOSHIMURA PRINCESS ...
...IS OBSCENELY ATTACHED TO A SERVANT...
SO YOU ARE THE ROOT OF THIS EVIL.
FATHER!
THAT WAS THE REASON I CAME BACK.
SAYAKA.
YOU ARE DISMISSED, NARUTAKI.
I DECIDED THAT I WOULD PROTECT YOU...
YOU WILL BE COMING TO AMERICA WITH ME.
FATHER !!

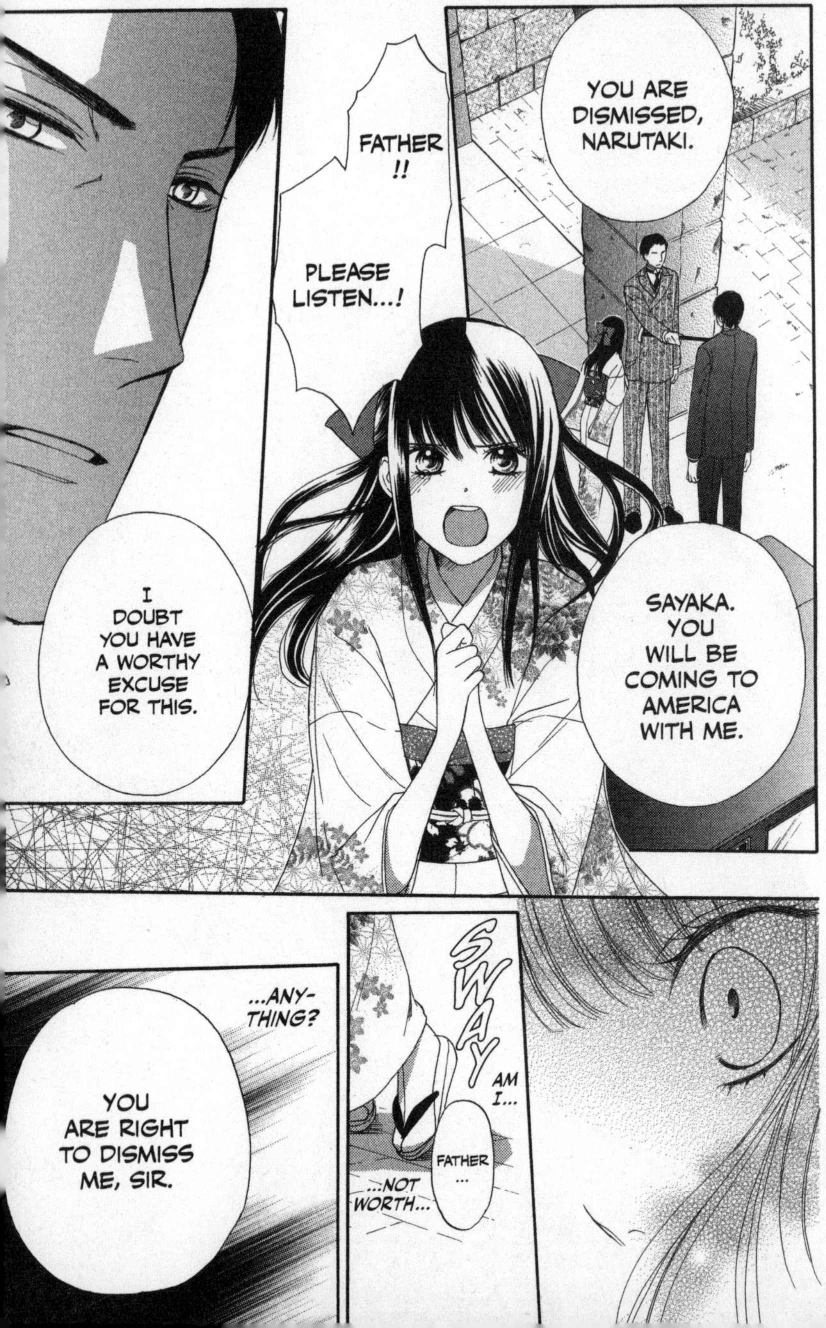
YOU ARE DISMISSED, NARUTAKI.
FATHER!!
PLEASE LISTEN...!
SAYAKA. YOU WILL BE COMING TO AMERICA WITH ME.
I DOUBT YOU HAVE A WORTHY EXCUSE FOR THIS.
SWAY
FATHER...
AM I...
...NOT WORTH...
...ANY-THING?
YOU ARE RIGHT TO DISMISS ME, SIR.

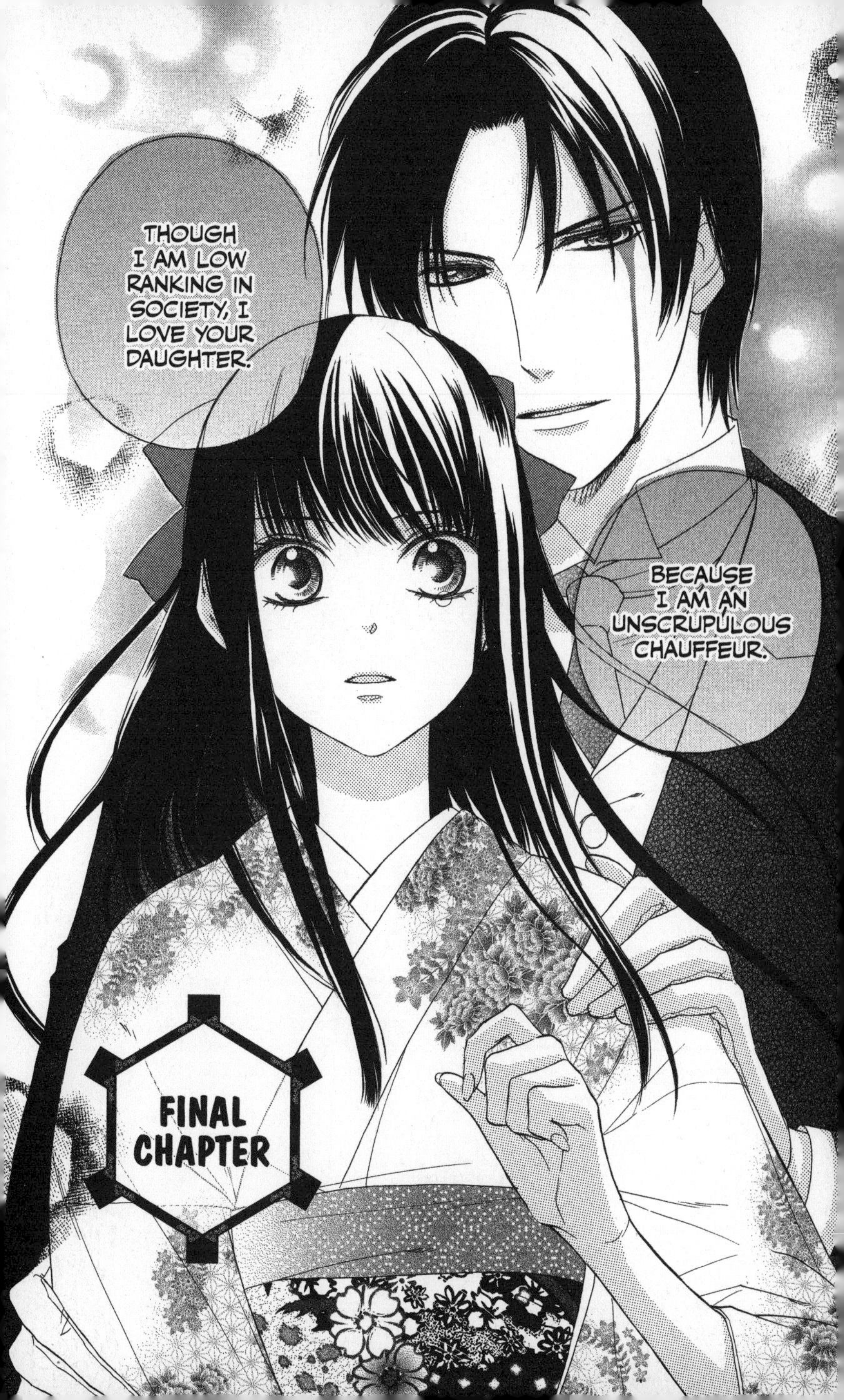
THOUGH I AM LOW RANKING IN SOCIETY, I LOVE YOUR DAUGHTER.
BECAUSE I AM AN UNSCRUPULOUS CHAUFFEUR.
FINAL CHAPTER

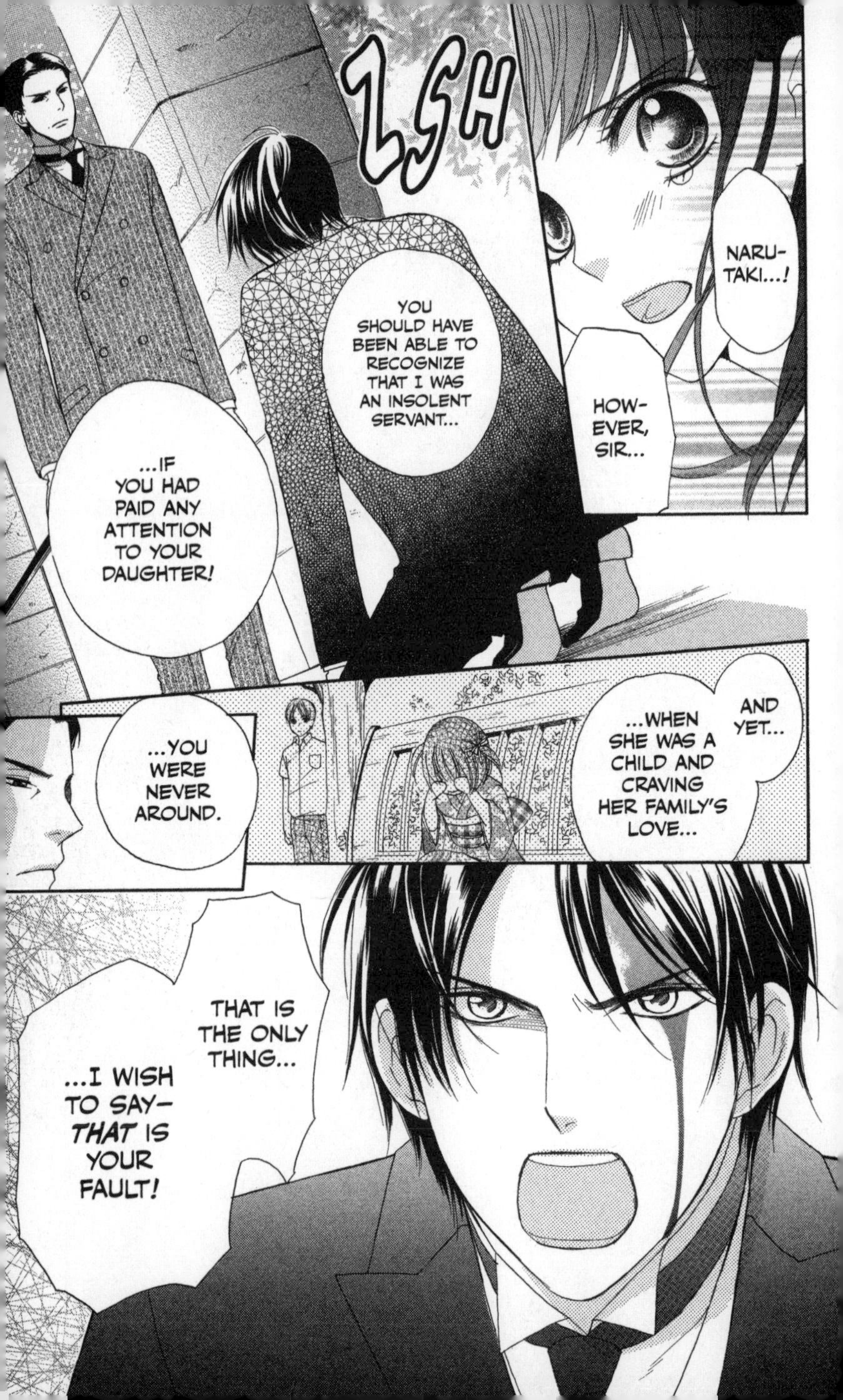
NARU-TAKI...!
HOW-EVER, SIR...
ZSH
YOU SHOULD HAVE BEEN ABLE TO RECOGNIZE THAT I WAS AN INSOLENT SERVANT...
...IF YOU HAD PAID ANY ATTENTION TO YOUR DAUGHTER!
AND YET...
...WHEN SHE WAS A CHILD AND CRAVING HER FAMILY'S LOVE...
...YOU WERE NEVER AROUND.
THAT IS THE ONLY THING...
...I WISH TO SAY—*THAT* IS YOUR FAULT!

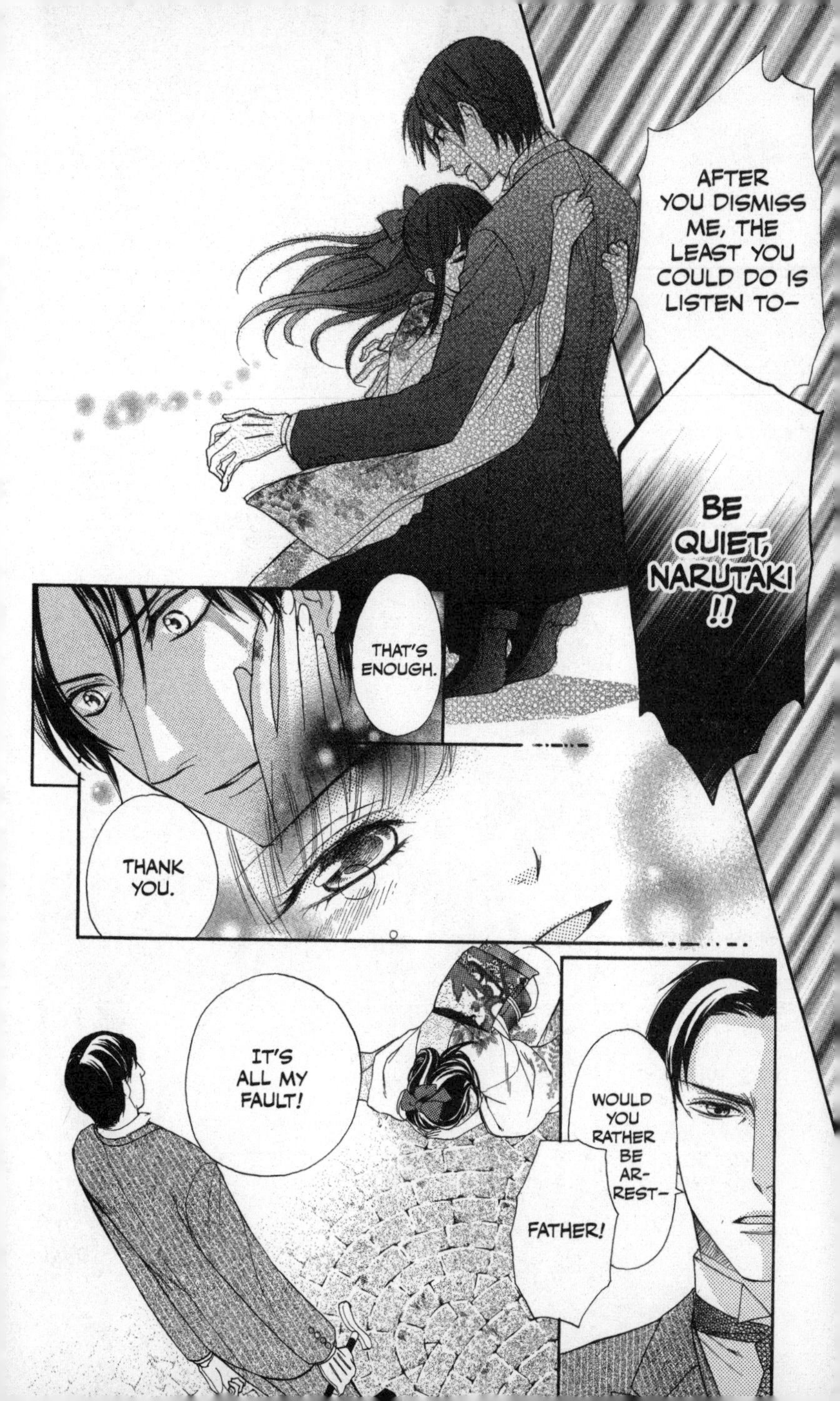
AFTER YOU DISMISS ME, THE LEAST YOU COULD DO IS LISTEN TO–
BE QUIET, NARUTAKI!!
THAT'S ENOUGH.
THANK YOU.
WOULD YOU RATHER BE AR-REST–
FATHER!
IT'S ALL MY FAULT!

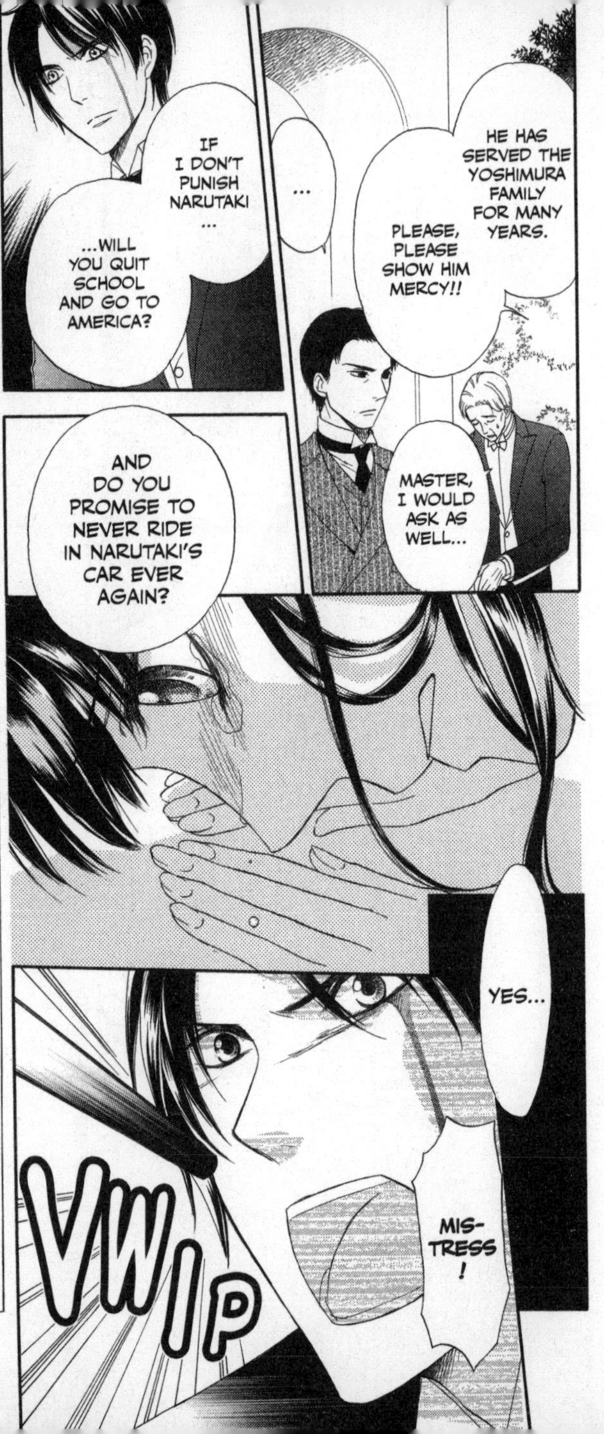
HE HAS SERVED THE YOSHIMURA FAMILY FOR MANY YEARS.
PLEASE, PLEASE SHOW HIM MERCY!!
...
MASTER, I WOULD ASK AS WELL...
IF I DON'T PUNISH NARUTAKI...
...WILL YOU QUIT SCHOOL AND GO TO AMERICA?
AND DO YOU PROMISE TO NEVER RIDE IN NARUTAKI'S CAR EVER AGAIN?
YES...
MISTRESS!
VWIP

ABOUT THE BASIS OF THIS STORY ②

Sadly, Yoshiko died in an accident at an early age. I think she had been happy though. When I was drawing the first chapter, I was thinking that if I were able to continue writing this story, I'd have them elope at the end like Yoshiko did.

However, this story ended up continuing for many more chapters. When I was talking to my editor about ending the series with an elopement, my editor said, "It's not like Sayaka to just throw everything away and run off." So that made me realize, "Yes, I think you're right."

I hadn't thought of any ending other than an elopement, but my editor was one step ahead of me and thought about the characters rationally. So the ending changed, but the basis of the Tadas still lives on in the story.

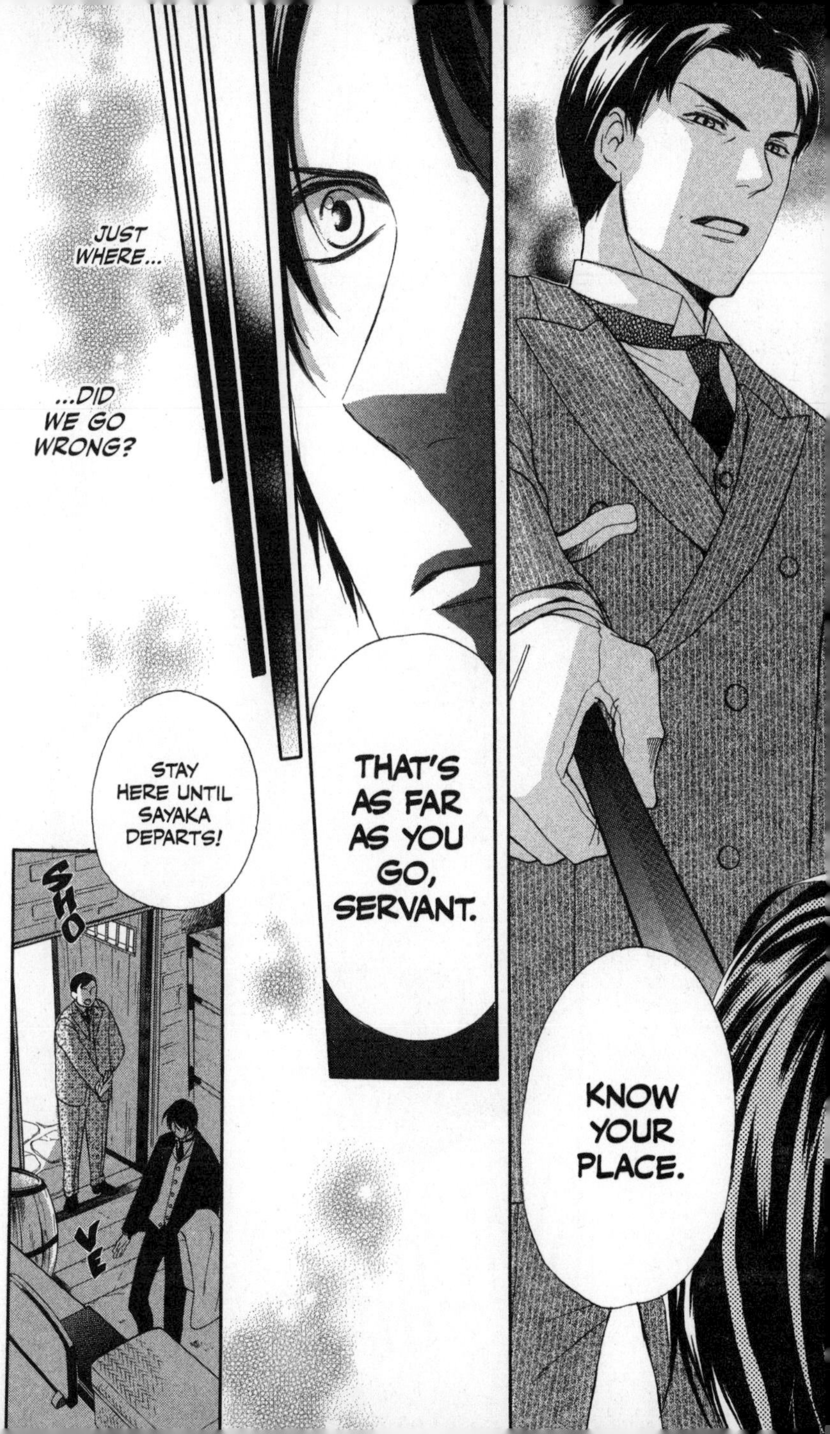
THAT'S AS FAR AS YOU GO, SERVANT.
KNOW YOUR PLACE.
JUST WHERE...
...DID WE GO WRONG?
STAY HERE UNTIL SAYAKA DEPARTS!
SHOVE

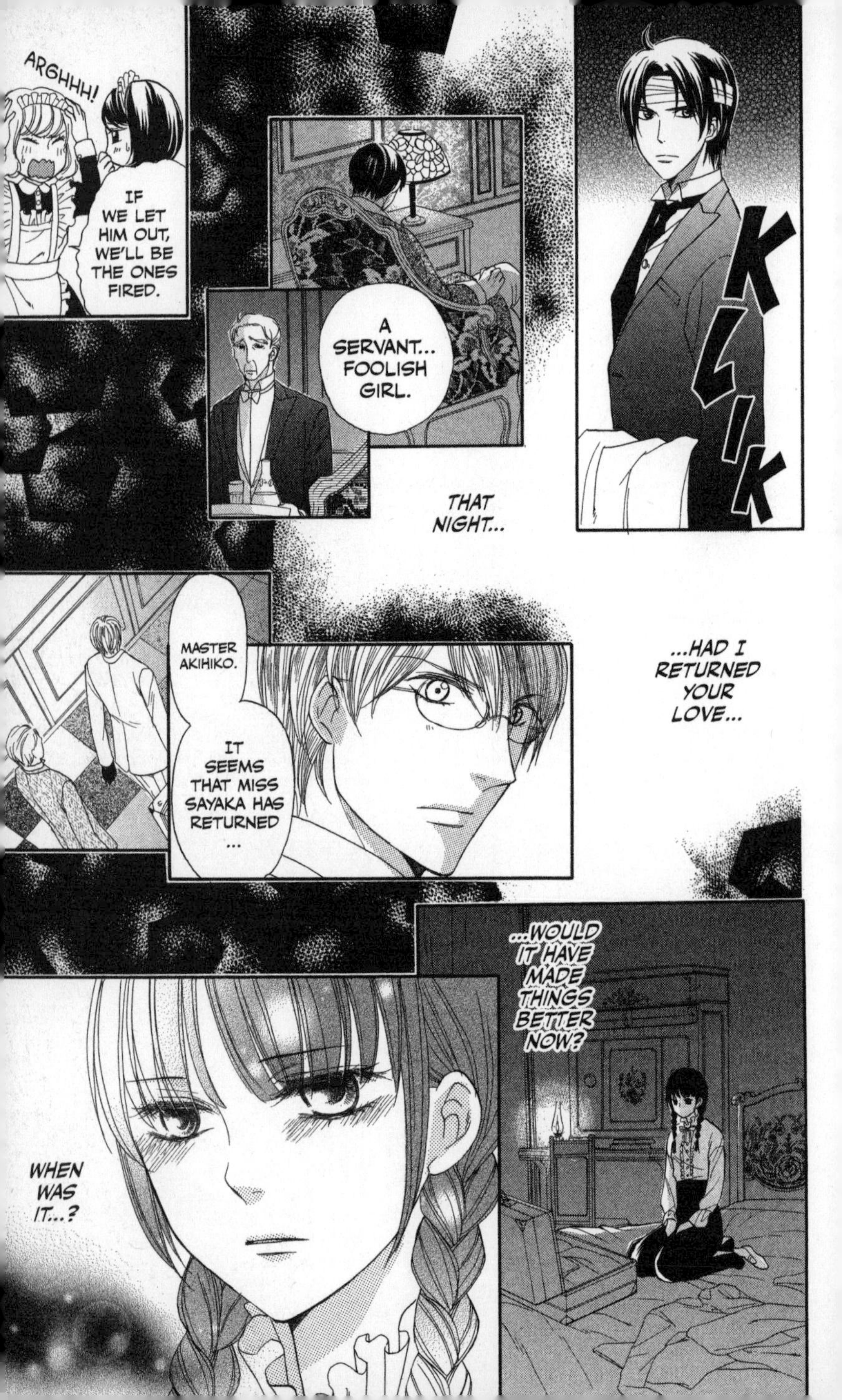
KLIK
THAT NIGHT...
A SERVANT... FOOLISH GIRL.
ARGHHH!
IF WE LET HIM OUT, WE'LL BE THE ONES FIRED.
...HAD I RETURNED YOUR LOVE...
MASTER AKIHIKO.
IT SEEMS THAT MISS SAYAKA HAS RETURNED ...
...WOULD IT HAVE MADE THINGS BETTER NOW?
WHEN WAS IT...?

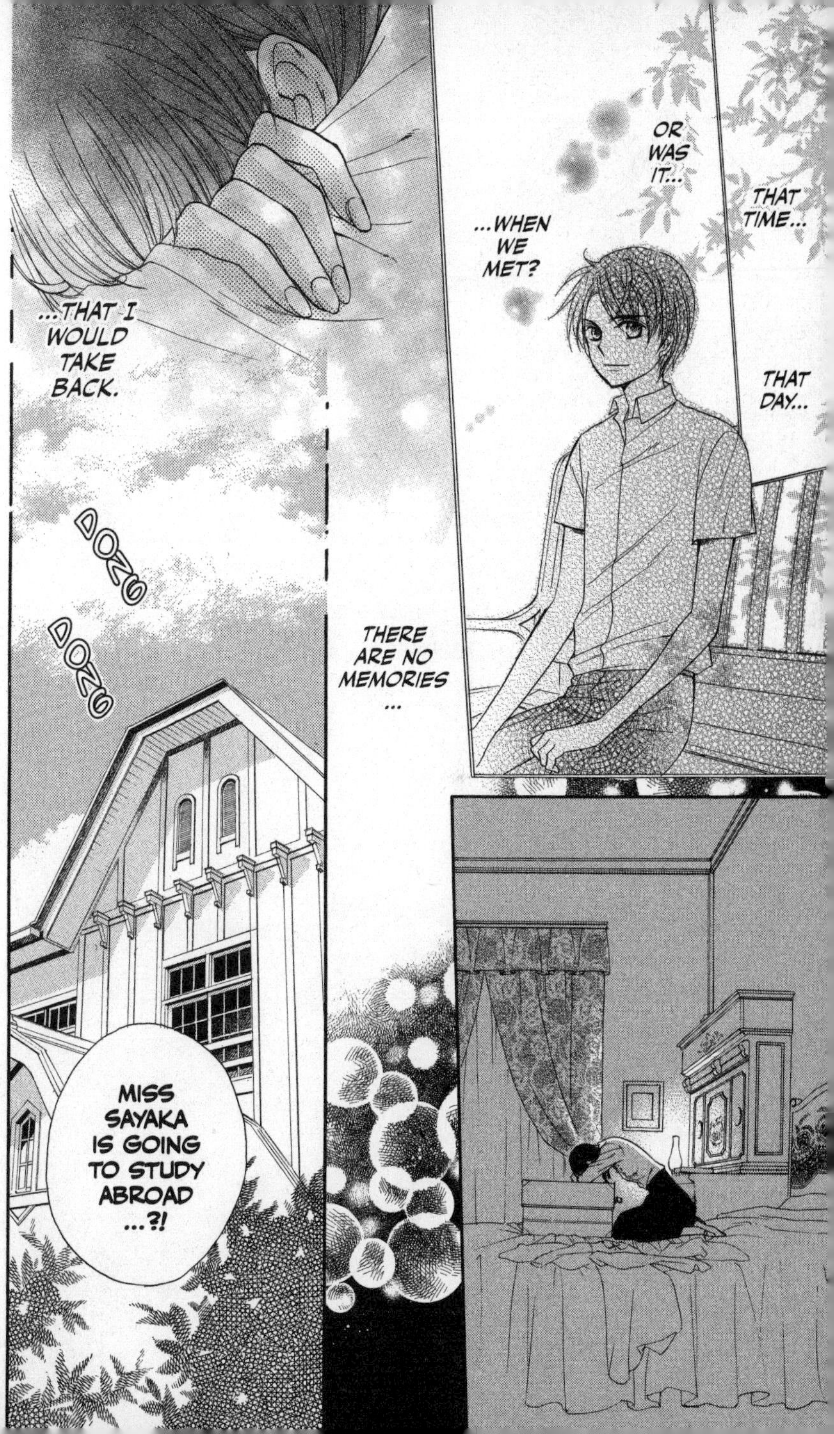
THAT TIME...
THAT DAY...
OR WAS IT...
...WHEN WE MET?
THERE ARE NO MEMORIES...
...THAT I WOULD TAKE BACK.
DONG
DONG
MISS SAYAKA IS GOING TO STUDY ABROAD...?!

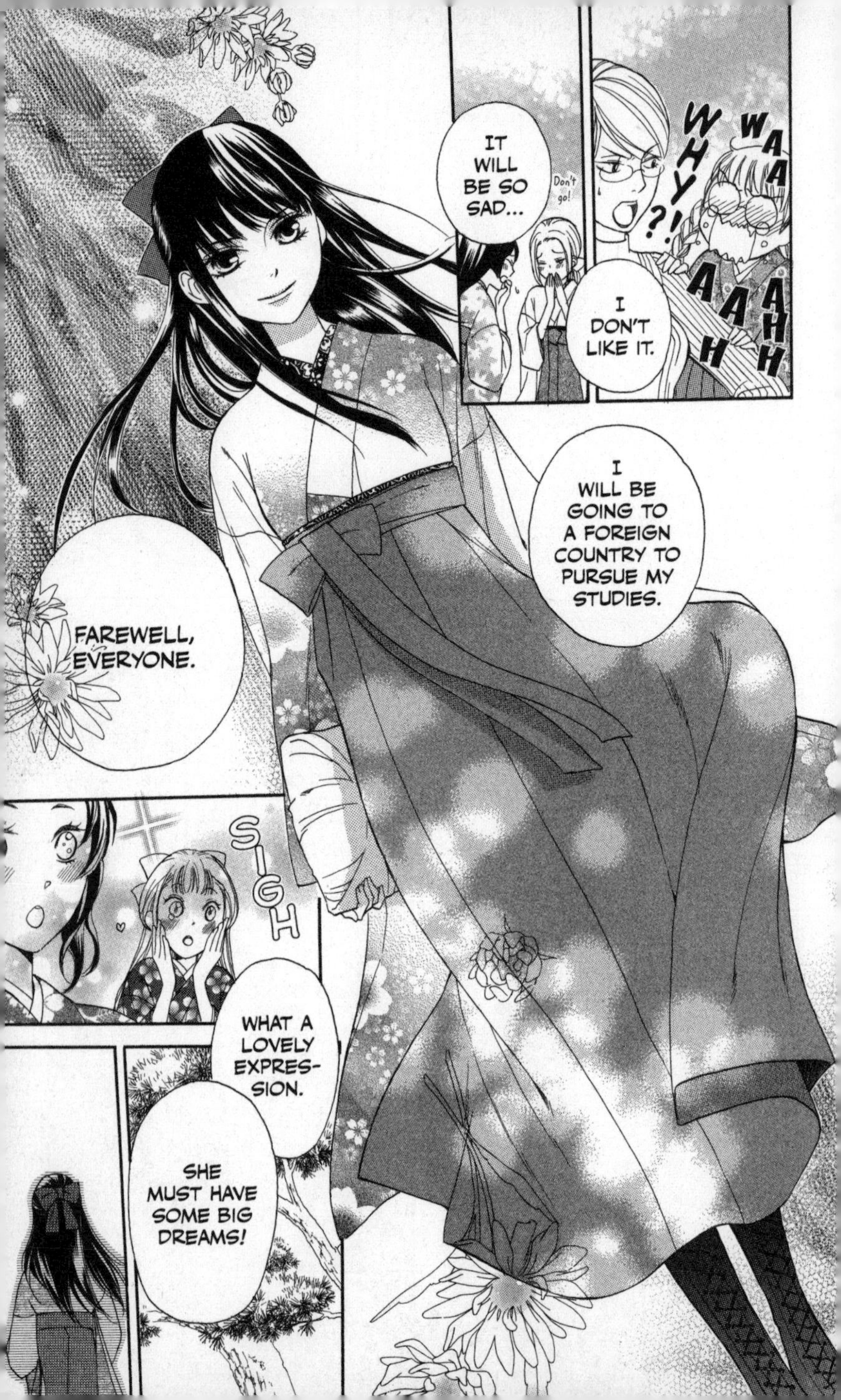
WAAAAHH
WHY?!
I DON'T LIKE IT.
IT WILL BE SO SAD...
Don't go!
I WILL BE GOING TO A FOREIGN COUNTRY TO PURSUE MY STUDIES.
FAREWELL, EVERYONE.
SIGH
WHAT A LOVELY EXPRES-SION.
SHE MUST HAVE SOME BIG DREAMS!

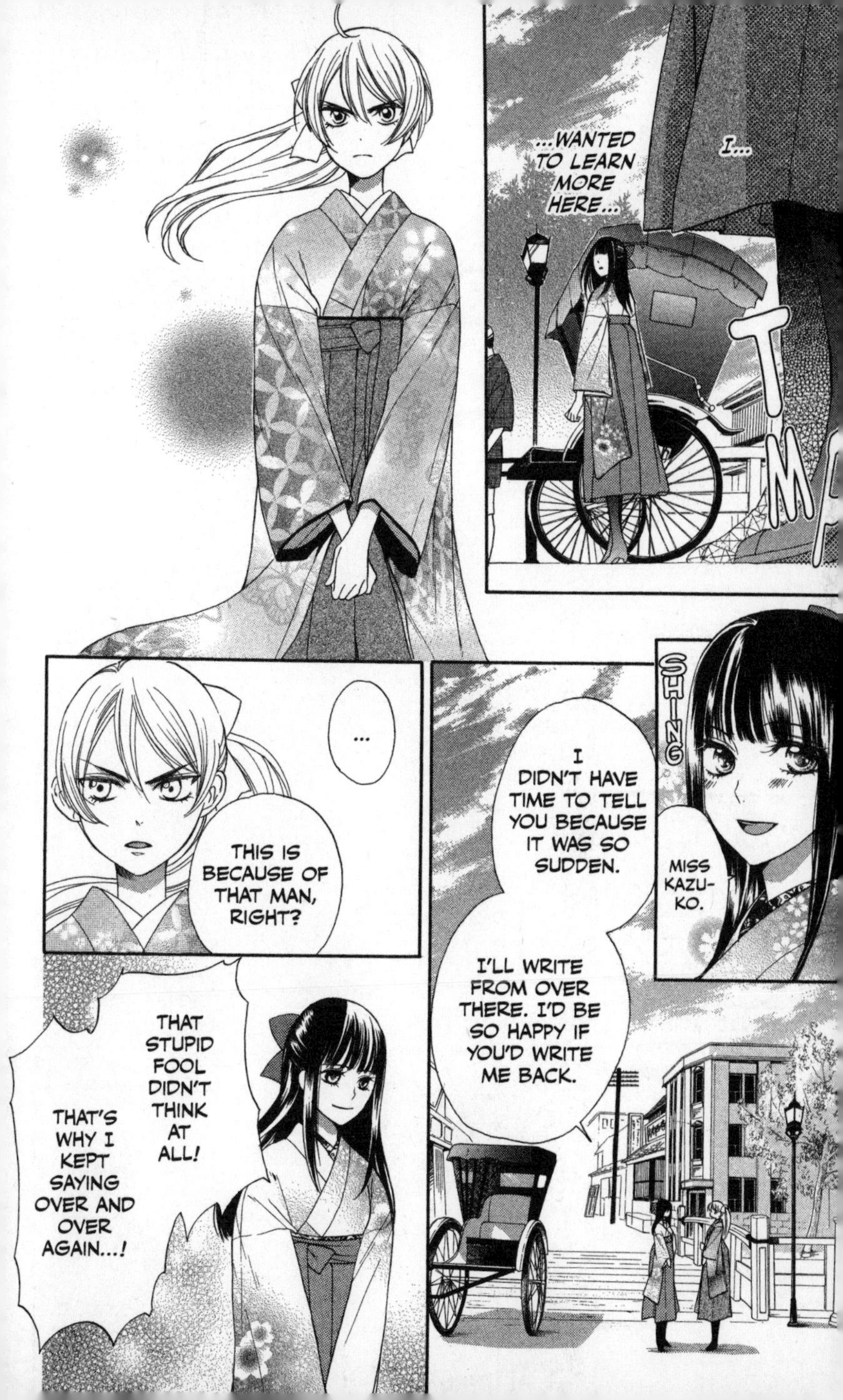
I...
...WANTED TO LEARN MORE HERE...
SHING
MISS KAZUKO.
I DIDN'T HAVE TIME TO TELL YOU BECAUSE IT WAS SO SUDDEN.
I'LL WRITE FROM OVER THERE. I'D BE SO HAPPY IF YOU'D WRITE ME BACK.
...
THIS IS BECAUSE OF THAT MAN, RIGHT?
THAT STUPID FOOL DIDN'T THINK AT ALL!
THAT'S WHY I KEPT SAYING OVER AND OVER AGAIN...!

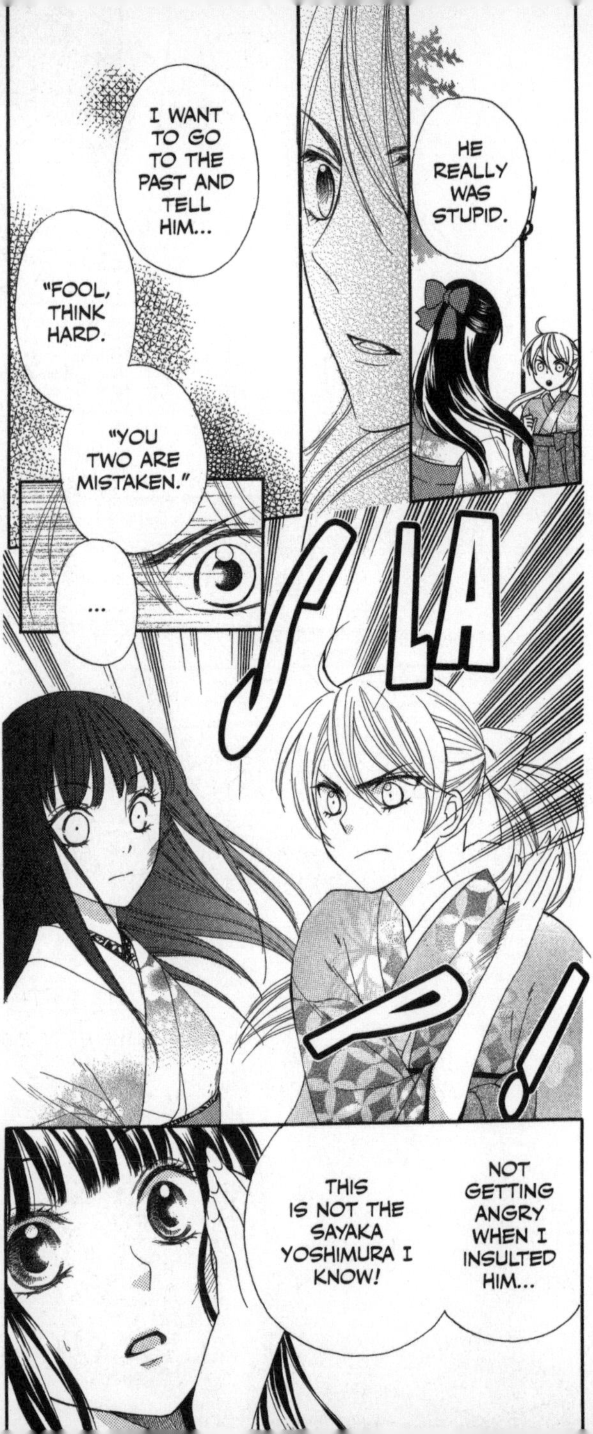
HE REALLY WAS STUPID.
I WANT TO GO TO THE PAST AND TELL HIM...
"FOOL, THINK HARD.
"YOU TWO ARE MISTAKEN."
...
LA
NOT GETTING ANGRY WHEN I INSULTED HIM...
THIS IS NOT THE SAYAKA YOSHIMURA I KNOW!

FINAL CHAPTER

I got sick during production, so this last chapter was really difficult.

When I was writing the storyboards, I felt so sad and got teary eyed thinking that I'd never get to write about these two again. But during the drawing phase, I was in such a rush that I didn't have time to get sad. It was over before I knew it. Because of the page count, I had to put the chapter title on a regular page. That was really disappointing.

I had decided that the illustration on all the chapter title pages would have them touching somewhere. I really wanted to stick to that concept and thought a lot about it.

I was able to finish drawing without any problems because of all the support I received from people around me. Thank you very much.

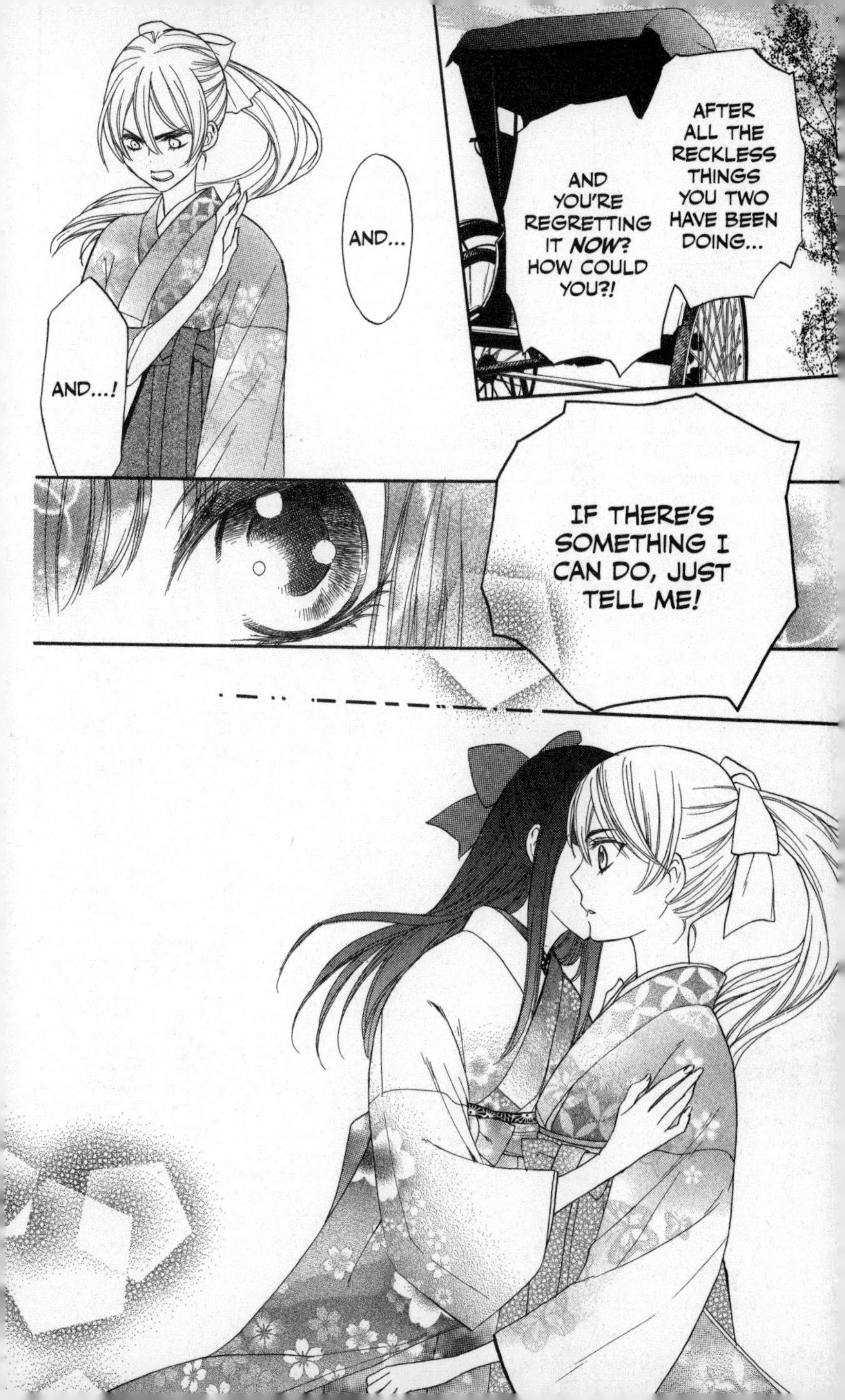
AFTER ALL THE RECKLESS THINGS YOU TWO HAVE BEEN DOING...
AND YOU'RE REGRETTING IT *NOW*? HOW COULD YOU?!
AND...
AND...!
IF THERE'S SOMETHING I CAN DO, JUST TELL ME!

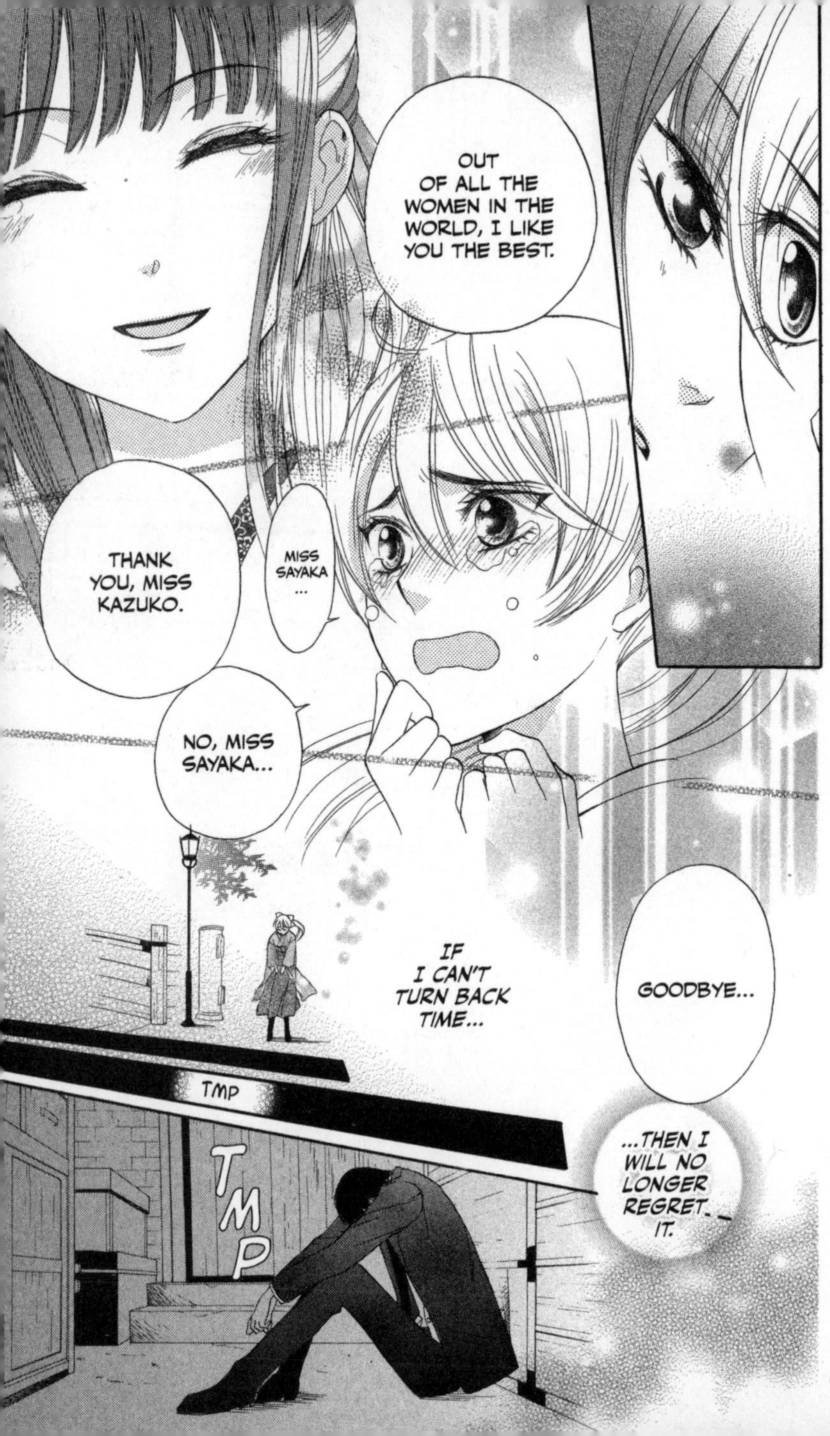
OUT OF ALL THE WOMEN IN THE WORLD, I LIKE YOU THE BEST.
MISS SAYAKA...
THANK YOU, MISS KAZUKO.
NO, MISS SAYAKA...
GOODBYE...
IF I CAN'T TURN BACK TIME...
TMP
TMP
...THEN I WILL NO LONGER REGRET IT.

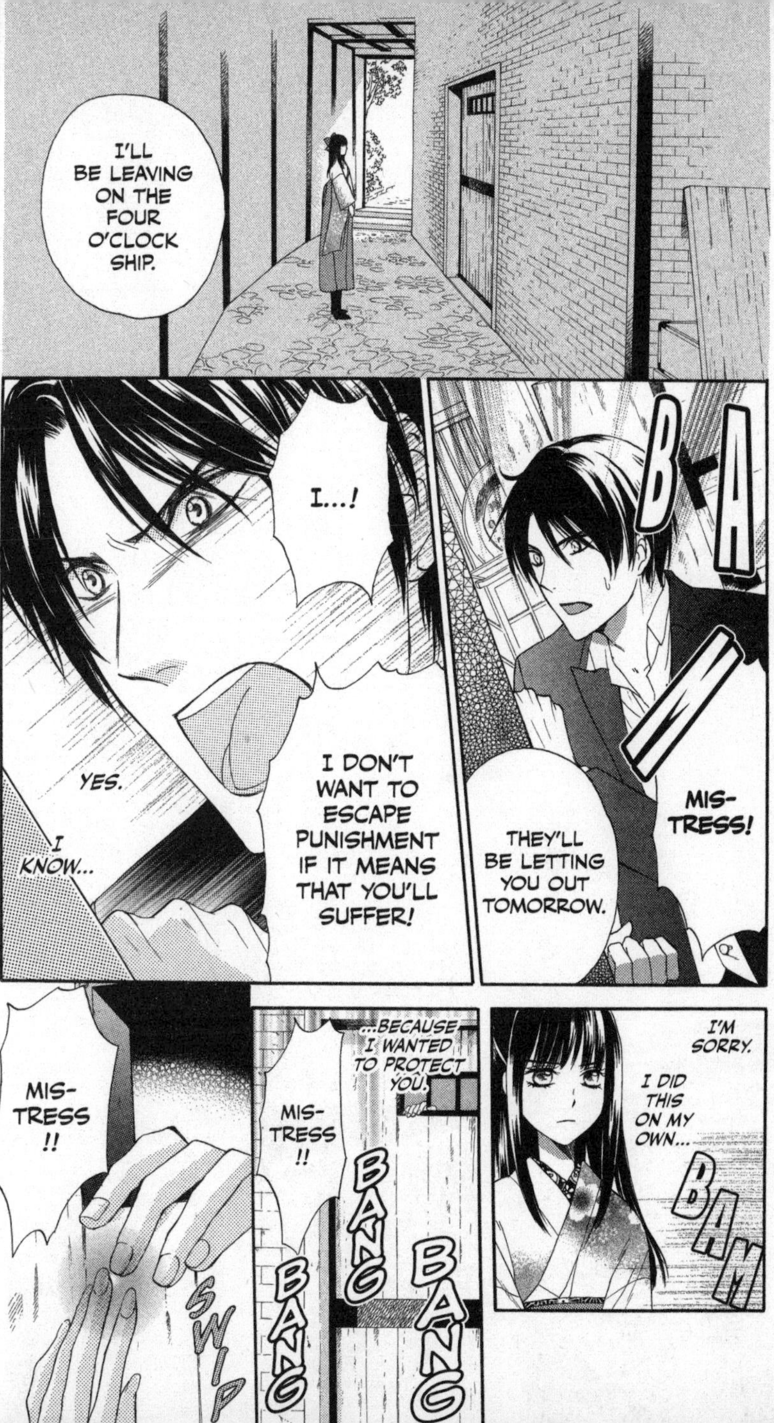
I'LL BE LEAVING ON THE FOUR O'CLOCK SHIP.
BAM
MIS-TRESS!
THEY'LL BE LETTING YOU OUT TOMORROW.
I...!
I DON'T WANT TO ESCAPE PUNISHMENT IF IT MEANS THAT YOU'LL SUFFER!
YES.
I KNOW...
I'M SORRY.
I DID THIS ON MY OWN...
BAM
...BECAUSE I WANTED TO PROTECT YOU.
MIS-TRESS !!
BANG
BANG
BANG
MIS-TRESS !!
SWIP

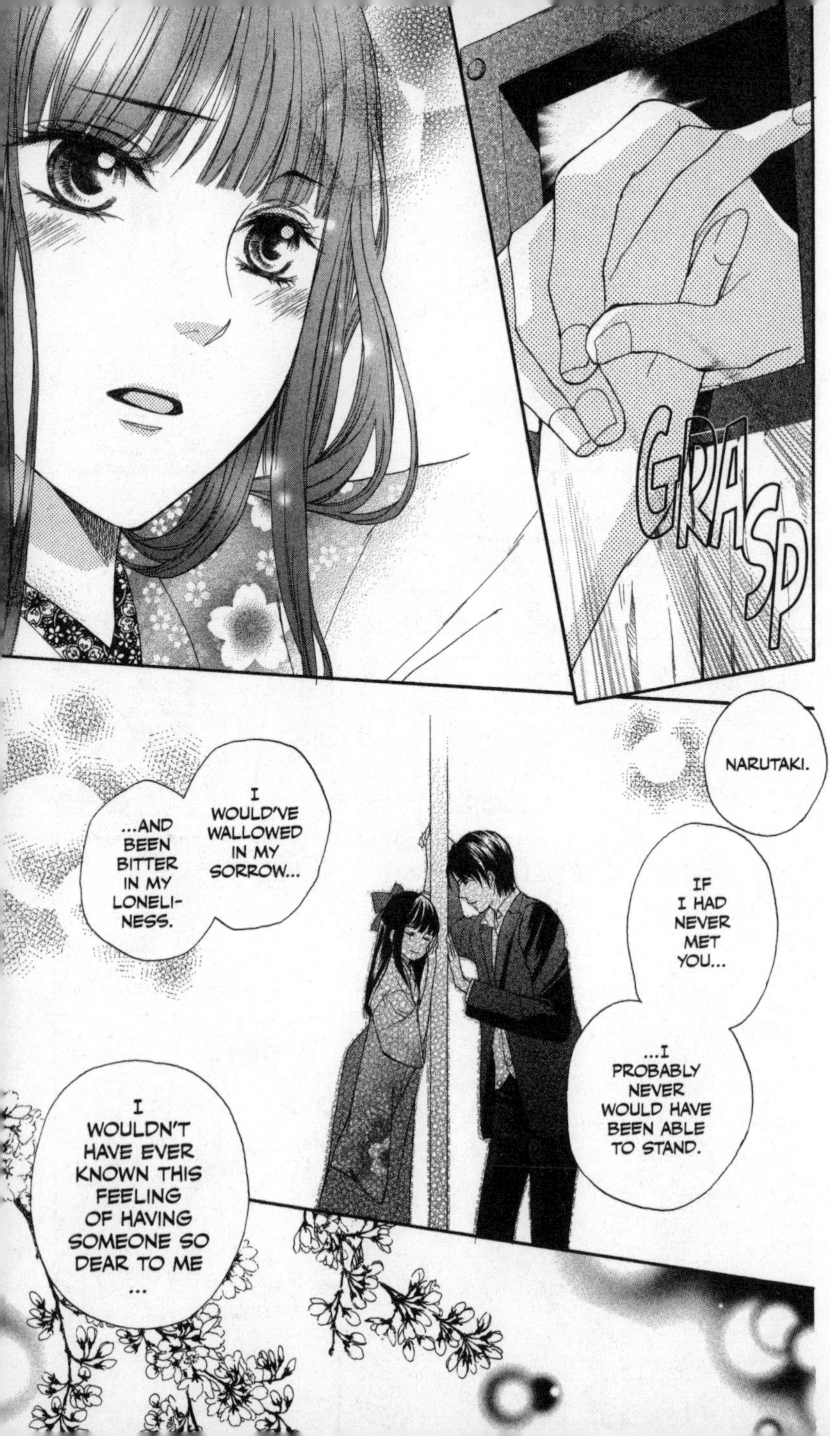
GRASP
NARUTAKI.
IF I HAD NEVER MET YOU...
...I PROBABLY NEVER WOULD HAVE BEEN ABLE TO STAND.
I WOULD'VE WALLOWED IN MY SORROW...
...AND BEEN BITTER IN MY LONELINESS.
I WOULDN'T HAVE EVER KNOWN THIS FEELING OF HAVING SOMEONE SO DEAR TO ME ...

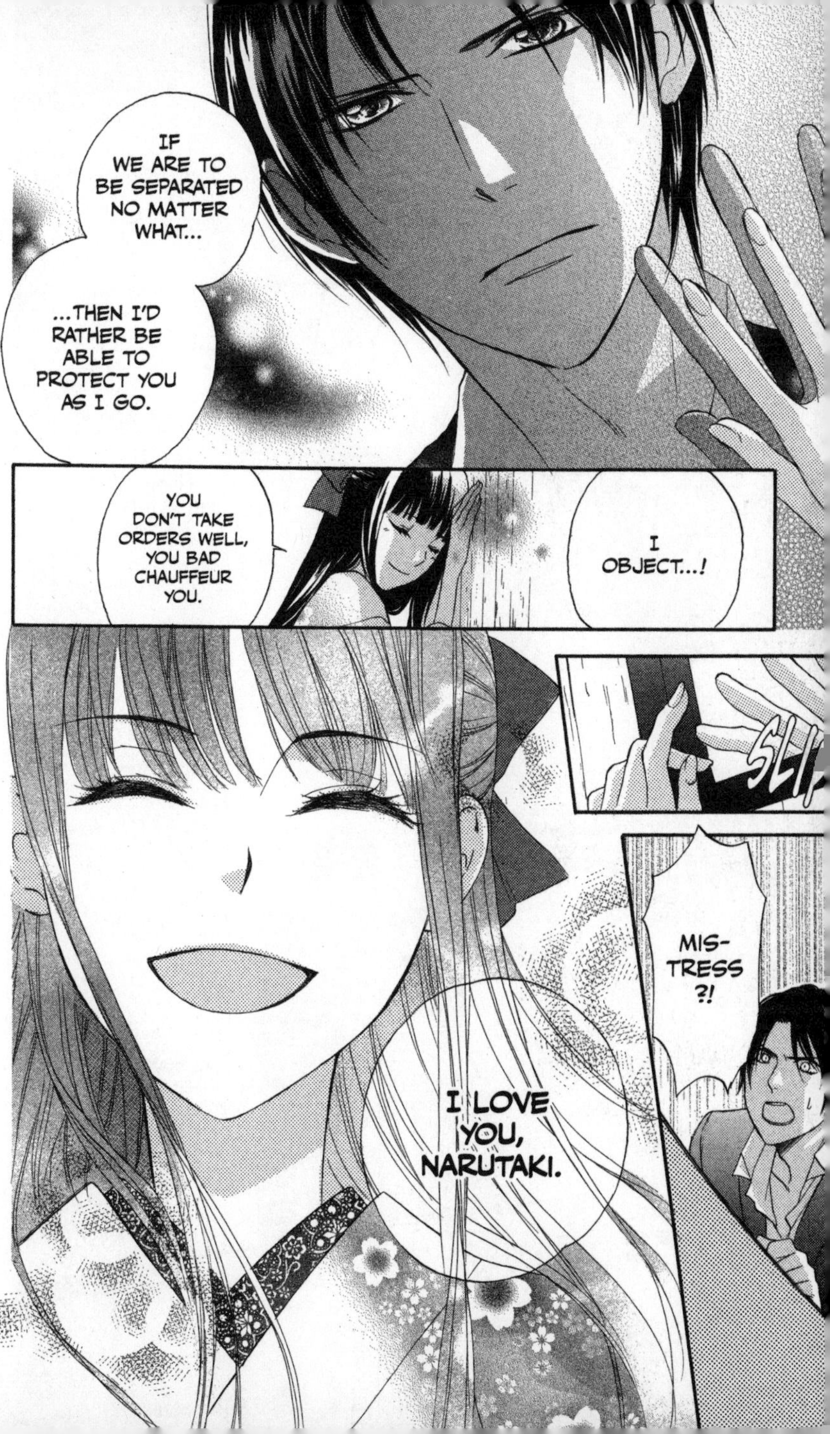
IF WE ARE TO BE SEPARATED NO MATTER WHAT...
...THEN I'D RATHER BE ABLE TO PROTECT YOU AS I GO.
I OBJECT...!
YOU DON'T TAKE ORDERS WELL, YOU BAD CHAUFFEUR YOU.
SLI
MIS-TRESS ?!
I LOVE YOU, NARUTAKI.

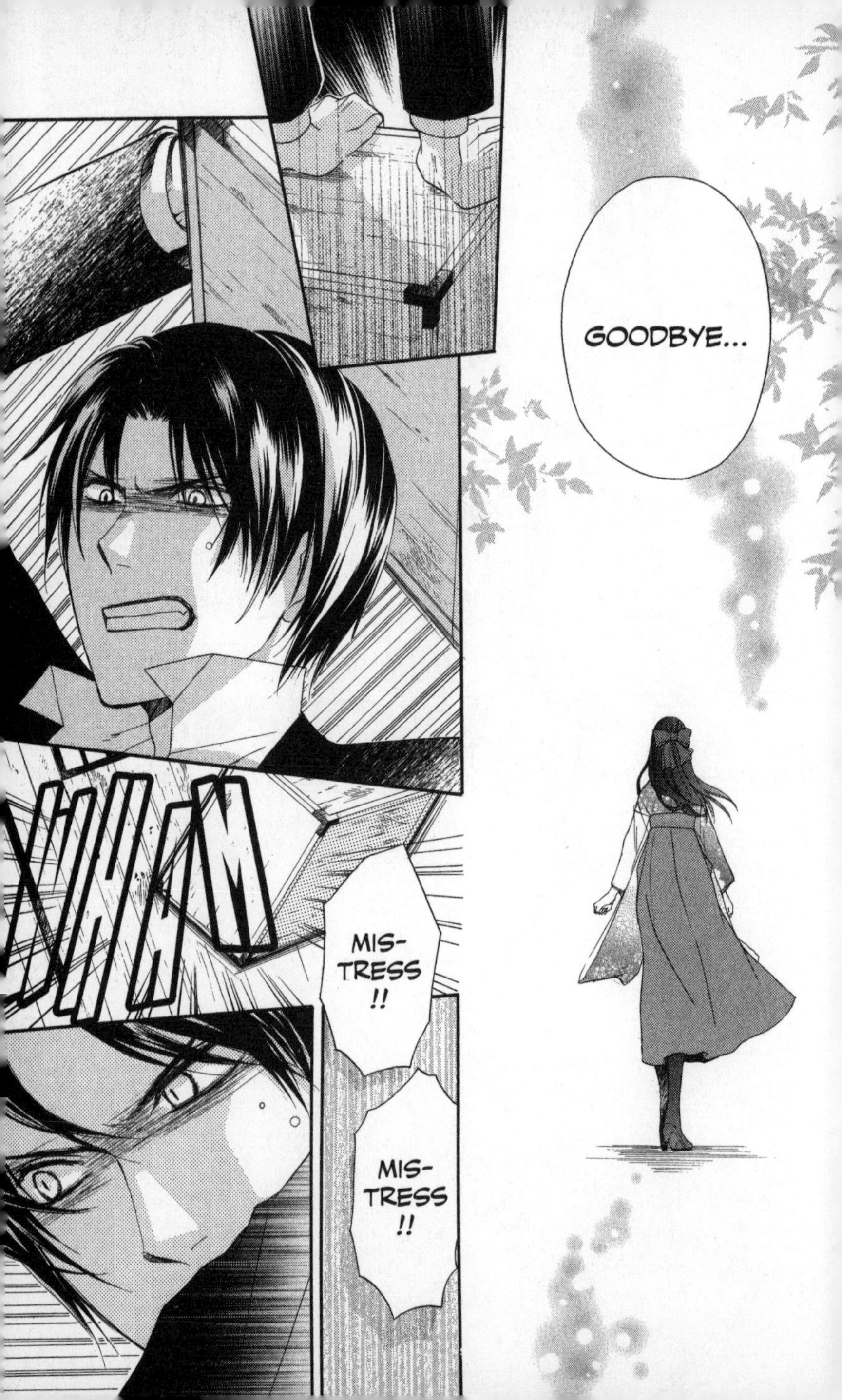
GOODBYE...
WHAM
MIS-
TRESS
!!
MIS-
TRESS
!!

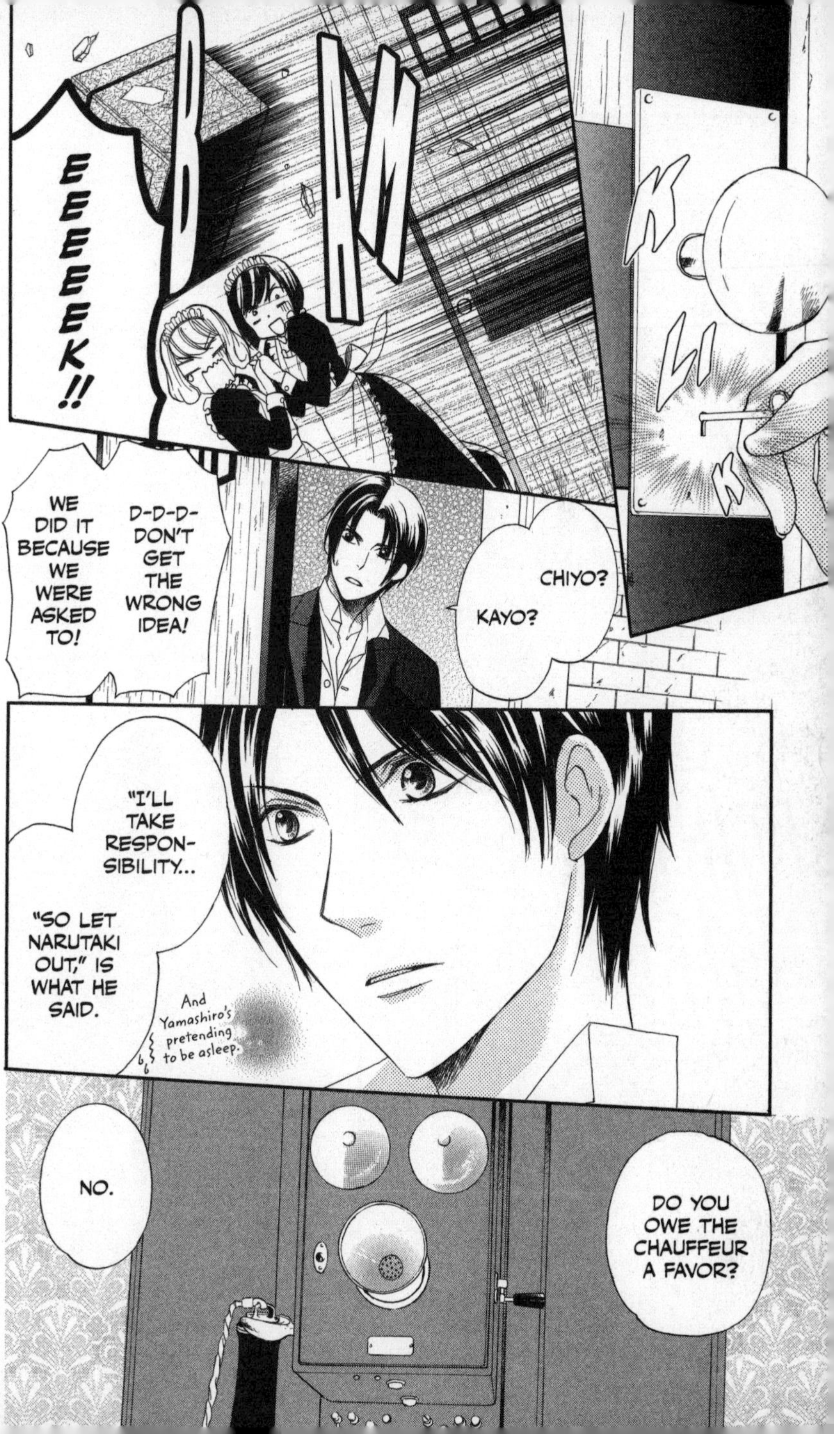
KLIK
BAM
EEEEEK!!
CHIYO?
KAYO?
D-D-D-DON'T GET THE WRONG IDEA!
WE DID IT BECAUSE WE WERE ASKED TO!
"I'LL TAKE RESPONSIBILITY...
"SO LET NARUTAKI OUT," IS WHAT HE SAID.
And Yamashiro's pretending to be asleep.
DO YOU OWE THE CHAUFFEUR A FAVOR?
NO.

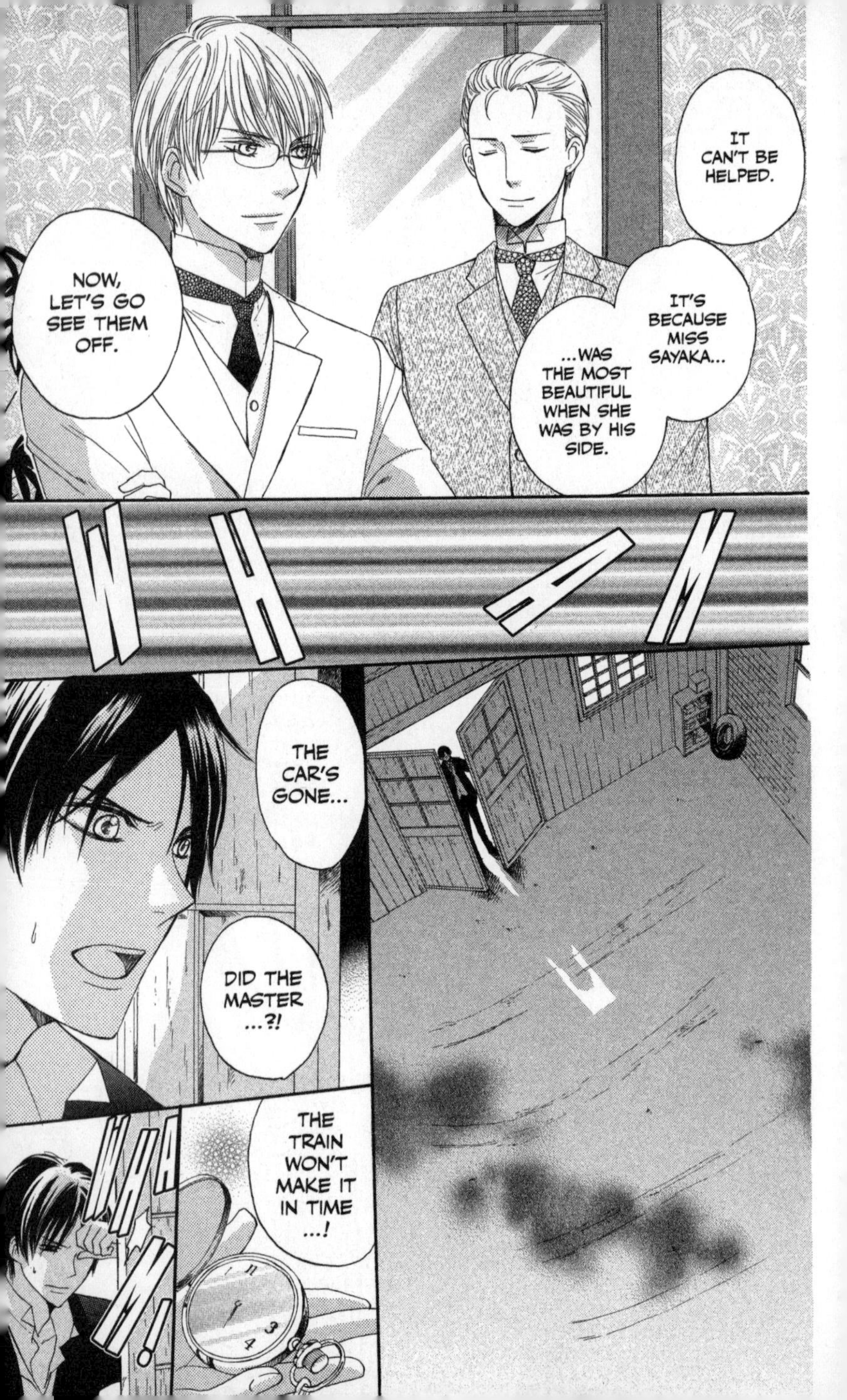
IT CAN'T BE HELPED.
IT'S BECAUSE MISS SAYAKA...
...WAS THE MOST BEAUTIFUL WHEN SHE WAS BY HIS SIDE.
NOW, LET'S GO SEE THEM OFF.
WHAM
THE CAR'S GONE...
DID THE MASTER ...?!
THE TRAIN WON'T MAKE IT IN TIME ...!
WHAAMM!

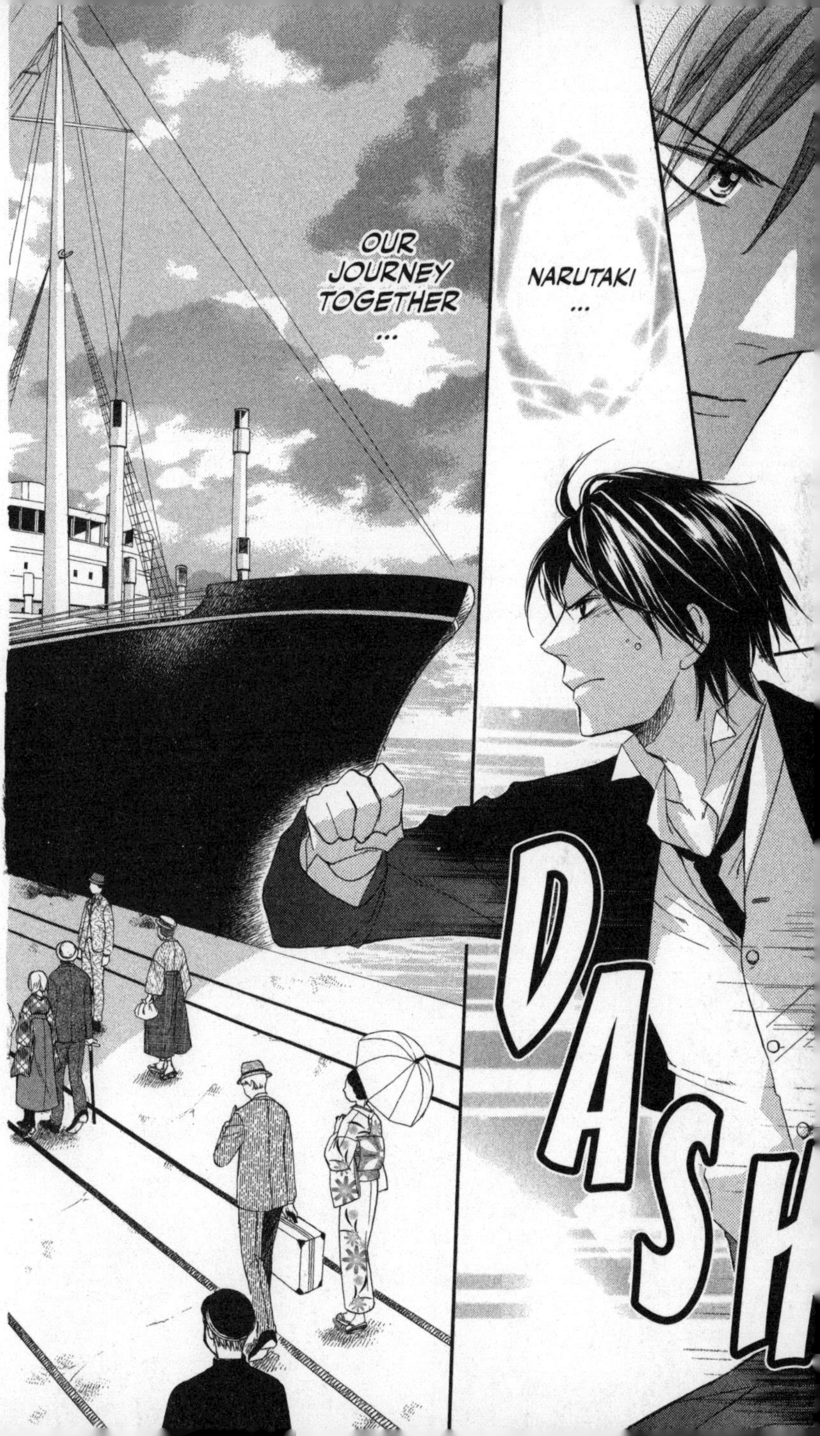
NARUTAKI ...
DASH
OUR JOURNEY TOGETHER ...

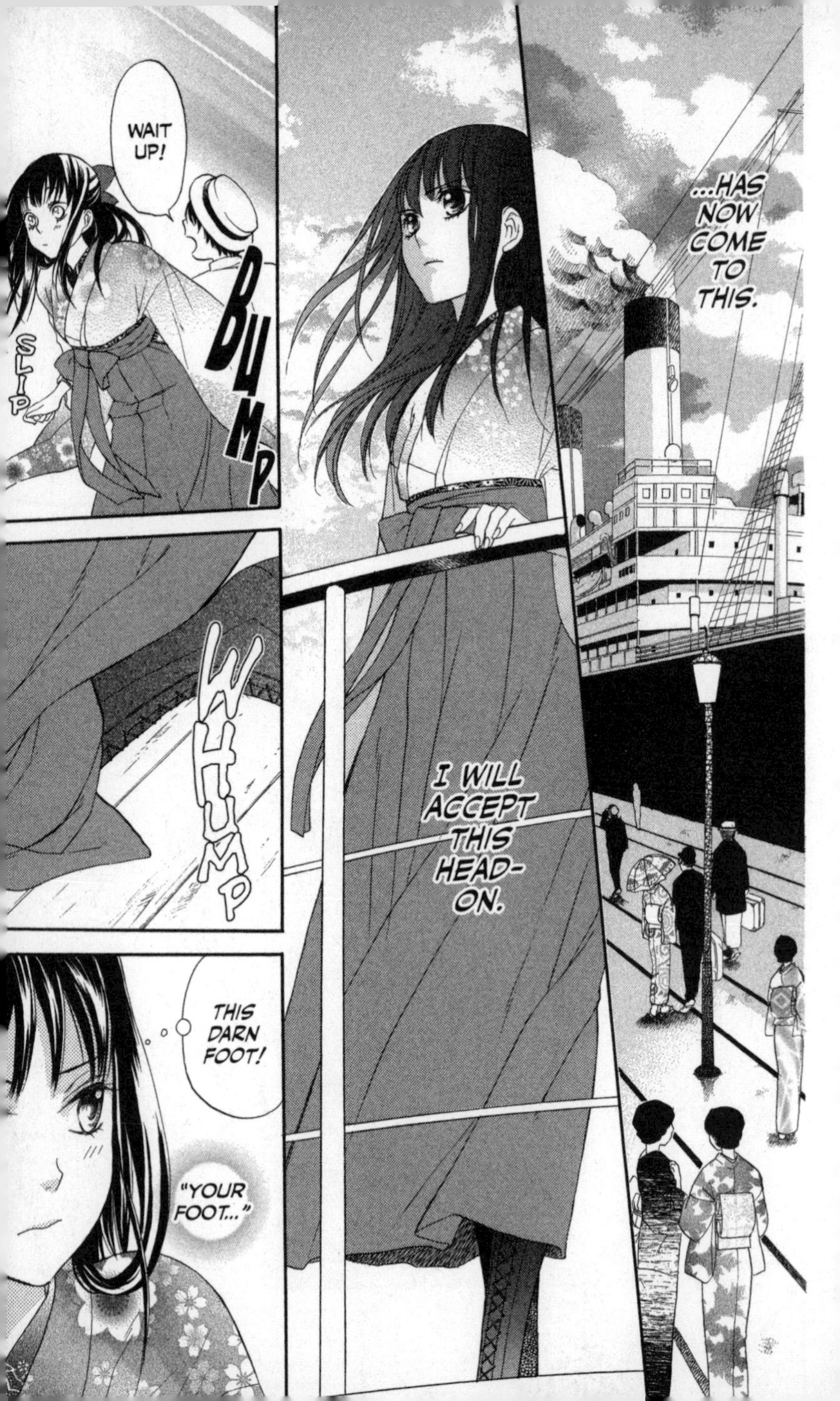
...HAS NOW COME TO THIS.
I WILL ACCEPT THIS HEAD-ON.
WAIT UP!
BUMP
SLIP
WHUMP
THIS DARN FOOT!
"YOUR FOOT..."

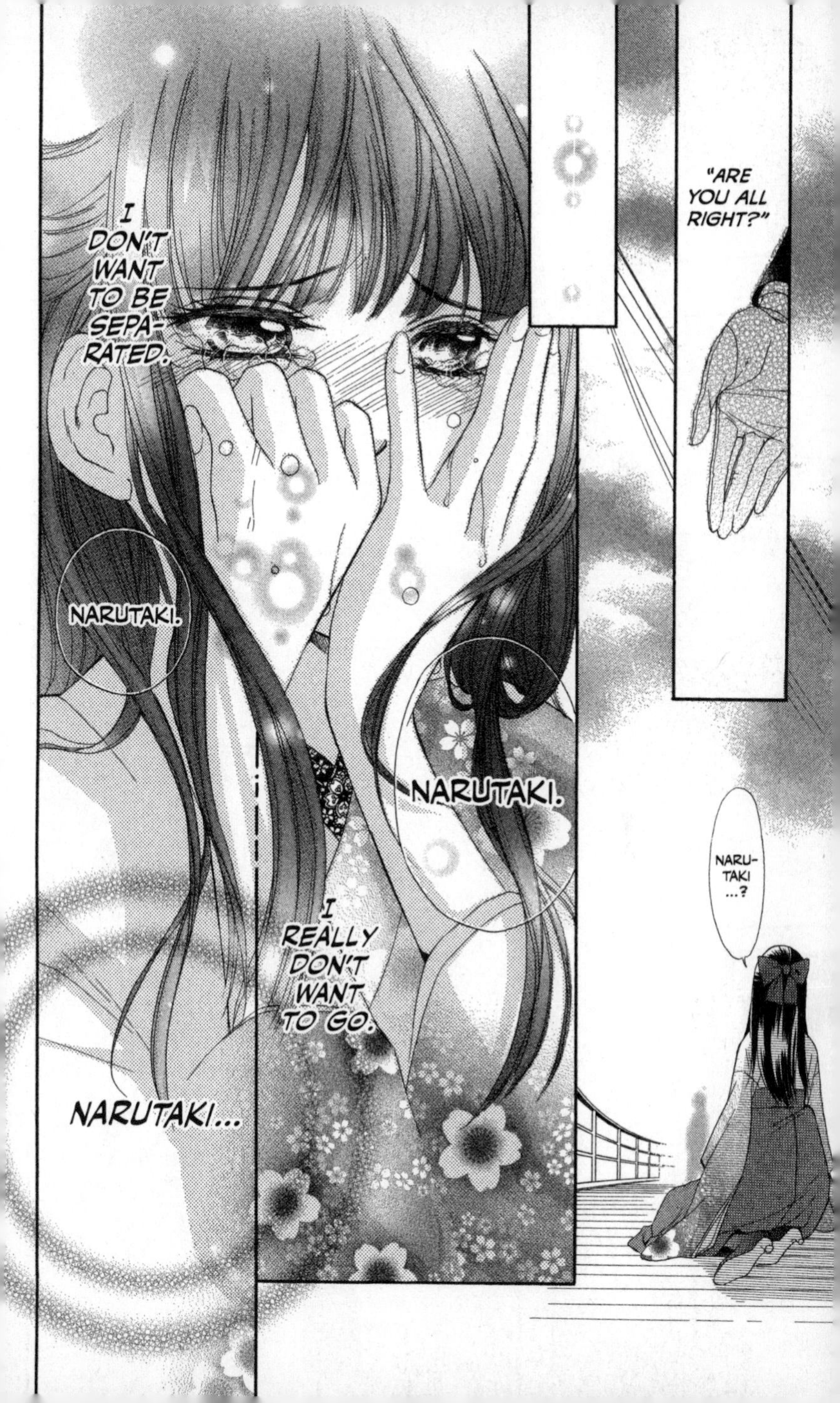
"ARE YOU ALL RIGHT?"
NARU-TAKI ...?
I DON'T WANT TO BE SEPA-RATED.
NARUTAKI.
NARUTAKI.
I REALLY DON'T WANT TO GO.
NARUTAKI...

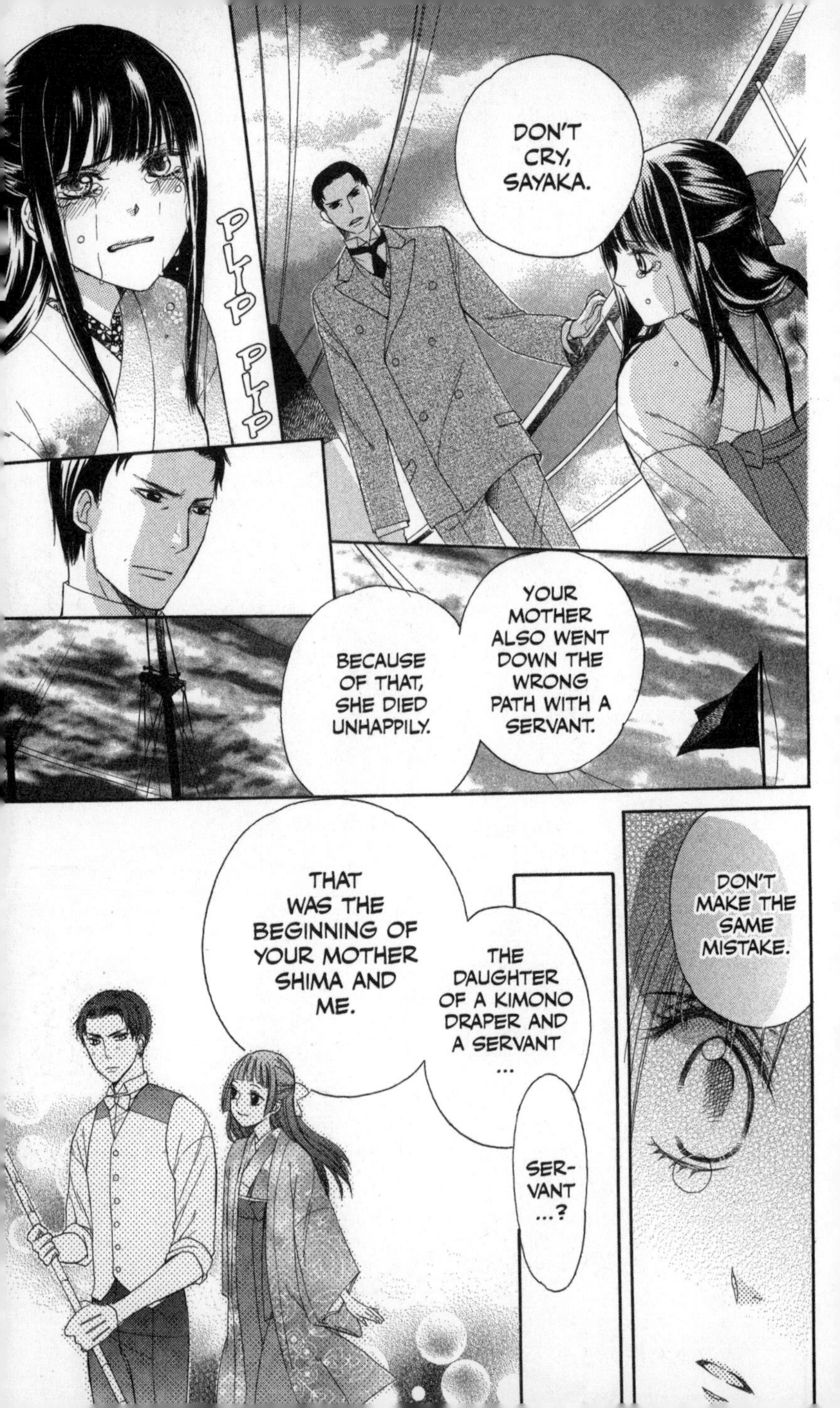
DON'T CRY, SAYAKA.
PLIP PLIP
YOUR MOTHER ALSO WENT DOWN THE WRONG PATH WITH A SERVANT.
BECAUSE OF THAT, SHE DIED UNHAPPILY.
DON'T MAKE THE SAME MISTAKE.
THAT WAS THE BEGINNING OF YOUR MOTHER SHIMA AND ME.
THE DAUGHTER OF A KIMONO DRAPER AND A SERVANT ...
SER-VANT ...?

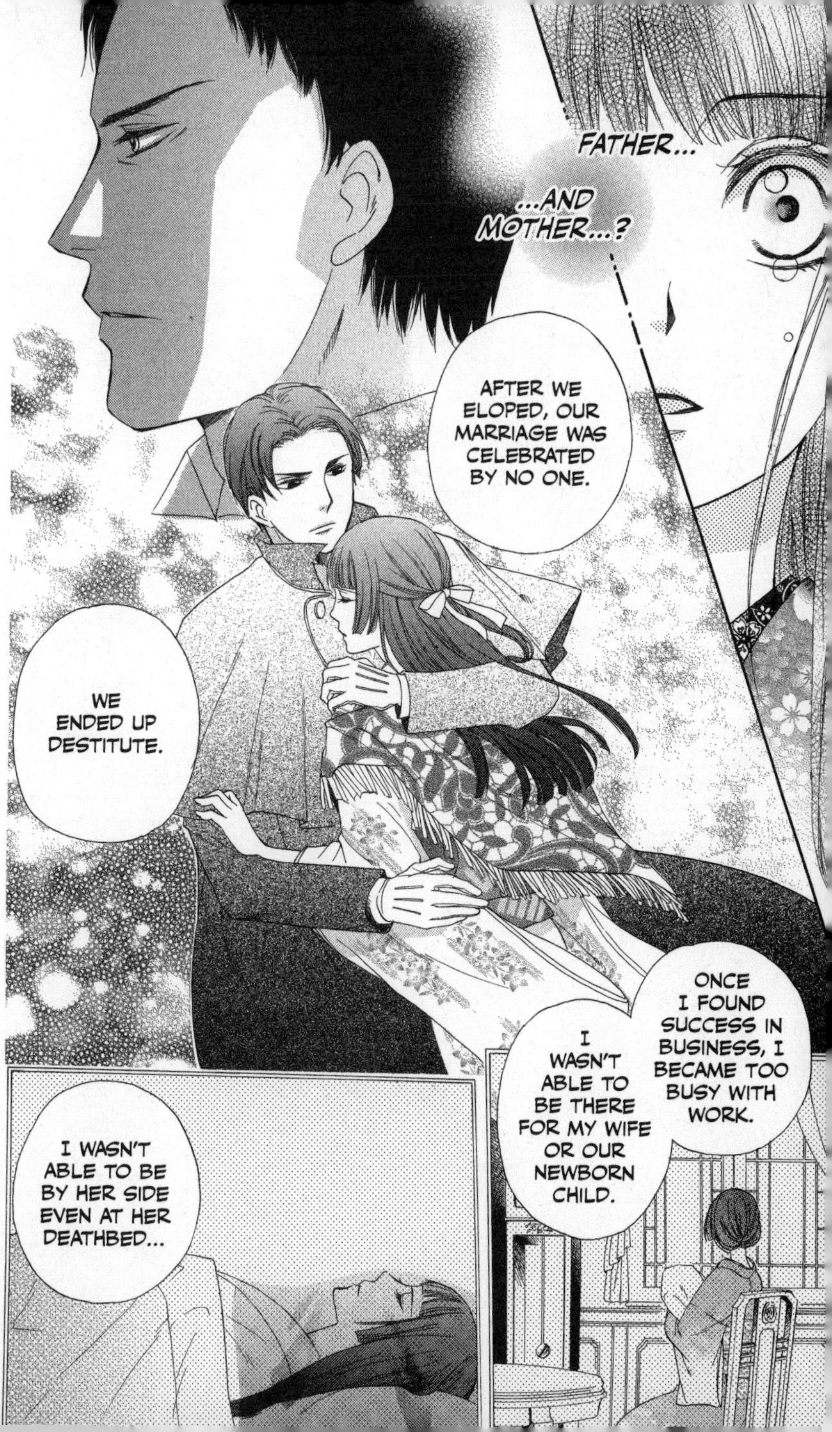
FATHER...
...AND MOTHER...?
AFTER WE ELOPED, OUR MARRIAGE WAS CELEBRATED BY NO ONE.
WE ENDED UP DESTITUTE.
ONCE I FOUND SUCCESS IN BUSINESS, I BECAME TOO BUSY WITH WORK.
I WASN'T ABLE TO BE THERE FOR MY WIFE OR OUR NEWBORN CHILD.
I WASN'T ABLE TO BE BY HER SIDE EVEN AT HER DEATHBED...

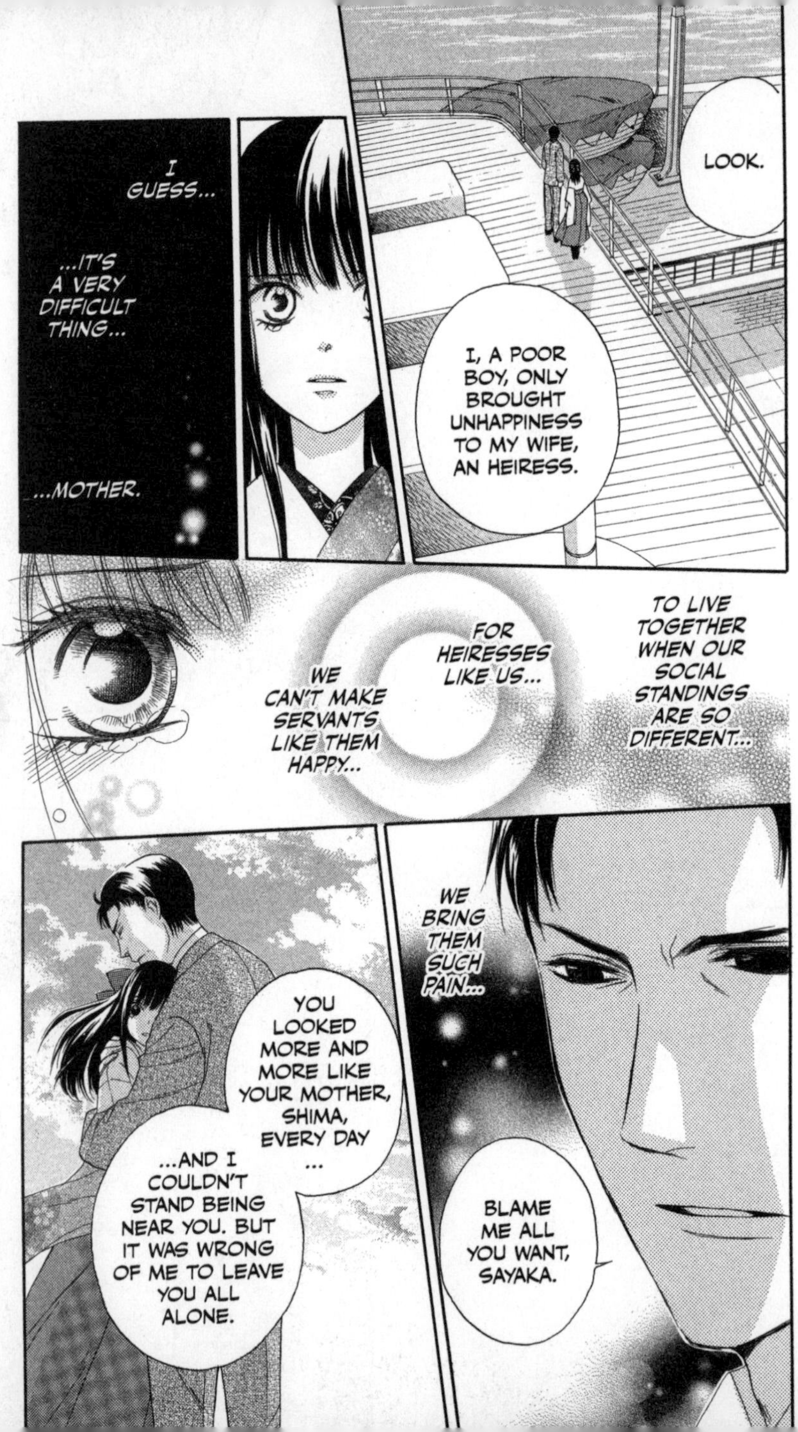
LOOK.
I, A POOR BOY, ONLY BROUGHT UNHAPPINESS TO MY WIFE, AN HEIRESS.
I GUESS...
...IT'S A VERY DIFFICULT THING...
...MOTHER.
TO LIVE TOGETHER WHEN OUR SOCIAL STANDINGS ARE SO DIFFERENT...
FOR HEIRESSES LIKE US...
WE CAN'T MAKE SERVANTS LIKE THEM HAPPY...
WE BRING THEM SUCH PAIN...
BLAME ME ALL YOU WANT, SAYAKA.
YOU LOOKED MORE AND MORE LIKE YOUR MOTHER, SHIMA, EVERY DAY ...
...AND I COULDN'T STAND BEING NEAR YOU. BUT IT WAS WRONG OF ME TO LEAVE YOU ALL ALONE.

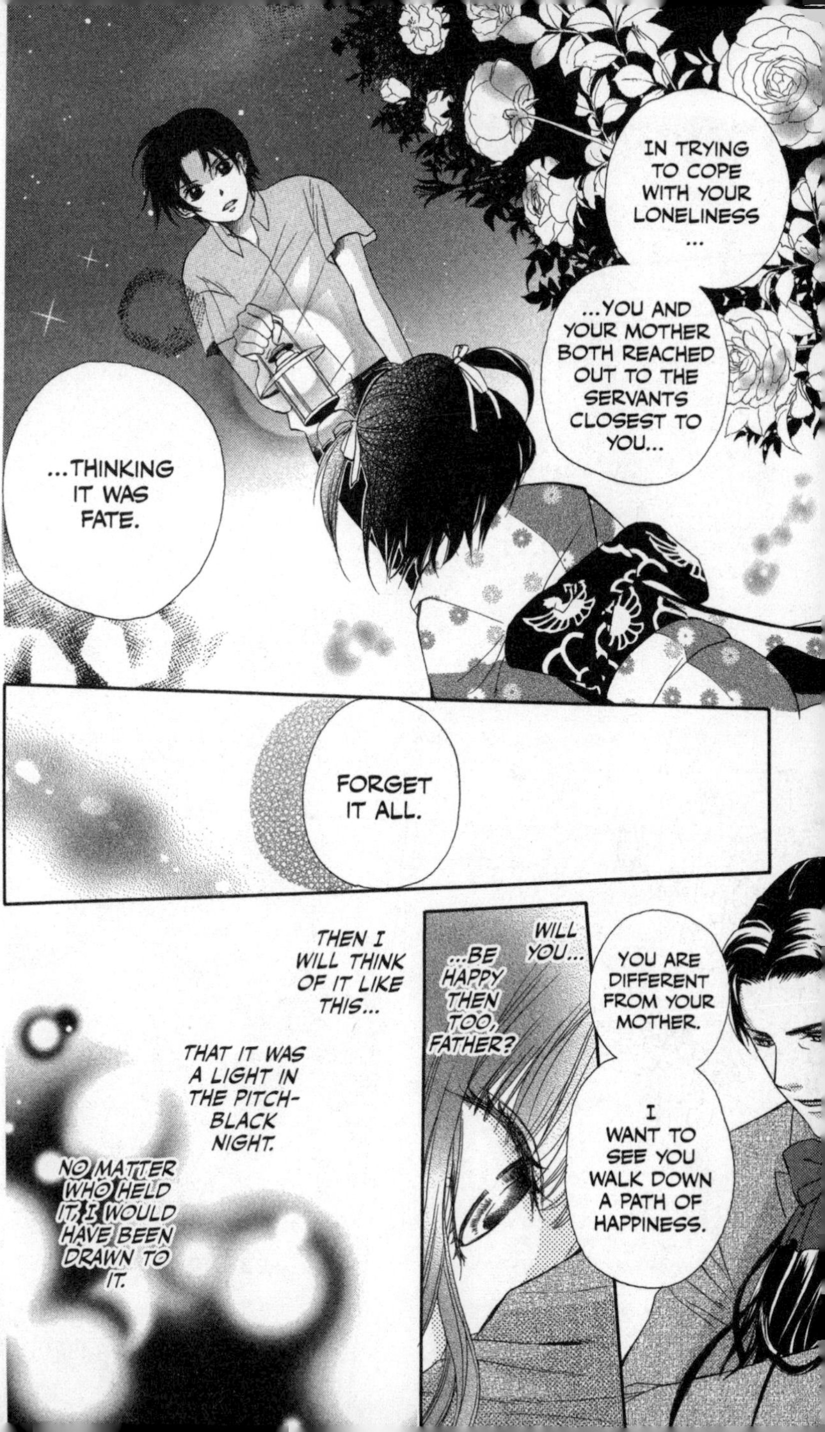
IN TRYING TO COPE WITH YOUR LONELINESS ...
...YOU AND YOUR MOTHER BOTH REACHED OUT TO THE SERVANTS CLOSEST TO YOU...
...THINKING IT WAS FATE.
FORGET IT ALL.
YOU ARE DIFFERENT FROM YOUR MOTHER.
I WANT TO SEE YOU WALK DOWN A PATH OF HAPPINESS.
WILL YOU...
...BE HAPPY THEN TOO, FATHER?
THEN I WILL THINK OF IT LIKE THIS...
THAT IT WAS A LIGHT IN THE PITCH-BLACK NIGHT.
NO MATTER WHO HELD IT, I WOULD HAVE BEEN DRAWN TO IT.

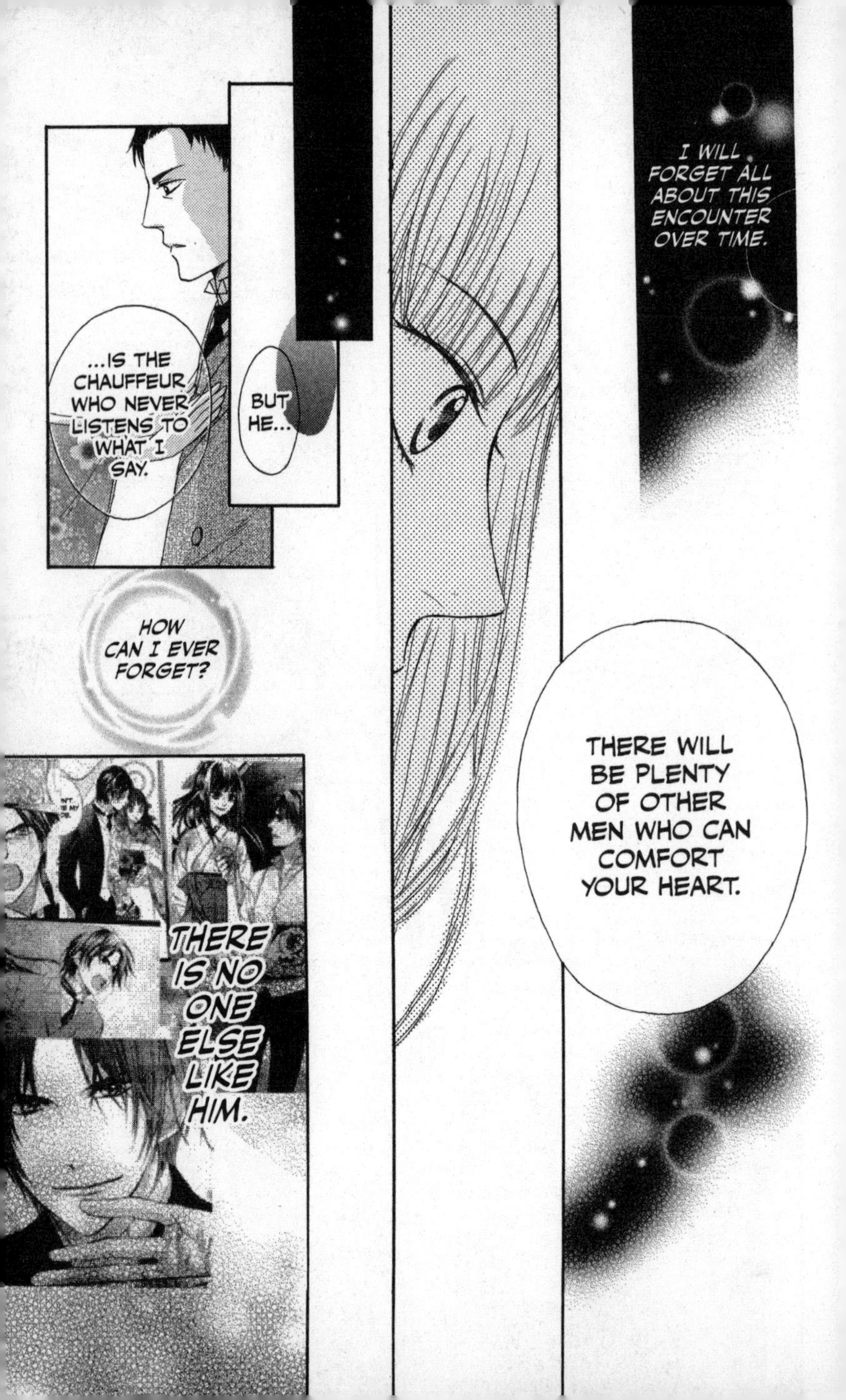
I WILL FORGET ALL ABOUT THIS ENCOUNTER OVER TIME.
THERE WILL BE PLENTY OF OTHER MEN WHO CAN COMFORT YOUR HEART.
BUT HE...
...IS THE CHAUFFEUR WHO NEVER LISTENS TO WHAT I SAY.
HOW CAN I EVER FORGET?
THERE IS NO ONE ELSE LIKE HIM.

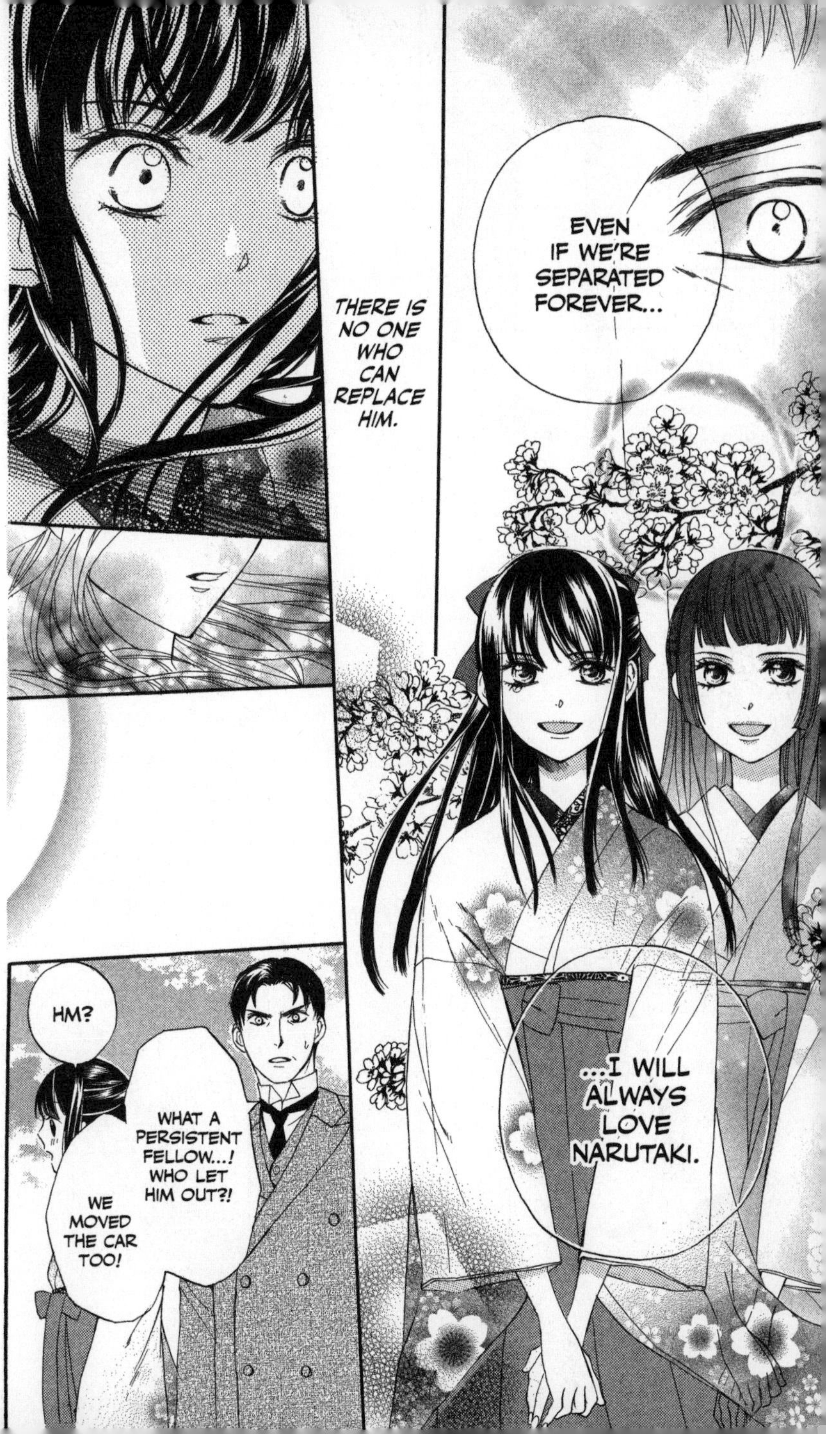
EVEN IF WE'RE SEPARATED FOREVER...
...I WILL ALWAYS LOVE NARUTAKI.
THERE IS NO ONE WHO CAN REPLACE HIM.
HM?
WHAT A PERSISTENT FELLOW...! WHO LET HIM OUT?!
WE MOVED THE CAR TOO!

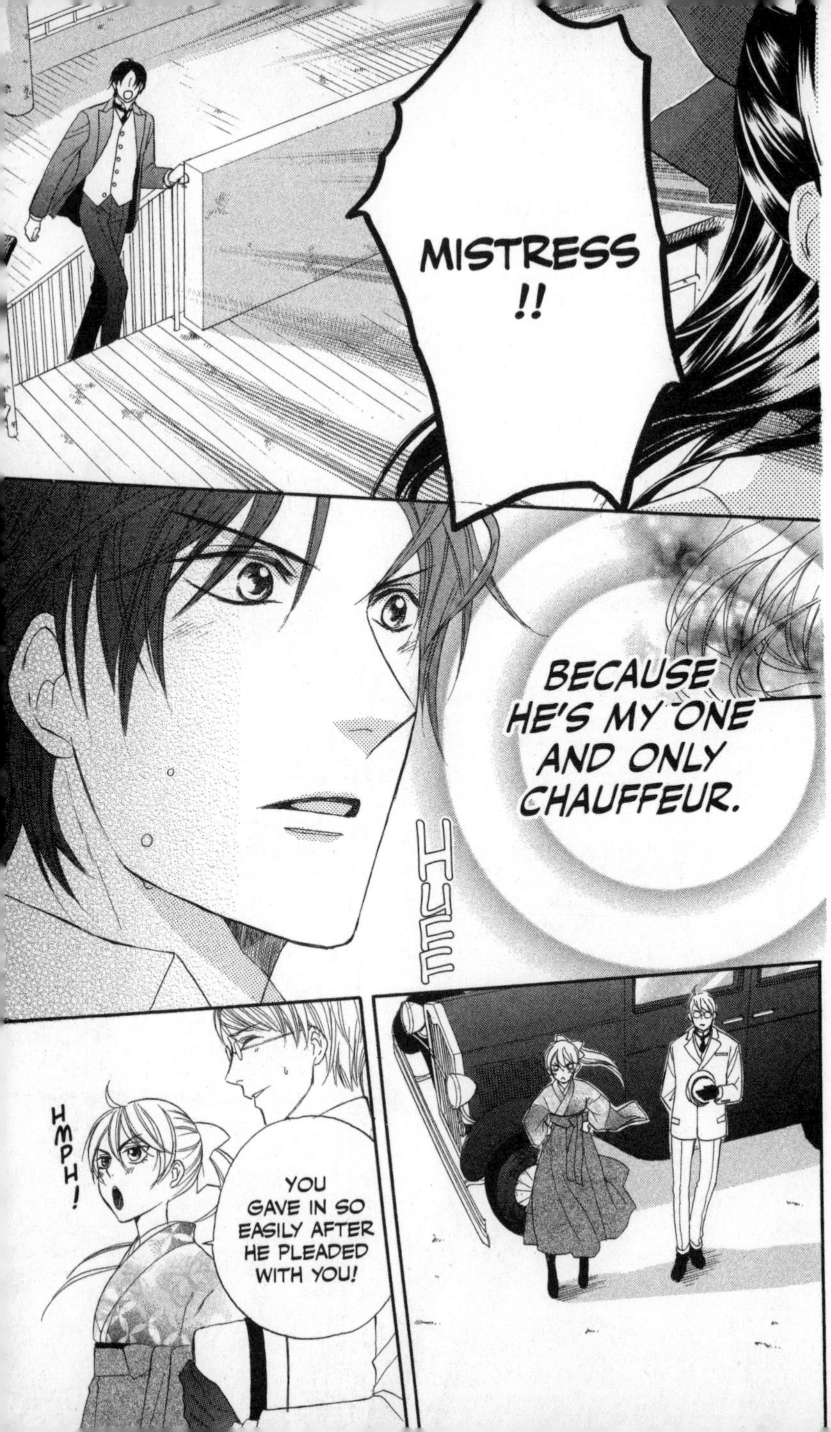
MISTRESS !!
BECAUSE HE'S MY ONE AND ONLY CHAUFFEUR.
HUFF
YOU GAVE IN SO EASILY AFTER HE PLEADED WITH YOU!
HMPH!

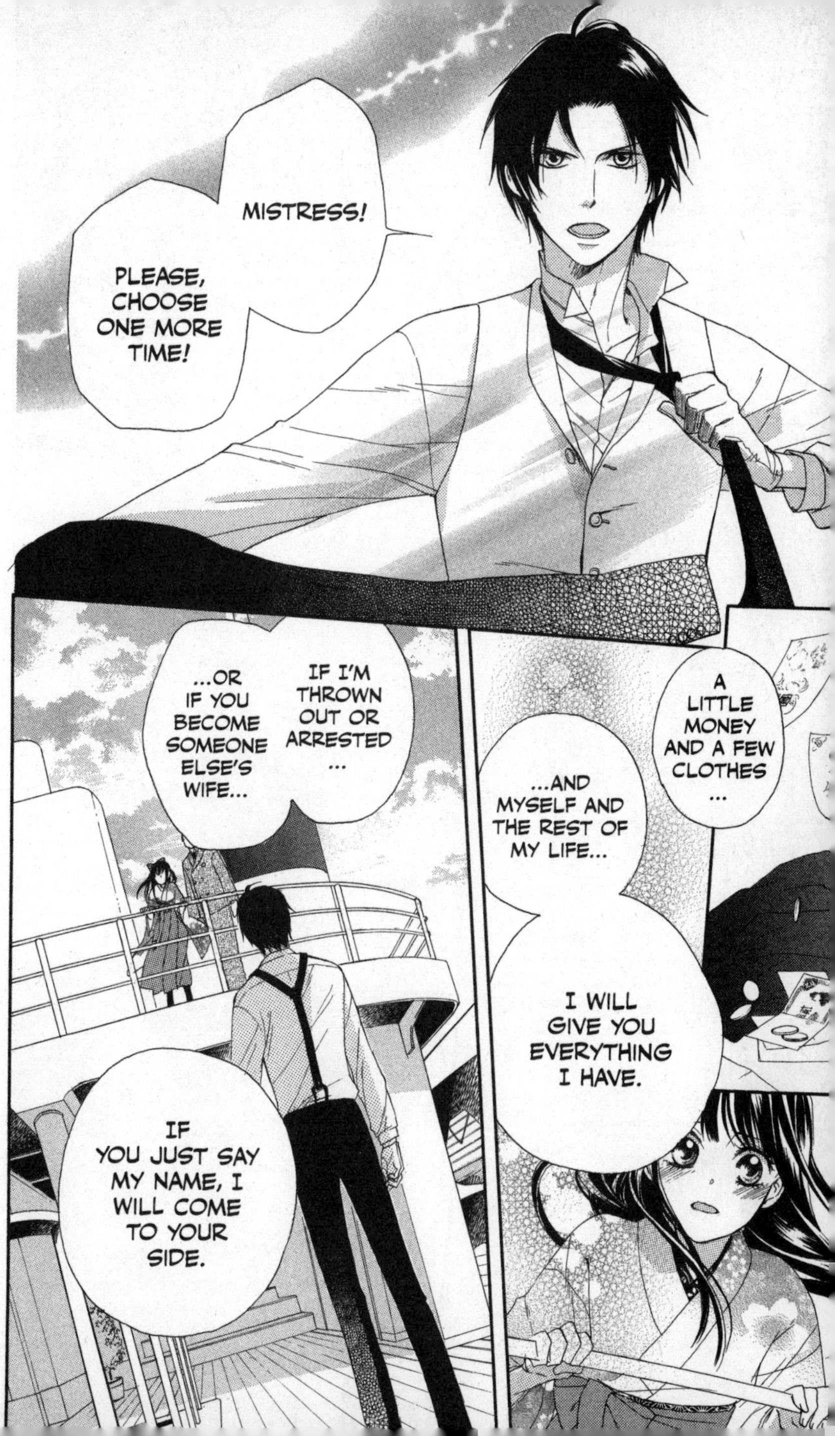
MISTRESS!
PLEASE, CHOOSE ONE MORE TIME!
A LITTLE MONEY AND A FEW CLOTHES ...
...AND MYSELF AND THE REST OF MY LIFE...
I WILL GIVE YOU EVERYTHING I HAVE.
IF I'M THROWN OUT OR ARRESTED ...
...OR IF YOU BECOME SOMEONE ELSE'S WIFE...
IF YOU JUST SAY MY NAME, I WILL COME TO YOUR SIDE.

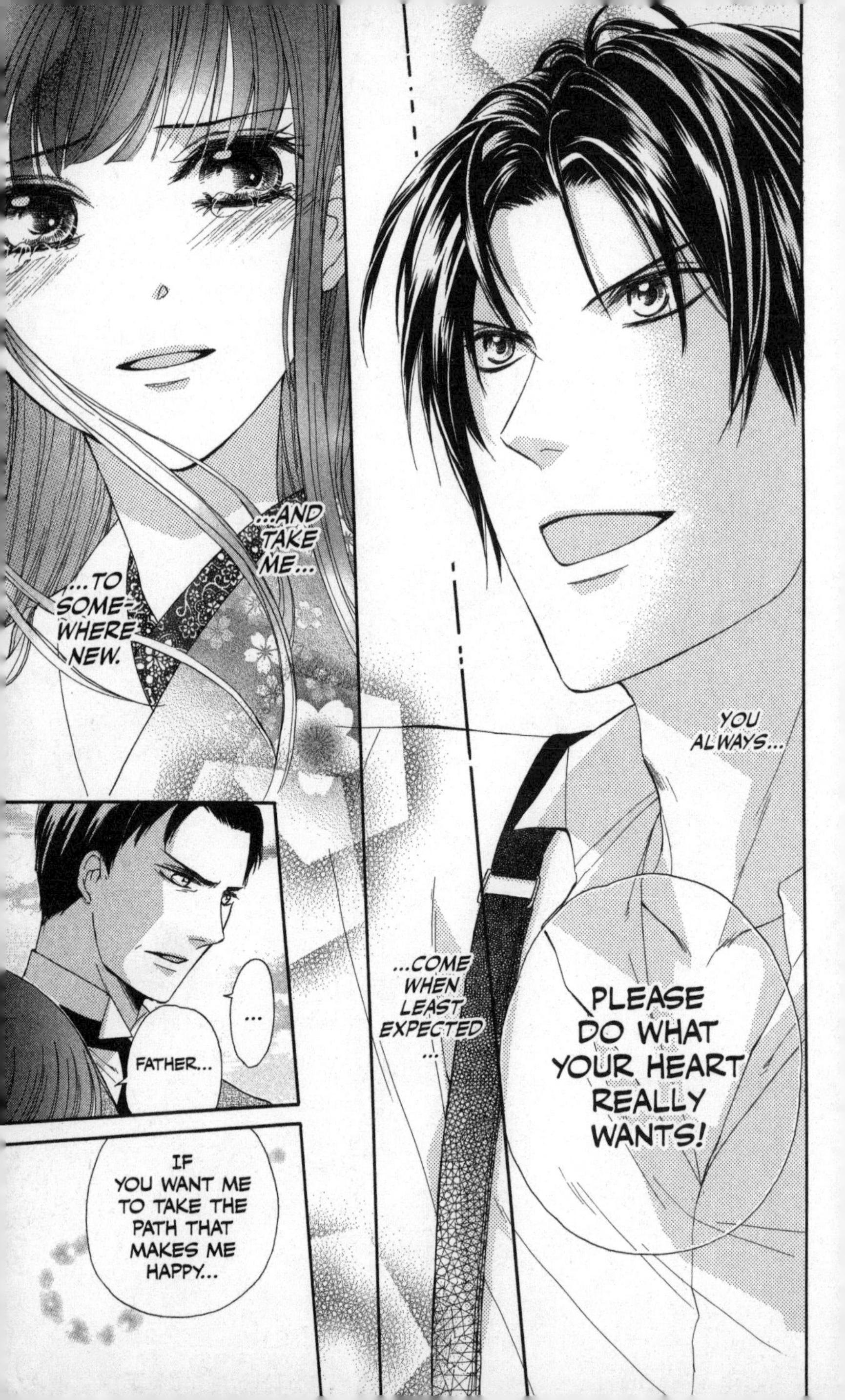
YOU ALWAYS...
...COME WHEN LEAST EXPECTED...
PLEASE DO WHAT YOUR HEART REALLY WANTS!
...AND TAKE ME...
...TO SOMEWHERE NEW.
...
FATHER...
IF YOU WANT ME TO TAKE THE PATH THAT MAKES ME HAPPY...

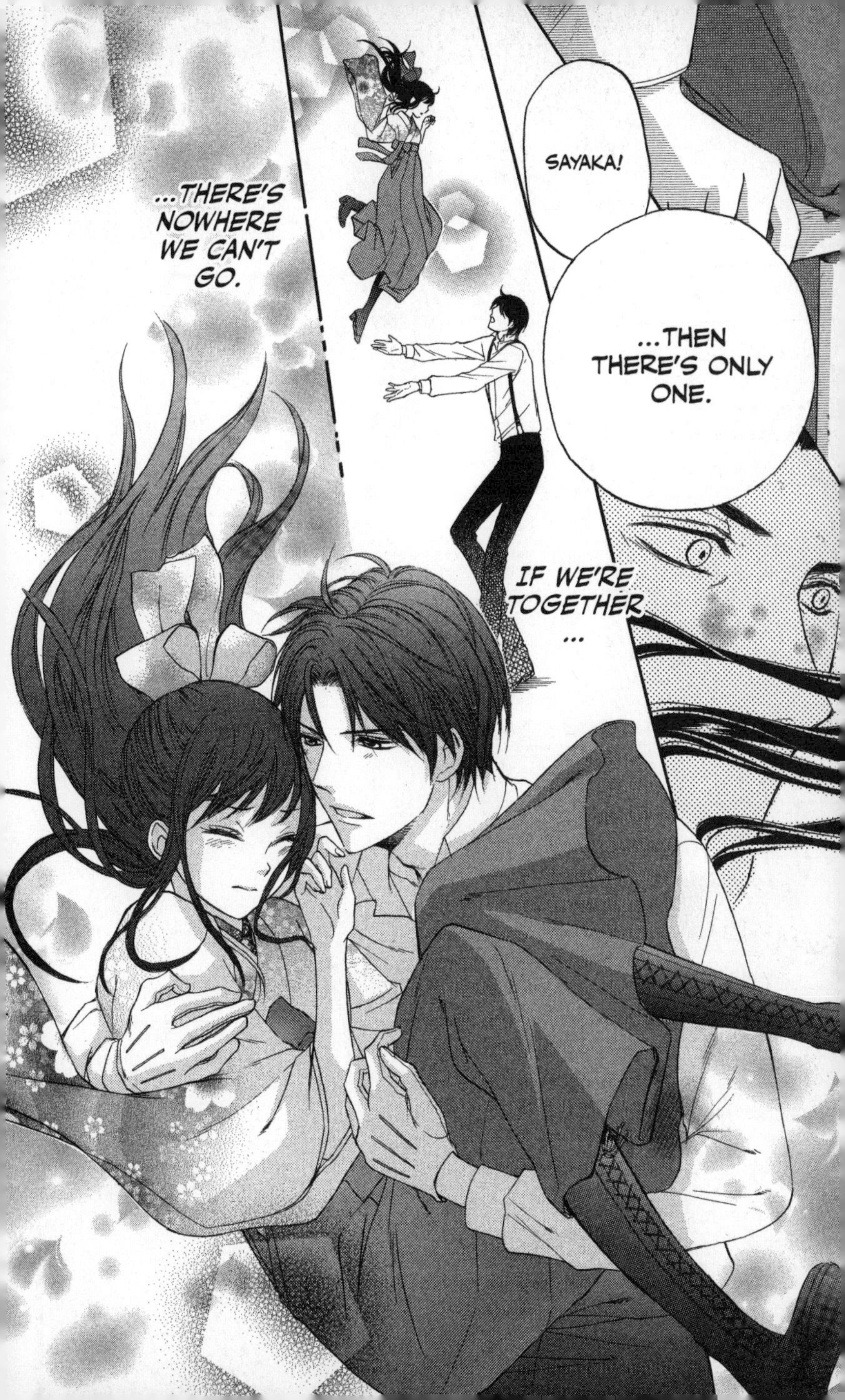
SAYAKA!
...THEN THERE'S ONLY ONE.
IF WE'RE TOGETHER...
...THERE'S NOWHERE WE CAN'T GO.

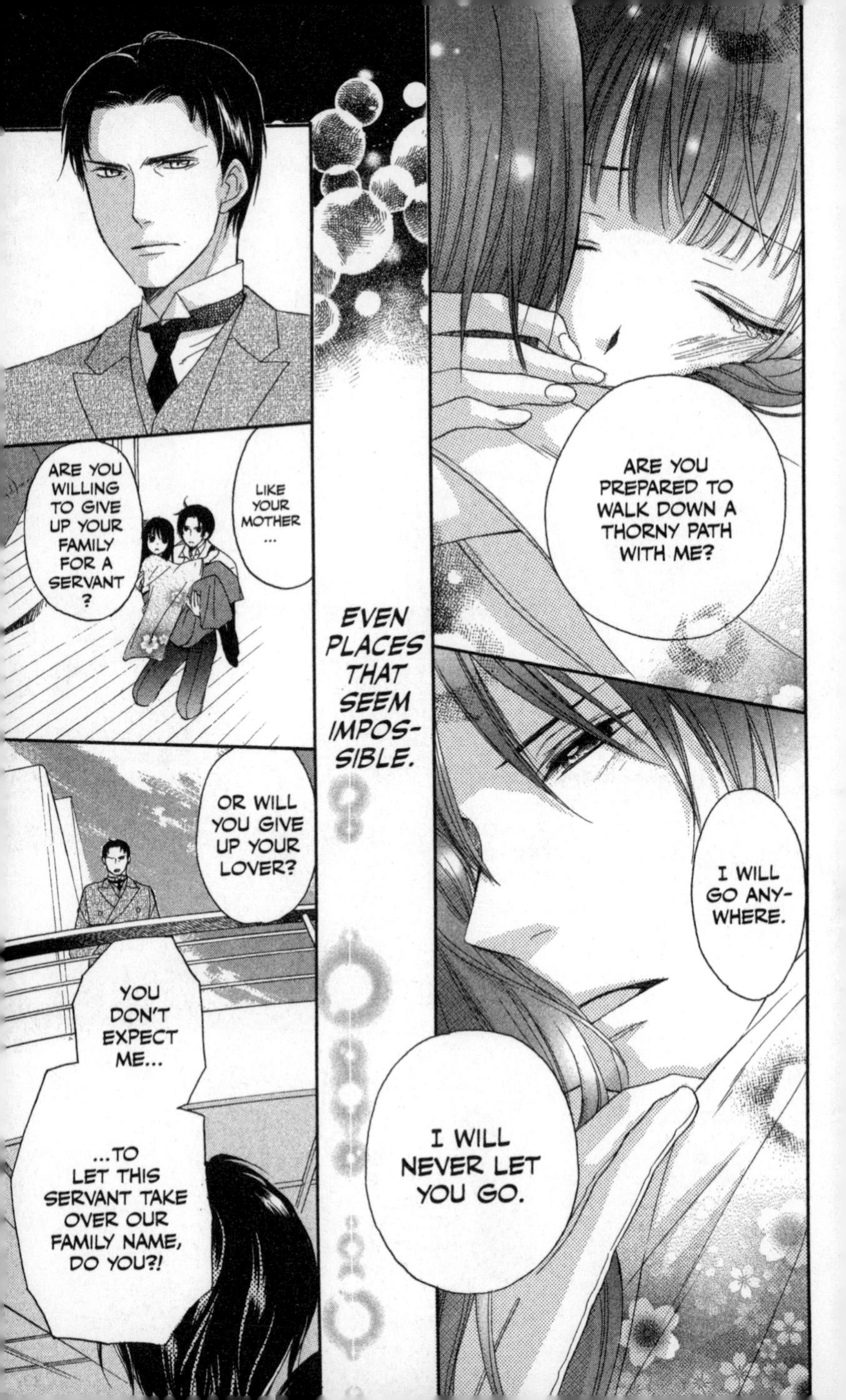
ARE YOU PREPARED TO WALK DOWN A THORNY PATH WITH ME?
I WILL GO ANYWHERE.
I WILL NEVER LET YOU GO.
EVEN PLACES THAT SEEM IMPOSSIBLE.
LIKE YOUR MOTHER...
ARE YOU WILLING TO GIVE UP YOUR FAMILY FOR A SERVANT?
OR WILL YOU GIVE UP YOUR LOVER?
YOU DON'T EXPECT ME...
...TO LET THIS SERVANT TAKE OVER OUR FAMILY NAME, DO YOU?!

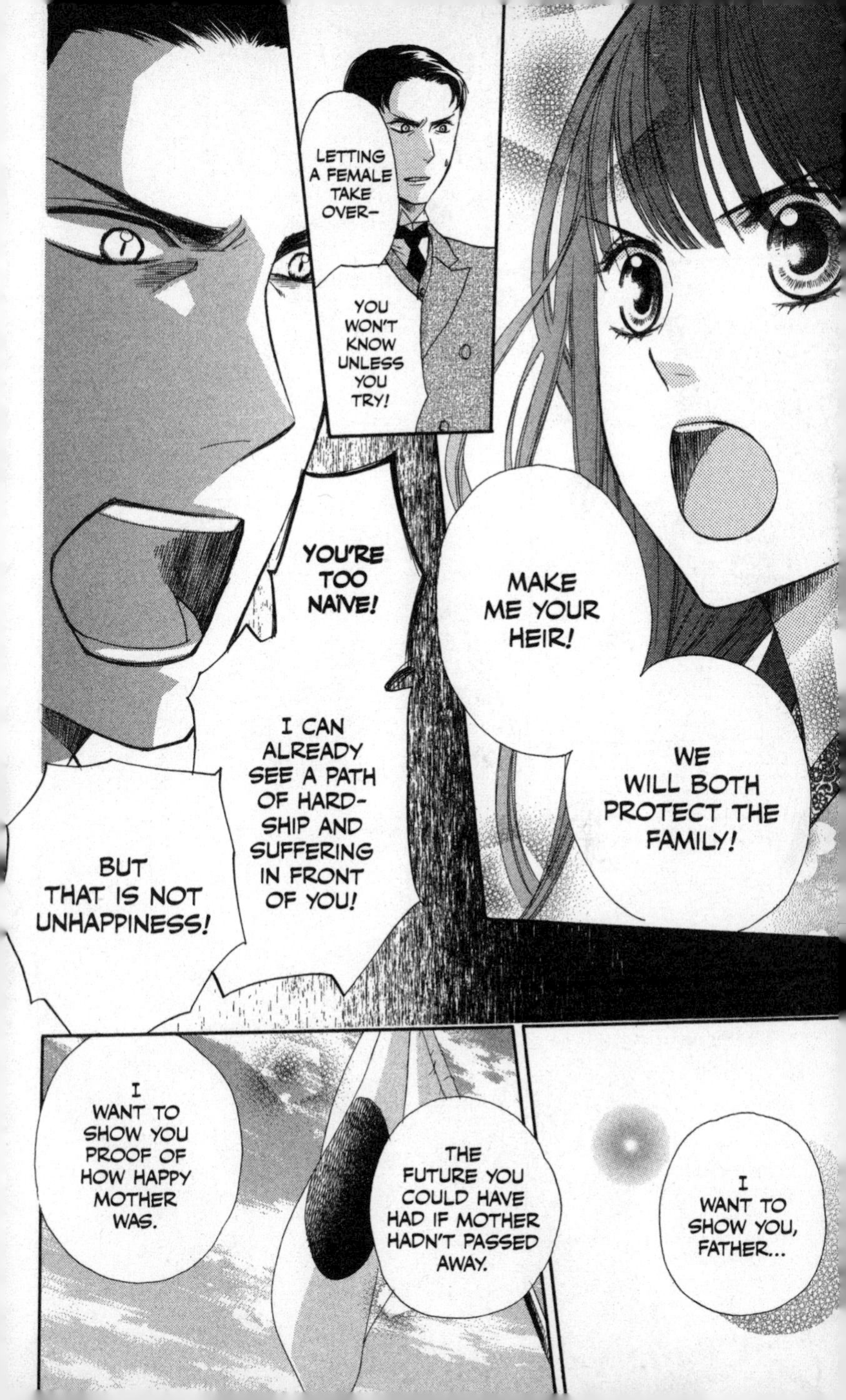
MAKE ME YOUR HEIR!
WE WILL BOTH PROTECT THE FAMILY!
LETTING A FEMALE TAKE OVER—
YOU WON'T KNOW UNLESS YOU TRY!
YOU'RE TOO NAÏVE!
I CAN ALREADY SEE A PATH OF HARD-SHIP AND SUFFERING IN FRONT OF YOU!
BUT THAT IS NOT UNHAPPINESS!
I WANT TO SHOW YOU, FATHER...
THE FUTURE YOU COULD HAVE HAD IF MOTHER HADN'T PASSED AWAY.
I WANT TO SHOW YOU PROOF OF HOW HAPPY MOTHER WAS.

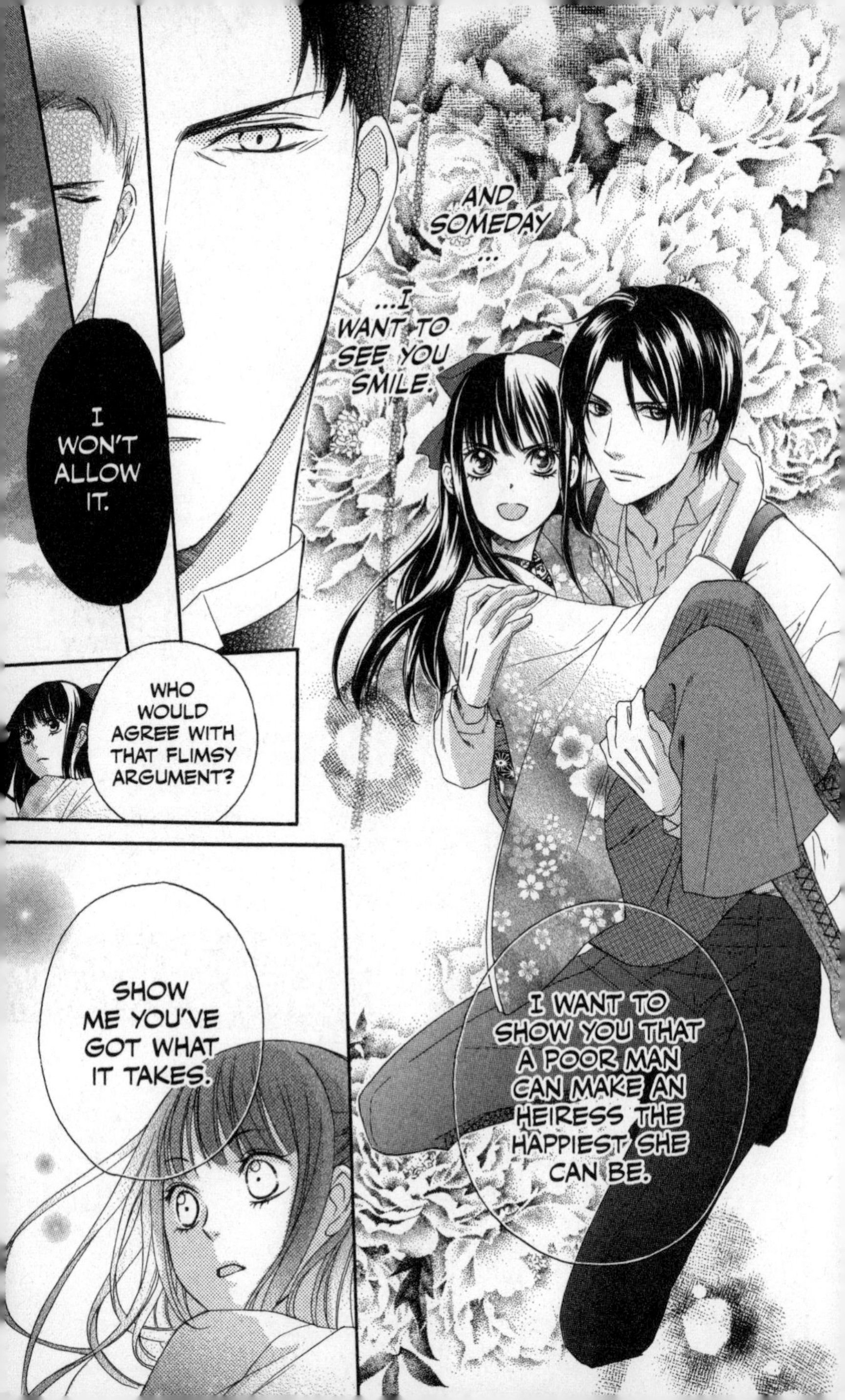
AND SOMEDAY...
...I WANT TO SEE YOU SMILE.
I WANT TO SHOW YOU THAT A POOR MAN CAN MAKE AN HEIRESS THE HAPPIEST SHE CAN BE.
I WON'T ALLOW IT.
WHO WOULD AGREE WITH THAT FLIMSY ARGUMENT?
SHOW ME YOU'VE GOT WHAT IT TAKES.

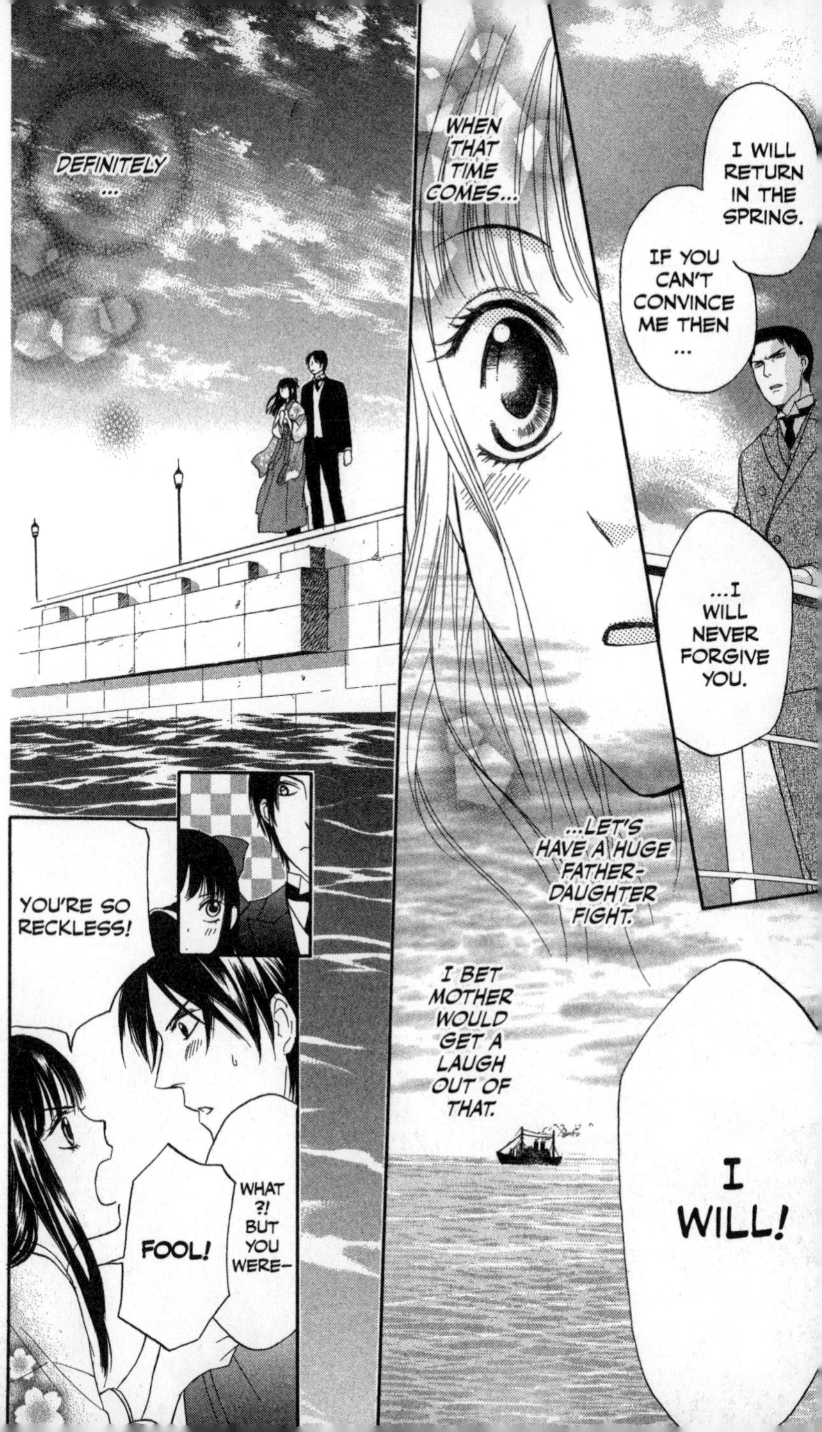
I WILL RETURN IN THE SPRING.
IF YOU CAN'T CONVINCE ME THEN ...
...I WILL NEVER FORGIVE YOU.
WHEN THAT TIME COMES...
...LET'S HAVE A HUGE FATHER-DAUGHTER FIGHT.
I BET MOTHER WOULD GET A LAUGH OUT OF THAT.
I WILL!
DEFINITELY ...
YOU'RE SO RECKLESS!
FOOL!
WHAT?! BUT YOU WERE-

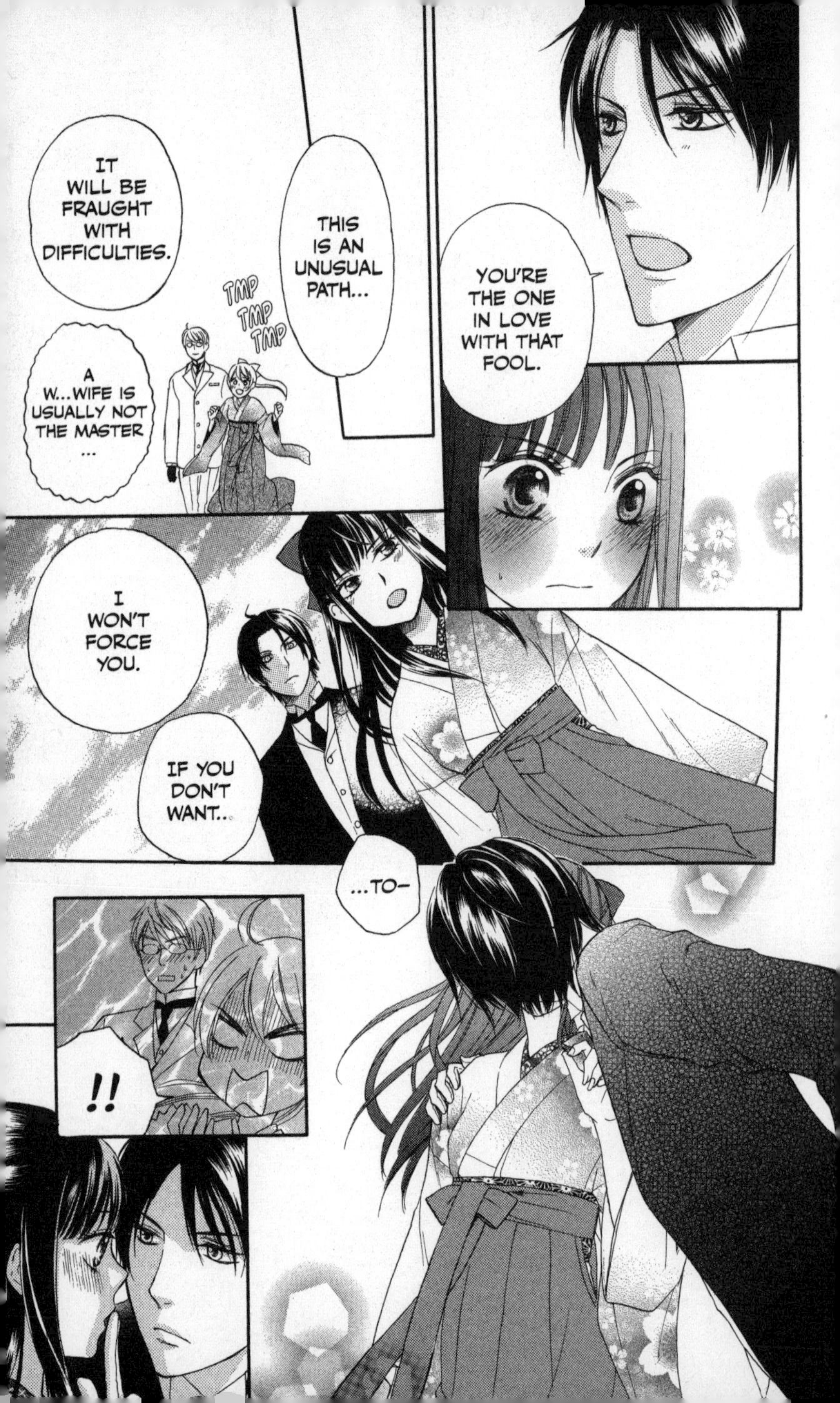
YOU'RE THE ONE IN LOVE WITH THAT FOOL.
THIS IS AN UNUSUAL PATH...
IT WILL BE FRAUGHT WITH DIFFICULTIES.
TMP TMP TMP
A W...WIFE IS USUALLY NOT THE MASTER ...
I WON'T FORCE YOU.
IF YOU DON'T WANT...
...TO-
!!

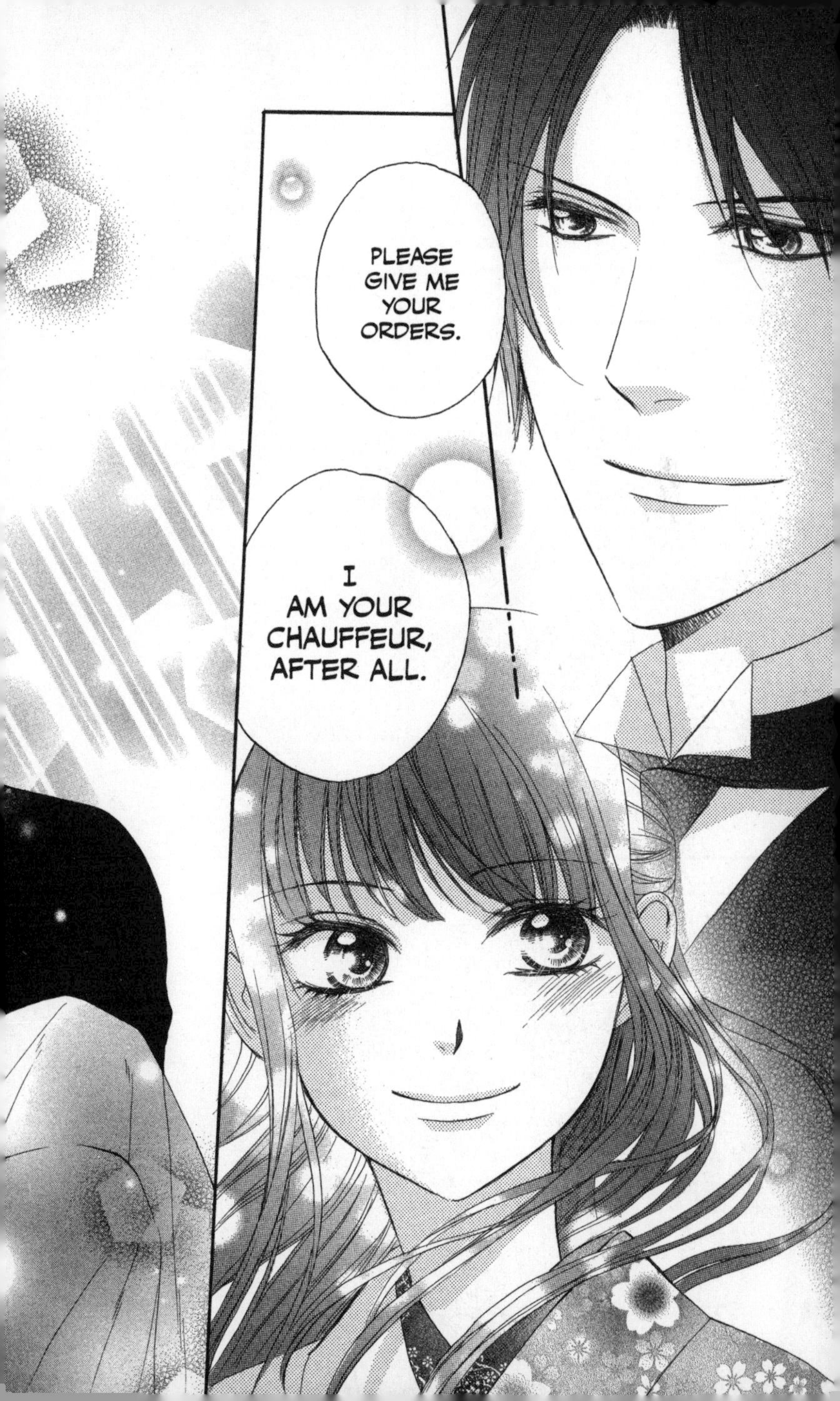
PLEASE GIVE ME YOUR ORDERS.
I AM YOUR CHAUFFEUR, AFTER ALL.

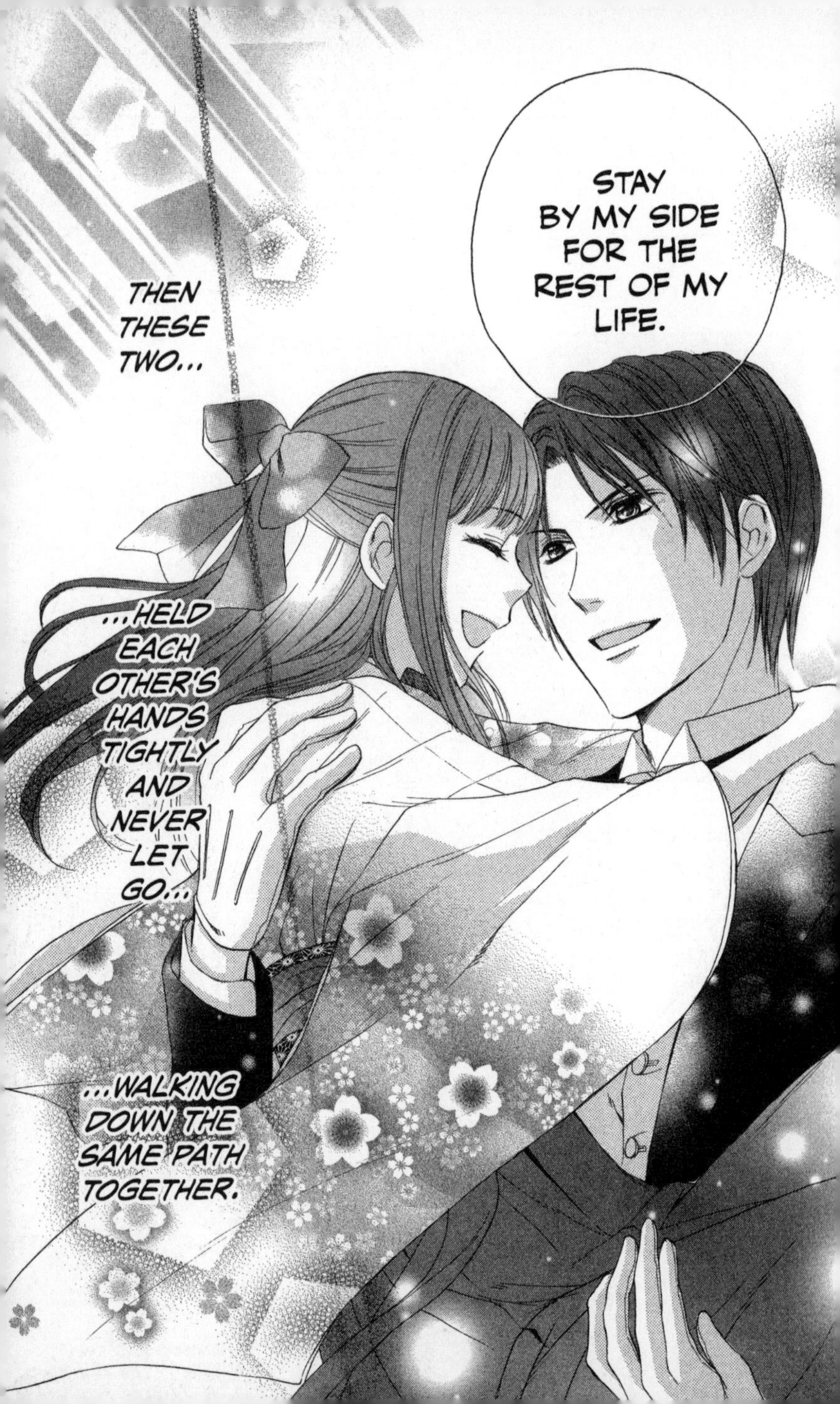
STAY BY MY SIDE FOR THE REST OF MY LIFE.
THEN THESE TWO...
...HELD EACH OTHER'S HANDS TIGHTLY AND NEVER LET GO...
...WALKING DOWN THE SAME PATH TOGETHER.

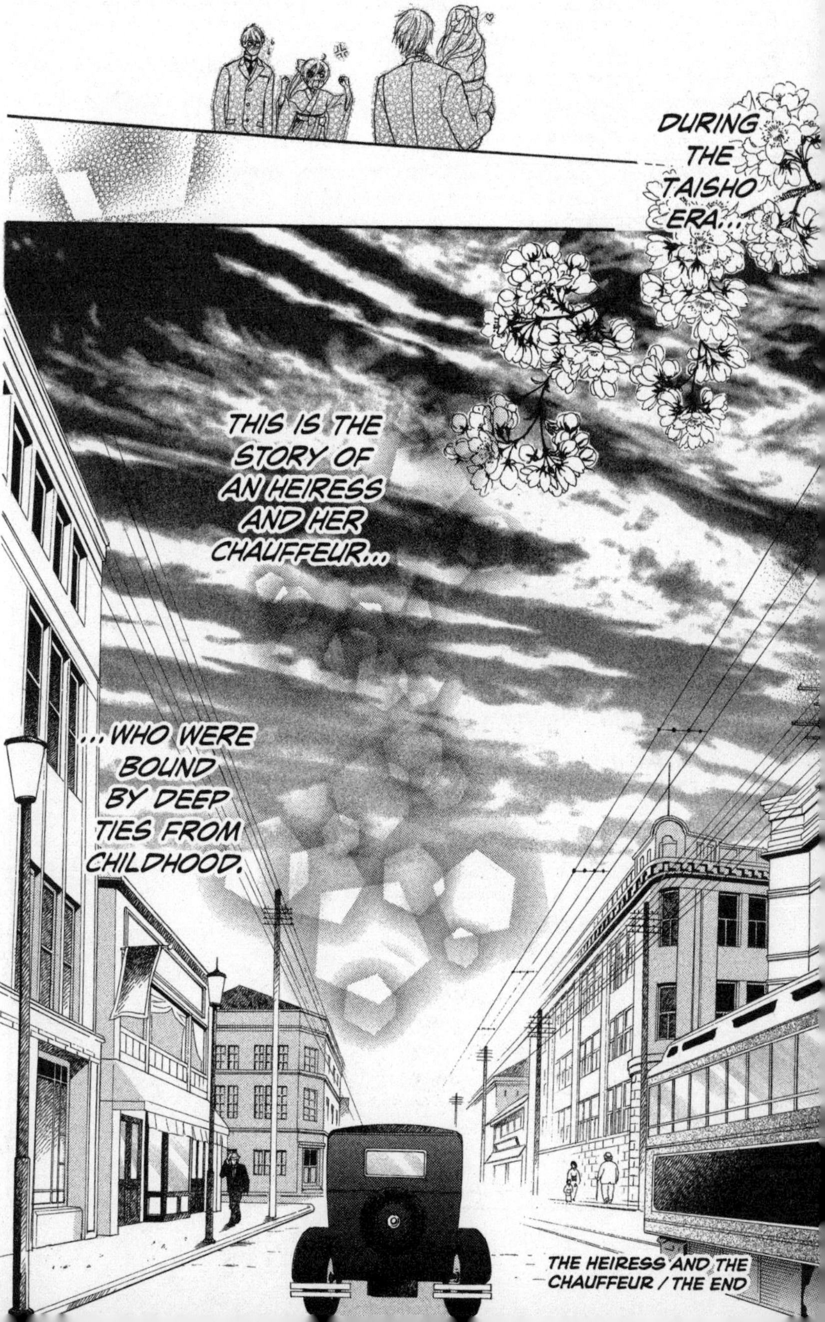
DURING THE TAISHO ERA...
THIS IS THE STORY OF AN HEIRESS AND HER CHAUFFEUR...
...WHO WERE BOUND BY DEEP TIES FROM CHILDHOOD.
THE HEIRESS AND THE CHAUFFEUR / THE END

AFTERWORD

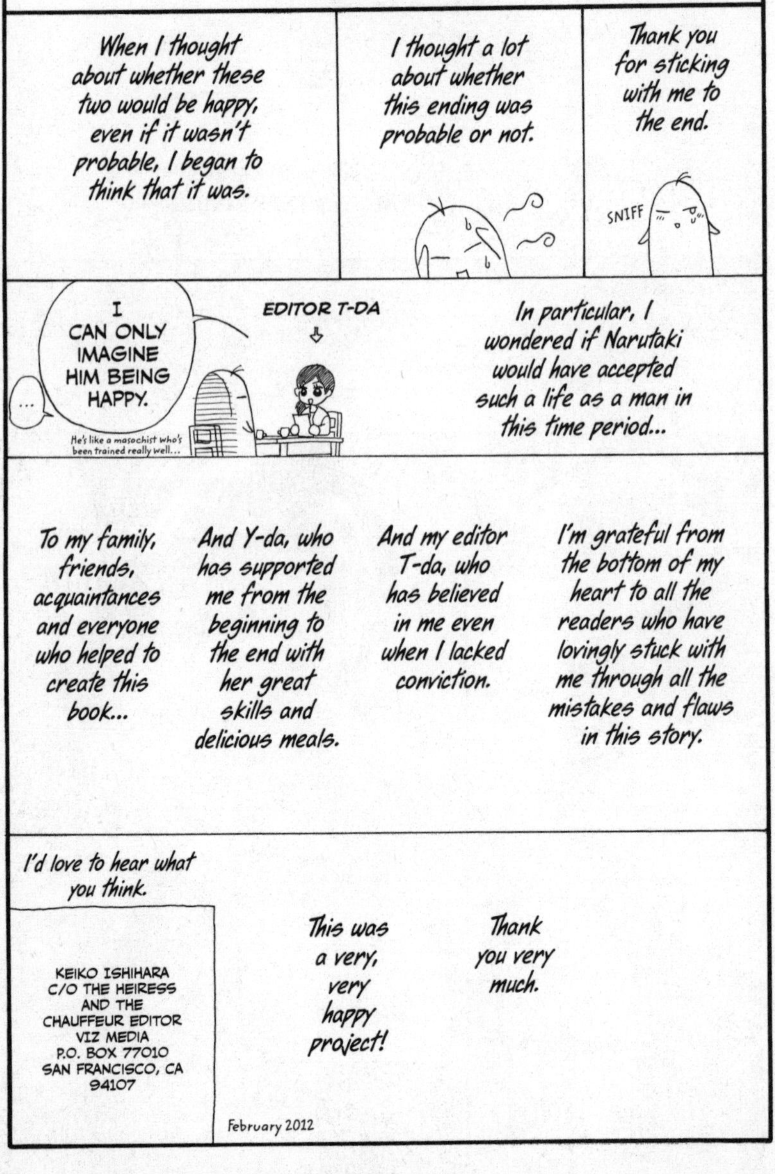

Thank you for sticking with me to the end.
SNIFF
I thought a lot about whether this ending was probable or not.
When I thought about whether these two would be happy, even if it wasn't probable, I began to think that it was.
In particular, I wondered if Narutaki would have accepted such a life as a man in this time period...
EDITOR T-DA
I CAN ONLY IMAGINE HIM BEING HAPPY.
...
He's like a masochist who's been trained really well...
I'm grateful from the bottom of my heart to all the readers who have lovingly stuck with me through all the mistakes and flaws in this story.
And my editor T-da, who has believed in me even when I lacked conviction.
And Y-da, who has supported me from the beginning to the end with her great skills and delicious meals.
To my family, friends, acquaintances and everyone who helped to create this book...
Thank you very much.
This was a very, very happy project!
I'd love to hear what you think.
KEIKO ISHIHARA
C/O THE HEIRESS AND THE CHAUFFEUR EDITOR
VIZ MEDIA
P.O. BOX 77010
SAN FRANCISCO, CA 94107
February 2012

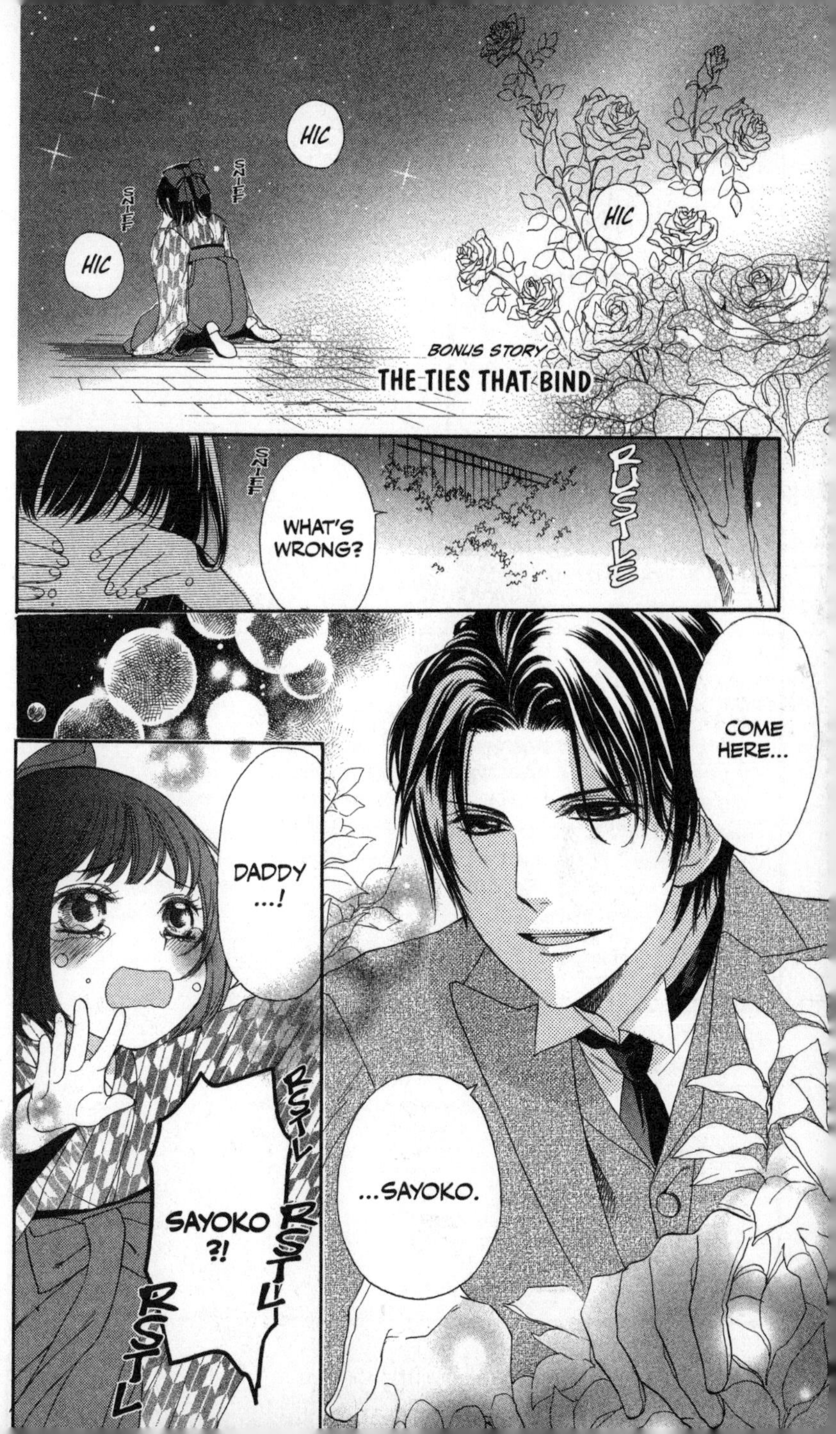
HIC
HIC
SNIFF
SNIFF
HIC
BONUS STORY
THE TIES THAT BIND
RUSTLE
WHAT'S WRONG?
SNIFF
COME HERE...
...SAYOKO.
DADDY ...!
RSTL
RSTL
SAYOKO ?!
RSTL

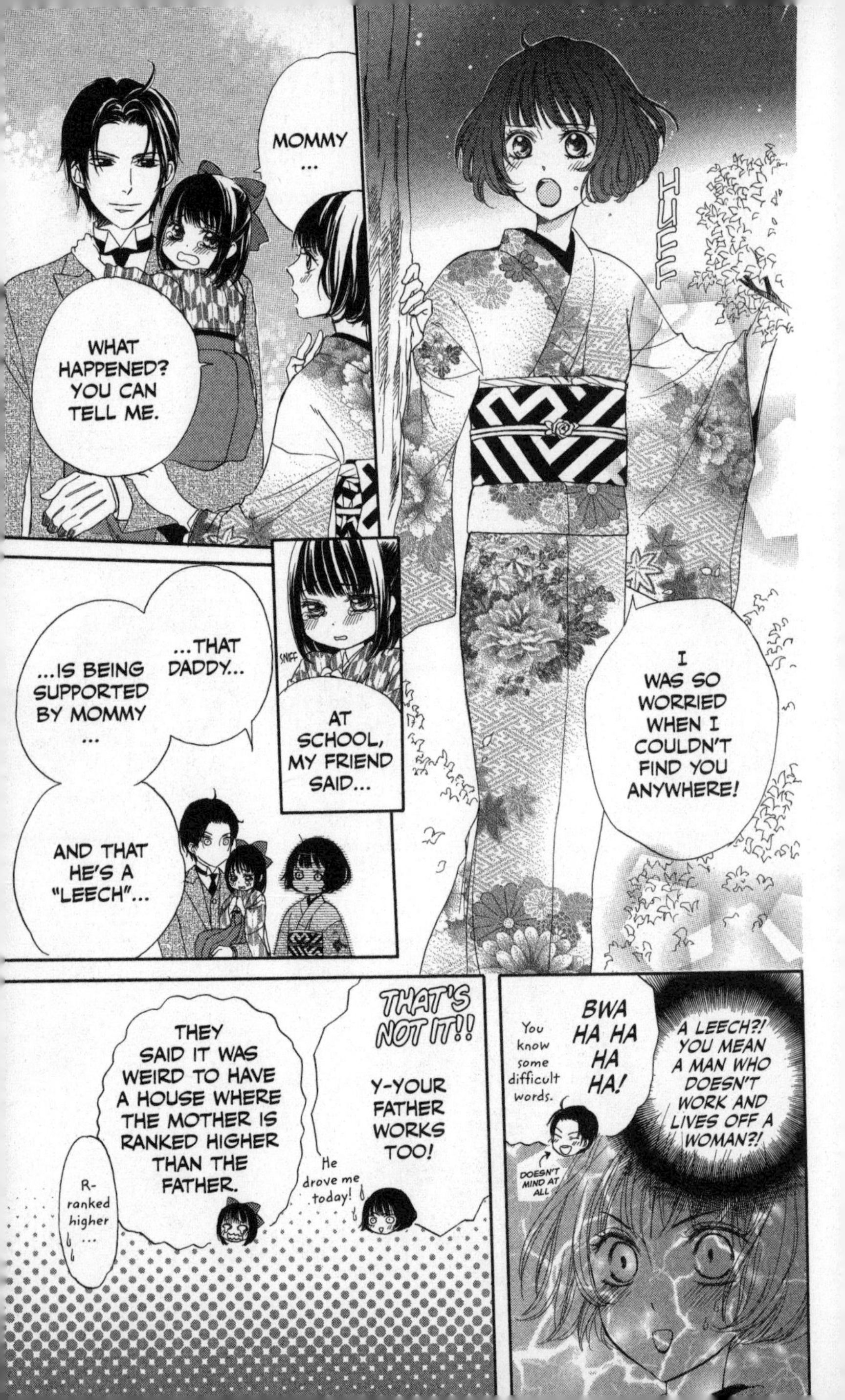
HUFF
I WAS SO WORRIED WHEN I COULDN'T FIND YOU ANYWHERE!
MOMMY ...
WHAT HAPPENED? YOU CAN TELL ME.
SNIFF
AT SCHOOL, MY FRIEND SAID...
...THAT DADDY...
...IS BEING SUPPORTED BY MOMMY ...
AND THAT HE'S A "LEECH"...
A LEECH?! YOU MEAN A MAN WHO DOESN'T WORK AND LIVES OFF A WOMAN?!
BWA HA HA HA HA!
You know some difficult words.
DOESN'T MIND AT ALL
THAT'S NOT IT!!
Y-YOUR FATHER WORKS TOO!
He drove me today!
THEY SAID IT WAS WEIRD TO HAVE A HOUSE WHERE THE MOTHER IS RANKED HIGHER THAN THE FATHER.
R-ranked higher ...

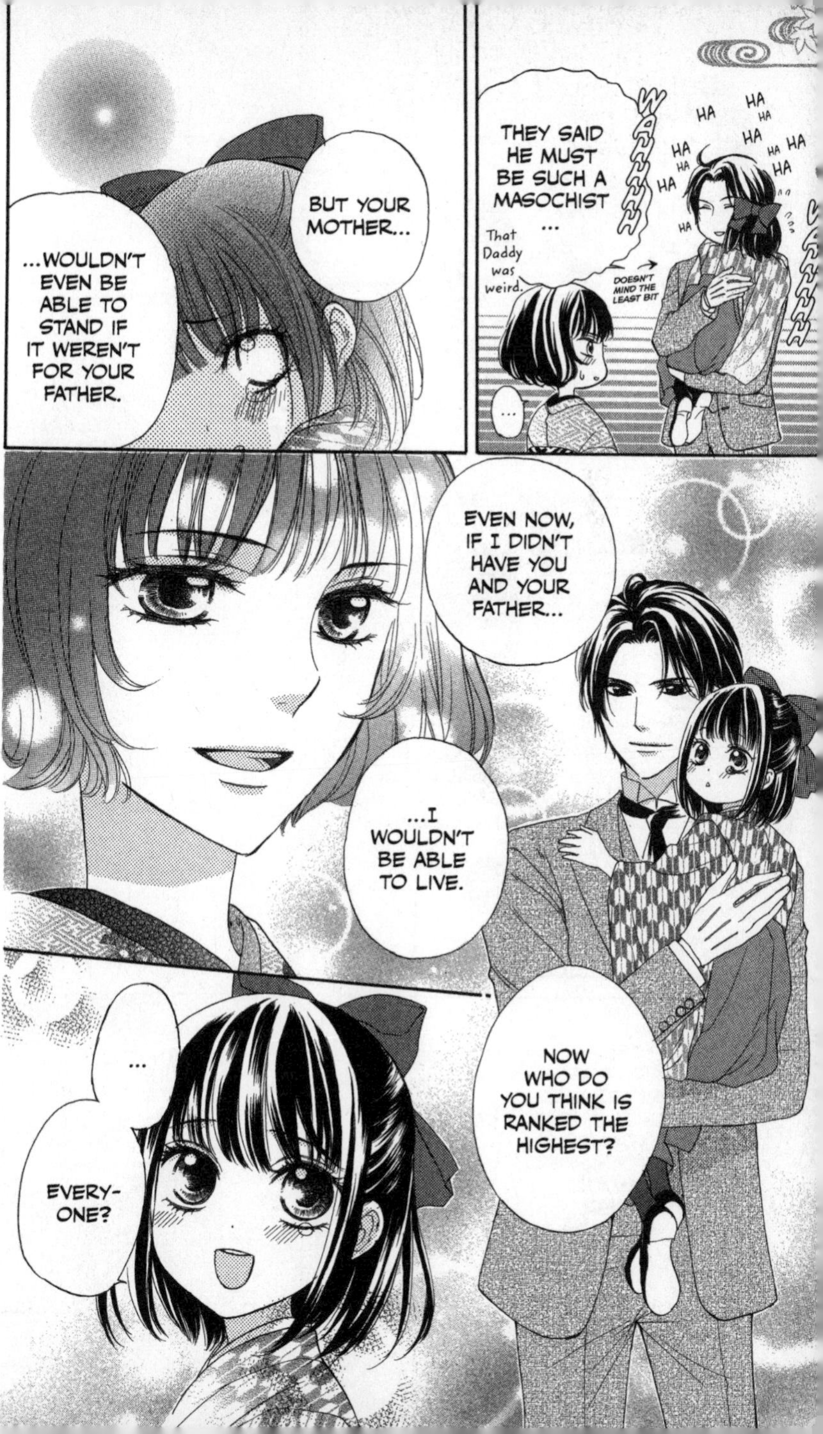

HA HA HA HA HA HA HA HA HA HA HA
WAHHHHH
THEY SAID HE MUST BE SUCH A MASOCHIST ...
That Daddy was weird.
DOESN'T MIND THE LEAST BIT
...
BUT YOUR MOTHER...
...WOULDN'T EVEN BE ABLE TO STAND IF IT WEREN'T FOR YOUR FATHER.
EVEN NOW, IF I DIDN'T HAVE YOU AND YOUR FATHER...
...I WOULDN'T BE ABLE TO LIVE.
NOW WHO DO YOU THINK IS RANKED THE HIGHEST?
...
EVERY-ONE?

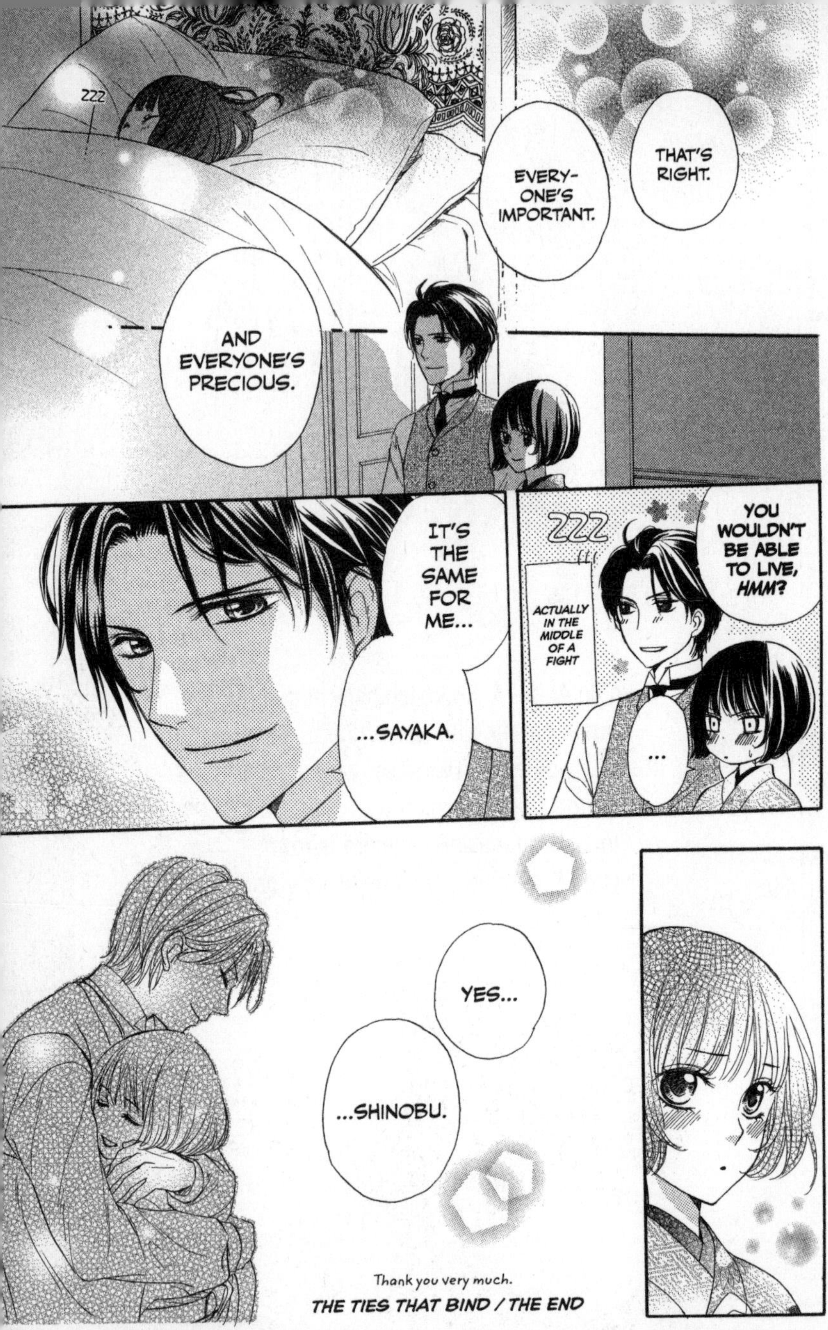
THAT'S RIGHT.
EVERY-ONE'S IMPORTANT.
ZZZ
AND EVERYONE'S PRECIOUS.
ZZZ
YOU WOULDN'T BE ABLE TO LIVE, *HMM?*
ACTUALLY IN THE MIDDLE OF A FIGHT
...
IT'S THE SAME FOR ME...
...SAYAKA.
YES...
...SHINOBU.
Thank you very much.
THE TIES THAT BIND / THE END

Born on April 14, Keiko Ishihara began her
manga career with *Keisan Desu Kara*
(It's All Calculated). Her other works include
Strange Dragon, which was serialized
in *LaLa* magazine. Ishihara is from
Hyogo Prefecture, and she loves cats.